Satirical Apocalypse

Recent Titles in
Contributions to the Study of World Literature

Writing the Good Fight: Political Commitment in the International Literature of the Spanish Civil War
Peter Monteath

Money: Lure, Lore, and Literature
John Louis DiGaetani, editor

Smollett's Women: A Study in an Eighteenth-Century Masculine Sensibility
Robert D. Spector

English Country Life in the Barsetshire Novels of Angela Thirkell
Laura Roberts Collins

Bakhtin, Stalin, and Modern Russian Fiction: Carnival, Dialogism, and History
M. Keith Booker and Dubravka Juraga

Aspects and Issues in the History of Children's Literature
Maria Nikolajeva, editor

Reluctant Expatriate: The Life of Harold Frederic
Robert M. Myers

The Decline of the Goddess: Nature, Culture, and Women in Thomas Hardy's Fiction
Shirley A. Stave

Postcolonial Discourse and Changing Cultural Contexts
Gita Rajan and Radhika Mohanram, editors

Prometheus and Faust: The Promethean Revolt in Drama from Classical Antiquity to Goethe
Timothy Richard Wutrich

English Postcoloniality: Literatures from Around the World
Radhika Mohanram and Gita Rajan, editors

The Vonnegut Chronicles
Peter Reed and Marc Leeds, editors

SATIRICAL APOCALYPSE

An Anatomy of Melville's *The Confidence-Man*

JONATHAN A. COOK

Contributions to the Study of World Literature,
Number 67

GREENWOOD PRESS
Westport, Connecticut • London

Library of Congress Cataloging-in-Publication Data

Cook, Jonathan.
Satirical apocalypse : an anatomy of Melville's The confidence-man / Jonathan A. Cook.
p. cm. — (Contributions to the study of world literature, ISSN 0738-9345 ; no. 67)
Includes bibliographical references (p.) and index.
ISBN 0-313-29404-6 (alk. paper)
1. Melville, Herman, 1819–1891. Confidence-man. 2. Apocalyptic literature—History and criticism. 3. Satire, American—History and criticism. 4. Swindlers and swindling in literature.
5. Millennialism in literature. I. Title. II. Series.
PS2384.C63C66 1996
813'.3—dc20 95–40033

British Library Cataloguing in Publication Data is available.

Library of Congress Catalog Card Number: 95–40033
ISBN: 0–313–29404–6
ISSN: 0738–9345

First published in 1996

Greenwood Press, 88 Post Road West, Westport, CT 06881
An imprint of Greenwood Publishing Group, Inc.

Printed in the United States of America

The paper used in this book complies with the Permanent Paper Standard issued by the National Information Standards Organization (Z39.48–1984).

10 9 8 7 6 5 4 3 2 1

Copyright Acknowledgments

The author and publisher gratefully acknowledge permission to reprint the following:

Excerpts from *The Age of Enterprise: A Social History of Industrial America* by Thomas C. Cochran and William Miller. Copyright 1942 by Macmillan Publishing Company, renewed 1970 by Thomas C. Cochran and William Miller. Reprinted with the permission of Simon & Schuster.

Excerpts from *Correspondence*, edited by Lynn Horth. Copyright 1993 by Northwestern University Press and the Newberry Library. Reprinted with the permission of Northwestern University Press.

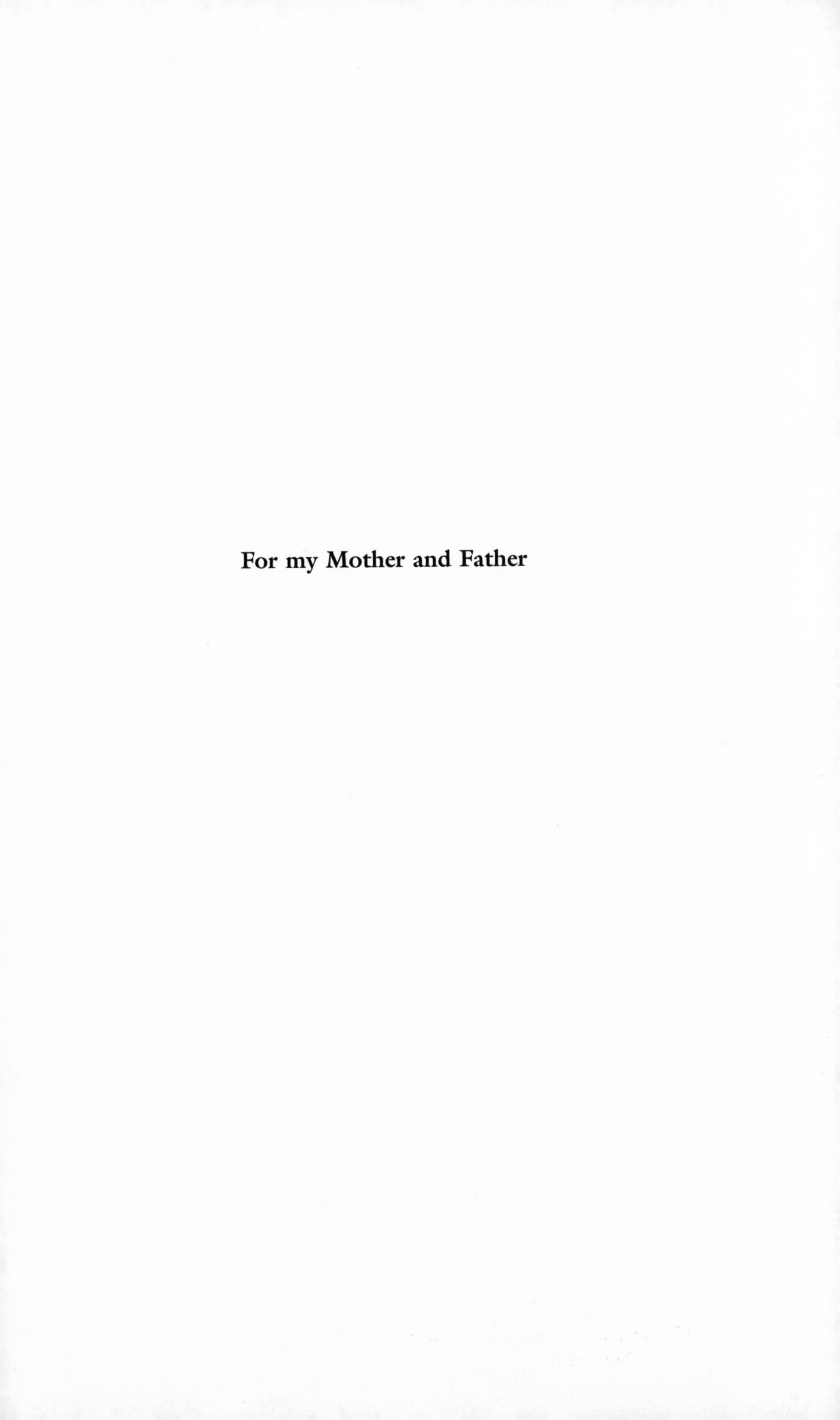

For my Mother and Father

Contents

Preface

> But no man can be a good critic of any book, who does not read it in a wisdom which transcends the instructions of any book, and treats the whole extant product of the human intellect as only one age revisable and reversible by him.
>
> Emerson, "Thoughts on Modern Literature" (1840)

Although *The Confidence-Man,* like Melville's other major fiction, has attracted a significant, and even daunting, amount of critical commentary—in the process becoming something of a "cult" book among both academic and common readers—so far there has been little consensus on the novel's meaning and it continues to be the author's most problematic and potentially forbidding text. Conflicting views begin with the protean characterization and shifting symbolic identity of the novel's protagonist, and extend to differing assessments of its generic affiliation, its relation to its historical context, its potential use of biographical models, and, finally, the overall nature of Melville's religious and philosophical vision in this, his last work of fiction to be published in his lifetime. In response to this critical disarray, the present study of *The Confidence-Man* seeks to provide a comprehensive new guide to the novel by interpreting it as a "satirical apocalypse" subsuming a broad range of biographical, social, and religious implications. An April Fools' Day apocalypse ironically answering the widespread millennial expectations of nineteenth-century America, *The Confidence-Man* was written to express Melville's accumulated animus against his family and friends, the literary profession, the nation at large, and the Christian faith. With such an all-encompassing subversive agenda, Melville was forced to employ a complex strategy of disguise and allegorical indirection to attain his ends.

In broad outline, then, this study seeks to situate *The Confidence-Man* in its relevant biographical, historical, and theological contexts. Chapter 1 provides an introductory overview of America in the 1850s, Melville's life and literary career during this period, and the development of his religious beliefs as they relate to the writing of *The Confidence-Man*. Chapter 2 sets forth some of the theoretical issues involved in the study of satire and explores the novel's parodic incorporation of a wide range of formal ingredients. Relating the novel to its historical milieu, Chapter 3 investigates Melville's indictment of America's socioeconomic transformation and corruption in the years preceding the Civil War. In keeping with the encyclopedic energies of satire, the novel focuses on a number of specific targets, including gambling and financial speculation, drinking and temperance, slavery, evangelical religion, education, law, medicine, science, philosophy (Transcendentalism), money, and banking.

As a survey of the novel's allegorical component, Chapter 4 interprets the symbolic identity of the Confidence Man as a reflection of Melville's recurrent preoccupation with the problem of theodicy, which led him to a skeptical, heterodox, and morally equivocal conception of the deity. A theological coincidence of opposites, the figure of the Confidence Man embodies an allegorical compound of Christ and Satan, with trickster and Dionysian archetypes giving him other distinctive features. The novel, moreover, constitutes a typological parody of the Bible framed by the first and second coming of Christ.

Chapters 5 and 6 demonstrate that *The Confidence-Man* incorporates a strategically displaced representation of Melville's personal and literary milieux. Continuing the work of critics who have identified Emerson, Thoreau, and Poe as subjects for satirical caricature in the novel, I show that virtually *all* of the major characters have identifiable models. The guises of the Confidence Man are implicitly autobiographical, embodying the successive phases of Melville's literary career; the other character models, in turn, are divided between members of Melville's immediate and extended family—Melvilles, Gansevoorts, and Shaws—and his literary peers—Emerson, Thoreau, and Poe, as well as Duyckinck and Hawthorne, Melville's closest literary friends. A survey of the biographical models for characters in the novel draws attention to Melville's troubled relation to his family, friends, and literary contemporaries at the end of his professional career as a writer.

The last two chapters of this study focus on the novel's narrative and discursive interludes: Chapter 7 analyzes *The Confidence-Man*'s four interior fables in relevant biographical, social, and religious contexts, while Chapter 8 examines its three interpolated essays as a tripartite satirical "defense" and a formal statement of Melville's poetics of fiction. Finally, an Epilogue follows Melville on the trip to Europe and the Levant that he took upon completing composition of the novel, and briefly comments on its contemporary reception and legacy.

While drawing on previous criticism of the novel, the present study represents a fresh interpretation of *The Confidence-Man* that attempts to render it more accessible and engaging as a work of literary artistry. Since this is an essay in practical criticism, I go into some detail in order to elucidate the complex layers of Melville's text, many of which remain to be brought to light. For, as one of the novel's ablest expositors, Elizabeth Foster, wrote over four decades ago, *The Confidence-Man* "keeps its secrets because its submerged meaning, it seems probable, was deliberately hidden. It needs to be decoded. Furthermore, it can be" (xlvi). The work of fiction that emerges here is more closely related to its author's life and times and is more subversive in its narrative strategies and thematic concerns than previously believed. Yet Melville might have said about his last published novel what he once remarked to Hawthorne of *Moby-Dick:* "I have written a wicked book, and feel spotless as the lamb."

As more fully recorded in the text and notes, my chief debt here is to the many Melville scholars of the past half-century whose patient researches and critical insights have made this endeavor possible. I am also grateful for the assistance of librarians at the New York Public Library, the Massachusetts Historical Society, and the Berkshire Atheneum, and the libraries at Columbia, New York University, and Harvard. In addition, I would like to thank Professor Robert Ferguson of Columbia University for his assistance on this project at an earlier stage of development. I would like to thank, too, those friends who have read all or parts of the manuscript, or who have discussed with me some of its contents: James Bednarz, John Bryant, Lucy Collins, Elena Latici, Larry Reynolds, Stafford Reynolds, and John Wenke.

Abbreviations

The following abbreviations refer to the series *The Writings of Herman Melville*. General ed. Harrison Hayford, Hershel Parker, and G. Thomas Tanselle. Evanston and Chicago, Ill.: Northwestern University Press and the Newberry Library, 1968– .

M	*Mardi* (1970). Ed. Harrison Hayford, Hershel Parker, and G. Thomas Tanselle.
R	*Redburn* (1972). Ed. Harrison Hayford, Hershel Parker, and G. Thomas Tanselle.
WJ	*White-Jacket* (1970). Ed. Harrison Hayford, Hershel Parker, and G. Thomas Tanselle.
MD	*Moby-Dick* (1988). Ed. Harrison Hayford, Hershel Parker, and G. Thomas Tanselle.
P	*Pierre* (1972). Ed. Harrison Hayford, Hershel Parker, and G. Thomas Tanselle.
IP	*Israel Potter* (1982). Ed. Harrison Hayford, Hershel Parker, and G. Thomas Tanselle.
PT	*The Piazza Tales and Other Prose Pieces, 1839–1860* (1987). Ed. Harrison Hayford, Alma A. MacDougall, Hershel Parker, and G. Thomas Tanselle.
CM	*The Confidence-Man* (1984). Ed. Harrison Hayford, Hershel Parker, and G. Thomas Tanselle.
Cl	*Clarel* (1991). Ed. Harrison Hayford, Alma A. MacDougall, Hershel Parker, and G. Thomas Tanselle.
C	*Correspondence* (1993). Ed. Lynn Horth.
J	*Journals* (1989). Ed. Howard C. Horsford with Lynn Horth.

Also used is:

Log	Jay Leyda. *The Melville Log: A Documentary Life of Herman Melville, 1819–1891.* 2 vols. 1951. Rpt. with a new supplement, New York: Gordian Press, 1969.

1

Introduction

"It will be well for all those persons who have been defrauded by the 'Confidence Man,' to call at the police court, Tombs, and take a view of him." So ends the notice in the New York *Herald* on July 8, 1849, describing the first appearance of the "Original Confidence Man," a figure whose manipulation of his victim's trust was hardly original but whose operation was so remarkably simple as to require the invention of a journalistic sobriquet. The respectable-looking "William Thompson" engaged a stranger in conversation, requested his "confidence" in connection with the temporary "loan" of his watch (the "mark" assumed some previous acquaintance), and then exited the scene with both confidence and chronometer. In the midst of a summer of intensive creative effort that produced *Redburn* by early July and *White-Jacket* two months later, Melville could have spared only a passing glance at news of this overnight criminal celebrity who, in the ensuing weeks, inspired a (now lost) popular comedy at Burton's Chambers Street Theatre and a prolonged series of comments in the press. In one widely reprinted article appearing three days after his initial arrest, for example, a journalist for the *Herald* caustically argued that the operation of the "Confidence Man" was merely a miniature version of those used by the city's *nouveau riche:* "His genius has been employed on a small scale in Broadway. Theirs has been employed in Wall street. That's all the difference." The writer concluded his trenchant social commentary by ironically dismissing the "Confidence Man" as a fraud and a failure compared to the contemporary capitalist who commits the same crimes on a more grandiose scale: "Success, then, to the real 'Confidence Man.' Long life to the real 'Confidence Man'!—the 'Confidence Man' of Wall street—the 'Confidence Man' of the palace uptown—the 'Confidence Man' who battens and fattens on the plunder coming from the poor man and the man of moderate means! As for the 'Confidence Man' of 'the Tombs,' he is a cheat, a humbug, a delusion, a sham, a mockery! Let him rot!" Striking an opposing, sentimental note over a month later, Melville's close friend, Evert Duyckinck, reprinted in his own weekly, the *Literary World,* an article from the *Merchant's Ledger* that viewed the "Confidence Man" not as a symptom of a larger social corruption but as a potentially redemptive figure, an agent to test men's charity: "That one poor swindler, like the one under arrest, should have been able to drive so considerable a trade on an appeal to so simple a quality as the confidence of man in man, shows that all virtue and humanity of nature is not entirely extinct in the nineteenth century. It is a good thing, and speaks well for human nature, that, at this late day, in spite of all the hardening of civilization, and all the warning of newspapers, men *can be swindled.*"[1]

The newly christened "Confidence Man" was clearly both a satirical mirror and moral barometer of midcentury America, and Melville no doubt appreciated his wide-ranging significance. *The Confidence-Man* would in fact later incorporate the antithetical reactions, both cynical and sentimental, noted above. But for a writer increasingly aware of the conflict between the commercial, convention-bound nature of the contemporary literary profession and the subversive content of his own imagination, the operations of the "Confidence Man"—a man who asked his victim's confidence before, in effect, picking his pocket—might have evoked a special shock of recognition. So, too, for a writer facing a maturing crisis of faith, there might have been something particularly suggestive about a fraudulent promoter of "confidence" who was temporarily on view at the "Tombs." Yet whatever may have been Melville's reaction at the time, nearly six years after the Confidence Man's first advent, his reappearance in Albany in late April 1855 executing the same type of ploy clearly provided the catalyst for Melville's final published work of fiction—a satire in which personal, social, and theological concerns are fused into a seamless whole. As an inducement to sum up his increasingly sardonic view of literary career, country, and Christian deity, the "second coming" of the "Confidence Man" that April was a literary godsend.

While the term "Confidence Man" was a local New York invention that soon entered the language, the character type it describes obviously had an extensive cultural history previous to his American incarnation. Elizabethan coney-catching pamphlets, seventeenth- and eighteenth-century criminal biographies, the literature of roguery and the picaresque—all these documented different specimens of this class of criminal-imposter who took advantage of his victim's gullibility or greed, the victim becoming a co-conspirator in his own duping. Yet there were special reasons for the official emergence of the "Confidence Man" in mid–nineteenth-century America. The most outstanding of these was the egalitarian environment of the Jacksonian era which had created unprecedented commercial opportunities and social mobility in the nation, as the "self-made man" was launched in pursuit of the "almighty dollar" (to use two terms coined in the 1830s). The fluid social environment of antebellum America was consequently creating a nation of strangers for whom questions of confidence and distrust were becoming increasingly problematic. As one commentator notes, "Once a land of semi-sufficient localities, America was becoming part of a new, interdependent economic order. The old ethics, based on the personal relations of men in small communities, squared badly with a market become radically impersonal. Mobility in space and society destabilized the relations between men who knew each other, and bound their fortunes to other men they knew not at all" (Wilson Carey McWilliams, 225). This problem of "confidence" was especially apparent in the nation's fast-growing urban centers. Conditions were therefore auspicious for the appearance of an "Original Confidence Man" in mid-nineteenth-century New York, the nation's burgeoning commercial capital, at a time when the country was engaged in the unsettling ordeals of modernization and the creation of a national market economy based on industrial capitalism.[2]

Yet the appearance of the "Confidence Man" was symptomatic in another important respect, for during much of the 1840s and 1850s the invocation of "confidence" constituted a virtual password on the way to wealth. It is worth recalling that at the time Melville was writing his last published novel, America had witnessed a decade of extraordinary commercial and continental expansion; and whatever ominous shadows of sectional conflict were hovering on the horizon, the country was flush with prosperity:

> By 1850, the vestiges of the long depression after the panic of 1837 had vanished. Victory in the Mexican War, the flow of California gold, the rapid growth of population and its steady movement to the rich and virgin West created a new tide of confidence. In the next four years every line of business boomed; commodity prices started their ascent, and profits kept the pace. In response, often with railroad stock as collateral, manufacturers borrowed to expand their plants, merchants borrowed to allow their western debtors longer credits. Both were joined by doctors, lawyers, teachers, writers, in gambling on precarious margins in Wall Street or State Street or through brokers' offices in the hinterlands connected by telegraph with the great exchanges in the East. To meet these new and continuing demands upon their resources, the banks of the country, besides issuing notes, created new instruments of credit in the form of call loans and deposits. Between 1848 and 1854, these three items—notes, loans, deposits—jumped from $538,000,000 to $950,000,000. By 1856 they had soared to $1,042,000,000. (Cochran and Miller, 82)

It goes without saying that these boom times—the dollar amounts noted above should be multiplied by thirty-five to forty times to approximate their current value (Derks, 2)—acted as a smokescreen for a number of social ills, in particular the divisive issue of slavery; in fact, the new prosperity also helped precipitate the commercial chicanery, social atomization, political gridlock, and emerging aura of corruption that marked America's drive to continental empire. In New York City, for example, the early 1850s produced what Edward Spann has called an Age of Gold: "Political corruption, corporate power, big wealth, social cleavages and tensions—in retrospect, it is evident that the Age of Gold ushered in a new era in New York which made the peculations and social troubles of the period before 1850 look like the emblems of innocence" (297). He continues:

> Although the new metropolis did not invent human corruption, the nature of its prosperity weakened public morals in both the business and political worlds. The boom brought a jump in the scale of wealth for which society was morally unprepared. The near doubling of the assessed value of real and personal property from some $254 to nearly $487 million between 1848 and 1855 combined with the California gold strikes to reinflame the get-rich-quick enthusiasms that earlier had been dampened by memories of the Panic of 1837. (305–306)

The scramble for wealth, with its attendant weakening of public morals, was occurring on the national level as well. In an important revisionary study, *The Plundering Generation,* Mark Summers has documented the widespread financial and political corruption of the decade, as generated by rapid commercial expansion and the increasingly entrenched spoils system in politics: "If by corruption we mean 'the use of public position for private advantage or exceptional party profit, and the subversion of the political process for personal ends'—a definition that covers all the wrongs that most Americans would have listed as corrupt in 1850—then the evidence is overwhelming. In every way the decade before the Civil War was corrupt. . . . In the 1850s, corruption was given an apocalyptic importance, and orators used the most extreme terms to explain it" (14, 18). Such a finding may surprise those who regard the decade of the 1850s as dominated by the political struggle over slavery.

On the other hand, however much a growing sense of corruption, anticipating a later Gilded Age, infected the 1850s, the traditional view of America's special destiny as a nation continued to exert a powerful influence on the culture. In this view, progress and providence went hand in hand to make America the world's "redeemer nation," the modern Israel whose history was covenanted with the Creator. Americans of the nineteenth century thus considered themselves the hope of the world for the universal transmission of their republican government and evangelical faith, a belief that has been called America's sense of "mission," or its "civic millennialism." Many accordingly believed that their country was destined to bring about the millennium forecast in the Book of Revelation, the thousand years of peace and prosperity envisioned in Christian eschatology.

Combined with a secular faith in progress with which it easily blended, millennial perfectionism manifested itself in virtually all spheres of antebellum life and constituted a major ingredient in its general spiritual "ferment." As social and religious historians such as Alice Felt Tyler, Timothy L. Smith, Ronald Walters, and (most recently) Robert Abzug have amply documented, the many reform movements that characterized American society during the Jacksonian and antebellum eras—antislavery, temperance, sabbatarianism, peace, criminal justice, mental illness, women's rights, education, social welfare, health, and diet—were fostered by a spirit of millennial hope and evangelical perfectionism, the latter in keeping with Christ's injunction, "Be ye therefore perfect, even as your Father which is in heaven is perfect" (Matt. 5:48). The dramatic transformations of the antebellum economy were also viewed, not only as a means for greater distribution of wealth, but also as a means of moral improvement. From an evangelical perspective, railroads and telegraphs figured as potential heralds of the "good news" of an increasingly Christianized republic on the road to conversion of the world.

The Second Coming of Christ was an implicit religious index of this perfectionist ideology. According to a standard division in eschatological theory that first developed during the eighteenth century, the Second Coming was thought to occur through either of two scenarios, "premillennialist" or "postmillennialist," according to whether Christ's return would occur before or after the millennium. The first scenario envisioned Christ's Second Advent as a sudden apocalyptic intervention not conditioned by human effort; the second envisioned an incremental movement toward perfection within history. As literal believers in New Testament apocalyptic, premillennialists expected imminent judgment on the world and heavenly reunion with their redeemer; as more figural readers of biblical prophecy, postmillennialists were optimistic believers in Christ's promise of this-worldly redemption. The most conspicuous contemporary premillennialists were followers of William Miller (1782–1849), a self-taught Baptist preacher from upstate New York who, relying on the Books of Daniel and Revelation, predicted the Second Coming for the year 1843—a prophecy that gained a significant number of adherents in the early 1840s but that inevitably led to what was called the "Great Disappointment" and a general discrediting of premillennialist date-setting for some time to come. Postmillennialism, on the other hand, encompassed a broader constituency of evangelical and lay proponents of progress through conversion and reform, individuals who saw the nation's moral improvement as a portent of millennial things to come. The moral crusades of the 1830s to the 1850s were thus in large measure a product of postmillennial impulses, which gained additional strength from the failure of the Millerite movement, as Timothy L. Smith notes:

> The most significant millenarian doctrines of the mid-nineteenth century were not those of William Miller, but those which grew out of evangelical Protestantism's crusade to Christianize the land. Revivalistic Calvinists like Edward and Henry Ward Beecher and Albert Barnes, Oberlin perfectionists, and Methodists great and small were ardent postmillennialists, bent like John the Baptist on preparing a kingdom for the King. Social reforms of all sorts fit into their scheme. The chief result of the Millerite excitement seems to have been to hasten the acceptance of this doctrine among Baptists and Presbyterians previously attached to the premillennial view. That clergymen identified the popular belief in America's mission with the Christian hope and drifted steadily toward Arminianism, with its emphasis upon free will and human ability, strengthened the trend. (236)

In sum, if premillennialism and postmillennialism were poles on a spectrum of contemporary belief, postmillennialism was the dominant credo, being more in keeping with the optimistic tenor of the times.[3]

The Confidence-Man was, in part, Melville's satirical response to this pervasive ideology. That Melville was preoccupied at this time by the disparity between American ideals and realities is confirmed by his remark to George W. Curtis in September 1857 when Melville was about to go on the lecture circuit: "I have been trying to scratch my brains for a Lecture. What is a good, earnest subject? '*Daily progress of man towards a state of intellectual & moral perfection, as evidenced in history of 5th Avenue & 5 Points*' " (*C*, 314). Using the sardonic voice of his most recent literary protagonist, Melville undercuts America's perfectionist faith by citing the contrasted, but implicitly synonymous, glitter and squalor of contemporary New York City. In his *American Jeremiad,* Sacvan Berkovitch has remarked that "Melville's options, given his commitment to America, were either progress toward the millennium or regression toward doomsday. He simply could not envision a different set of ideals . . . beyond that which his culture imposed" (193). Yet in a novel featuring the premillennial advent of a postmillennial Christ figure, Melville paradoxically charted the simultaneous moral perfection and doomsday regression of his culture aboard a ship of state, ship of faith, and ship of fools.

Whatever Melville's underlying stake in the national ideology, there were other, more personal reasons for him to assume the role of satirist in his last published novel. Prominent among these would be the fact that while the rest of the country boomed and a new class of feminine authors produced lucrative new best sellers, Melville was being slowly "damned by dollars."

Indeed, the decline of his reputation in the early 1850s following his early literary successes confirmed Melville's awareness of the disparity between making a living as a writer and telling the "truth" to America. The writing and publication of *Moby-Dick* would be a key event in this progressive disillusionment. Thus in September 1850, in the midst of composing his greatest work of fiction, Melville had purchased a house and farm in Pittsfield with the help of a $3,000 loan from his father-in-law, Lemuel Shaw, and a $1,500 mortgage from the former owner of the property, Dr. John M. Brewster. Then in April 1851, hoping to soon capitalize on his new whaling novel, Melville had requested an advance from his publishers, the Harper Brothers, but was refused, partly on the grounds that he already owed them $695.65 (*Log,* 1:410). That May, Melville had instead borrowed $2,050 (for five years at 9 percent interest) from a Lansingburgh family friend, Tertullus D. Stewart (*C,* 182, 291). But the publication of *Moby-Dick* in November 1851 failed to produce a commercial success, and by May 1852 Melville had defaulted on the semiannual interest payments of Stewart's loan; for the next four years the loan was to hang over Melville's head like a sword of Damocles. With the critical and commercial disaster of *Pierre* in the summer and fall of 1852, Melville's income from his writings came to a halt. After being unable to publish his next novel, *The Isle of the Cross,* Melville by the spring of 1853 was looking for a consular appointment in the Pierce administration; despite the influence of Hawthorne with the new president, Melville failed to obtain a suitable position and was only able to continue his writing career at this point by turning to the reduced format of *Harper's* and *Putnam's* new monthly magazines.

Even so, debt and disaster seemed to dog his steps. In November 1851 Melville was $422.82 in debt to the Harpers; in March 1853 the sum was $298.71; in March 1856 it was $348.51 (*Log,* 1:438, 468, 2:513). From the end of 1853 to 1864, all of Melville's profits from sales of his books went to pay off his debt to his publishers, while his income from his short fiction appearing between 1853 and 1856 amounted to only about $1,329 (*PT,* 494). In addition, a fire at the Harper Brothers warehouse in December 1853, which destroyed a quarter of a million dollars of stock, consumed approximately 2,300 bound and unbound copies of Melville's books worth about $1,000 in royalties (*Log,* 1:482, 492; *C,* 294). Although it was well-received as a serial in *Putnam's,* the book publication of *Israel Potter* in March 1855 did not translate into a commercial success. In the summer of 1855 Melville was unable to sell his Pittsfield Farm to a commission looking for the site for a new state mental asylum (*Log,* 2:506). In September 1855 Melville for the first time had defaulted, in the sum of $90, on his $1,500 mortgage to Brewster, and by early 1856 Tertullus Stewart was threatening to take legal action for repayment of his $2,050 loan (*C,* 290–95). With a family of four children by March 1855, Melville was more dependent than ever on the good graces of his wealthy father-in-law.

To Melville's struggle to make a living as a writer was added the burden of intellectual isolation and illness. Starting in 1852, Melville had become estranged from his closest literary friends, Evert Duyckinck and Nathaniel Hawthorne, and the laconic nature of his correspondence in the mid-1850s, largely confined to bulletins to his publishers, attests to an absence of friendly rapport. Melville had also been ill in the spring of 1853 and again in 1855 when he was disabled first by rheumatism in February and then by sciatica the following June. In mid-September 1855, the *Berkshire County Eagle* reported that Melville was "just recovering from a severe illness" (*Log,* 2:507). *The Confidence-Man* thus emerged from a writer who might well have envisioned himself a martyr to his vocation—a literary Job or Christ being tested by his culture, if not the deity.[4]

Melville's last published novel would also dramatize the author's increasingly ambivalent relation to his literary audience. If Melville's early career was marked by the hope for an intimate rapport between author and public, such a confidence in direct communication eventually gave way to the discovery that telling the "truth" was not always welcome to the American public. Melville's mature literary aesthetic was formulated in his 1850 review of Hawthorne's *Mosses from an Old Manse.* Classifying Hawthorne with Shakespeare, Melville argued that these two writers were, in effect, literary confidence men who hid potentially subversive truths under a protective facade of entertainment and amusement: "For in this world of lies, Truth is forced to fly like a scared white doe in the woodlands; and only by cunning glimpses will she reveal herself, as in Shakespeare and other masters of the great Art of Telling the Truth,—even though it be covertly, and by snatches" (*PT,* 244). Melville's message here thus enshrines irony, allegory, and indirection as necessary vehicles of truth-telling. Taken to an extreme in the case of *Pierre,* this double agenda produced an incongruous blend of a popular romantic plot with an outspoken critique of both American society and the Christian faith. In his subsequent short fiction of the mid-1850s, however, Melville exhibited a more controlled mode of "double writing" that attempted to insinuate provocative moral and metaphysical truths beneath an unexceptionable narrative framework. In his last work of this period, Melville's cumulative alienation from his audience led him to the domain of satire, the literary mode of unpopular, disagreeable, or even dangerous truths. As Frank Goodman (ironically) complains midway through *The Confidence-Man,* "something Satanic about irony. God defend me from Irony, and Satire, his bosom friend" (*CM,* 136).

As we might expect, *The Confidence-Man,* which probably was originally planned for serial publication in *Putnam's* magazine (*CM,* 277–79), also grew out of the themes and methods of Melville's short fiction of the 1850s. Many of his tales from this period explored issues of failure, hardship, and the need for charity in a society in which success, progress, and optimism were the national norm. Consequently, they often featured contrasted views of American life in which downtrodden or defeated individuals served as an index of larger social and religious values. The three so-called diptychs from among these stories, which presented thematic oppositions between American and English societies, also anticipate the bipartite structure of *The Confidence-Man,* a novel in which the protagonist mimics various aspects of American society in the first half and then plays the role of international "cosmopolitan" in the second. The picaresque *Israel Potter* offered still another potential rationale for the social criticism of *The Confidence-Man,* for its historical exploration of the origins of the American Republic chronicled the betrayal of revolutionary ideals in the career of a representative common man. If *Israel Potter* was subtitled "A Fourth of July Story" during serial publication, Melville's next novel was an April Fools' Day narrative depicting the equivocal result of the American experiment.[5]

While the biographical and social dimensions of satire in *The Confidence-Man* suggest the close relation between Melville's literary discontents and his growing criticism of the nation, there remains to be considered his theological satire in the novel, the dimension that provides an overarching perspective on all else. According to Frank Clark Griffith, by the time he was writing *Moby-Dick,* Melville faced a "four-part religious predicament—an acute awareness of temporal evil, a conviction that the universe is either Godless or governed by a malicious God, an unwillingness to live with such terrifying alternatives, [and] the consequent need for religious knowledge" (152). Melville's religious predicament was partly a product of the Calvinism he imbibed in his youth. In the deterministic moral economy of Calvinism, with its ascription of absolute sovereignty to a God who operated both vengefully and providentially, the deity unofficially subsumed the function of the devil, inexplicably condemning some individuals to damnation and others to salvation according to an inscrutable plan. Yet in an attempt to answer the traditional issue of theodicy—why if God was all-powerful and all-good He sanctioned the existence of evil—Melville turned the punitive features of the Calvinist God into an indictment of God as an evil or amoral creator, the "author of sin" (hence the infuriated absolutism of Ahab). On the other hand, based on his early exposure to polytheistic beliefs in Polynesia, and his later reading in such skeptical savants as Montaigne and Bayle, Melville questioned whether anything positive might be known about God, given the seemingly relativistic nature of all truth (hence the open-minded agnosticism of Ishmael). Melville was, in short, a divided soul: a skeptic by temperament but a believer at heart.[6]

This internal conflict was the irresolvable moral and metaphysical dilemma that caused Melville constantly "to reason of Providence and futurity, and of everything that lies beyond human ken," as Hawthorne reported in November 1856; for Melville could "neither believe, nor be comfortable in his unbelief and he is too honest and courageous not to try to do one or the other" (*Log*, 2:529). In this battle of head and heart, Melville could neither believe in traditional Christianity nor accept the traumatic implications of a godless or malign universe; both the theme and form of the novel he had just completed reflected this division in his thought. Like his other "metaphysical" fictions, *The Confidence-Man* is a literary theodicy dramatizing the author's obsession with the problem of evil, the existence of God, and man's limited capacity to know God or comprehend the truths that would justify the ways of God to man.[7]

Beginning with John Shroeder and Elizabeth Foster, and continuing with Hershel Parker and others, a persistent assumption among influential interpreters of the novel has been that the figure of the Confidence Man represents an incarnation of the devil. Yet this reading overlooks the heterodox nature of Melville's religious beliefs and fails to do justice to the complexity of the novel's vision. For the characterization of the Confidence Man suggests that good and evil, Christ and Antichrist, are ultimately part of one divine entity but that any proof of such a conjunction or other positive knowledge of the divine nature is seemingly impossible. Moreover, as the bipartite structure of the novel demonstrates, God may appear to be a satanic swindler of man's confidence, but in the person of Christ He can also incarnate a faith of the heart that provides the necessary basis for human fellowship and so may redeem the evil in man.

Melville's placing of the action of *The Confidence-Man* on a ship of fools on April Fools' Day is symptomatic of his religious predicament. While a preoccupation with fools and folly is a late medieval and Renaissance phenomenon found in Sebastian Brandt's *Ship of Fools*,[8] Erasmus's *Praise of Folly*, and the fools of Rabelais and Shakespeare, Melville's ultimate locus of inspiration for this theme was undoubtedly St. Paul. At the beginning of his first letter to the Corinthians, Paul insists that "the foolishness of God is wiser than men" (1:25), for "God has chosen the foolish things of this world to confound the wise" (1:27). Moreover, "If any man among you seemeth wise in this world, let him become a fool, that he may be wise" (3:18–19); in short, "We are fools for Christ's sake" (4:10). The only problem with such a formulation is that being a fool of Christ could mean either becoming redemptively "wise" or else falling prey to a pious hoax created by an evil or amoral creator.

While the setting of Melville's novel on April Fools' Day implicitly creates a drama of religious skepticism, the very mechanics by which the drama is enacted arise from an April Fools' Day custom native to the Scotland of Melville's paternal ancestry:

> What compound is to simple addition, so is Scotch to English April fooling. In the northern part of the island, they are not content to make a neighbour believe some single piece of absurdity. There, the object being, we shall say, to befool simple Andrew Thomson, Wag

> No. 1 sends him away with a letter to a friend two miles off, professedly asking for some useful information, or requesting a loan of some article, but in reality containing only the words:
>
> 'This is the first day of April
> Hunt the gowk [cuckoo, fool] another mile'
>
> Wag No. 2, catching up with the idea of his correspondent, tells Andrew with a grave face that it is not in his power, &c.; but if he will go with another note to such a person, he will get what is wanted. Off Andrew trudges with this second note to Wag No. 3, who treats him in the same manner; and so on he goes, till some one of the series, taking pity on him, hints the trick that has been practiced on him. (Chambers, 461)

Such sequential fooling is precisely the kind performed by the Confidence Man in the first half of the novel, as the passengers on the *Fidèle* succumb to fooling by the successive guises of Melville's hero. Conversely, in the second half of the novel, the Confidence Man as cosmopolitan is the intended dupe for an interlinked series of knaves who are species of confidence men in their own right.[9]

This scenario is enhanced by the novel's typological grounding in the Parousia or Second Coming of Christ. This event was prefigured in the Book of Daniel, announced in the Gospels in Christ's "Little Apocalypse" (Matt. 24–25, Mark 13, Luke 21), reaffirmed in several of the Epistles, and symbolically enacted in the Book of Revelation. In Christ's own prediction in the Olivet discourse or "Little Apocalypse," the Second Advent was to be heralded by a time of general calamity characterized by wars, earthquakes, and famine (in Christian eschatology, this period is known as the Tribulation or Apostasy); it would also be marked by the appearance of "false Christs and false prophets" who "shall deceive the very elect" (Matt. 24:24). Accompanying this prophecy of signs of the end-times, however, was the assertion that Christ's advent was going to be completely unexpected, "for in such an hour as ye think not the Son of man cometh" (Matt. 24:44).

Selected passages in the rest of the New Testament re-worked various strands of Christ's prophecy, including the expectation of satanic deceivers as heralds of the end-time. In the important eschatological discussion in his two letters to the Thessalonians, for example, St. Paul wrote, "Let no man deceive you by any means: for *that day shall not come*, except there come a falling away first, and that man of sin be revealed, the son of perdition; / Who opposeth and exalteth himself above all this is called God, or that is worshipped; so that he as God sitteth in the temple of God, shewing himself that he is God" (II Thess. 2:3–4). The possibility of being led astray by a satanic deceiver or Antichrist in the "last days" was also apparent in the Book of Revelation, when Satan, having been temporarily defeated during a thousand-year period (the millennium), "shall go out to deceive the nations" during a "last loosening" before his final destruction (Rev. 20:7–10)—a period analogous to Satan's earlier activities during the Apostasy or Tribulation.

The ambiguous nature of Christ's Second Advent, including the epistemological dilemma of not being able to detect the false from the true Christ, forms an integral part of the theological basis for Melville's last published novel. Indeed, the inscrutability and ambiguity associated with the apocalyptic advent of Christ evokes Melville's long-standing belief in the enigmatic and ambivalent nature of God. Also playing a part in Melville's fictive adaptation of Christian eschatology is the analogy between the unexpectedness of Christ's Second Coming and that of a thief. In the Olivet discourse, Christ said, "But know this, that if the goodman of the house had known in what watch the thief would come, he would have watched, and would not have suffered his house to be broken up. / Therefore, be ye also ready" (Matt. 24:43–44; Luke 12:39–40). In the epistles of Paul and Peter, the message of the parable emerges as the familiar slogan, "the day of the Lord cometh as a thief in the night" (I Thess. 5:2; II Peter 3:10). Finally, in St. John's Revelation the apocalyptic warning appears as "I will come on thee as a thief" (Rev. 3:3) and "Behold, I come as a thief" (Rev. 16:15). In *The Confidence-Man* Melville made a provocative association between the traditional metaphor of Christ's unexpected advent like that of a thief, and the figure of the thievish "Original Confidence Man," whose reappearance in Albany in April 1855 after his previous arrest in New York (and subsequent stint in Sing Sing prison) did indeed constitute a kind of "second coming."

The apocalyptic framework of Melville's novel has not gone unnoticed by critics. In a pioneering essay on apocalyptic symbolism in modern American fiction, for example, R.W.B. Lewis argues that *The Confidence-Man* is "the pivotal text in the history of apocalyptic literature in America. . . . It is a conventional inspection of humanity during the last loosening of Satan: but its perspective is profoundly and almost shatteringly comic" ("Days of Wrath," 210–11). While Lewis's essay provides a useful introduction to the apocalyptic frame of the novel, it too closely equates the Confidence Man with the devil and too narrowly schematizes the novel's plot. For in fact *The Confidence-Man* re-creates the Parousia and Apostasy, the Second Coming of Christ and Last Loosening of Satan as a single event; it also synthesizes a dense variety of allusions to the Book of Revelation, the New Testament, and the Bible as a whole.[10]

Lewis and others have read *The Confidence-Man* as a "comic" or "ironic" apocalypse, but "satirical apocalypse" is actually a more useful generic designation, for the novel synthesizes its apocalyptic scenario with the ironic tactics, topical references, comic devices, and moral concerns of satire. Significantly, classical satire and Christian apocalypse are, in several respects, coterminous literary forms: both enact protests against contemporary fraud and corruption; both are premised on a prophetic dialectic of crisis, judgment, and potential renewal; both employ allegorical indirection. (Appropriately enough, Juvenal—the most outspoken and well-represented Roman satirist—and St. John the Divine—the founder of Christian apocalyptic—were contemporaries, both of them reacting against the tyranny and decadence of late first-century imperial Rome.) In English and American literature, works such as Langland's *Piers Plowman,* Pope's *Dunciad,* Byron's "Vision of Judgment," and Hawthorne's "The Celestial Railroad" have variously synthesized narrative or verse satire with apocalyptic, allegorical "dream" vision, the latter form having its ultimate generic model in the Book of Revelation. As a complex embodiment of this hybrid tradition, Melville's April Fools' Day apocalypse paradoxically undercuts America's worldly corruptions and millennial faith while calling into question the whole superstructure of Christian belief.[11]

In addition to the novel's apocalyptic frame, its April Fools' Day setting has still another implicit bearing on the underlying mythical structure of the narrative. As an ancient, pan-European celebration with a cognate tradition in the Hindu festival of Huli, April Fools' Day jocularity has been traced to celebrations commemorating the rebirth of nature and the return of the sun at the vernal equinox. (The Christian holiday of Easter, with its "good news" of spiritual rebirth, was partly an outgrowth of the same tradition: Easter was named after the Anglo-Saxon goddess of spring, Eostre or Ostara, whose holiday was celebrated at the vernal equinox.) In *The Confidence-Man* Melville implicitly draws on a symbolic association between the Resurrection, the Second Coming, and pagan myths of saviors "reborn" in the spring to ensure human and natural fertility. The Confidence Man is thus both Son and Sun, the novel being evenly divided between day and night according to the equal division of day and night at the equinox. In keeping with this mythical paradigm, the first guise of the Confidence Man, the Christ-like "man in cream-colors," is initially compared to the Inca sun god, Manco Capac; even the designation "cream-colors" evokes the color spectrum contained in white light.[12]

The relevance of the novel's setting on April Fools' Day also applies to another of the Confidence Man's important mythical affiliations, that of trickster god. The trickster is an inconsistent, amoral embodiment of knavery and foolishness, a figure with a traditionally close relationship to the satirist. While episodes in both *Moby-Dick* (Ch. 49) and *Pierre* (Bk. XIV) on occasion hint that the deity is a type of trickster, only in *The Confidence-Man* does Melville's shape-shifting protagonist formally assume the mythological lineaments of a traditional trickster god. "The trickster's outstanding characteristic is that he functions ambivalently. . . . Because he knows that God and the Devil are holding hands behind the scenes, *sub specie eternitatis,* he is able to rise above the consistency sanctioned by conventional, societal values. He moves from one role to another with great facility because his insight permits him to play all roles with delight" (Baim, 81–82). The trickster god thus plays both knave and fool in a cosmic masquerade like that of Melville's Confidence Man, whose identity as a "trickster" effectively distances him from too close an association with the devil.

Finally, the ambiguous ethical import of Melville's hero must be seen in the context of the well-known Victorian crisis of faith, a crisis Melville shared more with his English contemporaries like Tennyson and Arnold than his fellow Americans, although many American writers and intellectuals of the postbellum era would later cover the same ground as Melville in the 1850s. Even before the publication of Darwin's *Origin of Species* in 1859, the possible extinction of Christian belief due to the development of contemporary science (especially geology) and the higher criticism of the Bible threatened to place mankind in an alien, capricious, and potentially terrifying universe; in the words of D.H. Meyer, "the age-old assumption that nature is an intelligently and purposefully designed system—fabricated by a benevolent Creator to serve Higher Ends—had eventually to be consigned to the rubbish heap. Purpose and order were replaced by randomness, chance, and the blind operation of natural laws" (588). Deprived of belief in a transcendent providential deity, mankind was seemingly cast adrift in a world governed by the selfish and materialistic interests of Mammon. But before we investigate Melville's image of this world in *The Confidence-Man,* we must look at the novel's formal structure.[13]

2

Satirical Form: Parodic Masquerade

Just as the enigmatic identity of the Confidence Man has provoked longstanding critical controversy, *The Confidence-Man*'s generic affiliation has also remained in doubt. For even though the novel is one of Melville's most tightly constructed and stylistically sophisticated performances, it has often been considered a work that ultimately defies literary classification. And while a number of critics have recognized that *The Confidence-Man* possesses a large measure of satirical ingredients, relatively few attempts have been made to examine it specifically from this perspective. Yet critical examination of *The Confidence-Man* as satire demonstrates that many of its apparent anomalies of form and content are explicable in light of this generic affiliation.[1]

For present purposes satire may be defined as an attack on vice and folly by means of wit, irony, or ridicule; combining comic invention with moral judgment, humor with censure, satire presents a schematic, largely topical representation of individuals and societies corrupted by moral abuses. Set on April Fools' Day on a riverboat denominated a "ship of fools" and characterized by a wide variety of frauds and swindles, *The Confidence-Man* patently exhibits the traditional moral concerns of satire, vice and folly. Indeed, in the figure of the Confidence Man Melville has created both an embodiment of contemporary moral abuses and a satirical agent for their exposure in others. In its latter half, moreover, the novel features a sustained attack on the dominant philosophical creed of its era, Transcendentalism, which is depicted as a self-centered, dehumanizing species of idealism. Such an attack on a contemporary "school" of philosophy is a regular feature of satiric tradition and can be found in the writings of Aristophanes, Juvenal, Lucian, Rabelais, Swift, and Huxley.[2]

Yet despite the salience of its satirical themes, the novel still poses at least two important questions for any attempt to characterize it as a satire. The first relates to the vexed question of satirical form, for satire is notorious for the variety of literary forms it appropriates: "The word satire is said to come from *satura,* or hash, and a kind of parody of form seems to run all through its tradition" (Frye, 233). While satire is often termed a literary "mode" or is classified as a characteristic tone or attitude, two main traditions of satire as genre, both with classical origins, have generally been recognized. The first is formal verse satire, the tradition stemming from Horace and Juvenal, in which the satirist (or satiric persona) directly attacks a particular manifestation of vice or folly. The second is Menippean (i.e., discursive, principally prose) satire, the tradition stemming from Lucian, which typically employs a borrowed structure or "fable" in which the author *qua* satirist plays a more oblique or even invisible role.

If this classification serves a useful function of identifying satiric types and establishing their lineages, it nevertheless tends to obscure basic continuities between formal verse and Menippean satire. Stressing such continuities, Leon Guilhamet has recently suggested a system of classification that distinguishes not between formal verse and Menippean, but between "simple" and "complex" satire, noting of the latter:

> Complex satire begins in the same way as simple satire, with a host structure—rhetorical, belletristic, or popular. Like simple satire, it deforms the host structure by means of modal satire, comic ridicule, and ironic devices. The only difference is the much more elaborate use of additional genres and styles so that the form becomes preeminently mingled satire. As in all satire, the introduction of formations contradictory to the purposes of the host genre de-forms the structure and transforms it into satire. The dynamic of complex satire consists of more than one formal strategy working in relation with one another. Complex satire thus differs from the simple kind only in its much more ambitious use of competing formations and its tendency to become encyclopedic, if not in bulk, then at least in the range of its satiric applications. (14)

The Confidence-Man may be said to constitute a "complex" Menippean narrative satire, given the obliquity of the author's role as satirist, the encyclopedic range of its applications, the philosophical issues it debates (a typical feature of Menippean satire), and the variety of host structures it subsumes. These host structures, or subgenres, include apocalyptic vision, pilgrimage allegory, Platonic dialogue, stage comedy, quest romance, picaresque fiction, and theatrical masquerade.[3] While some of these subgenres are discussed later in this chapter and in Chapter 4 below, we might pause here to note the novel's incorporation of two in particular, chivalric quest romance and the picaresque. Like one of Spenser's heroes, the Confidence Man is closely identified with a Christian virtue, which he proceeds to test throughout the novel in a series of episodic encounters or "wit combats." Like an Arthurian hero, he ends his career with a parody of the finding of the Grail, here a chamber pot *qua* life preserver situated under a "clean, comely, old man," whose characterization recalls the fact that guardians of the Grail were required to be pure in mind and body.

The Confidence-Man also exhibits a number of the characteristic elements of the picaresque, including several of the "low" character types found in this tradition like the quack doctor and the barber. Its shape-shifting hero similarly conflates the eighteenth-century English picaro's polarized identity as either larcenous knave or hapless fool—either a Jonathan Wild or a Lancelot Greaves, a Count Fathom or a Joseph Andrews. Still another resemblance to picaresque stems from the fact that Melville's novel re-creates the prolonged eighteenth-century debate on human nature that pitted Hobbesian cynicism against Shaftesburyean benevolism, a debate that shaped the mixture of satire and sentiment found in English picaresque fiction. In particular, the central Indian-hating chapters in the middle of Melville's novel are analogous to the story of the misanthropic Man of the Hill in the middle of *Tom Jones.* Melville's three interpolated essays (Chapters 14, 33, and 44) are also Fieldingesque, while his narratological confidence games parallel the method of Sterne. Yet despite this overlap of both matter and method, *The Confidence-Man* should not be primarily classified as a picaresque fiction because its plot is more static and schematic, its narrative texture more allegorical, its themes more philosophical, and its historical context more immediately topical than picaresque fiction typically demonstrates.[4]

Not only does *The Confidence-Man* subsume a range of parodic subgenres, but its "plot" also exhibits a common structural design of a class of narrative satires. Ronald Paulson has characterized the episodic form of such satiric "fictions" as being analogous to the seemingly unplotted movement of Roman verse satire (*satura*):

> The narrative equivalent of *satura* is the journey. A protagonist's wanderings allow for independent satires within a frame, permitting a catalog form and an ironic reference to the more idealized journeys of romances. The accumulation of encounters is a good approximation of the "characters" and anecdotes in *satura,* conveying something of the same claustrophobic feeling of the crowd welling up around the satirist standing on his street corner. A more static narrative is the dinner party, ship, carriage, or some such gathering in which a group of different types can be analyzed in relation to a general vice. But whenever a narrative action is desired, the protagonist must leave the dinner party and go to different places or meet different people, and the progression of his journey is either unplotted or borrows a plot (e.g., from romance) bearing an ironic relation to the real satiric ac-

> tion, which is only a movement from one kind of folly to another or from bad to worse. (43)

The protagonist of *The Confidence-Man* similarly enacts a static journey through a broad social landscape, repeating a formal pattern of encounter that both mirrors a romance "plot" (as earlier noted) and progresses from bad to worse, that is, from the fools of the first half to the knaves of the second. The novel's apparent lack of closure is also consistent with the formal conventions of narrative satire, for as Alvin Kernan notes, "It is clear that satire never offers that direct, linear progression which is ordinarily taken as plot. Instead, we get collections of loosely related scenes and busyness which curls back on itself—darkness never really moves on to daylight but only to intensified darkness" (*Plot of Satire,* 100).[5]

Finally, the novel's formal heterogeneity also subsumes a diverse array of discrete parodic ingredients. As Paulson points out, "Satire enjoys the episodic forms, the collection of stories or anecdotes, the list, the large dinner party or the group conversation, the legal brief, the projector's pamphlet, the encyclopedia, and the calendar" (5). In *The Confidence-Man,* we find an equivalent range of forms, including the stories and anecdotes making up the novel's four interior fables, Black Guinea's list of character witnesses, the vinous "symposium" of Frank Goodman and Charlie Noble, the legal agreement by the barber and Goodman, the projector's schemes of the man in gray, the encyclopedic discussion between Charlie Noble and Frank Goodman, and finally the temporal/calendrical scheme of the novel's April Fools Day setting progressing from dawn to midnight. Other forms parodied include the sermon (delivered by John Truman to Henry Roberts), the panegyric (Charlie Noble's salute to the "press"), the tall tale (the story of John Moredock), and the tract (the Story of China Aster). On a smaller scale, we find samples of lyric poetry (an "Ode on the Intimations of Distrust in Man"), nursery rhyme ("Hey diddle diddle"), epitaph (China Aster's tomb), apothegm (the barber's quotation from Ecclesiasticus), and innumerable tags from Shakespeare and the Bible—an admixture that evokes the traditional origins of Menippean satire in a mixture of verse and prose. The novel's profusion of formal ingredients is also accompanied by a varied rhetorical and stylistic repertoire of assonance, alliteration, onomatopoeia, paranomasia, litotes, parallelism, and *reductio ad absurdum,* such variety being a hallmark of satirical style.[6]

The other chief difficulty some critics face in considering *The Confidence-Man* a satire stems from their inability to perceive what kind of moral norm it implies. In fact, many people assume that a literary work can only be judged a satire if it contains a clearly defined norm, often thought to be some standard of "reason." In Melville's novel, on the other hand, in the Hobson's choice between having "confidence" or "charity" and being duped, and having none of either and losing one's humanity, there would seem to be no "reasonable" alternative. Yet it should be noted that the bipartite structure of the novel—featuring a negative critique of confidence and charity in the first half, followed by a more positive presentation in the second, and a return to the initial critical mode at the end of the novel—conforms to the dialectical structure of formal verse satire, a structure often repeated in Menippean or narrative satire as well: "The fact has long been recognized that formal verse satire as a poetic form breaks sharply into two markedly disproportionate divisions—thesis and antithesis, destruction and construction, black and white—with the latter portion being ever the weaker and less striking of the two" (Randolph, 369n). It is thus a moot point whether Melville's novel argues the need for Christian charity or else demonstrates its impracticability or obsolescence in the modern world. As one commentator remarks, "The ambiguity of Melville's position is plain in his use of the Christian ethic to condemn a world in which that ethic is clearly inoperable. This ethic is too good to be true, but none other is good enough" (Hoffman, *Form and Fable,* 311). The novel accordingly exemplifies what might be called a paradoxical moral norm.[7]

Recent criticism of satire has in fact discredited the older notion that satire teaches clear moral precepts and substituted a more ambiguous or unresolved moral framework. Thus Frank Palmeri points out the "dialogical" nature of narrative satire in which different modes of discourse are strategically juxtaposed, while Dustin Griffin highlights satire's tendency to effectuate a process of ongoing ethical "inquiry" and "provocation": satire often works "not by drawing a clear line between 'Good' and 'Evil' but by teasing readers with the play of contraries" (60). It is increasingly being recognized, too, that many well-known satires leave the matter of a moral norm ambiguous or otherwise in doubt, especially when irony makes the author's viewpoint inconsistent or duplicitous. Erasmus's mock encomium, *Praise of Folly,* for example, exhibits a paradoxical norm comparable to the one found in *The Confidence-Man;* for if at the beginning of her encomium Folly's self-praise is patently ironic, it eventually becomes associated with the positive spirituality of the wise fool or the Pauline fool of Christ. Swift's satirical strategies also create normative ambiguity. Thus *The Tale of a Tub* and *Argument Against Abolishing Christianity* send the reader on a wild goose chase for a clearly articulated ethical precept, while *Guilliver's Travels* systematically inverts our perspective on its paradigmatic world with each successive book. Significantly, the experiences chronicled in Gulliver's final voyage subvert any ostensible norm of "reason" by showing the predominance of man's animal nature (the Yahoos), while simultaneously revealing the seeming impossibility of mankind ever living up to an effective standard of reason (the Houyhnhnms). In twentieth-century satire, which has been largely subsumed within the domain of the novel, the question of satire's moral norm has been rendered even more problematic by the disintegration of supernaturally sanctioned principles of order and authority. So in the novels of Huxley, Waugh, and Orwell in England, and West, Pynchon, and (most recently) Tom Wolfe in America, we find a variety of satiric, frequently apocalyptic narratives depicting the modern world as threatened by the forces of cosmic chaos or social corruption. The ethical universe of *The Confidence-Man* is thus situated between the ambiguous or paradoxical norms of its satiric predecessors and the absurdist, annihilative vision of the twentieth century.[8]

Another important consideration arising from an analysis of the novel's form concerns its relation to the theatre. Most readers can hardly fail to notice the many theatrical motifs that characterize *The Confidence-Man*, especially in the protean performance of its hero. For example, the Confidence Man begins his career on the *Fidèle* by approaching a "placard" warning of a "mysterious imposter," a sign the crowds examine as "if it had been a theatre-bill." In the second chapter of authorial commentary (Chapter 33), the narrator invokes the theatre as the relevant metaphor for the Confidence Man's actions, as well as the reader's experience of the novel. Subtitled a "masquerade" and largely composed of a medley of dialogues, Melville's fiction effectively incorporates a wide variety of motifs from classical, Renaissance, and contemporary dramatic traditions. Taken together, these theatrical elements confirm the mixed nature of the novel's satirical structure, while also hinting at larger questions relating to the novel's philosophical vision.[9]

A number of critics have remarked that *The Confidence-Man* exhibits the Aristotelian "unities" of time, place, and theme; but the extent to which the "plot" of the novel is also based on a classical comic scenario has not been noticed. For in the schematic conflict between the man in cream colors and the barber in the first chapter, the barber represents a traditional comic "blocking" character whom Melville's protagonist eventually overcomes at the end of the "drama." In classical New Comedy (Menander, Plautus, Terence), the model for most later European comedy, the protagonist is typically a young man whose ambitions are blocked by a money-conscious father, miser, or pimp. The hero achieves his goal, usually a young woman, with the help of a "witty slave" or "designer of wiles" whose manipulative freedoms are partly a function of the social liberties of holiday license. Overcoming the financial interests and moral objections of his adversaries through trickery, the young man is reconciled to his alienated father at the end of the comedy. If we substitute *agape* for *eros* as the object of the protagonist's quest, unite the young man and witty slave into one protean personality, and translate the father into a patriarchal persona, *The Confidence-Man* may be said to conform to this classical model. The novel also parodies the conventional classical *anagnorisis* or "recognition" scene when, in the final chapter, the Confidence Man is for the first (and only) time explicitly identified by an offstage voice. Finally, the setting of Melville's novel on April Fools' Day evokes the ritual origins of classical comedy in Dionysian and Saturnalian celebrations, continued in the association of later European comedy with Christmas revels or pre-Lenten Carnival.[10]

Within the realm of Renaissance drama, the "comical satire" of Jonson and Shakespeare provided the model for another salient theatrical motif in *The Confidence-Man.* A central feature of "comical satire" involved the introduction of an outspoken character who embodied a dramatic version of the aggressive authorial persona of Elizabethan formal verse satire. The abrasive personality of this persona stemmed from the erroneous belief that Roman satire developed from the scurrilities and obscenities of the mythological "satyr" as depicted in the ancient Greek satyr play. The figure of Thersites in *Troilus and Cressida* is perhaps the best known dramatic satyr-satirist; Jonson's Asper-Macilente from *Every Man Out of His Humor* is another representative figure. In keeping with this theatrical tradition, *The Confidence-Man* features a satyr-satirist in the wooden-legged man of Chapters 3 and 6, who may be considered a modern version of Thersites: both are physically disabled; both are abrasive, lewd, and vengeful; both call everyone around them fools; both evoke the primitive origins of satire in the formulaic curse, which was thought to be able to injure or even kill the satirist's victims. And just as the satyr-satirist aspired to blister the skin or flagellate the body of his adversaries, the wooden-legged man in Chapter 3 dubs himself a "Canada thistle" and later tells the man in gray of his desire to expose Black Guinea: " 'I'm just in the humor now for having him found, and leaving the streaks of these fingers on his paint, as a lion leaves the streaks of his nails on a Caffre' " (*CM,* 32). Yet although he can see through Black Guinea's minstrel paint, the "discerning eye" of the wooden-legged man fails to see that the same enigmatic personality is standing before him in the latter scene. The wooden-legged man is thus unable to injure his protean adversary, who is himself a satirist by inversion and indirection and so escapes the penalties exacted on the wooden-legged man as a cynical malcontent. A scapegoat figure and "satirist-satirized," the wooden-legged man serves as a monitory example of the fallibility of the satirist's judgment, the potential ostracism of the satirist as social critic, and the low-mindedness that was associated with the satirist's vocation.[11]

In general, if Ben Jonson's protean world of knaves and fools bears a notable resemblance to that depicted in *The Confidence-Man,*[12] Shakespearean drama exerted a more direct influence on the novel. The universality of acting, the mutability of human behavior, the problem of appearance and reality, the mystery of iniquity—all these were lessons Melville eagerly assimilated from the writer he once called the "divine William" (*C,* 119). In addition to direct quotations from a number of plays, several Shakespearean characters and motifs appear in *The Confidence-Man* as, for example, in the story of Goneril, whose malignity is parodically related to her Shakespearean prototype, or in the series of allusions throughout the novel to the misanthropy typified by Timon of Athens. The second half of the novel is particularly informed by Shakespearean drama: as a figure in motley, the cosmopolitan plays the fool like Touchstone and Feste; as a Prospero-figure, he casts a spell over Charlie Noble; as a Hamlet-figure, his tale of Charlemont functions as a moral "mousetrap" for Noble. In the cosmopolitan's encounter with Egbert, moreover, the two enact a play within a play like that found in *As You Like It;* Egbert's citation of Jacques' famous lines on the "world as stage" at the end of the encounter confirms the connection. Shakespeare's characters and authorial intentions are also directly "canvased" during the cosmopolitan's encounter with Charlie Noble. Noble hysterically attacks Polonius as a morally rotten character, but the transparent irony here is that Noble is himself Polonius-like in his physical decay, manipulative behavior, and cynical morality. Goodman's subsequent evaluation of Autolycus, however, represents a more ambiguous critique. For if Goodman's remarks notify Noble that he is aware of his friend's manipulative con game, they also hint at his kinship with Shakespeare's genial rogue. Yet in their larger import, they ultimately suggest that Shakespeare's moral ambiguity in the creation of Autolycus and other subversive characters is a model both for Melville as literary creator and for the potentially nihilistic universe depicted in the novel. Melville is essentially restating the insight of Keats, who speculated on Shakespeare's equal delight in creating an Imogen and an Iago.[13]

Finally, as a reflection of contemporary theatrical motifs, the novel subsumes various features from pantomime, minstrelsy, and farce. The physical comedy of farce actually frames the novel, from the flattening of the mute's hat in the first chapter to the cosmopolitan's chamber pot joke in the last. The pale-looking mute in cream colors also implicitly assumes the role of Pierrot, one of the stock characters of pantomime, the popular silent theatre that developed out of French commedia dell'arte. As Helen Trimpi notes, "Pierrot was typically mute, young, and dressed in white; he carried nothing because he owned nothing, was generally poor and friendless, was the butt of physical buffoonery, and was mocked as half-witted; he was associated with the moon and with romantic idealism about love and *le peuple*" ("Harlequin-Confidence-Man," 168). The French associations of the opening scene of the novel—the city of St. Louis, the steamer *Fidèle,* the "chevaliers" on her decks—are thus well suited to the mute's assumption of the innocent, otherworldly part of Pierrot.[14]

In contrast to this initial figure of pallid innocence, the Confidence Man's next guise plays on the duplicity latent in the art of minstrelsy, the leading popular entertainment of antebellum America, in which white actors in blackface imitated the music, dance, and comic routines of black slaves. With his physical deformity, coal-sifter tambourine, devious sense of humor, and ability to ridicule his audience while amusing them as a comic butt, Black Guinea plays the role of Brother Tambo, the tambourine-beating "endman" of the minstrel lineup. "Minstrels made extensive use of nonsense humor, fantasy, and animal fables that they almost certainly derived from Afro-American folk song and narrative, which relied heavily on animal symbolism, used indirection and guile to voice protests or attack adversaries, and featured victories for the weak over the strong" (Toll, 48).[15] Guinea's witty exchange with the drover thus conforms to Tambo's facetious dialogue with his straight-man "interlocutor"; Guinea's subsequent "pitch penny" game of catching coins in his mouth like an "elephant in a menagerie" also suggests a novelty act within the minstrel show framework. Significantly, both menageries and minstrel shows were featured at P.T. Barnum's American Museum in New York City, which functioned as an emporium of antebellum entertainment. And as David Reynolds points out, "The first chapter of the novel shows immediately that Melville had reached the same conclusion about American society that many humorists of the 1850's had: in the Barnumesque carnival of popular culture, all is reduced to theater and entrepreneurial manipulation" (552).[16]

While all of these theatrical elements confirm the close relation between satire and theatre, and contribute to the satirical mix of formal ingredients in *The Confidence-Man,* the larger implications of the novel's theatricality arise out of Melville's philosophical skepticism. As several critics have noted, *The Confidence-Man* ultimately suggests the fictiveness of both human and cosmic "reality." The novel accordingly evokes the epistemological confusions and ironic incongruities of the "grotesque" while anticipating the modern literature of the "absurd." Consonant with this philosophical vision is the novel's underlying metaphor of the world as stage, or *theatrum mundi.* The idea was first articulated by the Pre-Socratics, embraced by Roman Stoicism, and established during the Middle Ages as a Christian paradigm in which God was viewed as the divine author and stage manager invisibly presiding over the evolving human drama. Yet as Jean-Christophe Agnew remarks, "Melville revived the epistemological anxieties of the medieval *theatrum mundi* without offering the corresponding consolations of otherworldliness or utopia" (203). Melville's novel thus performs a satirical exposure of the universe itself, showing it to be a cosmic masquerade with possibly nothing behind it. From this perspective, the novel's masquerade of parodic forms corresponds to the apparent fictiveness of both human and cosmic reality.[17]

3

Historical Context: Mirror of Man

In the preceding chapter we examined how *The Confidence-Man* exemplifies satirical form; in this chapter we turn to a consideration of its satirical content. What specific targets is Melville attacking in his last published novel? Critics have suggested a wide range of answers. In an early appreciation Richard Chase interpreted the novel as an ironic evaluation of American "liberalism" in which the Confidence Man mimicked various facets of the national character, the American "booster" in particular. In the introduction to her pioneering 1954 Hendricks House edition of the novel, Elizabeth Foster argued that *The Confidence-Man* offered an encyclopedic critique of the nation's heritage of optimistic philosophy, including Shaftesburyean benevolism, Benthamite utilitarianism, Enlightenment and Romantic cults of nature and progress, and Emersonian idealism. In her view the novel was an American *Candide*. In the late 1960s Johannes Bergmann identified the "Original Confidence Man" who served as Melville's historical prototype, thereby providing a better understanding of the genesis of the novel and some of its topical resonances. A decade later, Carolyn Karcher argued that *The Confidence-Man* constituted an apocalyptic judgment on the national "sin" of slavery. In the early 1980s Tom Quirk explored Melville's literary adaptation of some of the criminal tactics employed by contemporary swindlers and confidence artists, including the figure earlier identified by Bergmann. In the last ten years, Mary Jean Northcutt has interpreted *The Confidence-Man* as a satire on the deficiencies of the democratic mind in America, as diagnosed by de Tocqueville: rejecting traditional notions of authority and social hierarchy in favor of the wisdom of the people (otherwise known as the "tyranny of the majority"), America developed characteristic modes of cultural expression such as sentimentalism and sensationalism that Melville systematically exposes to ridicule. Finally, in a recent study of narrative satire, Frank Palmeri has analyzed Melville's novel as a dialogical conflation of Christian and commercial modes of discourse, while Michel Imbert has similarly highlighted the symbolic correspondence in the novel between financial credit and divine credibility.

Although these and other studies have shed light on *The Confidence-Man*'s philosophical, socioeconomic, and general cultural contexts, it largely remains to be seen how the novel reflects many of the specific features of its immediate historical era. As Edward Rosenheim reminds us, "All satire is not only an attack; it is an attack upon *discernible, historically authentic particulars.* The 'dupes' or victims of punitive satire are not mere fictions. They, or the objects which they represent, must be, or have been, plainly existent in the world of reality; they must, that is, possess genuine historical identity" (25). In order to discover how the novel reflects the historical particulars of the antebellum era, we will begin by examining the significance of its setting on a Mississippi riverboat. We will then go on to examine how it focuses attention on an extensive roster of contemporaneous social issues and institutions including race and slavery, religion, education, law and criminal justice, medicine, science, philosophy, money and banking. In keeping with the satirist's traditional role of anatomizing the moral abuses of his era, *The Confidence-Man* presents an encyclopedic catalogue of national vice and folly.[1]

Melville's setting the novel on a Mississippi steamer along the nation's western frontier was suited to both his general thematic and immediately topical aims. The "West" was traditionally viewed as the realm of the future in America, Jefferson's "empire for liberty" in which the nation's democratic ideals would find their most representative embodiment. As Melville had earlier affirmed in *Israel Potter,* "the western spirit is, or will yet be (for no other is, or can be) the true American one" (*IP,* 149). Yet in *The Confidence-Man* he goes on to depict the nation's western frontier as tainted with fraud and corruption, a "sardonic inversion of the values his culture conventionally attributed to the frontier," as Edwin Fussell remarks (304). Melville's ironic portrait was actually symptomatic of the tensions and disjunctions of American life by the 1850s, an era when a triumphant materialism and economic individualism coincided with America's incipient fulfillment of its "manifest destiny" in the West. For the novel dramatizes America's increasingly hypocritical attempt to serve both God and Mammon, as the Confidence Man's evangelical rhetoric offsets an intricate series of depredations and deceptions.

The novel's opening tableau, which juxtaposes the mute's pleas for "charity" with the barber's announcement of "No Trust" (i.e., no credit given), typifies the basic opposition between Christian and commercial values found throughout the novel. The contrast points to the contemporary belief that in the absence of traditional forms of authority, only the ethics of Christianity could keep a democratic society like America from disintegrating into a collection of autonomous individuals driven by predatory self-interest. Douglas T. Miller notes that

> the rapid settlement of the West during the first half of the nineteenth century weakened such earlier institutions of social control as the family, church, bench and bar, landholding and merchant elites, and the state. Many persons, of course, welcomed these changes as the fruition of democratic individualism—the triumph of the self-reliant common man. Emersonian transcendentalism epitomized this faith in a society of free individuals operating without institutional restraints. But for others the image of such an unchecked individualism conjured up fears of anarchy and immorality. (*Birth of Modern America,* 54–55)

With a professional role of giving "shaves" to his customers—to "shave" has been a cant term for cheating or taking advantage of someone since the time of Chaucer—the barber is an emblematic figure of both the prudential morality and exploitative self-interest that characterizes many of the *Fidèle*'s passengers. Confirming this Hobbesian view of contemporary American society is the initial image of the *Fidèle* as a "whitewashed fort on a floating isle" as well as the various "hunters" who make up the passenger list (*CM,* 8, 9).

Yet in addition to its larger symbolic significance as the American ship of state, the *Fidèle* as a Mississippi steamer provided a recognizably topical setting for Melville's sardonic representation of American society, for this particular mode of transportation would have evoked the notorious vices of riverboat travel in the 1840s and 1850s:

> Thousands of gamblers, cheats and blacklegs followed river gambling for a livelihood. Formerly they had remained stationary in the river towns, and there took advantage of landing flatboatmen and travelers. Captains were supposed to watch out for those rascals and to see that none of their passengers were tricked, and if a blackleg got aboard [the captain] had instructions from the owners to "bank" him at once. Few precautions, however, were actually taken, and gambling on board the steamboats was as commonplace as stopping for wood. Sometimes the boats' officers were *en league* with the sharpers, and always put them off at the "right time" and at the "right woodyards." Next to gambling, excessive drinking and the "entertainment halls" were notorious vices of river travel. These two evils combined were the means of many innocent "gulls" losing personal fortunes within the scope of a short voyage. (Clark, 92; citations omitted)

The moral perils of gambling and drinking are also evident on the *Fidèle.* Indeed, they provide the thematic frame for related narrative sequences in the first and second halves of the novel as the Confidence Man diddles a foolish Henry Roberts and then a knavish Charlie Noble. These sequences bear examination in some detail since they complement each other in both theme and structure, and act as satirical caricatures of contemporary commercial and social relations.[2]

The Confidence Man actually diddles Henry Roberts three times, first as Black Guinea, then as John Ringman, and finally as John Truman, each encounter dramatizing an increasingly complex interplay between charitable appearances and predatory realities. While Black Guinea elicits Roberts' first act of charity as a spontaneous gesture of pity to a social inferior, his subsequent guise of John Ringman draws on a more elaborate ploy derived from the "sentimental" ethos of the merchant's own middle-class culture. The logic of antebellum sentimental culture posited the domestic sphere as a protected realm of feeling, safe from the calculated interests and acquisitive energies of the market. Yet the actions of the Confidence Man demonstrate that such a division of cultural labor is potentially flawed, for John Ringman's masquerade of bereavement constitutes a clever manipulation of sentimental culture by means of its conventions of mourning. Karen Halttunen has analyzed the importance of mourning in sentimental culture as a demonstration of genteel social status:

> By conforming to the explicitly defined rules of mourning dress and etiquette, the bereaved and their sympathetic acquaintances enacted publicly a genteel performance of their deep sensibility. In other words, mourning was subject to the same civilizing process shaping other aspects of bourgeois conduct. But once again, middle-class efforts to embody private feelings in established cultural forms aroused deep anxieties about the conflict between social form and sentimental content and gave rise to a sentimental attack on the hypocrisies of middle-class life. Sentimentalists feared that the struggle for bourgeois gentility was poisoning even mourning with calculated self-interest and transforming mourning ritual into a masquerade of affected sensibility. Any confidence man or woman, it was feared, could easily assume the proper mourning dress and etiquette, stage a deceptive performance of deep grief, and thus establish a false claim to genteel social status. (124–25)

John Ringman performs precisely this ploy, not only tricking Roberts into making a charitable contribution during their initial encounter but also setting him up for a future encounter with John Truman by letting Roberts know that Truman is ready to sell undervalued coal company stock. Having thereby stimulated Robert's greed, Ringman is ready for his ensuing manipulation of Roberts in his future guise of Truman, during which the "game" of confidence turns into a multifaceted act of fraud, revealing the potential corruptions latent within both the public world of business and the private world of the home.

Significantly, the sequence involving Henry Roberts and John Truman beginning in Chapter 10 transpires in a cabin where card-sharping is the order of the day, as revealed by the narrator's unobtrusive mention of the "philosophes" who are observing the various games, no doubt commissioned by their fellow card sharks. Indeed, the atmosphere of deceit in this gambling hall is the subject of attack by a mysterious elderly Quaker (the Confidence Man in a cameo role) who distributes throughout the cabin a mock-Wordsworthian "Ode on the Intimations of Distrust in Man." After enacting the traditional confidence artist's use of conspiratorial plants, the Confidence Man as genial John Truman enters the premises, ready to initiate a game of cards. But failing to find a partner, he sits next to Henry Roberts to watch as two "unpolished youths" play cards with a pair of soberly dressed card sharpers whom the narrator, with Chaucerian disingenuousness, characterizes as "decorously dressed in a sort of professional black, and apparently doctors of some eminence in the civil law" (i.e., blacklegs). Roberts rightfully suspects that some cheating is in progress, but Truman criticizes the merchant's suspiciousness and the merchant is able to regain his "confidence" in a pattern that is repeated several times throughout this sequence.

Truman's ensuing manipulation of the merchant's credulity by selling him stock from the Black Rapids Coal Company extends the gambling motif from cards to the stock market. The underlying rationale for connecting the two stems from the fact that they not only were—and still are—viewed as analogous activities, but also because of their metaphorical associations with hell: gambling halls were commonly referred to as "hells" in nineteenth-century England and America. (Melville had earlier depicted a London gambling "hell" in Chapter 46 of *Redburn.*) The name of Truman's company also patently evokes the idea of hell, a fact earlier brought out by John Ringman's description of the fluctuations of Black Rapids stock in terms of Satan's fall in *Paradise Lost.* Gambling, stock manipulation, greed, and hell are in fact all associated here in a symbolic configuration that was based on the corruptions of the contemporary stock market:

> In the fifties, with the growth of corporations, speculation in the ups and downs of stocks became the respectable avenue to great fortunes, the occupation of leaders of society. Stocks were "bulled" with dividend announcements or rumors of government largesse, after insiders had purchased in low markets; or "beared" with horrendous gossip which sent prices tumbling and short sellers buying. Often the dividends were paid out of capital, the gossip manufactured in the

> "Street." Out of the fluctuations they set in motion the great financiers got rich, the little margin traders got fleeced.
>
> Such activities generally were accepted in the spirit of roulette or faro. A game among plungers, "Playing the Market" gave spice to the drab mercantile existence, attracted little Daniels to the lions' den. More important to the business community were the frauds perpetrated through the market. Uninspected at issue, fake stocks encountered no barriers if the company in whose name they were issued was listed. Thus Robert Schuyler, President of the New York and New Haven Railroad, could sell at par for his own benefit, in 1854, 20,000 unauthorized shares of stock—$2,000,000 worth—in his own company. In the same year, Alexander Kyle of the Harlem Railroad issued forged stock to the tune of $300,000 for his own purse, Parker Vein Coal Company officials flooded the market with five times as many shares as their charter authorized while President Edward Crane of the Vermont Central Railroad for his own profit scattered 10,000 illegitimate shares so widely that they were irretrievable, forcing the legislature to increase the authorized capitalization of his road to save his victims from being fleeced.
>
> These operations, when discovered, created a financial panic in 1854. They depressed prices, made the investing public wary, and temporarily frightened capital away from private corporations. Only the most flagrant offenders, however, were punished. The rest were soon excused. Business, the art of making money, had by the fifties "ceased to be a mere occupation which must be carried on in accordance with the moral code. It had itself become part of that code. Money-making having become a virtue, it was no longer controlled by the virtues, but ranked *with* them, and could be weighed against them when any conflict occurred." (Cochran and Miller, 74–76; citation omitted)

Developments in the contemporary stock market thus provide us with the immediate historical context for Truman's scam. For instead of dismissing Truman's coal company as a fraud, as some critics do, we should regard Truman's stock as "unauthorized" shares of a legitimate company. In addition, Truman himself is modeled on those market manipulators—including corporate officers—whose corrupt practices may be taken as an index of the debasement of moral values in the nation in general, and in its commercial capital in particular.[3]

The ostensible role of "chance" in the encounter of Truman and Roberts underlines a continuing motif of gambling as Truman proceeds to diddle his victim. Truman draws the merchant's attention to his stock book by "chancing to expose the lettering on the back" and then hastening away from his place while leaving his book behind. As a result, the merchant recognizes the name of the company that John Ringman had earlier recommended and is thus lured into buying Black Rapids stock, the metaphorical equivalent of selling his soul to the devil. Given the symbolic context here, it is not surprising that after purchasing his stock Roberts sinks into a gloom, citing the cases of the miser, Black Guinea, and Goneril as evidence that the world is full of unmerited suffering, despite the appealing "spectacle" of the scene around them. The sentimental merchant is apparently unaware of the fact that all of his examples evoke the existence of hell: the miser lying in his tortured bunk, Black Guinea sleeping in his "baker's oven," and the lascivious she-devil, Goneril, ruining her husband's life. The story of Goneril in particular causes Roberts' interlocutor to engage in a concerted effort at Christian apologetics in order to gloss over the story's darker implications. In fact, the ensuing discussion, in which Truman repeatedly attempts to prove that the story of Goneril is susceptible to a positive or providential interpretation, constitutes a *Candide*-like mock theodicy in which Truman's Panglossian insistence on human and divine justice is actually an ironic indictment of the unreliability of divine providence.

Despite Truman's sermonizing, the merchant's persistent "doubts" again erupt when the two are quaffing champagne, at which point the merchant involuntarily confesses, " 'Ah, wine is good, and confidence is good; but can wine or confidence percolate down through all the stony strata of hard considerations, and drop warmly and ruddily into the cold cave of truth? Truth will *not* be comforted. Led by dear charity, lured by sweet hope, fond fancy essays this feat; but in vain; mere dreams and ideals, they explode in your hand, leaving naught but the scorching behind!' " (*CM*, 67). While these sentiments are comically apt for someone who has put his confidence in bogus coal company stock, in the process making a symbolic investment in "hell," they also suggest an emerging moral consciousness in the merchant, even though framed in terms of both masturbatory indulgence ("explode in your hand") and diabolic high jinks ("scorching behind"). For Roberts has looked into the abyss within man's moral nature, and in this respect it is probably no coincidence that he discovers "the queer, unaccountable caprices of his natural heart" in Chapter 13 of the novel.[4]

In the merchant's multifaceted encounter with the Confidence Man, then, Melville plays on the symbolic connections between a vice typical of riverboat travel, the calculated deceits of both sentimental culture and the antebellum marketplace, the unreliability of providence, and finally, the moral darkness latent even within the "good" merchant, the representative fool of the first half of the novel.

While the climax to the scene between Truman and Roberts occurs as the two are quaffing champagne, it is only in the later encounter of Frank Goodman and Charlie Noble that the other prominent vice of riverboat travel, drinking, is fully dramatized. As two confidence men of unequal capacities, Goodman and Noble enact an elaborate ritual of deception in a classic frontier scenario of the "bitter-bit" while drinking each other's health in spurious wine. Noble initiates the drinking as a means of getting his mark "fuddled," little knowing that Goodman is a formidable adversary who will play the role of Socratic *eiron,* or self-deprecating ironist, to Noble's inept *alazon,* or foolish self-deceiver. Moreover, gifted like Socrates with a "hollow leg," Goodman directs this frontier symposium through an exposure of false friendship in which wine serves as a factitious vehicle of social communion.

It is important to keep in mind that not only does this scene evoke both the perils of riverboat drinking and the pervasiveness of alcohol consumption in nineteenth-century America, but it also plays on topical issues arising from the current temperance movement which was reaching a climatic phase of development in the 1850s. Due to the zealous lobbying of Neal Dow, the first statewide law of prohibition was passed in Maine in 1851, with a number of New England and midwestern states soon following suit. John Gough was also barnstorming the nation as a leading temperance orator, while Timothy Shay Arthur's best-selling *Ten Nights in a Bar-Room* (1854) sought to do for temperance what *Uncle Tom's Cabin* (1852) had recently done for the cause of antislavery. Although disagreeing whether fermented drinks like beer, wine, and hard cider ranked with distilled "ardent spirits" like whiskey and rum as equal menaces to the nation's welfare, the temperance movement branded most alcoholic beverages as poisonous to health and happiness and touted the virtues of pure *cold* water. (The presumed virtues of *cold* water are ironically evoked in *The Confidence-Man* during Frank Goodman's encounter with the chilly transcendental mystic, Mark Winsome, in Chapter 36.) Moreover, as a dramatization of issues raised by the temperance crusade—including whether wine, despite its role in Christian communion, should be included in the general ban on liquor—the symposium of Goodman and Noble also plays on the current belief that many alcoholic beverages, especially wine, were chemical concoctions marketed by unscrupulous producers and retailers. The prohibitionists' argument that all alcoholic beverages were harmful inevitably bolstered this belief, which had a legitimate basis in fact:

> Purveyors were finding it profitable to mix expensive wine with cheap whiskey to create a fortified product that was 20 to 30 percent alcohol. This concoction was sometimes cut with water to produce a still potent beverage and large profits. Indeed, fortification, watering, and adulteration were so common that it was estimated that Americans drank five times as much "Madeira" as was imported. The high potency and adulteration of the wine sold in America led antispirits crusaders to sacrifice it on the altar of teetotalism. (Rorabaugh, 106)[5]

The subject of the adulteration of wine arises at the beginning of the drinking bout between Frank Goodman and Charlie Noble, when Noble remarks:

> "Ill betide those gloomy skeptics who maintain that now-a-days pure wine is unpurchasable; that almost every variety on sale is less the vintage of vineyards than laboratories; that most bar-keepers are but a set of male Brinvillierses, with complaisant arts practicing against the lives of their best friends, their customers."
>
> A shade passed over the cosmopolitan. After a few minutes' downcast musing, he lifted his eyes and said: "I have long thought, my dear Charlie, that the spirit in which wine is regarded by too many in these days is one of the most painful examples of want of confidence. Look at these glasses. He who could mistrust poison in this wine would mistrust consumption in Hebe's cheek. While, as for suspicions against the dealers in wine and sellers of it, those who cherish such suspicions can have but limited trust in the human heart. Each human heart they must think to be much like each bottle of port, not such port as this, but such port as they hold to. Strange traducers, who see good faith in nothing, however sacred. Not medicines, not the wine in sacraments, has escaped them. The doctor with his phial, and the priest with his chalice, they deem equally the unconscious dispensers of bogus cordials to the dying."
>
> "Dreadful!"
>
> "Dreadful indeed," said the cosmopolitan solemnly. "These distrusters stab at the very heart of confidence. If this wine," impressively holding up his full glass, "if this wine with its bright promise be not true, how shall man be, whose promise can be no brighter? But if wine be false, while men are true, whither shall fly convivial geniality? To think of sincerely-genial souls drinking each other's health at unawares in perfidious and murderous drugs!"
>
> "Horrible!" (*CM,* 161)

The mordant irony of this situation depends on the justifiable assumption that the wine the two are drinking is indeed spurious, if not drugged. The ambiguous label of "P.W." on the bottle earlier hinted at both cheap viticulture and poisonous adulteration; and Charlie Noble's "slight involuntary wryness to the mouth" when first drinking and his subsequent reluctance to imbibe effectively confirm the wine's dubious purity. As symbolic counterparts, a false-hearted Noble and a debased vintage here together convey a potent message of falsity at the heart of social relations.

Noble's mention of the possible spuriousness of wine is actually a prelude to Goodman's systematic exposure of Noble as a con artist and hypocrite whose identity is "shady" in more senses than one. For Noble is surrounded with hints that he may actually be a hobgoblin or demonic agent. As critics have noted, the name "Charlie Noble" is naval slang for a galley smokestack. Noble accordingly shows signs of being both a smokey apparition and a mechanical "stiff." Noble's initial description is in fact so equivocal that no distinct image of him emerges other than that of possessing false teeth, ill-fitting clothes, a garish vest, and a simulated "florid cordiality." Noble is thus a shady character, greedy hobgoblin, and teetotaling "departed spirit" combined into one.[6]

Goodman and Noble's symposium ranges over a number of topics, but in every instance we find Noble inadvertently exposing himself as a fraud. The exposure gets under way when Goodman initiates a discussion of humor by suggesting that " 'a man of humor, a man capable of good loud laugh—seem how he may in other things—can hardly be a heartless scamp.' " However, when Noble goes on to laugh at a poor pauper in big boots, he inadvertently reveals that he is indeed a heartless scamp; contrary to Goodman's theory, laughter is an ambiguous index of the human "heart."[7] When Noble subsequently brings up the subject of the "press," he evokes another potential vehicle of affirmative social values; but again his actions belie his assertions. Noble's earlier performance as Judge Hall speaking to the "press" on Indian-hating was actually a burlesque distortion of the historical James Hall and his writings in the interest of Noble's stratagem of ingratiation. Similarly, Noble's recitation of a panegyric on the wine "press" inverts the warning against wine contained in the passage from Proverbs (23:29–32) that Noble is parodying. Noble's panegyric actually travesties a contemporary temperance speech, which typically cited scriptural strictures against wine (often the very passage from Proverbs that Noble is inverting) and then concluded with a poetic tribute to cold water.[8]

On the surface, Goodman and Noble's conversation registers a steadily increasing intoxication with a utopian vision of universal "geniality." In reality, Noble is obsessed with getting Goodman drunk while evading his share of the drinking and smoking. The spuriousness of the wine-bibbing is thus a match for the spuriousness of this geniality which, according to Goodman's confident projection, will soon affect all professions, even—in a sardonic *reductio ad absurdum*—that of the common hangman. Goodman's vision of a golden or millennial age of geniality is a bombastic parody of the pervasive nineteenth-century belief in the inevitability of progress. However, the inevitable proof that human nature remains immune to improvement finally obtrudes when Goodman calls Noble's bluff and requests a loan, thereby bursting the speculative "bubble" the two have inflated and exposing Noble for a scheming sharper.

Given Noble's symbolic status as a treasure-seeking hobgoblin, it comes as no surprise that Goodman is able to conjure back Noble's "geniality" using his gold coins as proof that he was only joking; hence a new round of drinking promises to ensue. However, Goodman's story of Charlemont, with its oblique commentary on Noble's false friendship, puts an end to the discussion as Noble beats a hasty retreat. Noble blames his indisposition on the wine, which he denominates a "confounded elixir of logwood," thereby inadvertently confirming the sham that has fueled his whole performance in this reference to a current topical joke on the red "logwood" dye allegedly used to give color to wine.[9] In his evocation of the adulterated port wine as a bogus "elixir"—a substance thought to be capable of changing base metals into gold or of prolonging life—Noble paradoxically confirms the relevant adage, *in vino veritas,* while admitting that the wine was indeed as false as himself.

The Confidence Man's prolonged encounters, then, with a foolish Henry Roberts and a knavish Charlie Noble dramatize two prominent vices of riverboat travel that typify larger cultural mores. Both encounters play on mock-diabolic motifs that serve as satirical indices of the natural depravity latent in Roberts and Noble; in both sequences, the possibility of evil is insinuated under an official ideology of progress and providence. Both narrative sequences include an illustrative fable and inspire a chapter of authorial commentary on the novel's methods. Yet in addition to these two sequences highlighting contemporary commercial and social relations, *The Confidence-Man* also attacks a wide array of other explicit and implicit historical "targets," and it is to these that we now turn.

Issues of race and slavery first obtrude with the appearance of Black Guinea in Chapter 3 of the novel. A free Negro whose handicap necessitates a life of beggary, Black Guinea is a stereotypical "happy darky" of antebellum cultural convention, especially its minstrel show variety. Guinea's beggary similarly evokes an antebellum stereotype of the Negro as a child-like dependent who would be helpless in white society if freed from slavery; his destitution is in fact typical of the endemic poverty of the antebellum Negro, whether slave or free. As the "black bread" amidst "nice white rolls," or a "black sheep nudging itself a cozy berth in the heart of the white flock," Black Guinea typifies the black man as a permanent alien in white America. In keeping with his culturally degraded condition, Guinea's charitable cause is ineffectual until he makes himself the equivalent of a performing circus animal for the crowds on the *Fidèle.*

Carolyn Karcher has argued that Guinea represents an "apocalyptic nemesis" figure who enacts a symbolic revenge on the passengers of the *Fidèle* for the sinfulness of slavery. In her interpretation, Guinea fulfills Melville's vision of an America tainted by Negro servitude and thus deserving of the alleged judgment figured in the apocalyptic structure of the novel.[10] Yet if Guinea's performance dramatizes the hardships facing blacks in antebellum America, his obsequious behavior and gleeful duping of his audience vitiate much of the pathos we feel for his plight. As a disguise of the Confidence Man, moreover, Guinea is in all probability a fake Negro impersonated by a "white operator" (he may even be the devil himself; see next chapter). Edward Grejda aptly remarks that Guinea is at once "a grinning darky, a deserving object of the white man's abuse; as a white man assuming the stereotypical characteristics of the darky he is an indirect criticism of the whites who see the Negro as a formula; his treatment by the whites, who deny him charity and trust, dramatically illustrates the negative view of man advanced by the book" (129). With such a multifaceted identity, exemplifying Melville's paradoxical moral vision in the novel, Guinea is an ambiguous index of racial injustice—but a reliable index of human selfishness—on the *Fidèle.*

Issues of race and slavery are nevertheless raised again during the man in gray's encounter with the gentleman with gold sleeve-buttons in Chapter 7. In this case, Karcher has more persuasively argued that the depiction of the gentleman conforms to the traditional image of the Southern Cavalier, the genteel character type developed by popular culture and literary convention to celebrate the happy plantation life of the South as a desirable alternative to the degrading material interests of the North (*Shadow,* 126–37). The encounter of the man in gray with the gentleman thus effectuates a meeting of sectional stereotypes, the man in gray incarnating Northern missionary uplift and economic calculation in contrast to the gentleman's Southern patriarchal conservatism and indulgent prodigality. It is useful to note that by 1860 three-fifths of the richest 1 percent of the population were Southern slaveholders (Levine, 58). Hence Melville's ostentatiously dressed planter as the *Fidèle*'s representative aristocrat is historically justified.

Melville's satirical strategy in the depiction of the gentleman is to demonstrate that even the most ostensibly "charitable" individual on the *Fidèle* is inherently tainted with corruption. For while the gentleman at first conveys an aura of consummate "goodness," this quality is gradually subverted in his ensuing characterization, at the end of which the narrator asserts that "it is still to be hoped that his goodness will not at least be considered criminal in him." The motive for this *reductio ad absurdum* of the gentleman's ostensible "goodness" is provided by his white attire, which hints at a mysterious association of good and evil in its bearer:

> The inner-side of his coat-skirts was of white satin, which might have looked especially inappropriate, had it not seemed less a bit of mere tailoring than something of an emblem, as it were; an involuntary emblem, let us say, that what seemed so good about him was not all outside; no, the fine covering had a still finer lining. Upon one hand he wore a white kid glove, but the other hand, which was ungloved, looked hardly less white. Now, as the Fidèle, like most steamboats, was upon deck a little soot-streaked here and there, especially about the railings, it was a marvel how, under such circumstances, these hands retained their spotlessness. But, if you watched them a while, you noticed that they avoided touching anything; you noticed, in short, that a certain negro body-servant, whose hands nature had dyed black, perhaps with the same purpose that millers wear white, this negro servant's hands did most of his master's handling for him;

> having to do with dirt on his account, but not to his prejudice. (*CM,* 36)

We may at first read this passage as an ironic attack on the worldly vanities and moral obliquities of the wealthy, whose insularity from the world's "dirt" is a symptom of their privileged condition. Yet for the reader alert to antebellum stereotypes, the reference to a Negro servant as better adapted to demeaning manual labor would evoke a current Southern justification for slavery. Officially denominated the "mudsill" theory of society by James Henry Hammond of South Carolina, this popular belief postulated a permanent servant class of blacks to perform the drudgery necessary to produce a higher civilization among whites. In his study of the slave culture of the South in the mid-1850s, Frederick Law Olmsted wrote that this ideological defense of slavery

> assumes that by having a well-defined class set apart for drudging and servile labour, the remainder of a community may be preserved free from the demeaning habits and traits of character which, it is alleged, servile and menial obligations and the necessity of a constant devotion to labour are sure to fix upon those who are subject to them. Hence a peculiar advantage in morals and in manners is believed to belong to the superior class of a community so divided. I am inclined to think that there is no method of justifying slavery, which is more warmly cherished by those interested to maintain it, than this. I am sure that there is none which planters are more ready to suggest to their guests. (514)[11]

In the gentleman's portrait, then, Melville is effectively parodying the contemporary "mudsill" theory, showing that the gentleman's supposed "goodness" and immunity from evil are premised on mere accident and the doctrinaire degradation of the African race. In sum, in the gentleman's emblematic illustration of Melville's belief in the enigmatic link between good and evil, the generous-hearted Southern Cavalier, one of the most outwardly attractive antebellum American character-types, is revealed to be tainted with sin.

Significantly, the gentleman's portrait is framed in specifically religious terms, his putative goodness contrasted with the man in gray's evangelical righteousness. The gentleman is surrounded by hints that he is a pharisaical exemplar of law untouched by grace. The narrator in fact draws on Paul's letter to the Romans—a key exposition of the transformation of law into grace provided by Christ—in order to confirm that the gentleman is merely "good" without being in any way "righteous." To underline this point, the gentleman is compared to Pontius Pilate and dissociated from William Wilberforce (1759–1833), the wealthy English evangelical reformer best known for his work for the abolition of British colonial slavery. And while the initial image of the gentleman's immaculate appearance evokes Christ's denunciation of the scribes and pharisees as "whited sepulchres" (Matt. 23), the equivocation of the narrator over the gentleman's "goodness" would also seem to mimic the protracted antebellum debate over whether slaveholding was a sin and whether the slaveholder could be a Christian. The slavery issue had already divided the largest American denominations, the Baptists and Methodists, into independent Northern and Southern organizations by the mid-1840s. The next largest, the Presbyterians, had split in 1837 into Old and New School divisions, while the New School offshoot would again fragment over slavery in 1857. The narrator's convoluted defense of the gentleman's "goodness" in Chapter 7 of *The Confidence-Man* in effect suggests the contradictory response, both condemnatory and apologetic, that slavery elicited from contemporary institutional Christianity.

Yet whatever moral judgment is being rendered here, it should be noted that the gentleman's association with Southern slavery is only implied, not asserted. Why should Melville be so elliptical in this era of *Uncle Tom's Cabin* and "Bleeding Kansas"? One answer would be that in the portrait of the *Fidèle*'s gentleman Melville is attempting to unite satirical specificity with allegorical suggestiveness. Thus from a theological perspective, the gentleman's moral condition could be read as analogous to that of the Christian deity, for like the gentleman, God is able to remain spotlessly pure by having the devil do his dirty work for him. From a sociological perspective, the gentleman's peculiar moral condition might be considered emblematic of all those wealthy individuals whose privileged lives are dependent on a class-based "sinning by deputy." They accordingly remain in bondage to the "world" even in their acts of charity because such charity doesn't alter a worldly status quo. Like Bunyan's Worldly Wiseman (also known as the "gentleman") or Hawthorne's Judge Pyncheon, both of whom he resembles, Melville's gentleman with gold sleeve-buttons might be considered a type of hypocritical patrician benevolence.

The encounter depicted in Chapter 7 of the novel is also notable as a satirical critique on the contemporary "benevolent empire" of philanthropical or reformist enterprises promoted by evangelical ministers and their lay supporters. This movement is exemplified by the entrepreneurial man in gray, collector for a Seminole Widow and Orphan Asylum and a World's Charity. As the operator of a domestic charity, his alms-seeking for Seminole widows and orphans incongruously evokes America's most expensive and protracted nineteenth-century Indian war, the Seminole War of the 1830s, together with the sanctimonious "asylum" movement on behalf of the criminal, the insane, and the destitute. In his capacity as international evangelical reformer, the man in gray embodies the millennial faith that led Protestants to promote global philanthropies and missions in preparation for the Second Coming of Christ, in keeping with Christ's apocalyptic assertion: "And this gospel of the kingdom shall be preached in all the world for a witness unto all nations; and then shall the end come" (Matt. 24:14).

Melville parodies America's millennial mission in the man in gray's description of the genesis of his World's Charity at the first "world's fair" in London in 1851. Officially known as the "Great Exhibition of the Works of Industry of All Nations" and held in what was dubbed the "Crystal Palace," this "world's fair" was a mid-Victorian monument to the benefits of free trade and technological progress. Attending the "Fair" to exhibit a "Protean easy-chair" that promises unlimited ease to both body and mind—a spoof on the thousands of machines, home furnishings, art, and other "improvements" on display at the fair—the man in gray has been inspired to come up with a charitable scheme commensurate with his surroundings. Hence on the fourth day he issued his prospectus for a "World's Charity," thereby burlesquing God's summoning of light on the fourth day of creation (Gen. 1:14–19). In keeping with this miraculous precedent, the titanic philanthropical projects and missionary efforts of the man in gray parody the overweening ambitions of the contemporary evangelical enterprise. "It is remarkable how increasingly," writes Perry Miller, "at least down to about 1850, the immense American missionary effort was presented as something basically *radical*, of a piece with the titanic entrance into the world of steam and electricity. . . . Over and over again, to the point of tedium, but never to satiety, orators identified missions with the industrial 'scene of astonishing activity' " (*Life of the Mind*, 52).[12]

A salient problem, however, with the man in gray's ambitious schemes is that they require the utilization of noticeably worldly means to accomplish their spiritual ends. First, the man in gray would institute a "grand benevolence tax upon all mankind" of a dollar a head, thereby ignoring the problem of the poor contributing to the relief of their own poverty, as the gentleman quickly points out. Second, the man in gray would quicken his missions with the "Wall street spirit" of competitive bidding, thereby ignoring the corruption that might ensue from such an unlikely partnership of God and Mammon. The man in gray's "World's Charity" is in fact a Swiftian satire on a contemporary "spiritual projector" who is attempting to unite worldwide benevolence with the benefits of laissez-faire capitalism and free trade. It should be noted that Melville's satire here is actually applicable to both England and America, for mid-Victorian confidence in the sovereign virtues of free trade nurtured the climate of overweening optimism that the man in gray personifies—hence the relevance of the man in gray's visit to the London "world's fair." Nevertheless, his concluding demonstration of a "spirit of benevolence which, mindful of the millennial promise, had gone abroad over all the countries of the globe," is a distinctively American ambition, founded on the nation's tradition of civic millennialism.

Confirmation that the "Wall street spirit" is not a proper vehicle for benevolence can be found in the Confidence Man's two encounters with the college sophomore in Chapters 5 and 9, a sequence that adds education to the roster of Melville's satirical targets. In Chapter 5 the sophomore is an effete-looking collegian with a Byronic affectation in dress, as evidenced by his open-collar shirt, Greek-letter fraternity pin, and copy of Tacitus in hand. Here the Confidence Man as John Ringman, a sentimental "man of feeling," approaches the sophomore and after examining his reading matter launches into an attack on Tacitus. The ensuing scene amounts to a Swiftian "battle of the books" as Ringman tries to get the sophomore to throw away his copy of Tacitus, whom he denounces as a dispenser of "moral poison," along with other classical writers such as Horace, Juvenal, and Lucian (satirists all). Ringman's alternative text is a more agreeable "modern," the poet-physician Akenside. Adding a touch of comic absurdity to this miniature "battle of the books" is the fact that the names of the two authors carried by Ringman and the sophomore are puns on their owners' behavior: Ringman is introduced as having "his hand to his side like one with the heart-disease" (ache-in-side), while the sophomore remains largely silent throughout Ringman's assault on Tacitus.

Ringman makes a fool of the sophomore as a timid, tongue-tied young man whose eventual flight is largely motivated by fear of some impending impropriety. When the Confidence Man as John Truman encounters the sophomore in Chapter 9, however, he is able to dupe the sophomore because he is a now a cheerful man of business instead of an emotive sentimentalist. Moreover, Truman now appeals to the sophomore's material self-interest instead of his moral well-being. The underlying joke throughout this scene is that Ringman needn't have worried about the sophomore being corrupted by Tacitus because he has already been corrupted by a precocious materialism that thrives on "fellows that talk comfortably and prosperously" like Truman.

Playing on the sophomore's greedy, cynical nature, as manifested by his eagerness to do business and his impatience with Truman's appeals on behalf of the "unfortunate man" (Ringman), Truman argues that all gloomy philosophers, " 'whether in stocks, politics, bread-stuffs, morals, metaphysics, religion—be it what it may—trump up their black panics in the naturally-quiet brightness, solely with a view to some sort of covert advantage' " (*CM,* 48). The double irony here is that Truman is taking advantage of the sophomore by behaving like a cheerful philosopher. Moreover, Truman's appeals on behalf of Ringman are implicitly motivated by self-interest, the sophomore's boasted *modus operandi.* The sophomore ultimately damns himself by preferring to buy stock in the Black Rapids Coal Company rather than the "New Jerusalem," while his final desire to see the "unfortunate man" thrown overboard merely confirms the sophomore's selfishness, which Truman wryly labels a "dry" sense of humor.

The college sophomore might be taken as Melville's satirical rebuttal of Emerson's prescriptions for an "American Scholar" not beholden to the

European past but reliant on his own intellectual resources and actively engaged with the life of his times. Self-consciously asserting his masculinity during his conversation with Truman, the sophomore aggressively conforms to the Emersonian ideal of worldly engagement, but with a precocious worldliness that might have surprised the sage of Concord. For in Melville's portrait of a sophomoric American scholar, the classical past has become an empty standard of value, replaced by the money-making speculations of the present. Significantly, the sophomore reveals himself to be a more astute reader of Truman's stock pamphlets than of the classical literature he himself carries. Not surprisingly, he refuses to invest in the New Jerusalem despite the fact that it has a total of *twenty* lyceums! With his expensive tastes and drawling speech, the sophomore is the beneficiary of an education based on privilege, not knowledge; his Greek-letter fraternity pin highlights the fact that brotherhood in his world is for "members only."[13]

The sophomore's callous attitude to the "unfortunate man" anticipates to some extent the Confidence Man's later encounter with the alms-seeking "soldier of fortune" in Chapter 19, an encounter that renders an indictment of the nation's legal and criminal justice system. As the witness to a class-based murder at a political rally in City Hall Park in New York City—either an anti-British demonstration during the agitation for the Oregon territory in the early 1840s or a later patriotic rally during the war with Mexico—an impecunious Fry has become an invalid because he was left stranded in the Tombs prison after being unable to come up with bail money. Modeled on an Egyptian temple, the Tombs was in fact notorious for its insalubrious environment, having been built on what was formerly a swamp.[14] Unable to attract charity by revealing the true reason for his infirmity (which would appear too unflattering to the national self-image to be believed), Thomas Fry instead passes as a disabled Mexican War veteran. Juxtaposing the demagogic politics of manifest destiny with the social conflicts of the nation's commercial capital, the story of Thomas Fry exemplifies the sacrifice of the "common man" within a political and legal system that deferred to class privilege despite its supposed egalitarian basis. The historical conditions for such a development arose with the stratification of social classes in Eastern cities that accompanied industrial growth. As Douglas T. Miller writes, "The social and economic changes that brought a wealthy plutocracy to the pinnacle of Northern society in the period before the Civil War were not accepted without resentment. As the rich became richer and the poor more numerous, hostilities and even open class conflicts frequently occurred, particularly in New York" (*Jacksonian Aristocracy*, 184).[15]

Fry had witnessed the murder of a pavior in City Hall Park by a "gentleman" who pushed the pavior because of the pavior's "beastly" habit of chewing tobacco. When the herb doctor notes that the pavior "tried to maintain his rights" by pushing back, Fry counters with the assertion that "he undertook something above his strength," a claim the herb doctor appears not to understand. The implication of Fry's remark, however, is an ironic inversion of the formula that might makes right: the pavior is physically stronger than the gentleman and has a better claim to justice, but the gentleman represents the greater power of vested interests, as his acquittal for the murder subsequently demonstrates. The upshot is a grotesque contrast between the fate of the gentleman and the innocent third party, for the gentleman is "hung" with a gold chain by his friends upon acquittal, while Fry is eventually "hung" between a pair of crutches.

Like another "small fry" of American history, Israel Potter, the story of Thomas Fry shows that America was in danger of betraying its Revolutionary ideals, as some social commentators at this time were in fact remarking. Fry belongs to that class of working-class artisans, mechanics, and factory operatives who saw their economic status declining in the ostensibly prosperous 1840s and 1850s. His futile trip to find his brother in Indiana shows that the familiar panacea of "going west" was potentially another hollow promise of American life. Now "drifting down stream like any other bit of wreck," Fry is a representative "common man" who sinks instead of rising with the tide of national prosperity, a victim of the growing rift between rich and poor, and the increasing atomization of American life, especially in its major cities.

We have seen that in the character of John Ringman, Melville satirizes America's sentimental culture; in the man in gray, its evangelical commitment to global reform; and in John Truman, the corruptions of its new corporate capitalism. The Confidence Man's subsequent appearances as a nostrum-peddling herb doctor and a shady-looking employment agent satirize other aspects of America's commercial culture, parodying trades and professions marked by abuses of trust under the guise of fostering benevolence.

In the appearance of the herb doctor, Melville launches a prolonged attack on the national faith in "nature" by means of a critique of its patent medicine industry. As a patent medicine salesman, the herb doctor is the agent for a growing industry that offered innumerable cures for cancer, consumption, venereal disease, dyspepsia, fever and ague, catarrh, and virtually all known and imaginary ailments. The herb doctor's relentless promotion of his products reflects the fact that the development of the advertising profession in America in the 1840s and 1850s was partly dependent on promoting the many patent remedies then flooding the market. "There was no end to the variety and quantity of ingredients available," remarks James Harvey Young, "and there were soon more pills and potions than Americans could swallow conveniently. The medicine man's key task quickly became not production but sales, the job of persuading ailing citizens to buy his particular brand from among the hundreds offered. Whether unscrupulous or self-deluded, nostrum makers set about this task with cleverness and zeal"

(166). The claims of patent medicine advertising were thus evidence of the optimistic tenor of nineteenth-century American life and a reminder of the marketability of that optimism. Consider an advertisement that repeatedly ran in Melville's local paper, the *Pittsfield Sun,* in 1855:

> Devine's Compound Pitch Lozenge. A Beautiful Remedy For Cold, Coughs, Costiveness &c., and facts show that this simple, pleasant and cheap medicine cures what is by respectable Physicians called Consumption
>
> Despair had blistered my spirit with its fiery smart!
> These Tidings my pulses thrill, and Hope hath touched my heart!
> Yes—Here is Hope!

Although attacks on patent medicine quackery began to appear during the Jacksonian era, no effective regulation of the industry would occur until the first decade of the twentieth century when therapeutic laissez-faire in medicine finally yielded to scientific rigor in an era of reform. This was largely because the etiology of most diseases was a mystery until the development of Pasteur's germ theory in the later nineteenth century. Until then, a vague body of pseudo-science governed much of popular and even professional medical thought, a pervasive theory being that all diseases had one root cause and hence one universal remedy (a "panacea" or "catholicon") might be able to cure them all. The patent medicine industry also took advantage of trust in the herbal remedies developed by the American Indian, as well as religious faith in the efficacy of "natural" ingredients as curatives provided by God to offset the many diseases He put on earth.[16]

As he unabashedly touts his two products, Melville's herb doctor satirically mirrors the claims and procedures of the patent medicine industry. The magnitude of his claims, for example, is in blatant contrast to the incurable illnesses of his potential patients: a consumptive "sick" man, a melancholy "invalid Titan," a paralytic "soldier of fortune," and a moribund old miser with a "church-yard cough." The herb doctor's Omni-Balsamic Reinvigorator and Samaritan Pain Dissuader are also modeled on varieties of patent medicines, the Omni-Balsamic evoking the cure-all claims of many of these products as in Brandreth's purgative "Vegetable Universal Pills" (one of the most popular nineteenth-century remedies), and the Samaritan Pain Dissuader mimicking the pervasive use of religious motifs for brand names and promotion.[17]

The herb doctor's mode of operation also mimics the promotional techniques of the nostrum vendors. In his encounter with the sick man, for example, the herb doctor begins by attacking the practices of "chemical practitioners" and ends by warning the sick man against counterfeiters of his product. The constant downgrading of the medical profession as well as unscrupulous practices by competitors characterized the patent medicine business throughout the nineteenth century. The counterfeiting of remedies was in fact widespread, as commercial rivals and rogue operators stole both recipes and packaging in order to take advantage of a brand's success. The campaign against doctors also took advantage of a widespread distrust of the medical establishment, as Young notes:

> Year after year, nostrum advertisers told the layman about the failings of the doctors. Wherever regular physicians were weak, lo, there the nostrum maker was strong. Their therapy was brutal, his was mild. Their treatment was costly, his was cheap. Their procedures were mysterious, his were open. Their prescriptions were in Latin, his label could be read by all. Their attack on illness was temporizing, his was quick. Their approaches were cumbersome, his were simple. Their techniques led to the grave, his never failed. (169)

In short, the nostrum makers—and with them, Melville's herb doctor—drew on faith in the common man's private judgment and the easy exploitation of popular credulity that characterized America's democratic culture.

If the herb doctor promotes the beneficence of nature, the shabbily dressed representative of the Philosophical Intelligence Office (P.I.O.) promotes the goodness of human beings. Moreover, as the agent for a peculiar variety of antebellum "Intelligence Office" (i.e., employment bureau), the P.I.O. man claims to bring philosophical method to his business, which in this case consists of an attempt to "sell" Pitch a "boy" helper for his farm despite Pitch's reluctance to accept one. For Pitch's experiences with a long series of "boys" has convinced him that "boyhood is a natural state of rascality." Using a series of "scientific" examples to illustrate alleged universal principles of human development, the P.I.O. man's attempt to demonstrate that human nature is naturally good ultimately draws on America's Enlightenment belief in man as a perfectible being. The prolonged debate of the P.I.O. man with Pitch thus sets America's commitment to "progress" against its Calvinist heritage of belief in mankind's innate depravity.

The P.I.O. man's encounter with Pitch also touches on a variety of other social issues of the 1850s, including the debate over free and unfree labor, the rapid industrialization of the American economy, and the widespread "incorporation" of America. Believing that America has become a land of white wage slaves and black bond slaves, Pitch is a staunchly independent "frontier" character violently opposed to society in which the independent laborer was being replaced by the expendable factory worker and depersonalized office employee; perversely and paradoxically, he looks forward to the replacement of all human beings by machines. The P.I.O. man's operation, on the other hand, evokes the contemporary problem of guiding adolescents into suitable trades and professions, as attested by a cottage industry of young man's guides offering detailed instruction in behavior, reading, social relations, professional advancement, and general moral precepts. However, the elimination of moral blemishes in "boys" was not so easily assured, as the rise of juvenile delinquency in the nation's cities attested.[18]

Yet the chief focus of the debate between the P.I.O. man and Pitch is the question of whether human nature is innately good or evil. Throughout their conversation, the P.I.O. man draws on a gamut of arguments to prove that man's moral nature is susceptible to improvement, a position that mimics the pervasive contemporary belief in progress as an inevitable force in human history. In particular, he uses a number of organic analogies to show that the boy he has in mind for Pitch will naturally ripen into a morally unexceptionable helper, a caricature of nineteenth-century positivistic philosophy which considered human nature as subject to the same developmental laws as physical nature.

However, the P.I.O.'s other main source of analogical comparison, hagiography, also demonstrates that there is an implicit religious dimension to his argument. The P.I.O. man's remarks in fact rely on the influential "argument from design," the belief that the supposed perfect symmetry of the physical universe revealed the lineaments of the Creator. Contemporary science in America was still heavily influenced by the tenets of natural theology, most prominently exemplified at the time by the writings of William Paley (1743–1805). The P.I.O. man's analogical reasoning is thus suggestive of contemporary use of "scientific" analogy to affirm the ultimate benignity of the cosmos. In a study of Jacksonian science, George Daniels has remarked on the importance of analogical reasoning to bridge the gap between God and nature:

> The times cried out to the men of the early nineteenth century that there was a God and that he was a benevolent God. Since this was so, it seemed that His works must necessarily attest to His character. From this point, the argument developed inexorably toward the conclusion that since "one mind created the entire universe" there must be harmony in all its parts. Starting with the dogma of orderliness and adding to it the commonsensical approach of the Scottish philosophy, it was difficult for scientists to escape the conclusion that things which *look* alike must *be* alike. Furthermore, and most importantly, there was no such thing as a *chance* resemblance. As a corollary to this, there was no such thing as a resemblance that did not matter. The world was one grand plan of creation, each part manifesting purpose and bearing the lineaments of its Creator. (188–89)[19]

The underlying joke, however, throughout the debate between Pitch and the P.I.O. man is that the P.I.O. man actually represents the Confidence Man in one of his most overtly diabolical disguises, an association confirmed when the P.I.O. man suddenly exits at Cairo within sight of a landmark called the "Devil's Joke." The P.I.O. man is in fact a Mephistophelean casuist whose "mean" appearance and "canine" manner should have put Pitch on his guard against the P.I.O. man's analogizing. Still another irony to the P.I.O. man's encounter with Pitch stems from the fact that despite the P.I.O. man's commitment to "scientific" standards of evidence, he is ultimately persuaded to try a new boy because of the P.I.O. man's appeal to his emotions, namely, his vanity and self-esteem. When Pitch wakes up to his duping while contemplating the sickly environment of Cairo, he realizes that the rational basis for his choice was merely a symptom of a residual "genial" nature that inadvertently attests to his humanity. He is thus a transitional figure between the population of fools depicted in the first half of the novel, and the dehumanized knaves in the second half. Pitch's subsequent encounter with the cosmopolitan, whom he tries to identify as a fellow misanthrope, further plays on his vulnerability of "heart," but he is again deceived in his interlocutor.

Throughout his three encounters with the Confidence Man as herb doctor, P.I.O. man, and cosmopolitan, Pitch is nevertheless tenaciously skeptical of the Confidence Man's easy affirmations. Indeed, he is the most formidable intellectual adversary of Melville's protagonist. Seeing him as an embodiment of heroic resistance to the wiles of the Confidence Man, several critics have viewed him as Melville's spokesman, or else as an implied moral norm for the novel. In this view, Pitch's nay-saying to the Confidence Man constitutes a programmatic "No! in thunder" in keeping with Melville's well-known dissent from his culture's optimistic faith. But the problem with Pitch (as was earlier true of Ahab) is that his devotion to "truth" has overcultivated his head at the expense of his heart. As a result, he is a misanthropical bear of a man whose disillusionment with human nature has produced a callousness toward human life. Those who see Pitch as an ethical ideal must overlook the fact that he remarks to the miser that the miser is better off dead, anticipates the day when he can go "boy-shooting," and believes in the science fiction fantasy that machines are better company than human beings. In the end, Pitch's long debate with the P.I.O. man demonstrates that the ethical universe of *The Confidence-Man* offers no secure ground between foolish credulity and dehumanizing distrust.[20]

While the Confidence Man in the first half of the novel both incarnates and exposes the vices and follies of antebellum America through a variety of roles and gambits, in the second half he is himself the victim of a sequence of operators who dramatize the heartlessness of personal relations in a general cultural environment of laissez-faire capitalism and unfettered individualism. And if Charlie Noble would seem to typify the selfish passions some Americans feared would predominate in a materialistic culture unrestrained by Christian values, he also acts as a moral touchstone for the ensuing appearance of Winsome and Egbert, revealing them to be philosophical confidence men who rationalize and idealize the selfish impulses that motivated Noble. Thus Winsome first appears pronouncing a warning against Noble, but the two in fact share a number of character traits, including a dubious corporeality, abstention from social drinking, a defective sense of humor, and a militant uncharitableness.[21]

As a satirical type, Winsome represents the traditional figure of the *philosophus gloriosus,* an intellectual pretender whose ancestry includes Aristophanes' Socrates, Lucian's Alexander the Prophet, and Swift's Partridge the almanac maker. As will be discussed more fully in Chapter 6 of this study, Winsome is also a detailed satirical caricature of Emerson and so is full of oracularities and inconsistencies that echo Emerson's thought while playing on popular stereotypes of Transcendentalism. Yet despite the facetious side to Winsome's obscurantism, Melville's debunking of Emerson has a serious moral basis in the seeming justification found in his teachings for a ruthless pursuit of self-interest. And an unnoticed irony of much of Winsome's performance is that it represents an implicit parody of several key passages from the Sermon on the Mount, thereby transforming Winsome into a kind of burlesque Antichrist.

Thus Winsome imagines the pleasure of being a poisonous snake; Christ reaffirms the Mosaic law against murder: "whoever shall kill shall be in danger of the judgment" (Matt. 5:21). Winsome warns Goodman about Noble's character based on hearsay; Christ militantly enjoins trust and respect toward one's fellow man: "whosoever is angry with his brother without a cause shall be in danger of the judgment; and whosoever shall say to his brother, Raca, shall be in danger of the council: but whosoever shall say, Thou fool, shall be in danger of hell fire" (Matt. 5:22). (Winsome's incomprehensible Egyptian word for Noble mimics the epithet "Raca" here, an obscure Aramaic term of abuse.) Winsome's professing not to understand the term *favor* may be compared to Christ's antithetical policy: "Therefore if thou bring thy gift to the altar, and there rememberest that thy brother hath ought against thee; Leave there thy gift before the altar, and go thy way; first be reconciled to thy brother, and then come and offer thy gift" (Matt. 5:23–24). Winsome's claim that "Pharaoh's poorest brick-maker lies proudlier in his rags than the Emperor of all the Russias in his hollands" parodies Christ's assertion, "And yet I say unto you, That even Solomon in all his glory was not arrayed like one of these" (i.e., the "lillies of the field," which "toil not, neither do they spin") (Matt. 6:29). Winsome's indignant rejection of the crazy beggar is a violation of Christ's injunction, "Judge not, that ye be not judged. . . . And why beholdest thou the mote that is in thy brother's eye, but considerest not the beam that is in thine own eye?" (Matt. 7:1, 3). (Winsome hypocritically points out that the crazy beggar shows "one damning peep of sense.") Winsome's insistence that the spiritual and material aspects of life are easily reconciled flies in the face of

Christ's affirmation that these two realms cannot be bridged: "Ye cannot serve God and mammon" (Matt. 6:24). Finally, Winsome's philosophy as subsequently embodied in his practical disciple, Egbert, may be compared with Christ's warning against "false prophets": "Even so every good tree bringeth forth good fruit; but a corrupt tree bringeth forth evil fruit. . . . Wherefore by their fruits ye shall know them" (Matt. 7:17, 20).

While Winsome is implicitly propounding a new "law" of selfishness which supersedes Christian charity, Egbert is Winsome's authorized representative of this same law. Indeed, this "practical disciple" and Yankee trader acts out a textbook demonstration of transcendentalist ethics in action, as Melville reveals the tacit justification Emerson's philosophy would give to the rapidly developing business culture of the era. Moreover, just as Winsome earlier exhibited a number of similarities to Charlie Noble, Egbert actually adopts Noble's character when he plays the part of "Charlie" in a dramatic reenactment of Goodman's encounter with Noble. In effect, the selfishness of the young New England merchant proves to be identical to that of the broken-down Mississippi operator. With their prudential, anti-Christian morality, Winsome and Egbert are transcendental confidence men.

After his unrewarding debate with the frigid Egbert, the cosmopolitan's ensuing encounter with the barber, which focuses on the cosmopolitan's attempt to get the barber to take down his "No Trust" sign, represents a return to his earlier practice of deceptive gambits. Unlike the idealist philosophy of Winsome and his disciple, with its dehumanizing abstractions, the barber espouses a commonsensical view of human relations based on his personal experience in trade. Yet the barber ultimately emerges as a cynical pursuer of the main chance, for he secretly hopes to gain from the cosmopolitan's offer to insure him against any loss caused by his taking down his sign. The barber is in fact punningly associated with "sharp" practices early in his conversation with the cosmopolitan:

> "Are you competent to a good shave, barber?"
>
> "No broker more so, sir," answered the barber, whom the business-like proposition instinctively made confine to business-ends his views of the visitor.
>
> "Broker? What has a broker to do with lather? A broker I have always understood to be a worthy dealer in certain papers and metals."
>
> "He, he!" taking him now for some dry sort of joker, whose jokes, he being a customer, it might be as well to appreciate, "he, he! You understand well enough sir." (*CM,* 226)

To properly appreciate this punning exchange, the reader must know that in antebellum America to "shave" a note was a slang term for the exorbitant or unwelcome "discounting" of a promissory note or bank bill, a service performed by financial brokers. Moreover, without a standard paper currency (federal "greenbacks" were first issued during the Civil War), hundreds of state banks were the sole source of bank notes, and these constantly fluctuated in value, depending on the financial condition of the bank of issue, as well as the bearer's distance from the bank when seeking redemption. By 1860 about 7,000 different legitimate bank notes—approximately 1,600 of which were from defunct state banks—and about 5,000 counterfeits were in circulation. The national currency in the decades before the Civil War constituted a chaos of fluctuating values, all shored up by public confidence. Indeed, "by the time of the Civil War, the American monetary system was, without rival, the most confusing in the long history of commerce and associated cupidity" (Galbraith, 90).[22]

As Tom Quirk has shown, the debate between the cosmopolitan and barber plays on the comic ambiguities of such cant terms as to *shave* (cheat) and to *lather* (to *smooth talk*) in a confusion of the barber's trade with that of the sharp business operator or cheat. The barber seeks to justify his policy of "No Trust" by means of the practical experience that has taught him mankind's aptitude for fraud. Indeed, his trade includes the supplying of wigs to customers and thus has familiarized him with the dangers of trusting to appearances. Yet even though the barber may seem justified in his commercial *modus operandi,* his cynical estimation of mankind all too easily dovetails into a willingness to cheat his fellow man, as is demonstrated by his attempt to diddle the cosmopolitan out of a security deposit. In the end, the barber is emblematic of the cynical morality appropriate to a nation of strangers united only by their participation in depersonalized market transactions such as the "shaving" of the cosmopolitan.[23]

Whereas the barber is an exponent of a corruptive commercial morality, the old man encountered in the last chapter is a type of rural innocence whose simple-minded faith evokes twin stereotypes of the national character, the virtuous farmer and the American innocent. Yet the last chapter effectuates the subversion of the old man's confidence in both God and mankind, as the cosmopolitan undermines the authority of the Bible and the juvenile peddler arouses the old man's distrust in his fellow man through the sale of "security devices." While the old man's actions here might be said to epitomize the divided nature of American life by the 1850s—its evangelical ambitions incongruously blended with its aggressive economic individualism—his unconscious inconsistency in putting faith in both the Bible and the peddler's security devices is also in keeping with the Hobson's choice presented by the novel's moral universe. For in this climactic chapter, the worlds of both God and Mammon are being critiqued, with neither providing a secure source of value.

On the surface, the old man appears to be serving God, for the last chapter opens with him devotedly reading the Bible, an appropriate image for a nation founded on the Protestant principle of *scriptura sola.* Yet while the ensuing scene draws attention to the Bible as the ultimate cultural authority on the *Fidèle,* it simultaneously subverts that authority by revealing both the potential ambiguity of biblical truth and the culture's mere lip-service to its official faith. For after first demonstrating that the Bible is a potentially more complicated and subversive document than the old man realizes, the cosmopolitan goes on to note that the text of the Bible the old man is reading is in pristine condition because the "traveling public" largely ignores it. The untouched Bible here plays on the ubiquity of Bibles in antebellum America, particularly at the time Melville was writing. "The mid-fifties saw the American Bible Society at its greatest vigor," notes Carl Bode. "Between 1851 and 1856 the production of Bibles and New Testaments averaged almost three-quarters of a million a year. At the annual meeting of May 1856 the society boldly resolved, for the second time in its history, to place a free Bible in the hands of every poor family in the United States willing to take one" (143–44). In an aggressive effort to Christianize the nation, the nation's leading distributor of Holy Writ was literally flooding it with Bibles. Yet as the last chapter of *The Confidence-Man* demonstrates, the results of this Christian crusade were hardly a Christianized nation.

The irony of the public's lack of interest in the Bible here is dramatically underlined when the cosmopolitan notes that " 'in this land, and especially in these parts of it, some stories are told about steamboats and railroads fitted to make one a little apprehensive' " (*CM,* 250). The cosmopolitan is rightly concerned, for Western steamboat travel was plagued by serious accidents, with a snag, collision, fire, or (most feared) exploding boiler creating swift and sometimes apocalyptic destruction.[24] Foreign travelers during this period often noted the seeming indifference to human life in America, as evidenced by the numerous train and steamboat accidents resulting from carelessness or an obsession with speed. Steamboat accidents in particular could assume a portentous significance, especially when interpreted within the context of America's traditional millenarian beliefs, as Ernest Sandeen notes:

> Nineteenth-century society was very much like its most famous mechanical invention, the steamboat. Many millenarian newspapers in that day carried a column entitled "Signs of the Times," which contained news of ominous events and portents of the end of the world. One of the most common items in those columns was the notice of the explosion of a steamboat. The steamboat harnessed new power and moved with unprecedented rapidity. It was exciting, but it was also dangerous. The passengers knew that their voyage might possibly end by their being blown to smithereens. (117)

The apocalyptic ambience of the last chapter of *The Confidence-Man* must therefore be read in light of the dangers and anxieties caused by America's rapid economic and technological development. Moreover, the cosmopolitan's pious assurances to the old man, including his claim that a celestial "committee of safety" watches over them, implicitly ridicule America's belief in its providential destiny and protection. In like manner, the cosmopolitan's final assertion that the life preserver "stool" the old man has been sitting on represents a "special providence" is an obscene joke directed at the same cherished belief.[25]

Inasmuch as the cosmopolitan's interaction with the old man exposes the weaknesses of America's Christian faith, the old man's encounter with the juvenile peddler reveals the hazards and anxieties growing out of the country's rapid economic development. A "well-to-do farmer" who is able to afford a stateroom for the night, the old man is an appropriate customer for the peddler's security devices. Yet instead of giving him a sense of security, the patent lock and money belt draw attention to the dangers of thievery on the *Fidèle*. By the same token, the free counterfeit detector puts the old man into a hopeless quandary over the authenticity of his bank bill from the "Vicksburg Trust and Insurance Banking Company," a bill that is patently worthless; for as the site of some of the worst "wildcat" banking during the late 1830s, the state of Mississippi had actually prohibited all its banks from issuing notes from the mid-1840s up to the Civil War.[26]

In its evocation of contemporary currency problems, the peddler's counterfeit detector provides a climactic example of money as both a source and a symptom of national corruption. Because of the multiplicity of antebellum banking institutions and the relative ease with which their notes could be duplicated or altered, a host of bank note reporters and counterfeit detectors were marketed to alert the public concerning the shifting value of notes and the physical appearance of counterfeits. In 1855, for example, an exasperated individual in Massachusetts characterized the endemic problem of counterfeiting in an appeal to the state legislature, asking,

> how large a part of the community can begin to distinguish between good money and bad? Who stops even to examine? Who does not "go it blind"? Possibly if you offer a new or strange-looking bill for groceries, the grocer's boy wastes his time and yours by consulting that most popular of monthly journals, the Counterfeit Detector. How that periodical grows and flourishes! It bids fair to rival Webster's Dictionary in size, and eclipse it in practical utility. Did you ever consider what this curious detective literature proves? . . .
>
> The Counterfeit Detector is like a powerful optical instrument. It reveals to you, through the darkness of human hypocrisy, a dim outline landscape of a great system of counterfeiting, by which, however, you may know with perfect safety that it is nearly as extensive as our vastly ramified system of banks, and may be regarded as an image of that system reflected from the mirror of the depraved classes. (quoted in Glaser, 89)

Like this writer's example of a grocery boy wasting time over an unknown bill, the old man's quandary over his fraudulent bank bill captures the ironic disparity between an increasingly complex system of credit in the nation and the age-old problem of human iniquity. Moreover, by highlighting the corruptions associated with the country's currency, Melville is attacking a traditional target of the satirist while highlighting the role of marketplace values in the contemporary transformation of American culture.[27]

In the portrait of the old man, then, Melville is effectuating a representative climax to his satirical portrait of America. The heart of his critique, as we have seen, was the growing disparity between the country's millennial and material ambitions—its increasingly hypocritical attempt to serve both God and Mammon. The sociological basis for this development was the rise of economic and political individualism in the decades before the Civil War, with its promise of the fulfillment of America's democratic ideals, but with its attendant perils of social fragmentation owing to the ascendancy of laissez-faire and commercial values. Melville's fictive indictment of the nation is in fact consonant with other minority reports on the state of the Union by the mid-1850s. In the October 1855 *Putnam's,* for example, the same issue that contained the first installment of Melville's "Benito Cereno," a writer on the "Kansas Question" lamented the recent sea change in American life:

> A gross materialism, the success of trade, the progress of gain, an external expediency, is preferred to lofty ideal aspirations and spiritual truth. The grand and beautiful theory which lies at the center of our institutions, their noble humanitarianism, their just and magnanimous recognition of the dignity and worth of every human being, their utter and indignant disdain of the spirit of caste, of exclusion, of selfish aggrandisement,—no longer touch our hearts and kindle them into a fine and generous enthusiasm. Great deeds are not done among us. The atmosphere is cold, and ungenial. We speculate how to get rich; we build railroads and ships, to increase our stores; we spy out the neighboring lands which promise us luxurious harvests hereafter; . . . There is a time in the history of nations, as there is in the life of the individual, and as there was in the life of Christ, when the Devil carries them up into a high mountain, and offers them all the kingdoms of the earth, if they will but worship him. At such a time have we arrived in our national career. (431, 434)

In his fictionalized overview of this society—a society more typical of the industrializing North than the agrarian South—Melville exposes its pervasive moral abuses, in keeping with the satirist's role of cataloguing vice and folly through an encyclopedic series of negative examples. In the process, Melville creates a searching portrait of a society that is still very much with us in the late twentieth century.

A final, supplementary aspect of *The Confidence-Man*'s socioeconomic satire arises out of current social constructions of masculinity in relation to money. For the novel draws on contemporary belief in a "spermatic economy" that associated male physiology (especially the phobia concerning masturbation) with the ongoing revolution in the nation's economic life. While the link between money and semen has a long cultural history that lingers in the twin meanings of the verb "to spend," the newly developed market capitalism in nineteenth-century America gave this traditional metaphor new relevance as men entered the anxiety-ridden world of the marketplace while women were increasingly segregated in the home. The result was a heightened perception of the need for seminal self-control. G. J. Barker-Benfield has elucidated the implications of this "spermatic economy" in connection with the popular advice manuals of the Reverend John Todd (1800–1873), whose writings reflected the general beliefs of his era:

> During Todd's lifetime men were preoccupied with the fear of a loss of sperm, connected as it was to the whole question of manhood and to a man's hopes for some kind of immortality. The ancient connotations of sperm took on a particular significance in the nineteenth century; the context was the pressure on man's sexual identity. People believed in "pangenesis": each part of the body was believed to contribute a fraction of itself to the sperm by way of the blood. . . . It was this spermatic summary of man that Todd had in mind when he described the effects of ejaculation as debilitation of body and memory and the deterioration and weakening of the mind. Men believed their expenditure of sperm had to be governed according to an economic principle. (180–81)[28]

Evidence of the age's belief in a "spermatic economy" is evoked in the first chapter of *The Confidence-Man* in the juxtaposition of the pale man in "cream-colors" and the barber, William Cream. In effect, the man in cream colors is a purveyor of Christ's "engendering word" (*logos*) while the barber is an agent of spermatic economy. And if the man in cream colors attempts to plant the "seed" of Christian charity in the *Fidèle*'s passengers, the barber emblematizes the exploitative risks of the marketplace ("No Trust"), with its threat of emasculation (shaving) and the attendant need for seminal self-control. Yet just as the novel traces the incongruous intersection of God and Mammon on the American ship of state, the antithesis of "engendering word" and "spermatic economy" is satirically subverted in two scenes in the first and second halves of the novel, first during the man in gray's encounter with the gentleman with gold sleeve-buttons, and later during the cosmopolitan's encounter with the old man. (Another use of the spermatic economy in "The Story of China Aster" is discussed in Chapter 7.) In the process Melville continued to exploit the covert sexual symbolism that had informed his short fiction of the 1850s (Philip Young, Chs. 4–7), while giving it a new emphasis as part of his socioeconomic critique of the nation.

In Chapter 7 of *The Confidence-Man,* the emblematic characterization of the gentleman with gold sleeve-buttons conveys an image associating his wealth with the dynamics of male spermatic economy. While we have already commented on some of the ethical and sociological implications of the gentleman's emblematic attire, another figural meaning emerges if we notice his coat-skirts' pendulous position and seminal whiteness. The gentleman's interlocutor, the man in gray, is also notable for his implied seminal endowment, but in him the principle of spermatic economy is associated with his ambitious global evangelical projects to spread the "seed" of Christian charity. For the man in gray's performance is implicitly indebted to a soundly regulated spermatic economy. As the narrator remarks, if the man in gray's current "animation" when describing his projects contrasts with an earlier "unsprightly manner," this anomaly is explained by the observation that he had "already, in certain after colloquies, given proof, in some degree, of the fact, that, with certain natures, a soberly continent air at times, so far from arguing emptiness of stuff, is good proof it is there, and plenty of it, because unwasted, and may be used the more effectively, too, when opportunity offers" (*CM,* 38).

In keeping with this strategic use of his "stuff," the man in gray's program for a World's Charity is implicitly characterized as a colossal act of fornication: " 'You see, this doing good to the world by driblets amounts to just nothing. I am for doing good to the world with a will. I am for doing good to the world once for all and having done with it' " (*CM,* 41). When the gentleman doubts the efficacy of this colossal project, the man in gray makes the appropriate rejoinder: " 'And is the age of wonders past? Is the world too old? Is it barren? Think of Sarah.' " In his concluding remarks to the gentleman, the man in gray is again associated with seminal ambitions, for his conversation "revealed a spirit of benevolence which, mindful of the millennial promise, had gone abroad over all the countries of the globe, much as the diligent spirit of the husbandman, stirred by forethought of the coming seed-time, leads him, in March reveries at his fireside, over every field of his farm" (*CM,* 42). The man in gray's activities parody the supposed regenerative power of the "word" in conjunction with the potencies of hoarded semen, as Melville satirizes America's attempt to make Yankee dollars promote the global spread of the gospel in anticipation of the millennium.

The depiction of the "clean, comely, old man" in the last chapter provides another notable illustration of the workings of the spermatic economy in antebellum America. For during the old man's encounter with the juvenile peddler, the peddler's "patent lock" and "money-belt" form a set of symbolic genitalia that obliquely figure as guarantors of a sound spermatic economy. While performing his sales pitch, the peddler presents the classic "before" and "after" tableau of modern advertising:

> "All safe. Well. Now, about two o'clock in the morning, say, a soft-handed gentleman comes softly and tries the knob here—thus; in creeps my soft-handed gentleman; and hey, presto! how comes on the soft cash?"
>
> "I see, I see, child," said the old man; "your fine gentleman is a fine thief, and there's no lock to your little door to keep him out;" with which words he peered at it more closely than before.
>
> "Well, now," again showing his white teeth, "well, now, some of you old folks are knowing 'uns, sure enough; but now comes the great invention," producing a small steel contrivance, very simple but ingenious, and which, being clapped on the inside of the little door, secured it as with a bolt. "There now," admiringly holding it off at arm's-length, "there now, let that soft-handed gentleman come now a' softly trying this little knob here, and let him keep a' trying till he finds his head as soft as his hand. Buy the traveler's patent lock, sir, only twenty-five cents." (*CM,* 245)

The peddler's performance here is laden with sexual double entendres, for "soft-handed gentleman" here is, in part, a personification of the self-abuse which robs the body of its most precious commodity. However, with the lock firmly in place, this same nocturnal "gentleman" will succumb to a masturbation-induced "soft head," while the owner of the lock will retain his "soft cash." This covert illustration of the workings of the spermatic economy is followed by an equally provocative visual pun on the testicular source of masculine "soft cash":

> ". . . do you just buy one of these little jokers," producing a number of suspender-like objects, which he dangled before the old man; "money-belts, sir; only fifty cents."
>
> "Money-belt? never heard of such a thing."
>
> "A sort of pocket-book," said the boy, only a safer sort. Very good for travelers."
>
> "Oh, a pocket-book. Queer looking pocket-books though, seems to me. Ain't they rather long and narrow for pocket-books?"
>
> "They go round the waist, sir, inside," said the boy; "door open or locked, wide awake on your feet or fast asleep in your chair, impossible to be robbed with a money-belt." (*CM,* 246)

If by purchasing a money-belt the old man is involved—both literally and figuratively—in an obscene joke at his own expense, his approaching mortality nevertheless provides a larger significance to his purchase of security devices that double as mocking guarantors of spiritual potency through the hoarding of sperm. And if the man in gray earlier satirized an implied "spermatic economy" behind the evangelical mission of contemporary Christianity, the "clean, comely, old man" at the novel's end exemplifies its application to the individual Christian soul faced with the spiritual uncertainties of this world and the next.

4

Allegorical Structure: Mirror of God

In the previous chapter we surveyed the social and historical contexts for Melville's satire in *The Confidence-Man;* in this chapter we examine its allegorical structure. Critics have in fact disagreed on what kind of allegory is found in the novel, and indeed whether it is allegorical at all. Yet *The Confidence-Man* patently incorporates the basic schematic principles of a Dantean or Bunyanesque pilgrimage allegory as the *Fidèle,* the steamboat of the faithful, bears "that multiform pilgrim species man" down the Mississippi River, the stream of time that encompasses both American and western history. The journey of history is also the individual's journey through life, for *The Confidence-Man* begins with hints of birth imagery in the mute's sudden advent "at the water-side," and concludes with a Simeon-like old man being led off into the dark following a scene filled with hints of mortality. Moreover, like the idealized heroes of allegorical narratives such as Spenser's *Faerie Queene,* Melville's protagonist is identified with the Christian virtues of charity (*caritas,* love of mankind) and confidence (*fides,* faith in God). The ritual progression and wit combat of his encounters are also typical of allegorical narratives, "progress" and "battle" being the two chief modes of allegorical "symbolic action" according to Angus Fletcher. By the same token, Fletcher's characterization of the allegorical hero as a "daemonic agent" matches many characteristic qualities of Melville's shape-shifting protagonist. Finally, although critical attempts to relate the Confidence Man's successive guises to a fixed theological, philosophical, or cultural model have been unsuccessful, the schematized progress of the narrative nevertheless integrates a loose structure related to the Pauline virtues of faith, hope, and charity, while the novel itself constitutes a sustained parody of the Bible, as is shown in this chapter.[1]

Yet granted the existence of this allegorical framework, it may still be asked what the relationship is between allegory and apocalypse in the novel.

A partial answer to this question was provided some time ago by John Shroeder, who demonstrated that *The Confidence-Man* drew on the allegorical tradition of the Book of Revelation, Bunyan's *Pilgrim's Progress,* and Hawthorne's "The Celestial Railroad." "The Celestial Railroad" in particular provided Melville with a blueprint for his own satirical allegory, which, like Hawthorne's tale, ironically inverts Bunyan's representation of the schematized worldly progress of the Christian soul to the heavenly Celestial City, the apocalyptic New Jerusalem. Melville's novel thus directly refigures Hawthorne's satirical sketch, appropriating both individual incidents and Hawthorne's general thematic design indicting America's faith in its moral and material progress. The only danger in relating "The Celestial Railroad" and *The Confidence-Man* too closely arises from assuming, as did Shroeder, that Hawthorne's unctuous but diabolical Mr. Smooth-it-away—a version of Satan at his "last loosening" in Revelation 20—bears an equivalent allegorical identity to Melville's hero.

It is worth pointing out that Bunyan's allegory, like Hawthorne's, is itself a refiguration of the Book of Revelation, a text that has been a leading sourcebook for a host of early Christian, medieval, and Renaissance allegorists. The Book of Revelation thus stands as a kind of allegorical ur-text behind Hawthorne's tale and Melville's novel, both of which historicize its visionary scenario to demonstrate the deficiencies and delusions of their own era. (Only Melville, the religious radical, goes on to subvert the moral and metaphysical foundations of Christianity itself.) The assimilation of Revelation in both these texts is additionally significant in terms of its centrality as a source for the overarching "myth" of America as the potential site of the millennium and/or the new heaven and earth of St. John's vision. As interrelated satirical apocalypses, then, both "The Celestial Railroad" and *The Confidence-Man* manipulate the mythic origins of American cultural identity.

Like Hawthorne's sketch, too, Melville's novel is notable for its use of biblical typology. Typology constitutes the practice of interpreting the Old Testament as a repository of historical "types" for which the life the Christ provided the corresponding "antitypes." By employing this technique of exegesis, interpreters were able to read the Bible as an internally consistent narrative in which the Old Testament fulfilled itself in the New. The study of typology flourished in seventeenth-century England and America, the Puritan colonists believing themselves to be the New World antitype to the Old Testament Israelites. And as Ursula Brumm has shown, Americans of the nineteenth century inherited a well-developed tradition of typology that influenced those writers, like Hawthorne and Melville, intellectually shaped by the Puritan tradition. Narrative in *The Confidence-Man* actually occurs on three typological levels relative to the Bible as a whole, the New Testament alone, and the Book of Revelation. In the first typological paradigm, the novel figures the history of mankind from Genesis to Apocalypse, the first half of the novel transpiring under a rubric of Mosaic "law," typified by the barber's "No Trust" sign, the second under a rubric of Christian "grace," typified by the mute's messages of "charity." In the second paradigm, the novel moves from Christ's First Advent in the first chapter to his Second Advent in the last. Finally, in the third paradigm, the whole novel is an enactment of the Apocalypse, with the Confidence Man conflating true messiah and false prophet, Christ and Antichrist, Second Coming and Last Loosening of Satan.[2]

This complex allegorical layering is suggested by several features at the beginning of the novel. The mute's "advent" in the first chapter, for example, is both Christic and suggestive of the imagery of Genesis; his messages of charity, written on a portable slate, represent a figural antitype to the Mosaic tablets of the law. Equally evident is the fact that the beginning of the novel constitutes the onset of the Apocalypse. We have already noted that, in the ostensibly criminal identity of his hero, Melville plays on the traditional comparison of Christ's Second Advent to that of a thief. The mute's "flaxen" hair and "white fur" hat also reveal him as a type of Christ at the Second Coming, whose "head and his hairs were white like wool, as white as snow" (Rev. 1:14). Furthermore, when Melville's Confidence Man boards the *Fidèle* at sunrise, his sudden "advent" occurs "unsaluted," he is noted to be a "stranger" without luggage ("No porter followed him"), and he looks "as if, traveling night and day from some far country beyond the prairies, he had long been without the solace of a bed"—a characterization that directly evokes Christ's Parable of the Waiting Servant at the end of the "Little Apocalypse" in Mark 13:

> Take ye heed, watch and pray: for ye know not when the time is.
>
> For the Son of man is as a man taking a far journey, who left his house, and gave authority to his servants, and to every man his work and commanded the porter to watch.
>
> Watch yet therefore: for ye know not when the master of the house cometh, at even, or at midnight, or at the cock-crowing, or in the morning:
>
> Lest coming suddenly he find you sleeping.
>
> And what I say unto you I say unto all, Watch. (33–35)

The man in cream colors is also identified with a "mysterious imposter, supposedly to have recently arrived from the East," a reminder of Christ's claim in Matthew's "Little Apocalypse" that "as the lightening cometh out of the east, and shineth even unto the west; so shall also the coming of the Son of man be" (Matt. 24:27). And inasmuch as the procession of passengers described in Chapter 2 of the novel establishes the *Fidèle* as a type of the Ark, the significance of this allusion should also be read in the context of New Testament apocalyptic, for Christ invoked the Flood as a figure for the unexpectedness of his Second Coming (Matt. 24:37–41; Luke 17:26–36).[3]

By the same token, the beginning and end of the novel also share a common typological source in the writings of St. John, believed at the time to be the author of both the Fourth Gospel and the Book of Revelation. Thus the mute's written messages of charity in the first chapter suggest the image of Christ as Logos, the incarnate word of God (John 1:1); his advent with the dawn suggests the image of Christ as the true Light (John 1:9); his mistreatment by his fellow passengers recalls Christ's mistreatment when "He came unto his own, and his own received him not" (John 1:11); finally, the mute's lamb-like innocence suggests the well-known Johannine image of Christ as the "Lamb of God" (John 1:29). Counterpointing these allusions to the Gospel of John, the last chapter of *The Confidence-Man* represents a subversive parody of the eschatological drama depicted in St. John's Revelation, as will be shown at the end of this chapter.

We have previously suggested that the Confidence Man is a composite theological and mythological figure whose nature encompasses Christ and the devil, sun god and trickster. (A Dionysian archetype will also be demonstrated in this chapter.) Such a melding of symbolic identities and moral polarities makes him a syncretic figure uniting both Christian and classical archetypes, a synthesis characteristic of Melville's previous explorations of the divine nature in *Moby-Dick* and *Pierre*. *Pierre* in particular dramatizes the enigmatic interrelation of good and evil in both human and cosmic reality, as Mary E. Dichmann and others have argued; hence the Confidence Man's embodiment of both good and evil may be considered a direct outgrowth of the moral universe of *Pierre*.

The divided moral identity of the Confidence Man also conforms to a traditional mythological pattern. "The common perception of almost all mythologies," remarks Jeffrey Burton Russell, "is the coincidence of opposites, the ambivalence of the deity. The God is understood as light and darkness, good and evil. The gods who manifest this divinity are themselves coincidences of opposites, each god or goddess ambivalent in itself, or expressing the ambivalence by being paired with a doublet of opposite nature" (*Devil*, 54). Russell demonstrates that Judeo-Christian tradition similarly exemplifies a process known as "twinning" whereby the principle of evil was separated from God and made into an independent but interrelated entity, the devil. Beginning as an authorized agent of God, as in the Book of Job, Satan gradually became God's eternal adversary in the New Testament (*Devil*, Chs. 5–6). As a result of this conceptual fluidity, "Christianity is in fact a semidualist religion. On the one hand it rejects the full dualism that asserts the opposition of two eternal cosmic principles. But it has also generally rejected the monist complacency of the hidden harmony. The tension between monism and dualism has led to inconsistencies in Christian theodicy" (Russell, *Devil*, 228).

The ambiguous theological identity of the Confidence Man, then, illustrates the problem of Christian theodicy that stood at the center of Melville's life-long quest into the realm of religious "metaphysics." For Melville's last published novel dramatizes the idea that Christ and the devil—as exemplified by the trickster-like roles of Christ and Antichrist during the Apocalypse—are equally representative of God's divided moral nature and enigmatic identity. This conclusion accords with the findings of a group of critics—including Bruce Franklin, John Bernstein, Donald Schultz, John Seelye, Merlin Bowen, Alvin J. Seltzer, and Richard Boyd Hauck—all of whom variously affirm that Melville's Confidence Man is a paradoxical conflation of good and evil, Christ and Antichrist, God and the devil.[4] Richard Boyd Hauck, for instance, has summarized what he calls the "paradoxes" of Christianity to explain the Confidence Man's ambiguous apocalyptic role:

> That there can be no closed determination of the precise allegorical values in the Confidence-Man's masquerade confirms that it is designed to reflect several Christian paradoxes instead of the Apocalyptic sequence alone: at the time of the Apocalypse, Christ is indistinguishable from the Anti-Christ; as the Creator of the history depicted in Genesis and Revelation, God can be thought of as the author of darkness as well as light; God permits Satan freedom so that he can test the saints as he tested Jesus in the wilderness; Doomsday's chaos clears the way for a new divine order. Unlike most religions, Christian doctrine separates the figure of evil from the figure of good, but residual ambiguities in Christian myth suggest that the distinction is not absolute. ("Nine Good Jokes," 251–52)

In sum, by depicting the divine nature as inconsistent and ambivalent, Melville makes God the master of ceremonies in his satiric universe, adducing the vices and follies of mankind as counterparts to the divided nature of the deity. But we must now examine the composite allegorical identity of the Confidence Man in detail in order to discover how Melville has encoded his hero's apocalyptic mission.

The first chapter of *The Confidence-Man* introduces Melville's protagonist in his first guise, the mute man in cream colors; and while it is generally recognized that the mute represents a Christ figure, it has not previously been noticed that his performance actually constitutes a displaced parody of Christ's life. Thus as he comes aboard the *Fidèle,* the mute's appearance suggests the Nativity (Luke 2:1–20), for he exhibits a "fair" cheek, a "downy" chin, "flaxen" hair and wears a white fur hat "with a long fleecy nap"; his lack of luggage and his look of being "in the extremist sense of the word, a stranger" further evoke Christ's lowly birth in a manger in Bethlehem. A parody of the Journey and Adoration of the Magi (Matt. 2:

1–12) is next suggested by the announcement warning the passengers on the *Fidèle* of the arrival of a "mysterious imposter, supposed to have recently arrived from the East," while the "chevaliers" hawking books based on the lives of murderous Mississippi bandits recall the Flight into Egypt and Slaughter of the Innocents (Matt. 2:13–18).

Writing his messages of charity on a "small slate" to figure forth the principal ethical teaching of Christianity, the mute subsequently enacts a condensed version of Christ's ministry. Meanwhile, the mute's ideological opponent, the aproned and slippered barber, puts out a "No Trust" sign, a hint of those legalistic interests that opposed themselves to Christ's mission and ultimately brought about his crucifixion. Immediately after the barber's appearance, the crowd on the *Fidèle* begins to abuse the mute, leading to a reenactment of the Passion and Crucifixion (Matt. 27:1–54). Jeering, pushing, and punching him, the crowd vents its hostility until the mute is suddenly "hailed from behind by two porters carrying a large trunk" that is "accidentally or otherwise swung" against him, "nearly overthrowing him." This event constitutes a mock crucifixion, for the act of being "hailed from behind" contains a pun on hail/hale, while the "trunk" referred to here offers another potential pun on the arboreal "trunk" used for the crucifixion. Furthermore, the "peculiar inarticulate moan" the mute gives after his violent encounter with the "trunk" evokes Christ's famous remark in Aramaic on the cross, "Eloi, eloi, lama sabachthani" ("My God, why hast thou forsaken me?") (Matt. 27:46).

The Descent from the Cross and Entombment (Matt. 27:57–66) are subsequently mimed as the mute proceeds to lie down in a "retired spot" under one of the *Fidèle*'s forward ladders and goes to sleep. After he lies down, the narrator notes that "his cream-colored suit had a tossed look, almost linty," a punning reference to the throwing off of the linen burial shroud as a prelude to the Resurrection ("linty" is etymologically derived from "linen"). A parody of the Resurrection and the rolling away of the stone at Christ's tomb (Matt. 28:1–8) is also suggested by the description of the mute's appearance: "His aspect was at once gentle and jaded, and, from the moment of seating himself, increasing in tired abstraction and dreaminess." Finally, the spread of Christ's gospel after the Resurrection and his posthumous appearances to his followers are evoked by the mute's image at the end of the chapter, as the "lamb-like figure relaxed, and, half reclining against the ladder's foot, lay motionless, as some sugar-snow in March, which, softly stealing down over night, with its white placidity startles the brown farmer peering out from his threshold at daybreak." Its "white placidity" evoking the traditional concept of Christ as the Prince of Peace, the "sugar-snow" here is a parody of Christ's redemptive presence radiating over the earth in a baptism of the spirit (John 1:33; Acts 1:5), a phenomenon commemorated at Pentecost or "Whitsunday."[5]

Following the mute's displaced parody of Christ's life and teachings during his First Advent, the Confidence Man's next two guises incorporate other aspects of Christ's identity. Although he is primarily a mock-diabolic figure, Black Guinea's "knotted black fleece" and comparison to a "half-frozen black sheep" also suggest Christ's symbolic role as the Lamb of God. Guinea might in fact qualify as one of the "least" of the "brethren" with whom Christ identified in the Olivet discourse (Matt. 25:44). John Ringman, on the other hand, embodies the idea of Christ as the man of sorrows and the suffering servant (Isaiah 53:3; Phil. 2:7–8). In keeping with this association, Henry Roberts' thrice-repeated denial of previous acquaintance with Ringman covertly mimics Peter's triple denial of Christ (Karcher, *Shadow,* 209). Yet Ringman also embodies Christ's well-known typological conflation with Adam. As St. Paul wrote, "The first man Adam was made a living soul; the last Adam was made a quickening spirit. . . . The first man is of the earth, earthy: the second man is the Lord from heaven" (I Corin. 15:45, 47). Ringman punningly tells the merchant, " 'We are but clay, sir, potter's clay, as the good book says, clay, feeble, and too-yielding clay.' " Ringman plays the role of both the homeless Christ (Matt. 8:20) and the homeless postlapsarian Adam, the "weed" on his hat evoking the "herb of the field" that Adam must eat after disobeying God (Gen. 3:18). Ringman's hard-luck story, "a tale of singular interest, involving calamities against which no integrity, no forethought, no energy, no genius, no piety, could guard," ultimately refers back to the Fall.

The Confidence Man's subsequent guises in the first half of the novel continue his figural association with Christ. Thus the man in gray's global philanthropical efforts duplicate Christ's peripatetic ministry. In particular, his project for feeding the poor of London with "twenty thousand bullocks and one hundred thousand barrels of flour" mimics the feeding of the five thousand with loaves and fishes (Mark 6:30–34). Bearing a name evocative of Christ's claim to be "the way, the truth, and the life" (John 14:6) and carrying a book that suggests *the* Book, John Truman sells stock in the New Jerusalem and the Black Rapids Coal Company, heavenly and hellish-sounding enterprises. The herb doctor plays Christ's role as paraclete and miracle worker, and proves himself to be a Christ-like forgiver of injuries in this encounter with the invalid Titan in Chapter 17. Finally, Pitch's calling the P.I.O. man a "wordy" man recalls Christ's symbolic role as the incarnate word of John's gospel; the P.I.O. man confirms the association by asserting, " 'The best wisdom in this world, and the last spoken by its teacher, did it not literally and truly come in the form of table-talk?' " (*CM,* 125).

The Confidence Man's actions in the first half of the novel similarly parody various incidents from Christ's ministry. Thus the man in gray's encounter with the charitable lady in Chapter 8 mimics the story of the "widow's mites" (Mark 12:41–44; Luke 21:1–4); the twenty dollars the lady gives the man in gray recalls the two "mites" (pennies) given by the poor widow to the Temple treasury, which Jesus commended to his disciples. In a later scene, John Truman's charitable act of bringing water to the miser in his gloomy dormitory in Chapter 15 explicitly alludes to the parable of Lazarus and Dives (Luke 16:19–31), while also suggesting a version of Christ's legendary Harrowing of Hell (Eph. 4:8–10; I Peter 3:18–22, 4:6). However, the operative prooftext here is Christ's injunction, "For whosoever shall give you a cup of water to drink in my name, because ye belong to Christ, verily I say unto you, he shall not lose his reward" (Mark 9:41). Truman does indeed receive a "reward" of $100 from the miser, announcing that he will invest it in an enterprise that he characterizes as " 'A secret, a mystery—all I have to do with you is to receive your confidence, and all you have to do with me is, in due time, to receive it back, thrice paid in trebling profits.' " Truman's redemptive "mystery" parodies Christ's "mysteries of the kingdom of heaven" in Matthew 13 in which Christ compared heaven to a "pearl of great price" and a field with buried treasure.

While Chapter 15 satirizes the idea that Christian faith pays heavenly dividends, a sustained parody of one of Christ's well-known miracles can be found in the herb doctor's encounter with Thomas Fry in Chapter 19. Unjustly imprisoned in the Tombs, Fry has a biblical prototype in "the man dwelling among the tombs" possessed by an "unclean spirit" (Matt. 8:28–34; Mark 5:1–20; Luke 8:26–40). Just as the man with the unclean spirit is haunted by a "legion" of devils, so Thomas Fry is denounced by a fellow passenger as belonging to the "Devil's regiment," while to the herb doctor he is a "demoniac unfortunate." And just as Jesus conjured away the possessed man's "devils" by transferring them into a herd of swine, so the herb doctor exorcises Fry's misanthropy, first by ascribing the imperfections of human justice to the inexplicable workings of providence—a speech that Thomas Fry dismisses as "hog-latin"—and then by offering him a free sample of his medicine. Fry is last seen in a "soothed mood" that reflects his temporary release from his "devils."[6]

Still another narrative sequence in the first half of the novel plays on different aspects of Christian doctrine and institutions. Thus the coal company stock John Truman peddles symbolically represents damnation, while the herb doctor's two medicines figure as vehicles of salvation (literally, "health"). The medicines also symbolize the institutional division within Christianity of Protestantism and Catholicism, the Omni-Balsamic Reinvigorator evoking the activist evangelical ambitions of Protestantism, and the Samaritan Pain Dissuader, "ovally labeled with the engraving of a countenance full of soft pity as that of the Romish painted Madonna," suggesting the mystical anodynes of the Catholic faith, with its traditional mariolatry. The transformation of the herb doctor's medicines into symbols of religious faith was no doubt facilitated by the fact that ministers in antebellum America often endorsed patent remedies, religious journals carried their advertising, biblical references were used to promote them, and one minister, the flamboyant Universalist Lorenzo Dow, even marketed his own patented "Family Medicine" (James Harvey Young, 40, 69, 104–5, 128).

In his initial Protestant phase in Chapter 16, the herb doctor engages a mortally ill "sick man" in a long debate in an attempt to convert him to a belief in the herb doctor's "natural" remedy, the Omni-Balsamic Reinvigorator. Significantly, the herb doctor's argument against the "chemical practitioners" here functions interchangeably as both medical and theological polemic. Thus, in an implied parody of the Catholic sacrament of transubstantiation, the herb doctor asks, " 'though by natural processes, lifeless natures taken as nutriment become vitalized, yet is a lifeless nature, under any circumstances, capable of a living transmission, with all its qualities of a lifeless nature unchanged?' " In the same vein, his ensuing attack on the "tinctures, and fumes, and braziers, and occult incantations" of the chemical practitioners covertly casts aspersions on the formalized rituals of the Catholic service, with its incense fumes and incantatory Latin. Like any good Protestant who saw the Church of Rome as Antichrist, the herb doctor implies that such practices are in fact "atheistical." The herb doctor's boasted simplicity of procedure in going about nature "humbly seeking her cures" is in keeping with Protestant emphasis on the solitary communicant seeking salvation without priestly intervention.

If these covert attacks are aimed at Catholic dogma, the herb doctor terminates his spiel to the sick man by warning him against counterfeiters of the herb doctor's own quack remedy, a warning that can be interpreted as a spoof on the sectarian divisions within Protestantism itself. The herb doctor advises the sick man to hold the wrapper up to the light and look for a watermark reading "confidence," a procedure that covertly evokes the various dogmas that Protestant sects used to distinguish their particular brand of Christianity. The herb doctor's claim that only *he* sells the true product represents an ironic thrust at the follies of Protestant dissenters, each presumably blessed with the "true light."[7]

The herb doctor's subsequent appearance selling his Samaritan Pain Dissuader in Chapter 17 switches the allegorical focus from Protestantism to Catholicism. Here the herb doctor begins by enacting a parody of Catholic ritual when he holds up his remedy like a host at the mass: " 'Oh, Happiness on my right hand, and oh Security on my left, can ye wisely adore a Providence, and not think it wisdom to provide?—Provide!' (Uplifting the bottle)." The association is confirmed by the herb doctor's subsequent reception of the newly arrived "invalid Titan" and his child, "with both arms extended like a host's." The herb doctor's ensuing claims for his product eventually cause the Titan to assault him for his fraudulent promises of relief from pain. While an implied suggestion here is that the Catholic faith provides a sovereign remedy for any spiritual affliction, a related historical allegory is probably at work in this scene as well. For the Titan's mythic designation and initial association with a primeval forest setting evoke the chthonic, pre-Christian world of classical paganism. The Titan's conflict with the herb doctor thus suggests a contest of pagan "fate" with Christian "providence," the latter actually being the subject of the herb doctor's discourse when the Titan and his daughter board the *Fidèle*.

Following the Titan's attack on the herb doctor, two passengers, an "auburn-haired gentleman" and a man with a "hook nose," attempt to discover the "true character" of the herb doctor, an attempt that recalls still another historical development in early Christianity. Their discussion focuses on whether the herb doctor cynically dupes his customers for cash or does so because he himself believes in his own quack remedies—in short, whether he is a knave or a fool.[8] The situation, however, becomes more complicated when the herb doctor returns to dispense charity from the profits of his sales. The comprehensive theory now advanced by the auburn-haired man is that the herb doctor is a "knave, fool, and genius all together," or three persons in one. The dispute here parodies the debate over the meaning of the Trinity, a debate that split the early Christian church and is still officially beyond human understanding according to Catholic dogma. Since the herb doctor is in his Catholic phase, it is only appropriate that the discussion between the two men is joined by a third party, or *tertium quid,* who suspects the herb doctor to be "one of those Jesuit emissaries prowling all over our country." This topical allusion to the nativist, anti-Catholic movement, which produced a "Know-Nothing" party on the national political scene in 1854, effectuates a satirical climax to the discussion by suggesting that all three characters really "know nothing" about the mysterious character under scrutiny. Melville thus adapts a current political slogan to his recurrent skepticism about the individual's ability to know God.

Throughout the first half of the novel, then, the Confidence Man assumes various aspects of the symbolic identity of Christ, rehearses Christ's actions in the Gospels, and re-creates the historical development of Christianity. However, in keeping with the paradoxical nature of his identity, the Confidence Man's christological aspects are repeatedly shadowed by intimations of diabolism. And insofar as a doctrinal basis for the Confidence Man's Christ-like performance is the Redemption, an integral part of his satanic identity is his repeated rehearsal of the Fall. An obvious indication of this is the snake imagery that informs his appearance as John Ringman (*CM,* 27), the herb doctor (*CM,* 88), and the P.I.O. man (*CM,* 130), as well as allusions to Milton's Satan during the Confidence Man's performance as Ringman (*CM,* 22) and the P.I.O. man (*CM,* 130). Yet these references to Genesis and *Paradise Lost* constitute only one part of the traditional devil lore incorporated into the Confidence Man's demonic identity.[9]

As the diabolical foil to the mute's mock-Christ, Black Guinea is especially steeped in devil lore. Thus black is the color most often associated with the devil, who was often depicted as a Negro or Moor in European literature (Rudwin, 45; Russell, *Devil,* 64–66, 246–47). Guinea's physical disability also accords with legends of the devil as crippled by his fall from heaven or as disabled by his cloven hoof (Rudwin, 49–50). The drover calls Guinea "old boy," one of the many nicknames of the devil in English employing the epithet "old" such as "Old Horney" or "Old Hairy" or "the Black Bogey" (Rudwin, 32, 27). Guinea is even metaphorically given the horns of the devil when the drover puts "his large purple hand on the cripple's bushy wool, as if it were the curled forehead of a black steer." Guinea tells the drover that he sleeps "On der floor of der good baker's oven" where he constitutes the "black bread" alongside the baker's "nice white rolls," a remark that recalls the fact that the devil was sometimes considered a "baker" who put the damned into the "oven" (Rudwin, 27). Finally, Guinea's list of future sponsors (and potential guises) correlates with the devil's unlimited power to change his form (Rudwin, Ch. 4).

In keeping with his initial "diabolic" prototype, the Confidence Man's later guises draw on other aspects of the traditional iconography of the devil. John Ringman, the man in gray, and John Truman, for example, continue the color symbolism of blackness typified by Black Guinea. Ringman exhibits a gentlemanly and potentially satanic pride when requesting charity from the merchant, and subsequently enacts a parody of the temptation of Eve with the sophomore. The unctuous man in gray defends the authenticity of Black Guinea to the wooden-legged man while referring to the expression, "the devil is never so black as he is painted." Inasmuch as John Truman's position as agent for the Black Rapids Coal Company gives him the implied role of lord of the lower regions, his selling of shares to the sophomore and the merchant also evokes the traditional notion of a compact with the devil, made famous by the Faust legend (Rudwin, Chs. 15–17; Russell, *Mephistopheles,* 58–66, 157–67). The herb doctor's antic imitations of Christian doctrines and institutions suggest the devil's role as *simia dei* or "ape of God" (Rudwin, Ch. 12). The P.I.O. man's debate with Pitch draws not only on the popular notion of the devil as invincible casuist but also on the tradition of Southwestern humor involving a solitary frontiersman's confrontation with the devil.

Another aspect of the Confidence Man's diabolical identity in the first half of the novel arises out of the devil's traditional role of sexual tempter and scatological humorist. Black Guinea accordingly moves among the passengers of the *Fidèle* with "his knotted black fleece and good-natured, honest black face rubbing against the upper part of people's thighs." John Ringman approaches the effeminate sophomore by "softly sliding nearer, with the softest air, quivering down and looking up." The man in gray sits on the sofa next to the charitable lady, an appetizingly "plump and pleasant person" who drops her Bible as a sign that she is "not now unprepossessed." The P.I.O. man's sale of a boy to Pitch is pressed home by means of the phallic imagery of ripening corn cobs. As scatological humorist, the P.I.O. man breaks off his conversation with Pitch by saying that he must "look up the cook" he brought for "the inn-keeper at Cairo"; he then exits as the *Fidèle* passes a "grotesquely shaped bluff" called "the Devil's Joke." This "bluff" is both a verbal and a visual pun, the visual pun suggesting both a burlesque hell-mouth and the human fundament, a scatological double entendre that prefigures the chamber pot joke at the end of the novel.[10]

From our review of the Confidence Man's composite allegorical identity in the first half of the novel, we may draw several paradoxical conclusions. The first is that Melville's heterodox conception of the deity mandated a recognition that God was an inextricable blend of good and evil. Second, the Confidence Man plays on the ambiguous nature of Christ at his Second Coming: while enacting the role of Antichrist as an agent of deception, the Confidence Man also performs the Christ-like mission of revealing the "truth" of humanity's fallen condition. Third, the Confidence Man enacts a demonic parody of Christianity, revealing it to be a pious fraud; yet he also figures forth the genuine need for some form of faith as a condition for human survival. Fourth, the Confidence Man's ambiguous identity and protean nature confirm Melville's insistence on the inscrutability of God while raising the possibility that God is merely a projection of man's own ambiguous moral nature and thus a product of man's illusions.[11]

With the entry of the figure of the cosmopolitan in the second half of the novel, the allegorical matrix within which the Confidence Man moves incorporates another important mythical dimension. A number of critics have noticed that in the guise of the cosmopolitan, the Confidence Man assumes a more benevolent, even redemptive, aspect that contrasts with his earlier guises as a predatory deceiver. There are also obvious contrasts both of appearance and professional role between the cosmopolitan and the Confidence Man's earlier guises: the cosmopolitan is flamboyantly dressed in a mixture of international styles, and he represents no business or charity but that of universal human fellowship. He is, as he calls himself, " 'A cosmopolitan, a catholic man; who, being such, ties himself to no narrow tailor or teacher, but federates, in heart as in costume, something of the various gallantries of men under various suns. Oh, one roams not over the gallant globe in vain. Bred by it, is a fraternal and fusing feeling. No man is a stranger. You accost anybody. Warm and confiding, you wait not for measured advances' " (*CM,* 132). In broad terms, the most prominent differences between the Confidence Man in the first and second halves of the novel are those between a national and an international operator, and between the exploitation of the knave and the victimization of the fool.[12]

Yet any attempt to view the cosmopolitan as an unequivocally redemptive figure in the second half of the novel must ignore the hints of a more subversive identity in his dealings with Pitch, the barber, and the old man, in which he reproduces many of the deceptive, predatory gambits typical of the Confidence Man earlier in the novel. The cosmopolitan's performance is thus framed by the overarching ambiguities of the Confidence Man's divided moral identity. However, the cosmopolitan does differ from earlier allegorical associations of the Confidence Man in that to the Confidence Man's general Christic/diabolic, solar/trickster identities he adds a Dionysian component that gives him a number of distinctive features. In the character of the cosmopolitan, Melville, anticipating Nietzsche, explores the meaning of the Dionysian for modern, potentially post–Christian civilization.[13]

Originally a vegetation deity associated with fertility and later with wine and viticulture, Dionysus was a dying and reviving god whose nature encompassed a varied mythic history. According to some legends he was torn in pieces, buried, and consumed by the Titans, or else he was buried and then born anew in the spring. His Bacchic followers performed the same dismemberment (*sparagmos*) on animals in a communion-like meal (*omophagy*). Dionysus was regularly dubbed "the stranger," and his original cult was traditionally thought to be from Thrace or Asia Minor; yet the exact origins of his cult remained a mystery until recently when they were traced to the Greek mainland around Thebes. The youngest of the Olympian gods, Dionysus was conceived in the womb of a mortal, Semele, and so had a semi-divine status that was sometimes adduced to account for his fraternizing among mankind. A god of masks and irreducible strangeness, Dionysus was the instigator of orgiastic rites of Bacchic madness among his followers and thus was associated with subversion of the social order. Often depicted with a train of maenads, ithyphallic satyrs, sileni, and wild beasts, Dionysus and his cult reached all over the Mediterranean world and even India. Civilizer and destroyer, Dionysus was an ambiguous deity whose role was to give mankind access to the depths of the unconscious; his invasion of the psyche could bring either exaltation or mania, renewed life or violent death. Yet as a god of wine and viticulture, Dionysus was also considered a spiritual liberator and cultural benefactor. In Greece he was the mythical patron of the drama and the dithyramb; Greek drama was first developed at the Greater Dionysia held in the early spring.

Dionysus's mystery and moral ambiguity make him an appropriate archetypal model for the cosmopolitan, whose sobriquet of "citizen of the world" is suitable for a Greek god whose cult extended throughout the Mediterranean world and beyond. Like Dionysus, Frank Goodman is notable for his promotion of wine as a spiritual panacea and a means of fusing humanity into a fraternal mass and primordial whole. With its Eastern luxuriousness and predominantly red tonalities, the cosmopolitan's costume is also emblematic of Dionysus, as is his characterization as "a liberalist, in dress," a pun on "Liber," the Roman god of wine traditionally conflated with Dionysus. The cosmopolitan's pipe also suggests the Dionysian thyrsus, the pine-cone tipped scepter of the god.

The key to the transformation of the Confidence Man into the Dionysus-like cosmopolitan is the passage of the *Fidèle* into a night-time world at the town of Cairo, a domain associated with disease and death. Viewing Cairo from the *Fidèle,* Pitch is gradually made aware that he has been duped by the P.I.O. man, whom he now believes to be the devil. His subsequent meeting with the cosmopolitan is initiated with the cosmopolitan's greeting, "A penny for your thoughts," a request that recalls the Confidence Man's earlier contrivances for getting money out of his interlocutors, and may also allude to the penny that was required of the shades of the departed to enter Charon's boat in order to cross the Styx, the river of death in Greek mythology. The town of Cairo is thus a liminal realm where the Confidence Man undergoes a symbolic death and resurrection from the satanic and worm-like P.I.O. man to the butterfly-like citizen of the world, Frank Goodman, a version of Dionysus as dying and reviving god.[14]

The cosmopolitan's Dionysian persona is especially pronounced during his encounter with Pitch, whom he attempts to convert to a religion of wine-bibbing and revelry. As the cosmopolitan tells the backwoodsman early in their conversation, " 'This austerity won't do. Let me tell you too—*en confiance*—that while revelry may not always merge into ebriety, soberness, in too deep potations, may become a sort of sottishness. Which sober sottishness, in my way of thinking, is only to be cured by beginning at the other end of the horn, to tipple a little' " (*CM,* 134). The cosmopolitan's ensuing story of the old woman of Goshen's rejuvenation by means of "Santa Cruz" wine is, in effect, a parable of Dionysian conversion. The cosmopolitan's behavior here also suggests Dionysus's role as mythical patron of the drama. As he remarks to Pitch, " 'Life is a pic-nic *en costume;* one must take a part, assume a character, stand ready in a sensible way to play the fool' " (*CM,* 133). Finally, just as Dionysus's rites were celebrated in nocturnal orgies and revelry, the cosmopolitan makes his appearance at dusk, encourages Pitch to lighten up his mood, and even invites him to go dancing: " 'They are to have dancing on the hurricane-deck to-night. I shall fling them off a Scotch jig, while, to save the pieces, you hold my loose change; and following that, I propose that you, my dear fellow, stack your gun, and throw your bearskins in a sailor's hornpipe—I holding your watch' " (*CM,* 135).

Whereas the cosmopolitan's Dionysian nature is perhaps at its most obtrusive in his encounter with Pitch, the cosmopolitan's subsequent encounter with Charlie Noble is also clearly influenced by this mythical archetype. The two "boon companions" accordingly celebrate their new friendship over a bottle of port wine, while Noble's warbling of a tag from Leigh Hunt's "Bacchus in Tuscany" and his subsequent panegyric to the wine press constitute a dithyrambic performance appropriate for a Dionysian initiate. Yet the different capacity for drink evinced by Goodman and Noble during their symposium also suggests a contest between Dionysus and a reluctant convert, or even enemy, to the god. The relationship of Goodman and Noble has a mythical prototype in the story of Dionysus's encounter with pirates who abduct him on their ship in order to sell him for a slave, a legend recounted in both Dionysus's *Homeric Hymn* and Ovid's *Metamorphoses.* In this story, Dionysus magically causes a vine to grow from the deck and enfold the mast, while the ship's oars are turned into serpents and the pirates leap overboard to become dolphins. In Chapter 31 of *The Confidence-Man,* entitled "A metamorphosis more surprising than any in Ovid," we witness a comparable metamorphosis as the riverboat sharper, Charlie Noble, is transformed into a hissing serpent.

The cosmopolitan's ensuing conversation with Winsome similarly enacts a failed Dionysian communion, for the "mystic" prefers cold water to wine, an unequivocal indication of the "coldness" of his nature. Winsome's inhumanity is also conveyed by his refusal to give anything to the vinous-faced "crazy beggar." The cosmopolitan generously buys the "rhapsodical tract" of this broken-down devotee of Bacchic rapture, again showing his mythical affiliation as patron of wine and the dithyramb. The cosmopolitan's subsequent encounter with Egbert, on the other hand, is yet another exercise in failed conversion and communion.

Dionysian elements, then, implicitly inform the cosmopolitan's quest for friendship, vinous communion, and human solidarity throughout much of the second half of the novel. Yet as previously noted, the cosmopolitan also exhibits the same ambiguous blend of Christic and demonic traits that characterize the Confidence Man's appearances in the first half of the novel. The cosmopolitan's red attire actually suits both his Christic and diabolic identities, red being the color of the robe Jesus wore when scourged, and also of the "vesture dipped in blood" worn by Christ as the incarnate Word in Revelation 19; red is also, after black, the color most often associated with the devil (Rudwin, 46; Russell, *Devil,* 66). In a similarly ambiguous conflation, the cosmopolitan's surname, "Goodman," is both a nickname of the devil and a possible allusion to Christ's characterization as a "good man" (John 7:12). The cosmopolitan's behavior with Pitch hints at both symbolic identities, for the cosmopolitan's emphasis here on the brotherhood of man and the importance of wine ally him with Christian belief, yet his claim to be a "taster of races" also recalls the devil's role as a cannibalistic consumer of human souls.

The cosmopolitan's encounter with Pitch nevertheless ends as a failed conversion to a religion of human fellowship, as the cosmopolitan, claiming to be "an ambassador from the human race," proclaims a Christ-like mission of seeking "to conciliate accord between you and them."[15] And in a continuation of the novel's typological structure, the second half of the novel constitutes a displaced enactment of the last week of Christ's life, the complement to the Confidence Man's parody of Christ's ministry in the first half. Thus the cosmopolitan's boisterous interaction with Pitch corresponds to Christ's triumphant entry into Jerusalem on Palm Sunday. His subsequent encounter with Charlie Noble, on the other hand, constitutes an extended burlesque of the Last Supper. This encounter suggests the version of the Last Supper found in John's gospel in which Christ asserted as his chief commandment "that ye love one another, as I have loved you. / Greater love hath no man than this, that a man lay down his life for his friends" (15:12–13). In John's account, Christ also preached his famous "vine teaching": "He that abideth in me, and I in him, the same bringeth forth much fruit: for without me ye can do nothing" (15:5). From this perspective, Charlie Noble's failure to be redeemed arises from his failure to partake of the wine of Christian fellowship. Noble's subsequent betrayal of the cosmopolitan, moreover, casts him in the role of Judas; the cosmopolitan's awareness that Noble is trying to dupe him for money is also analogous to Christ's knowledge that Judas would betray him for thirty pieces of silver. The cosmopolitan's brief tale of Charlemont converts the same archetypal betrayal into a modern parable. Finally, in his later encounter with Egbert the cosmopolitan reproduces the same prototypical betrayal by the Judas-like Charlie, but his anguish over his rejection now evokes the Agony in the Garden, Christ's greatest spiritual torment prior to the Crucifixion. The flower symbolism associated with the two main characters of Egbert's story of "China Aster" is thus suited to a typological association with the garden of Gethsemane.

These re-creations of Christ's Passion represent an apparent vindication of one of the fundamental teachings of Christianity, brotherly love. Yet the cosmopolitan's encounter with the barber, with whom he enacts a parody of the Crucifixion, renders the teaching of Christianity once again problematic. Here the cosmopolitan triumphs over his initial symbolic adversary by getting him to take down his "No Trust" sign, a figural re-creation of Mosaic law superseded by Christian grace. A mock Lamb of God, the cosmopolitan is "shaved" in one of the barber's three throne-like, "high-backed and high-armed" chairs, the typological equivalent of the three crosses erected on Calvary ("the place of a skull") where the "king of the Jews" was crucified between two thieves. The punning cant that the barber and cosmopolitan exchange in effect conforms to this symbolic setting. The cosmopolitan on his "tonsorial throne" accordingly reenacts Christ's atonement—the cosmopolitan's ritual "shaving" hints at a displaced blood sacrifice—and thus the debate between the cosmopolitan and barber may be read as an attempt to convert the barber to a new faith predicated on Christ's sacrificial remission of sins.[16]

The scene with the barber would also seem to conflate the Sermon on the Mount with the Crucifixion, for the cosmopolitan's attempt to convince the barber to extend "trust" to his customers recalls Christ's injunction to forgive one's debtors, to lay up treasure in heaven, and to take no thought for the morrow (Matt. 6:12, 20, 34). The cosmopolitan's first words to the barber are in fact a blessing in imitation of the Beatitudes (Matt. 5:3–11). Yet the conversion of the barber into a practicing Christian is ultimately revealed to be a pious hoax at best, a diabolical joke at worst. For the whole scene is marked by a persistent undercurrent of the demonic, as suggested by the cosmopolitan's opening remark to the barber: " 'You call me *man*, just as the townsfolk called the angels who, in man's form, came to Lot's house; just as the Jew rustics called the devils who, in man's form, haunted the tombs. You can conclude nothing absolute from the human form, barber' " (*CM*, 225–26).

Despite this initial warning about human nature, the cosmopolitan goes on to argue on behalf of a moral absolute, "trust" in mankind. Adducing the case of a man seen at different angles and at different times of day, the cosmopolitan demonstrates that the barber's trust in his fellow man is based on relative criteria. And as we soon realize, the debate between the cosmopolitan and the barber typifies the conflict between the absolute values preached by Christianity and the relative values by which mankind actually lives. The cosmopolitan's encounter with the barber ultimately suggests that there can be no overlap between heavenly and worldly values, for a gain in one is clearly a loss in the other. To underline this point, the "security" the cosmopolitan offers the barber turns out to be a legal fiction. Moreover, the cosmopolitan actually convinces the barber to take down his sign only by means of magic, or more precisely, mesmerism. And although affirmed to be "benign," this mesmeric exercise is nevertheless compared to "the power of persuasive fascination—the power of holding another creature by the button of the eye" (*CM*, 234). In other words, the cosmopolitan hypnotizes his subject like a snake, a method that suggests both Christ's well-known injunction to his disciples to be as wise as serpents and harmless as doves (Matt. 10:15), as well as the persuasive powers of the serpent in Eden.

As a larger allegory of Christian faith, the underlying doctrinal basis for this scene is the supersession of an old covenant of law by Christ's new covenant of grace. To seal their new covenant, the cosmopolitan and barber sign an agreement ensuring the barber against any loss that might accrue from his newfound faith in mankind. Yet while Melville thus obliquely draws attention to the legalistic origins of the biblical concept of covenant, the open-ended obligation of the divine party is made manifest when the cosmopolitan refuses to give security against the contractual claim to "make good" any loss that the barber may experience by trusting mankind. As if to confirm the shortcomings of such a faith, the cosmopolitan cheats the barber for the price of his shave, thereby confirming the "certain loss" that the barber adduces as a justification for a security deposit of fifty dollars. Hence far from converting the barber to faith in his fellow man, the cosmopolitan has merely performed another version of the frontier gambit of the biter-bit, or in this case, the shaver-shaved.

In the context of sacred history, the cosmopolitan's encounter with the old man necessarily follows from his encounter with the barber. For like

Christ, whose Crucifixion and Resurrection led to union with the heavenly Father, the cosmopolitan next encounters a sacred-looking old man reading a Bible, a text the cosmopolitan immediately designates as the "good news." Instead of the hopeful "good news" implied by Christ's resurrection, however, the cosmopolitan heralds a new gospel of ambiguity and annihilation. Indeed, the end of *The Confidence-Man* effectuates a radical subversion of Christianity within the general framework of Christian eschatology. While a number of critics have noted the apocalyptic atmosphere of the last chapter, neither its full allegorical significance nor its densely parodic relation to the Book of Revelation has been fully recognized. The conclusion to *The Confidence-Man* is in fact a heavily allusive enactment of "last things" in which the insecurity of man's worldly and spiritual predicament is subversively dramatized. In this mock "revelation" in which everything and nothing is revealed, good and evil are not schematically separated but ambiguously compounded.[17]

While the whole of *The Confidence-Man* may be considered a satirical figuration of the Second Coming of Christ, the last chapter is an epitome of that event as the Confidence Man's "masquerade" draws to a close at midnight, a time traditionally projected for Christ's Second Advent like a "thief in the night" (I Thess. 5:2; II Peter 3:10). In his capacity as a "well-to-do farmer," the old man evokes another traditional concept of the apocalypse as the "harvest day" of God, as found in both the Hebrew prophets and the Book of Revelation (Isa. 17:5; Jer. 51:33; Joel 3:13; Rev. 14:14–20). The old man's initial comment to the cosmopolitan, in which he alludes to "war-time," may also recall the "wars and rumors of wars" that were supposed to signal Christ's impending return (Matt. 24:6). The initial apocalyptic ambiance of this chapter is similarly conveyed by the "solar lamp" that illuminates the scene: "In the middle of the gentleman's cabin burned a solar lamp, swung from the ceiling, and whose shade of ground glass was all round fancifully variegated, in transparency, with the image of a horned altar, from which flames rose, alternate with the figure of a robed man, his head encircled by a halo" (*CM,* 240). A symbol of the Christian faith, the solar lamp here is inscribed with images evoking the Old and New Testaments: the horned altar of Moses which God commanded Moses to build in Exodus 27:1–2, and a haloed saint, almost certainly St. John the Divine, whose text repeatedly alludes to robed figures (Rev. 1:13, 6:11, 7:9–14) and who, as the putative author of the fourth gospel, began his account with a reference to his role as a transmitter of the "light" of Christian faith (John 1:6–9). The image of the lamp also derives from the conclusion of Rabelais' *Fifth Book* describing the Oracle of the Holy Bottle, an affirmative revelation of Christian faith that Melville obliquely parodies here.[18]

Significantly, the various other lamps that surround the solar lamp are described as "barren planets, which had either gone out from exhaustion, or been extinguished by such occupants of berths as the light annoyed, or who wanted to sleep, not see." Mankind's superannuated faiths, these "barren planets" evoke a traditional apocalyptic image of cosmic extinction (Matt. 24:29; Mark 13:24–25; Luke 21:25–26; Rev. 6:12–14, 8:12). The narrator reports that the "captain" has forbidden the passengers from turning out the one remaining lamp because of the danger of thieves, a reminder of the merely utilitarian value of Christian revelation after its metaphysical truths have been exhausted or discredited.

The equation of light and faith implied by the image of the solar lamp draws on the symbolic role of light in New Testament apocalyptic, especially in two of the principal sources for the setting of the last chapter, I Thessalonians and Matthew 25. In his first letter to the Thessalonians, St. Paul evoked the conditions of Christ's Second Coming:

> But ye, brethren, are not in darkness, that that day should overtake you as a thief.
>
> Ye are all the children of light, and the children of the day: we are not of the night, nor of darkness.
>
> Therefore let us not sleep, as do others; but let us watch and be sober.
>
> For they that sleep sleep in the night; and they that be drunken are drunken in the night.
>
> But let us, who are of the day, be sober, putting on the breastplate of faith and love; and for an helmet, the hope of salvation. (5:4–8)

This opposition between those illuminated with faith and those asleep in the dark appears in *The Confidence-Man* as the contrast between the old man reading his Bible under the lamp and the potentially damned sleepers who surround him, some of whom rudely advise him to go to bed. Having put on the spiritual armor of Christian faith (Eph. 6:11–17), the old man is thus a type of the faithful, although the array of security devices which he acquires by the end of this scene will make a mockery of such protection.

In the parable of the ten virgins (Matt. 25:1–13), Christ compared the unexpected hour of his Second Coming to the bridegroom who arrived late at night when the five foolish virgins had fallen asleep without making sure of their lamp oil, in contrast to the other five virgins who were adequately prepared and were admitted to the marriage feast. Radiantly illuminated when the cosmopolitan arrives "as any bridegroom tripping to the bridal chamber," the old man is ostensibly like one of the wise virgins in Christ's parable; yet the very ease with which he is duped suggests that he is a foolish virgin after all, his folly giving no hint of heavenly wisdom or reward.

In keeping with Melville's syncretic method throughout the novel, the image of the old man here actually incorporates a composite allegorical identity combining both classical and biblical archetypes. As a classical archetype, the old man represents an allegorical "genius" figure based on the original "genius" of Roman religion, a paterfamilias who represented a tutelary, generative spirit ensuring continued life for the individual, the family, and the nation. The accretion of meanings surrounding the Roman "genius" began with its association with male generative power: "accompanying each man from birth, it signified not only virility, but also life, energy, and even temperament or personality. Its early paternalistic affiliations encouraged its transfer to other 'fathers': the founding father of the city and institution, then the gods, the Emperor, and finally, the State. Eventually deified as the personal god of each man, this external double safeguarded his life and fortune and was worshipped on his birthday" (Nitzsche, 4). Thus, just as the Roman genius was an embodiment of health and vitality, the old man in Chapter 45 has a "hale look of greenness in winter" and is "fresh-hearted" as a boy of fifteen"; the preservative powers of the Roman genius are also ironically reflected in the old man's security devices. A sacred-looking paterfamilias, the old man is the "genius" of the *Fidèle*—an allegorical image of the Father as a guardian of life and a personification of the State.

A more subversive aspect of the old man's identity, however, arises from his covert biblical model, the Ancient of Days, the image of the deity as divine judge depicted in Chapter 7 of Daniel's apocalyptic vision—the Old Testament source for the theophany of God the Father in Chapter 4 of the Book of Revelation. As the author of Daniel writes:

> I beheld till the thrones were cast down, and the Ancient of days did sit, whose garment was white as snow, and the hair of his head like the pure wool: his throne was like the fiery flame, and his wheels as burning fire. . . .
>
> I saw in the night visions, and, behold, one like the Son of man came with the clouds of heaven, and came to the Ancient of days, and they brought him near before him. (7:9, 13)

In Melville's parodic refiguring of this scene, we find the solitary old man, "head snowy as the marble," sitting on a stool under a "solar lamp" whose beams brilliantly illuminate the circular table where he sits. Yet if the Ancient of Days is an aged figure of wisdom and reverence, the old man is a dim-witted fool whom the cosmopolitan eventually leads into the dark in search of his "stateroom." On a figurative level, the last chapter of *The Confidence-Man* dramatizes a displaced act of deicide, the ultimate subversion of authority on Melville's ship of fools.[19]

Combining prominent Old Testament and classical archetypes of the divinized Father, the old man also assumes the role of God the Father within the apocalyptic frame of the Book of Revelation, where he evokes the initial image of God on his heavenly throne, a book in his right hand, seven lamps of fire overhead, "and before the throne there was a sea of glass like unto crystal" (Rev. 4:6). The ensuing action in Revelation involves the unsealing of the seven seals of the book of life by the slain Lamb (Rev. 5:1–8:1), an action parodied in *The Confidence-Man* when the cosmopolitan "unseals" the Bible the old man reads by discovering in it the words of Jesus, the Son of Sirach, earlier quoted by the barber (" 'Believe not his many words—an enemy speaketh sweetly with his lips' "). Despite the fact that an offstage voice has termed the Bible "too good to be true" and then announced that the Confidence Man is the subject of the Son of Sirach's message, the old man evades these warnings by noting that the cosmopolitan's text is from the Apocrypha. Playing along with the old man's observation, the cosmopolitan remarks, " 'Fact is, when all bound up together, it's sometimes confusing. The uncanonical part should be bound distinct' " (*CM,* 243).

The Confidence Man's simulated confusion over truth and fiction in the Bible might be taken as a reminder of the recent appearance of the higher criticism in America, which was historicizing, and consequently problematizing, what had previously been thought the revealed word of God.[20] But Melville goes beyond a topical reference to the newly questioned authority of biblical inspiration, for what emerges from the old man's action here is not only a naive evasion of the reality of evil by the "genius" of America, but also the suggestion that both the Word of God and God Himself are ambiguous constructs with a message of duplicity at their core. The Bible thus functions here as a model not only for the old man's inconsistency (trusting the Bible while distrusting his fellow man) but also the equivocal natures of both the cosmopolitan and peddler; it thus typifies the whole moral universe of the novel in which good and evil are inextricably mixed.

Furthermore, the cosmopolitan's complaint that the *Fidèle*'s Bible should be "bound" differently to separate the true text from the false possibly evokes the "binding" of Satan during the millennium (Rev. 20:2–5), thereby foreshadowing the appearance of the satanic-looking peddler. And while the peddler enacts a concentrated version of the Confidence Man's own role of apocalyptic deceiver (as some of the peddler's conspiratorial remarks to the cosmopolitan imply), he also implicitly subsumes the three apocalyptic agents of Antichrist in the Book of Revelation: devil, beast, and false prophet. Thus, like the devil who is busy on earth because "he knoweth that he hath but a short time" (Rev. 12:12) and is to be "loosed a little season" (Rev. 20:3), the peddler enacts what proves to be a cameo role. His peculiar attire of red flannel shirt and yellow coat, which "flamed about him like the painted flames in the robes of a victim of *auto-de-fé*" (*CM,* 244), also suggests the casting of devil, beast, and false prophet into the "lake of fire" both before and after the millennium (Rev. 19:20, 20:10). Finally, with his face exhibiting a "polish of seasoned grime" and a laugh "disclosing leopard-like teeth," the peddler evokes the images of the two "beasts" from sea and land depicted in Revelation 13: The beast from the sea, who "was like a leopard" (Rev. 13:2), blasphemed God and made war on the saints, while the beast from land set his "mark" on the foreheads of those who belonged in his corrupt community (Rev. 13:16–17). On the other hand, the peddler also paradoxically displays features of Christ as the anonymous conquering knight depicted in Revelation 19:11–16: the peddler's red flannel shirt is like Christ's "vesture dipped in blood"; the "lustrous sparks" of his eyes are like Christ's eyes, which resemble "a flame of fire"; and his "leopard-like teeth" suggest the "sharp sword" coming out of Christ's mouth. The pathos of the boy's homelessness and poverty similarly hints at a Christ-like identity. Like the Confidence Man, then, the peddler is a radically ambiguous figure, both savior and destroyer, truth-teller and deceiver—an inextricable mix of good and evil.[21]

A composite figure, the peddler also mimics the role of the Greek trickster god, Hermes, as Edgar Dryden has demonstrated.[22] Hermes the herald was the boy-god of flocks, roads and doors, commerce and thieves; possessed of a magic wand, he was also the god of spells and eloquence, the inventor of a means for kindling fire (he was sometimes considered a "little Prometheus"), fabricator of the lyre, and guide of souls to the underworld or *psychopomp*. Hints of most of these traits can be found in the characterization of the peddler. For example, the peddler possesses Hermes' gleeful taste for deceit in his dealings with the old man; his selling of lock and money belt suggests Hermes' patronage of both commerce and thieves; his riddling words recall Hermes' association with verbal spells; finally, the "miniature mahogany door" which he "meaningfully held before the old man" might be interpreted as a hermetic symbol of death, the ultimate thief in the night.

In keeping with the underlying theme of death here, and in a continuation of the parody of the Book of Revelation found in the last chapter, the peddler's counterfeit detector enables the old man to perform a burlesque version of the Last Judgment (Rev. 20:11–15) in which the realms of God and Mammon have been satirically inverted: "Laying the Detector square before him on the table, he then, with something like the air of an officer bringing by the collar a brace of culprits to the bar, placed the two bills opposite the Detector, upon which, the examination began, lasting some time, prosecuted with no small research and vigilance, the forefinger of the right hand proving of lawyer-like efficacy in tracing out and pointing the evidence, whichever way it might go" (*CM,* 248). In this ironic transvaluation of Christian eschatology, money has replaced the souls of the dead. Moreover, unlike God at the Last Judgment, the old man finds it impossible to judge the authenticity of his patently fraudulent bank bill according to the counterfeit detector's specifications. Both the *Fidèle*'s Bible and the peddler's counterfeit detector thus constitute analogous texts exemplifying the duplicities latent within the realms of both God and Mammon.[23]

Immediately after the Last Judgment, the terminal chapters of the Book of Revelation describe the climax of Christian eschatology in the symbolic marriage of Christ and the New Jerusalem, the holy city of the faithful which descends out of the sky. A huge jewel-like construction, "the city was pure gold, like unto clear glass. / And the foundations of the wall of the city were garnished with all manner of precious stones" (Rev. 21:18–19). In the terminal moments of *The Confidence-Man,* however, instead of a golden city descending from heaven we find a tin chamber pot or "life preserver" emerging from under the old man's rear end. The excretory implications of the old man's "stool" clearly violate St. John's injunction that in the New Jerusalem, "there shall in no wise enter into it anything that defileth, neither whatsoever worketh abomination, or maketh a lie" (Rev. 21:27). While this ironic substitution of chamber pot for the New Jerusalem may be considered a blasphemous joke, it nevertheless possesses a deeper purpose here by implying that the old man's hope for a personal immortality is as dubious as the end of Christian history in an eternal New Jerusalem. On the contrary, all man faces at death is physical corruption and spiritual annihilation.

In keeping with this covert message, the cosmopolitan remarks of the chamber pot–life preserver: " 'the tin part,' rapping it with his knuckles, 'seems so perfect—sounds so very hollow.' " This oblique demonstration of the "hollowness" of heaven is also an implicit rebuttal of St. Paul's argument in I Corinthians that at the Second Coming mortal man will be rendered immortal:

> Behold, I shew you a mystery; We shall not all sleep, but we shall all be changed,
>
> In a moment, in the twinkling of an eye, at the last trump: for the trumpet shall sound, and the dead shall be raised incorruptible, and we shall be changed.
>
> For this corruptible must put on incorruption, and this mortal must put on immortality.
>
> So when this corruptible shall have put on incorruption, and this mortal shall have put on immortality, then shall be brought to pass the saying that is written, Death is swallowed up in victory. (15: 51–54)

Having been a reader of the Bible for seventy years, the old man is past that three score and ten which served as the biblical span of human life. Yet the old man's impending death, symbolized here by a quintessential element of corruption and decay (feces), effectively negates Paul's famous teaching.[24]

By the same token, despite the cosmopolitan's assurances of safety, the "hollow" life preserver that he gives the old man will not be an effective safeguard against a wreck. The Mississippi's snag-ridden waters thus constitute an ironic contrast with the heavenly New Jerusalem, where the faithful will find the "pure river of water of life, clear as crystal, proceeding out of the throne of God and of the Lamb," as well as the "tree of life" whose leaves "were for the healing of the nations" (Rev. 22:1–2). The heavenly

New Jerusalem is also full of its own eternal illumination: "And there shall be no night there; and they need no candle, neither light of the sun; for the Lord God giveth them light: and they shall reign for ever and ever" (Rev. 22:5). At the conclusion of the scene with the old man, on the other hand, the cosmopolitan extinguishes the expiring solar lamp while remarking, " 'But bless me, we are being left in the dark here. Pah! what a smell, too.' "

The extinction of the solar lamp is no doubt meant to symbolize the completion of a fictive Apocalypse. Nevertheless, the last sentence of the novel ("Something further may follow this Masquerade") suggests the continued existence of the world. We know that the cosmopolitan plans to see Charlie Noble "to-morrow"; moreover, the barber is reported to tell his night's adventures with the cosmopolitan to his friends "in after days." Yet we may assume that this post-apocalyptic world is also post-Christian; indeed, it hints at the fictive universe depicted by twentieth-century writers of the absurd.

As both a nihilistic vaudeville and a densely allusive burlesque of biblical apocalyptic, then, the final chapter of *The Confidence-Man* is an "endgame" prefiguring the universe of Samuel Beckett. The last chapter also demonstrates the "part and parcel allegoricalness" of the novel, for just as the first chapter subsumes an allegorical parody of Christ's First Advent, the last chapter contains a parody of his Second. Between these two typological coordinates, Melville mythologizes the life of Christ while narrating a satirical "fifth gospel" that transvalues the moral framework of Christianity. Such a fictive transformation was not unusual in the era of David Friedrich Strauss's mythologizing *Life of Jesus* (1835; English version by George Eliot, 1846) which Melville apparently knew of or had read (*J*, 97). Yet Melville's subversive mythologizing of the life of Christ may also be said to form a part of an American tradition of what Lawrence Buell has called "literary scripturalism." In the seventeenth and eighteenth centuries, this consisted primarily of a pietistic appropriation of Bible themes; but in the transitional theological and literary environment of the nineteenth century a new set of relations between literature and the Bible developed, leading to "a comparative mythological approach to Scripture that sometimes moved in the direction of debunking it as fabrication but sometimes led to an emphasis on the luminous meaningfulness of its symbolism or even to a campaign for literature as scripture" (*New England Literary Culture,* 185). Melville's literary appropriation of Christ's life paradoxically incorporates both a satirical act of "debunking" and an implied reverence for the power of its symbolism. In the latter respect, it bears a potential resemblance to *Uncle Tom's Cabin* in its ascription of sotereological symbolism to its hero and its exploitation of current millennialist ideology. But whereas Stowe's novel is a sentimental testament of faith, Melville's novel is a skeptical dramatization of agonized unbelief. Only the unpublished Emily Dickinson in nearby Amherst would share Melville's ambivalent attitude to the Christian god as a religious confidence man.

5

Biographical Models: Fathers and Sons

So far we have seen that *The Confidence-Man* subsumes a multifaceted satirical representation of both American society and the Christian religion. Does the novel satirize specific individuals as well? The question has been germane ever since the revival of interest in the novel half a century ago. At that time Egbert Oliver convincingly argued that the mystic, Mark Winsome, and his "practical disciple," Egbert, were modeled on Emerson and Thoreau. Oliver also argued that Fanny Kemble provided a model for Goneril, the wayward wife of John Ringman, the man with the weed. Not long thereafter, Harrison Hayford similarly demonstrated that a caricature of Poe appears in the anonymous peddler of a certain "rhapsodical tract" appearing in Chapter 36.[1] Several decades of criticism have not materially altered this roster of models, although a recent attempt has been made to identify originals for virtually every character in the novel by canvassing the political and historical arena. This is Helen Trimpi's book-length study, *Melville's Confidence Men and American Politics in the 1850s,* a misguided attempt to demonstrate that Melville was writing a political satire on the founding of the Republican party in the early 1850s.[2]

The fact, however, that at least four characters in the novel have biographical models might lead one to suspect there were more to be found, given the right frame of reference. A hint in this direction has been provided by Michael Paul Rogin, who has argued that in *The Confidence-Man,* "Melville placed the history of his family at the center of one of his fictions for the first time since *Pierre*" (249). This family history according to Rogin consists of Allan Melvill's financial transgressions and victimization in a developing laissez-faire market economy: Allan Melvill is the prototypical confidence man who "makes the fictional fragments of *The Confidence-Man* whole" (249).

While Rogin's analysis of Allan Melvill's troubled career suggests some of the buried autobiographical premises of the novel, his analysis stops short of a reading that would identify Melville's father or other family members as actual models for the novel's characters. We have already seen that Melville employed a complex allegorical code to reflect his subversive views of the deity. A similar use of coding and displacement is employed in Melville's exploitation of his family, friends, and literary brethren as biographical models for the characters in his last published novel. By the same token, Melville's own troubled literary career makes the fragmentary character of the Confidence Man whole. For the Confidence Man represents a continuation of the literary line of Melville's semiautobiographical heroes—Tommo, Omoo, Redburn, White-Jacket, Ishmael, and Pierre—while his shape-shifting manifestations reproduce Melville's evolution as an artist from the mid-1830s to the mid-1850s. As a writer deeply conscious of the rapidity of his own development (*C*, 193), Melville is covertly reenacting his own protean growth of mind in the eight guises of the Confidence Man. The fact that the guises of Confidence Man function as a displaced self-portrait confirms what some critics have assumed in a general way about the novel without realizing its practical application.[3]

Significantly, while reading the seventeenth-century French moralist, La Bruyère, in September 1862 Melville scored and underscored the observation, "Nothing helps a Man more to bear quietly the injuries he receives from *parents and friends* than a reflection of the vices of humanity" (*Log*, 654–55). In *The Confidence-Man,* Melville is perpetrating a belated, burlesque revenge on his personal and cultural milieux. The novel picks up where *Pierre* leaves off, substituting satire for melodrama and an April Fools' Day masquerade for the misguided martyrdom of Pierre, the fool of truth. Melville's conflation of satire and masquerade operated as both a creative and a self-protective strategy, for as Edward and Lillian Bloom have remarked in a study of eighteenth-century satire:

> The satirist, knowing he risked retaliation should his satire be too openly offensive, employed art and artifice to satisfy practical as well as literary need. To minimize sanctions, as we have already seen, he often transparently disguised his victims' identities and his own. And sometimes he donned masks as a mere pretense to point up the absurdity of masking, even while he damned individuals or institutions. He might take additional cover behind allegory and beast fable. And he might shield himself in metaphor or other linguistic armor. Often as cunning as his own *eiron,* the satirist either erased the visible authorial self or created himself anew through a sheltering persona. (209)

The "masquerade" depicted in Melville's last published novel was also a fictional counterpart to some of the summer festivities that took place during his Berkshire years, especially the September 1855 "fancy dress picnic" sponsored by Sarah Morewood at Broadhall, to which Melville brought his family in costume but went himself in normal attire (*Log,* 2:507). Leon Howard views the event as having a germinating influence on the novel's composition (226).

The present chapter details the series of self-images that Melville created to chart the fictive career of the Confidence Man, and then goes on to identify and analyze the family members Melville used as models; the next chapter explores Melville's use of his literary peers for a supplementary range of models. A small number of characters involves the use of more than one model; and all characters are blended with cultural, regional, or theatrical types so that an exact delineation of the line separating model and type is necessarily schematic. It should be noted, too, that the identification of models is not intended to make the novel into a one-dimensional *roman à clef.* Nevertheless, the cumulative and mutually corroborative effect of such identification confirms the case for satirical caricature in virtually all "major" characters. Finally, we may observe that Melville's use of biographical models is actually consistent with April Fools' Day jokes on one's intimates and associates. Melville violated comic, but not satiric, norms by making sure that he was the only one to understand every level of a complex joke, which is perhaps the ultimate testimony of his intellectual isolation by the mid-1850s and another reason why he stopped writing fiction at this point.

THE MAN IN CREAM COLORS

Although clearly a Christ-like persona, the first guise of the Confidence Man also conveys a displaced image of Melville in late adolescence. The mute's "downy" chin and youthful demeanor would in fact suggest the image not of a "man" but of a mature adolescent. The most explicit autobiographical detail about the mute is the white fur hat he wears, for between the ages of fifteen and seventeen (1834–1836), Melville sold fur caps and winter cloaks as a clerk and bookkeeper in the fur and cap business of his older brother Gansevoort. "In the summer he sold plain cloth caps and 'Brush Hats of the finest quality' and in the winter Morocco and Circassian caps, buffalo robes, and raccoon sleigh robes" (Gilman, 71). The Melville fur business went bankrupt during the Panic of 1837, and as a result of this personal and national calamity, a fatherless Melville was thrown into a state of prolonged genteel poverty and exile from his originally privileged social milieu. The emblematic contrast between the charity-seeking mute and the barber with his "No Trust" sign suggests Melville's encounter with the inexorable economic forces that produced the Panic of 1837 and its ensuing six-year depression. Moreover, as the figurative representative of note-shavers and money lenders, the barber advertises a policy of "no credit" that parallels a crucial event in the collapse of his family's fortunes: Melville's witness in April 1837 of his mother's $50,000 bond to the New York State Bank, where her older brother Peter was a director (*Log,* 1:69).

In the mute's didactic messages of charity, Melville is also seemingly drawing on his educational experiences in the mid-1830s at the Albany Classical School, the Albany Academy, and as a member of the Albany Young Men's Association for Mutual Improvement, all of which put the final touches on his secondary education. The mute's text from St. Paul conforms to a stated aim of the Albany Classical School, "the formation of character under the influence of the Christian religion" (quoted in Gilman, 71). According to one of his instructors there, Melville was distinguished as a composer of literary "themes" (*Log,* 1:64). The mute's forensic exercise is also in keeping with the activities of the Albany Young Men's Association where Melville participated in debates on topics such as "whether the poor laws ought to be abolished and whether genius is innate" (Gilman, 74).

Finally, the mute's pedagogical mission also conceivably parodies Melville's first teaching job in Pittsfield in the fall of 1837, at which time he was initiated into the mysteries of instructing a recalcitrant group of pupils of various ages. (Just as the mute on the *Fidèle* is subject to physical assault, Melville's students at one point allegedly attempted to "lick" him [*Log,* 1: 72].) As Melville wrote to his uncle Peter Gansevoort on December 30, 1837, "Orators may declaim concerning the universally-diffused blessings of education in our Country, and Essayests may exhaust their magazine of adjectives in extolling our systim of Common School instruction,—but when reduced to practice, the high and sanguine hopes excited by its imposing appearance in *theory*—are a little dashed" (*C,* 9). Such a perception of the gap between theory and practice is similarly illustrated by the opening chapter of *The Confidence-Man.*

BLACK GUINEA

Black Guinea represents a grotesque self-portrait of Melville as a social outcast and "Ishmaelite" outlaw in the late 1830s and early 1840s. As Guinea tells the "purple-faced drover," he lives an impoverished outdoor existence in and around St. Louis. Melville led a similarly impecunious, wandering life during these years as a school teacher, surveying student, merchant seaman, midwestern traveler, whaler, and beachcomber. Melville's 1840 summer visit to his uncle Thomas in Galena, Illinois, provides a biographical link between Guinea's home and the author at this period of his life. Indeed, since Melville apparently returned east that fall by steamboat via the Mississippi and Ohio rivers, he would necessarily have stopped off in St. Louis on the way home.

Melville's youthful "Ishmaelite" self-image corresponds to a number of Black Guinea's traits. In a facetious note to his brother Allan in early December 1839, for example, Melville dubbed himself "Tawney"—the name of a local Lansingburgh Negro—and wrote in Negro dialect (the only instance of this in his surviving correspondence): "Dear Sergeant: How is you? Am you very well? How has you been?—As to myself I haint been as well as husual. I has had a very cruel cold for this darnation long time, & I has had and does now have a werry bad want of appetisement" (*C,* 23). Guinea speaks in a similar dialect. Thus, replying to the drover's question about how he lives outside even in winter, Guinea remarks, " 'Den dis poor old darkie shakes werry bad, I tell you sar. Oh sar, oh! don't speak ob der winter' " (*CM,* 11). Guinea claims to be on the *Fidèle* in order to "see broder at der landing"; Melville's brother Allan lived a few miles downriver from Lansingburgh in Albany after 1838, and Melville would also have had to travel downriver to New York City see his brother Gansevoort after 1839.

As we have seen, Guinea is not only a stereotypical "darky," but he may also be the "black man" or devil. A biographical basis for Black Guinea's diabolical qualities can be found in Melville's involvement in a sophomoric squabble in 1838 regarding leadership of the Philo Logos Society, a debating club affiliated with the Albany Young Men's Association. Early that year Melville had returned to Albany from teaching in Pittsfield and had proceeded to reorganize the Society, a usurpation of prerogative for which he was violently attacked by a rival for leadership, Charles Van Loon. Melville and Van Loon thereupon traded insults through March and early April in a correspondence printed in the *Albany Microscope,* Melville's first appearance in print (Gilman, 91–96, 251–63; *C,* 10–19, 554–64). On March 10, for example, Melville was denounced as a devil by his rival:

> As the name of this individual does not admit of an ingenious analytical introduction into the columns of the Microscope, I will inform the members of the Philologos Society, that it is none other than he, whose "fantastic tricks" have earned for him the richly merited title "*Ciceronian baboon;*" but I shall lead him up before the public under the more romantic appellation of Hermanus Mel*villian*. Hermanus Melvillian, a moral Ethiopian, whose conscience qualms not in view of the most atrocious guilt; whose brazen cheek never tingles with the blush of shame, whose moral principles, and sensibilities, have been destroyed by the corruption of his own black and bloodless heart. (*C,* 555)

Melville answered such charges with his own overdramatized polemics; but he was still pronounced a "child of the devil, full of all subtility and all mischief" in a subsequent letter from Van Loon on March 31 (*C,* 558). Van Loon's next letter ended with an entreaty to Melville "to devote the talents thus basely prostituted in the service of satan; to higher, nobler, and more honorable purposes" (*C,* 561). As a "moral Ethiopian," Black Guinea conceivably recalls Melville's engagement in this early dispute and the beginnings of his future rebellion against the conventional values and religious beliefs of his culture.

Finally, Guinea's interaction with the passengers on the *Fidèle* suggests a parody of Melville's initial literary success with his "primitive" narratives of South Sea life, *Typee* and *Omoo,* thereby dramatizing Melville's habitual denigration of his debut in American letters as "the man who lived among the cannibals." Like Tommo in *Typee,* Guinea is an outcast from civilized society who suffers from lameness in the legs; like the beachcombing Omoo, Guinea lives outdoors under "dat good baker" the sun. Moreover, just as the reading public initially questioned the veracity of Melville's experiences depicted in *Typee,* the crowds on the *Fidèle* waver in their faith concerning Guinea's case. In sum, as a caricature of Melville's roving life as a young man and his debut as a writer, Guinea presents a portrait of the artist as "poor devil author" for a fickle American public.

JOHN RINGMAN

The melancholy "man with the weed," John Ringman, is a caricature of Melville as a newly married man and the author of *Mardi.* Melville married Elizabeth Shaw, the daughter of his father's friend, Judge Lemuel Shaw, on August 4, 1847, shortly before he set up house in New York City and began work in earnest on his third novel. In keeping with an underlying marital motif here, "ringman" is an obsolete dialect word for the ring finger (*OED*). In the character of the man with the "weed," moreover, Melville draws on the traditional association of love and death—an association he would later use in his long narrative poems, "The Scout Toward Aldie" and *Clarel*—while also satirizing the sentimental culture that he experienced during his marriage and domestic life in New York City in the later 1840s. The sentimental culture of facile emotionalism and "graveyard school" melancholy is evident during Ringman's encounters with the merchant and the sophomore, and is given a subversive *reductio ad absurdum* in the story of Ringman's wife Goneril. As Egbert Oliver has argued, the story of Goneril burlesques the notorious contemporary divorce case of Fanny Kemble Butler, whose readings of Shakespeare Melville attended in early 1849 just after the completion of *Mardi.*

In keeping with this biographical parallel, John Ringman and his wife recall aspects of the novel Melville was writing during the first year and a half of his marriage. For example, Henry Roberts's inability to remember an earlier meeting with Ringman causes Ringman to point out the mind's "ductile" qualities and to ask if Roberts has suffered a possible "concussion upon the brain." Such an interest in the brain's vulnerability recalls two adjacent scenes situated at the very center of *Mardi,* one describing Samoa's unsuccessful trepanning operation (Chapter 96) and the other relating his story of a man who lived for a year with a transplanted pig's brain (Chapter 98).

As Charles Haberstroh, Jr., points out, *Mardi* is notable for its ambivalent view of marriage and female sexuality, particularly in the domestic black comedy played out by Samoa and Annatoo early in the novel. Before their arrival in Mardi, Taji and Jarl encounter this strange couple on the derelict ship *Parki,* where Annatoo lords it over her one-armed spouse and exhibits a mysteriously perverse nature at odds with her generous-hearted husband. John Ringman's troubled relationship with his errant wife Goneril parallels this early episode in *Mardi.* For example, Annatoo, like Goneril, has a pathologically selfish nature and is "possessed by some scores of devils, perpetually inciting her to mischief on their own separate behoof" (*M,* 113). Like Goneril's mysterious "touches," Annatoo would give Jarl "sly pinches, and then look another way, innocent as a lamb" (*M,* 114). Finally, Annatoo, like Goneril, suffers an unexpected death when the *Parki* sinks, after which Samoa, like Ringman, grieves over his wayward wife. In the bizarre domestic life of John Ringman, then, Melville is rehearsing *Mardi*'s domestic black comedy while also burlesquing his own newly married status.

THE MAN IN GRAY

As the agent of various philanthropies, the man in gray caricatures Melville's life and literary career in the late 1840s. Melville is probably indirectly alluding to his assumption of paternity in February 1849 in the man in gray's collection for a Seminole Widow and Orphan Asylum. This charity may also recall Melville's purchase of his house and farm in Pittsfield in September 1850, which he christened "Arrowhead" after finding Indian artifacts on the property. In addition to these likely autobiographical associations, the man in gray as social reformer satirizes aspects of *Redburn* and *White-Jacket,* the novels he wrote in rapid succession during the summer of 1849. Acting the role of Christian reformer in these two novels, Melville highlighted the moral divide between contemporary society's Christian ideals and its blatantly un-Christian practices. Thus *Redburn* critiques the inhumane conditions of the poor in Liverpool, as well as in merchant vessels like Redburn's *Highlander,* with its steerage passengers crowded into unsanitary living quarters. In *White-Jacket* Melville's righteous indignation is directed against corporal punishment and the inhumanity of the articles of war, including the supreme immorality of war itself. The man in gray's reference to "that bloody spendthrift, War" (*CM,* 40) epitomizes the pacifist argument of *White-Jacket.*[4]

The man in gray acts as a collector for a Seminole Indian charity; allusions to the Seminole War of the late 1830s are found in both *Redburn* and *White-Jacket* (*R,* 101; *WJ,* 62). To emphasize the preacherly role he assumed at this point in his fiction, Melville gives the man in gray a white cravat, symbol of a ministerial calling. This preacherly identity evokes the navy chaplain depicted in *White-Jacket,* who is involved in some of the global missionary enterprises of the era: "Several times subscription papers were circulated among the crew of the Neversink, while in harbor, under the direct patronage of the Chaplain. One was for the purpose of a seaman's chapel in China; another to pay the salary of a tract-distributor in Greece; a third to raise a fund for the benefit of an African Colonization Society" (*WJ,* 158). We may compare this global network with the man in gray's international missionary projects, which he hopes to accomplish by means of competitive bidding: "So much by bid for converting India, so much for Borneo, so much for Africa" (*CM,* 40). The narrator's concluding characterization of the man in gray's millennial ambitions is also comparable to Melville's homage to the nation's civic millennialism in both *Redburn* (*R,* 169) and *White-Jacket* (*WJ,* 150–51).

JOHN TRUMAN

The "man with the book," John Truman, president and transfer agent of the Black Rapids Coal Company, represents a parody of Melville as the author of *Moby-Dick* and *Pierre,* his two most "blasphemous" literary productions. Truman's business affiliation accordingly suggests a symbolic conflation of both *Moby-Dick* and *Pierre,* for the "Black Rapids" in the company's name suggests a reductive parody of the white whale and its oceanic domain, while the reference to "coal" evokes the stone and petrifaction symbolism of *Pierre.* In like manner, Truman's name conceivably plays on Melville's belief in the vital truth-telling role he assumed in these novels; we may recall the fact that Ishmael affirmed the "truth" of his narrative in Chapter 49 of *Moby-Dick* ("The Affidavit"). The "man with the book" not only carries a large volume, but he also wears a traveling cap. This traveling cap may recall Melville's trip to England and the Continent from October 1849 to February 1850 immediately before he began writing *Moby-Dick* and initiated his major creative phase. Melville's evocation in his journal of the Dantean, infernal appearance of London from the Thames, with its coal barges and coal-like waters (*J,* 14), similarly anticipates John Truman's coal company affiliation.

In Ahab's vengeful pursuit of the God-like white whale, and Pierre's rebellion against social conventions in pursuit of a Christ-like mission, Melville dramatized a fictive subversion of Christian metaphysics and ethics, respectively. In a letter to Hawthorne, Melville baptized *Moby-Dick* in the name of the devil (*C,* 196); and an indignant Evert Duyckinck wrote of *Pierre:* "The most immoral *moral* of the story, if it has any moral at all, seems to be the impracticability of virtue; a leering demoniacal spectre of an idea seems to be peering at us through the dim obscure of this dark book, and mocking us with this dismal falsehood" (Branch, *Critical Heritage,* 301).

In the character of John Truman, Melville parodies his most "diabolical" fiction, which he now transforms into a commodity on the stock market. The variation in stock price about which Truman complains in Chapter 9 thus obliquely conveys Melville's protest over the mixed (*Moby-Dick*) or hostile (*Pierre*) reception and inadequate sales of his most profound works of fiction (Branch, *Critical Heritage,* 24–31, 251–322; Hetherington, 189–239). When in late March 1853 Melville received his account from his American publishers, he found that the royalties of *Pierre* only paid off a fraction of his $500 advance, while all sales of his books so far still left him in debt to the Harper Brothers for $298.71, an indebtedness that would increase to $319.74 by October 1854 (*Log,* 1:447, 468, 492).

Melville's awareness of the difficulties of promoting "confidence" in his literary productions was especially apparent in April 1852 when he tried to get better terms from his British publisher, Bentley, by arguing the merits of *Pierre.* (Melville's last four books had lost Bentley a total of £453 [*C,* 618.]) Because Bentley was offering reduced terms at the same time that Melville was facing increasing financial difficulties, Melville fell into a promotional vein in his correspondence with Bentley that was an obvious distortion of the true significance of *Pierre* (*C,* 226–27). Not surprisingly, Bentley declined *Pierre* and the book was never published in England. Meanwhile, the debacle of *Pierre*'s reception in America resulted in sales of only 283 copies in the first eight months and fewer than two thousand copies over the next thirty-five years; *Moby-Dick* had sold fewer than three thousand copies five years after publication. John Truman's success in disposing of his Black Rapids stock ironically enacts Melville's covert revenge on the unreceptive audience for *Moby-Dick* and *Pierre.*

THE HERB DOCTOR

The herb doctor conveys an image of Melville in the period 1853–1854, when for the first time he suffered from serious health problems brought on by his overexertions as an author and his declining literary reputation. As his wife noted in a chronology of her husband's life, "We all felt anxious about the strain on his health in the spring of 1853" (*Log,* 1:468). Probably as a result of the critical disfavor over *Pierre,* Melville was unable to publish his new full-length work, *The Isle of the Cross,* in the spring of 1853. In order to escape the psychological strains and financial liabilities of his declining status as an author, Melville sought a consular appointment under the new administration of Franklin Pierce. Melville's mother wrote to her brother Peter explaining the gravity of the situation:

> In my opinion, I must again repeat it Herman would be greatly benefited by a sojourn abroad, he would then be compelled to more in-

> tercourse with his fellow creatures. It would very materially renew, & strengthen both his body & mind.
>
> The constant in-door confinement with little intermission to which Hermans occupation as author compels him, does not agree with him. This constant working of the brain, & excitement of the imagination, is wearing Herman out, & you will my dear Peter be doing him a lasting benefit if by your added exersions you can procure him a foreign consulship. (*Log,* 1:469)

While the actions of the herb doctor evoke Melville's declining health at this juncture, they also caricature some of the leading themes of Melville's short fiction from the same troubled period. Just as the herb doctor encounters a series of ailing patients to whom he dispenses bogus "natural" medicines, much of Melville's short fiction presents a world of personal failure, incurable evils, and moral and spiritual paralysis.[5] For example, the genial lawyer-narrator of Melville's first published work of short fiction, "Bartleby, the Scrivener," is confronted with an eccentric individual of mysterious origins who inexplicably refuses to perform his duties; the narrator's belated charity to his copyist fails to save Bartleby from self-willed annihilation. The narrator of Melville's next published short story, "Cock-A-Doodle-Doo!," is himself pathologically obsessed with the sickly environment in which he lives. The only medicine capable of curing him of his "doleful dumps" is the crowing of a rooster owned by the Merrymusk family. However, they are all mortally ill and expire at the end of the story, as does the rooster. The transcendental cock crow in "Cock-A-Doodle-Doo!," like the herb doctor's Omni-Balsamic Reinvigorator, is a dubious "natural" remedy for incurable disease and chronic depression.

Melville's three so-called diptychs of this period also dramatize contrasts in physical and spiritual health in ways that potentially anticipate the actions of the herb doctor. Thus the first sketch of "Poor Man's Pudding and Rich Man's Crumbs" depicts an impoverished rural farming couple, the Coulters, whose starved life is fatuously misrepresented by the visiting poet Blandmour, for whom nature is invariably beneficent. The bachelors in "The Paradise of Bachelors" are similarly situated in a fool's paradise of physical gratification, in contrast to the dehumanized factory environment found in "The Tartarus of Maids." "The Two Temples," narrated by a physician, juxtaposes the stifling hypocrisy of upper-class American Protestantism with the healthy charity of a lower-class British theatre audience watching a play about a Catholic prelate. (The interplay of Protestantism and Catholicism here anticipates the religious associations of the herb doctor's two products.) In these and other works of short fiction, Melville depicted a physically and spiritually ailing world comparable to the de facto sick ward on the *Fidèle* where the herb doctor plies his trade.

THE P.I.O. MAN

The Philosophical Intelligence Office representative caricatures Melville in the mid-1850s when he was writing *Israel Potter* and subsequently suffering from both rheumatism and sciatica. In her chronology of Melville's life, Elizabeth Melville noted, "in Feb 1855 he had his first attack of severe rheumatism in his back—so that he was helpless" (*Log,* 2:498). The following June, Melville suffered an attack of sciatica, and Oliver Wendell Holmes was summoned to examine him (*Log,* 2:502). Sciatica is a disease characterized by pain in the great sciatic nerve that emerges from the pelvis and passes down the back of the thigh to the foot. The P.I.O. man is described as "a round-backed, baker-kneed man," the latter phrase indicating a stance characteristic of bakers, with one knee pointed inward at the other as though stooping under a heavy weight in one hand—a stance appropriate for someone suffering from the disabling effects of sciatica, as Melville was in 1855. Pitch suspects that the P.I.O. man is suffering from a like condition, for he asks the P.I.O. man in exasperation, " 'have you the spinal complaint? What are you ducking and groveling about?' " (*CM,* 115).

His first two initials reversing those of *I*srael *P*otter, the P.I.O. man can be related to Melville's eighth novel, specifically its historical portrait of Benjamin Franklin. Thus, just as Franklin employs Israel Potter as a courier, the P.I.O. man runs an employment agency. The P.I.O. man's meliorist argumentation is also in keeping with Franklin's Enlightenment faith in both human and technological improvement. In *Israel Potter* Melville remarked that "history presents few trios more akin, upon the whole, than Jacob, Hobbes, and Franklin; three labyrinth-minded, but plain-spoken Broadbrims, at once politicians and philosophers; keen observers of the main chance; prudent courtiers; practical magians in linsey-woolsey" (*IP,* 46–47). Dressed in a cheap attire, the P.I.O. man is a similarly shrewd "practical magian" and observer of the main chance. Franklin's advice to Potter at one point also anticipates the P.I.O. man's reaction to Pitch's misanthropy: " 'Sad usage has made you sadly suspicious, my honest friend. An indiscriminate distrust of human nature is the worst consequence of a miserable condition, whether brought about by innocence or guilt. And though want of suspicion more than want of sense, sometimes leads a man into harm; yet too much suspicion is as bad as too little sense' " (*IP,* 41). Finally, the P.I.O. man's duping of Pitch by selling him a "boy" recalls Franklin's manipulation of Potter when the Yankee sage removes his Otard brandy and banishes a pretty French chambermaid from his room: "Not till the first impression of the venerable envoy's suavity had left him, did Israel begin to surmise the mild superiority of successful strategy which lurked beneath this highly ingratiating air" (*IP,* 52). Pitch similarly awakes from the wiles of his ingratiating opponent while the *Fidèle* is docked at Cairo. In short, Melville drew on several key aspects of his portrait of Franklin for the character of the P.I.O. man.

FRANK GOODMAN

Since we have completed Melville's sequence of self-images up the time of the novel's composition in 1855–1856, Frank Goodman, who dominates the second half of the novel, necessarily represents its most displaced autobiographical persona. Consequently, for the cosmopolitan we must discard the chronological progression we have traced so far and consider him an ironic embodiment of Melville's spirit or "soul." We have already noted the cosmopolitan's covert mythological association with Dionysus. From a more historicizing perspective, John Bryant has demonstrated the association between cosmopolitanism and millennialism in antebellum America: proponents of the Second Coming like the Universalist Lorenzo Dow were self-styled antisectarian "cosmopolites" looking for their true home in the next world.[6] A skeleton key to the cosmopolitan's autobiographical associations, however, might be found in Melville's confession to Hawthorne in November 1856 at the beginning of his trip to the Holy Land that he had "pretty much made up his mind to be annihilated." Melville's remark implies, not that he was contemplating suicide, but rather that he had ceased to believe in the Christian afterlife, a fact of potentially momentous importance in the disintegration of his religious faith.[7] We should recall that the cosmopolitan extinguishes the solar lamp of biblical revelation at the end of the novel, thereby consummating Melville's rejection of the promise of Christian transcendence.

Insofar as the cosmopolitan is an embodiment of the author's "soul" as mythological demigod and spiritual citizen of the world, Melville has structured the autobiographical stratum of *The Confidence-Man* according to a Christian dichotomy of self and soul, associating each with antithetical realms of day and night, life and death, mutability and permanence. Examples of midcareer metamorphoses from Melville's earlier novels like that found in *The Confidence-Man* include the transformations of Taji and Pierre: when the narrator of *Mardi* reaches the allegorical world of Mardi, he assumes the guise of a sun god, Taji; in the latter part of *Pierre,* on the other hand, the rebellious hero figuratively transforms himself into a pagan god.[8] A more contemporaneous analogue to the cosmopolitan's symbolic identity is provided by Melville's last piece of magazine fiction, "The Apple-Tree Table," published in *Putnam's* in May 1856. This domestic comedy plays on contemporary interest in the viability of "spirits" and the possibilities of resurrection, as figured by the mysterious "birth" of a beautiful bug out of the wood of an old apple tree table. Just as this bug emerges out of the apparently demonic table and is thereupon figured as an emblem of resurrection, the colorfully dressed cosmopolitan is "hatched" like a butterfly out of the satanic-looking P.I.O. man and thereafter acts as an advocate of spiritual rebirth.

As we have seen, in addition to serving as stalking horses for the depiction of national vices and follies, the guises of Confidence Man schematically set forth the consecutive phases of Melville's life and creative development. This finding confirms the widely recognized axiom that Melville generally relied on either personal experience or historical fact for the creation of his fiction. The close tie between Melville's life and literary works here also confirms the principle that "the work of fiction was a vulnerable extension of his self, inseparable as a form from the whole problem of his identity," as Stephen Railton remarks (172). Yet if we accept the autobiographical elements informing the hero of *The Confidence-Man,* as I think we must, the question may nevertheless arise concerning the rationale by which Melville has blended his own self-images with those of the Confidence Man's religious archetypes. A reading of Melville's correspondence, however, shows that he alternately saw his vocation as a writer in both redemptively Christ-like and subversively satanic terms, as when he wrote to Hawthorne concerning *Moby-Dick:* "I have written a wicked book, and feel spotless as the lamb" (*C,* 212). Furthermore, Melville's fictive self-deification as the Confidence Man was symptomatic of the divinized self of American Romanticism, as found in Emerson's essays or Whitman's "Song of Myself." The Confidence Man's portmanteau identity—autobiographical, historical, and theological—thus belongs in the tradition of the polymorphous American ego in its high-romantic, mid–nineteenth-century incarnation.

Having related the various guises of the Confidence Man to Melville's self-images, we will now examine characters modeled on Melville's immediate and extended family. These characters will be examined in the order in which they appear in the novel, with the exception of characters who may be more conveniently examined in conjunction with one another. Although there is no exact adherence to chronology (especially in the case of the cosmopolitan and his interlocutors), the correlation between Melville's series of self-images and individuals relevant to a corresponding phase of his career is usually close. Our examination of models will begin with a cluster of characters derived from his wife's family, the Shaws, Melville's chief private patrons during his writing career and thus an appropriate target for a satire on the subject of charity.

THE GENTLEMAN WITH GOLD SLEEVE-BUTTONS

The gentleman with gold sleeve-buttons of Chapter 7 is an exceptional character on board the *Fidèle* by reason of his wealth, his generosity, and the moral equivocation surrounding his appearance hinting at some connection with the institution of slavery. The biographical model for the gentleman can be found in Melville's father-in-law, Lemuel Shaw (1781–1861), chief justice of the Massachusetts Supreme Court from 1830 to 1860. The implicit biographical dimension of this character has two foci, the first relating to Shaw's legal career and the second to Shaw's financial patronage of his son-in-law.[9]

As chief justice, Lemuel Shaw had an important impact on the evolution of the slavery question in the 1850s, for in early April 1851 Shaw enforced the rendition of Thomas Sims, the first fugitive slave to be returned from Massachusetts since the passage of the new Fugitive Slave Law incorporated into the Compromise of 1850. Leonard Levy notes that "Shaw's opinion was the first full-dress sustension of the constitutionality of the Fugitive Slave Act of 1850 passed by any court" (98). The rendition of Thomas Sims was an important event in testing the efficacy of this law, engineered by Shaw's friend Daniel Webster, who as President Filmore's secretary of state went to Massachusetts to see that the rendition was enforced. To make sure that no rescue by abolitionists could take place, which had in fact occurred during the attempted rendition of "Shadrach" only a few weeks before, heavy chains were wrapped around the Boston courthouse where Sims was detained. Lemuel Shaw presided over this court, bowing under the chains to enter and exit the courthouse, an exercise that seemed to possess a portentous significance and inevitably recalled an earlier British tyranny.[10] The contrast between Melville's grandfather, a participant in the Boston Tea Party, and his father-in-law, involved in upholding the constitutionality of the Fugitive Slave Law almost seventy years later, no doubt provided a striking historical contrast to Melville.

Several aspects of the gentleman with gold sleeve-buttons' characterization suggest Shaw's role in upholding the constitutionality of the Fugitive Slave Law. The gentleman is thus explicitly dissociated from the figure of William Wilberforce, the evangelical philanthropist best known for his role in the elimination of British colonial slavery in 1832. The gentleman's moral condition of "sinning by deputy" is also underlined by a reference to "the Hebrew governor" who "knew how to keep his hands clean" (*CM,* 36). Shaw had actually been called Pilate by William Lloyd Garrison's *Liberator* in connection with the *Latimer* rendition case of 1842, an important precursor to *Sims* (Levy, 82).[11] Moreover, Sims's rendition in 1851 might have also invited a comparison with Christ's martyrdom since the slave's final departure under heavy guard occurred the day before Palm Sunday. The biblical analogies regarding the gentleman's moral status continue in the ensuing distinction from St. Paul (Romans 5:7) between the righteous man and the merely good man: "when we repeat of this gentleman, that he was only a good man, whatever else by severe censors may be objected to him, it is still to be hoped that his goodness will not at least be considered criminal in him" (*CM,* 37).

The "severe censors" of Sims's rendition, and Shaw's action in helping to enforce it, make up a roll call of famous names: Whittier, Parker, Phillips, Emerson, Thoreau, Dana, Alcott, and Longfellow. Whittier's poem, "Moloch in State Street" was an impassioned response to the *Sims* case. In a sermon entitled "The Chief Sins of the People," Parker vociferated, "O justice! O republican America! Is this the liberty of Massachusetts?" (*Sins and Safeguards,* 37). Phillips castigated Shaw "in terms that a gentleman would hardly apply to a pickpocket" (*Daily Evening Transcript,* April 5, 1851; quoted in Levy, 95). Emerson noted in his journal, "What a moment was lost when Judge Shaw declined to affirm the unconstitutionality of the Fugitive Slave Law!"; he had earlier called the law a "filthy enactment" (quoted in Levy, 101, 102). In his 1854 lecture on "Slavery in Massachusetts," Thoreau called *Sims* a "moral earthquake" (*Reform Papers,* 93). The day after Sims's departure from Boston, Richard Henry Dana, Jr., who had been one of the lawyers defending Sims, wrote in his journal: "Judge Shaw actually went under the chain, to get to his court. . . . Our temple of justice is a slave pen! Our officers are slave hunters, & the voice of the old law of the State is hushed & awed into silence before this fearful Slave power wh[ich] has got such entire control of the Union" (Lucid, 2:424).[12]

There is no doubt that Melville's father-in-law was a "good" man, especially since Shaw's generosity had often benefited Melville and his family, both before and after Melville's marriage to Shaw's daughter in 1847. Shaw had actually been the fiancé of Melville's aunt Nancy, as well as a close friend of his father Allan, both of them prematurely deceased (Frederic Chase, 46–47; *Log,* 1:52). Moreover, Shaw was personally critical of slavery and had published an article condemning it in the *North American Review* during the Missouri crisis in 1820 (Levy, 59–61). He had even liberated slaves who had come through Massachusetts with their owners on two occasions, the cases of Med in 1836 and Robert Lucas in 1844 (Levy, Ch. 5). Yet in an important 1849 decision, he upheld the legality of segregated schools in Boston; this became the basis for many later decisions promoting the segregation of the races (Levy, Ch. 7).

A few other aspects of the gentlemen's portrait also suggest Shaw's participation in the growing crisis of the Union of the 1850s. The gentleman comments on the man in gray's philanthropies by expressing his regret "that so many benevolent societies as there were, here and there isolated in the land, should not act in concert by coming together, in the way that already in each society the individuals composing it had done, which would result, he thought, in like advantages upon a larger scale. Indeed, such a confederation might, perhaps, be attended with as happy results as politically attended that of the states" (*CM,* 37–38). Such a faith in the Union was an article of Lemuel Shaw's political credo: "With the passing years, the intensification of the slavery controversy made the security and peace of the Union Shaw's passion; long ago these values had been elevated in his mind to a case of political and even 'moral' necessity" (Levy, 91). Shaw was such a devout Unionist that he eventually led an attempt to appease the South when secession began in late 1860 (Levy, 106–108). The gentleman's belief in the Union is probably sincere, but by the time Melville was writing, the Kansas-Nebraska Act of 1854 had upset whatever sectional balance was achieved by the Compromise of 1850 and the nation was slowly gravitating toward violent conflict over slavery. The irony of Melville's presentation of the gentleman may in fact have been influenced by another violent sign of the times, the rendition of Anthony Burns, which convulsed Boston in late May and early June of 1854 shortly after the Kansas-Nebraska Act was signed into law by President Pierce (Frederic Chase, 175–77; Levy, 105–106; Shapiro). Although Shaw was not directly involved in this case, his 1851 ruling was cited as authority in U.S. Commissioner Loring's decision. Melville's friend Dana again served as counsel for the defense and on this occasion narrowly escaped serious injury after being bludgeoned by a local anti-abolitionist thug.

The man in gray's description of the Protean easy-chair he exhibited at the London "World's Fair" also suggests that the slavery issue may be an underlying target of Melville's satire here: " 'My Protean easy-chair is a chair so all over bejoined, behinged; and bepadded, everything so elastic, springy, and docile to the airiest touch, that in some one endlessly-changeable accommodations of back, seat, footboard, and arms, the most restless body, the most racked, nay, I had almost added the most tormented conscience must, somehow and somewhere, find rest' " (*CM,* 38). The fact that *Sims* was decided in the same year as the Exhibition may have appeared as a reminder of American culpability in regard to genuine human progress, despite the potential fallibility of such expressions of Victorian optimism as the Exhibition itself.[13]

As noted earlier, the portrait of the gentleman with gold sleeve-buttons also parodies Melville's financial dependence on this father-in-law. The gentleman is solicited by the man in gray on behalf of an Indian charity. From 1837 to his death in 1861, Shaw was president of the Society for Propagating the Gospel Among the Indians and Others in North America (Frederic Chase, 253; Levy, 27). Melville had dedicated his first book, *Typee,* to Shaw, even though *Typee*'s strictures on missionaries attacked a philanthropic enterprise that Shaw domestically promoted. *Typee*'s dedication made clear Melville's indebtedness to Shaw as a personal and family benefactor; his last novel ironically reflects back on that indebtedness. The man in gray works himself up to a frenzy of philanthropy, a role that is both a parody of the missionary zeal Melville had criticized in *Typee* and *Omoo* and probably a fictional displacement of Melville's discomfort at being a "charity case" to his wealthy father-in-law. The gentleman nevertheless remains skeptical of the efficacy of the World's Charity, but this doesn't keep him from making a further contribution before stepping off the *Fidèle* to go to his niece's wedding.

Reference to nuptials is further confirmation that Melville is indirectly playing upon his relationship with his father-in-law here. The gentleman in gold sleeve-buttons gives the man in gray three "virgin bills" for the Seminole Widow and Orphan Asylum; Shaw advanced Melville $3,000 in September 1850 to help him buy his house and farm in Pittsfield (*Log,* 1:395). Shaw was in Lenox holding court that month, thereby enabling him to approve the purchase in person. The pastoral image used in the characterization of the gentleman suggests a connection with this transaction: "There he stood apart and in repose, and yet, by his mere look, lured the man in gray from his story, much as, by its graciousness of bearing, some full-leaved elm, alone in a meadow, lures the noon sickleman to throw down his sheaves, and come and apply for the alms of its shade" (*CM,* 35). Another image would seem to obliquely reflect Shaw's patronage of his impecunious son-in-law: "Like the benign elm again, the good man seemed to waive the canopy of his goodness over that suitor, not in conceited condescension, but with that even amenity of true majesty, which can be kind to any one without stooping to it" (*CM,* 37). (The word "kind" here is a likely pun, while the repeated reference to the gentleman as an "elm" is conceivably wordplay on the name of *Lem*uel Shaw.)

The gentleman responds to the man in gray's plea "by producing an ample pocket-book in the good old capacious style." Melville was given such a "pocket book" by his in-laws in June 1848. Elizabeth wrote her stepmother at this time, while echoing her husband's mordant wit: "Herman was much pleased with his pocket book—and says 'he has long needed such an article, for his bank bills accumulate to such an extent he can find no place to put them' " (*Log,* 1:277). Having accumulated a small fortune before he took the modestly paid job of chief justice at the age of forty-nine, Lemuel Shaw was undoubtedly as affluent as the gentleman appears to be: "From 1823 on Shaw became a man of considerable affluence, holding a fairly large amount of insurance company and bank stock. . . . Webster states that Shaw's last years of practice brought him $15,000 to $20,000 annually, a phenomenal sum in those days" (Levy, 17). Shaw's estate at his death was valued at $114,320 (Charvat, 195). It is perhaps significant that one of Shaw's assets was several thousand acres of Kentucky lands, which may have facilitated his transformation into a Southern Cavalier in *The Confidence-Man.* The contrast between his father-in-law's substantial fortune and his own worsening financial situation at the time of the composition of *The Confidence-Man* no doubt aggravated Melville's feeling of familial dependency; indeed, two letters dated May 1856 from Melville to Shaw reveal Melville's attempt to protect his father-in-law's investment in Arrowhead, owing to Melville's continuing default on his loan from Tertullus Stewart, now threatening suit (*C,* 290–95).

An earlier piece of evidence linking Shaw with the novel's Mississippi setting is provided by the trip Shaw and his daughter Elizabeth made to

Chicago via the Great Lakes in the early summer of 1845. During this trip Shaw planned to visit Melville's uncle Thomas in Galena, Illinois, and to return east via the Mississippi River (Frederic Chase, 262; *Log*, 1:196; Puett, 34–35). It is almost certain, however, that he did not go to Galena; Thomas died that summer on August 1.[14]

Finally, the gentleman with gold sleeve-buttons' manner and appearance suggest something of Shaw, although there is not an exact similitude; yet it should be noted that Shaw read his son-in-law's fiction and might have recognized too close a fictional likeness.[15] The gentleman is described as being "tall, rosy, between plump and portly, with a primy [spring-like], palmy air." According to one biographer, Shaw was "large and powerful, although he was not tall in stature" (Frederic Chase, 23). Another biographer writes, "He was a formidable-looking man, squat and powerfully built" with a "huge peculiarly magnificent head" (Levy, 26).

If Lemuel Shaw did indeed provide the biographical model for the gentleman with gold sleeve-buttons, the question might nevertheless be asked how Melville could have used his father-in-law—a much admired individual whose generosity to Melville and his family had been unstinting—as the basis for a character of benign demeanor but suspect morality? One answer might be that the ambivalence we discern in the portrait is another example of Melville's oft-noted ambivalence to authority figures in his fiction, which may have been especially true when the model for such a character was both a surrogate father and father-in-law on whom he was financially dependent. Shaw's eminent position as an exponent of the official social order may also have contributed to Melville's satirical animus here. As Melville's friend Dana noted in April 1856, "The truth is, Judge Shaw is a man of intense & doating biases, in religious, political & social matters. Unitarianism, Harvard College, the social & political respectabilities of Boston are his idola specus & fori" (Lucid, 2:689). Melville's use of Shaw in *The Confidence-Man* was conceivably Melville's backhanded tribute to his father-in-law's support, however uncomfortable it felt to be its recipient. Shaw generously advanced Melville the money ($1,400 to $1,500) for his trip to Europe and the Levant in 1856–1857 so that Melville could recover from his over-exertions as an author, the source of "severe nervous affections" according to Shaw (*Log*, 2:521, 525; *C*, 674). In all this, Shaw was, like the gentleman with gold sleeve-buttons, "charitable to the last, if only to the dreams of enthusiasm" (*CM*, 42).[16]

THE CHARITABLE LADY

The charitable lady of Chapter 8 is a simple-hearted, sentimental widow who, after a flirtatious appeal by the man in gray, gives him twenty dollars for the Seminole widows and orphans. The biographical model for the charitable lady can be found in Melville's wife, Elizabeth Shaw Melville. Amy Puett has described "Lizzie" on the eve of her marriage:

> She was well suited to become a respectable gentleman's wife. She was not beautiful, because she had inherited her father's large nose, but she was charming, affectionate and kind. She was not brilliant, but she had been well educated, was fairly well traveled and had moved in rather elite social circles. Moreover, she would not be expected to go into marriage unendowed. Her father established a trust fund of $3,000 for her, and just a short time prior to her wedding she had inherited a little over $2,500 from her maternal grandfather, Josiah Knapp. This was not an exceedingly large dowry, but then, in addition to sharing her father's good name and reputation in Massachusetts, she would eventually inherit a portion of his considerable estate. (46)

A less flattering description of Melville's wife would be that she was "The epitome of dull, conventional, well-bred Victorian womanhood" (Karcher, *Shadow,* 8). Melville's granddaughter, Eleanor Melville Metcalf, describes her as "domestic in her tastes without proficiency"; however, "the strength of her character was a monumental strength—simply kindness" (55).[17] Whatever view we may take of Elizabeth Shaw Melville, it is fairly certain that after almost a decade of marriage Melville was well aware of his wife's limitations. Indeed, another decade would bring them to the brink of separation (Yannella and Parker). By caricaturing his wife as the simple-hearted "charitable lady," Melville is spoofing his wife's conventional nature as well as his own financial dependence on her through her wealthy father.

The characterization of the charitable lady exhibits several details that correspond to different guises of the Confidence Man, thereby hinting at the intimate relationship between their respective biographical models. First, the lady is reading from I Corinthians 13, the text the mute used for his messages of charity. Second, like John Ringman, she is in mourning for her spouse. Third, the tint of her "twilight dress, neither dawn nor dark" matches the gray color of her interlocutor's attire. Fourth, after her donation, the man in gray writes down her name in his book, a foreshadowing of the man with the book, John Truman, who appears immediately afterward. Fifth, she is described as "just breaking the chrysalis of her mourning," an entomological metaphor comparable to the P.I.O. man's caterpillar-like metamorphosis into the cosmopolitan.

Other aspects of this scene also evoke Melville's relationship with his wife. The point-blank solicitation of the man in gray ("She sat in a sort of restless torment, knowing not which way to turn") accords with Melville's alleged tendency to constantly "challenge" his wife in their domestic life (Metcalf, 259). Elizabeth Shaw Melville's reputed "kindness" also matches the charitable lady's demeanor, which "seems to hint that, if she have any weak point, it must be anything rather than her excellent heart." The man in gray seeks the lady out as a "sister of the church," a pious appeal suggestive of the fact that Melville and his wife were pewholders in Henry Bellows's Unitarian "Church of the Divine Unity" when they lived in New York in the late 1840s (Yannella and Parker, 12). Moreover, in the man in gray's sanctimonious approach to the lady, Melville is probably satirizing his wife's religious piety, for Elizabeth Melville was clearly more devout than her husband: "Her letters after her marriage reveal that she attended church with some regularity, wanted the children baptized and apparently took comfort in her religion. . . . The influence of the Bible on Elizabeth was always marked. Just as her future husband did, she read that book and absorbed much of what she read, its content as well as its rhythms" (Puett, 27). Significantly, a Bible serves as the vehicle for uniting the man in gray and the charitable lady when the man in gray picks up the "gilt testament" the lady had let fall. (The "kindness unadorned" of this gesture suggests another covert familial pun.)

Melville may be obliquely expressing gratitude to his wife in this scene for her family's support, for after he has gotten his twenty dollars the man in gray quotes St. Paul in a final benediction of the lady for her "confidence" in him (II Corin. 7:16). On the other hand, the man in gray is obviously taking advantage of the lady's generosity; as the narrator notes at one point, "The lady was, in an extraordinary way, touched." Melville is thus indirectly paying homage to his wife while concurrently depicting her as a weak-minded female who succumbs to the man in gray in a mock seduction scene.[18]

THE SOPHOMORE

The college sophomore whom John Ringman encounters in Chapter 5 appears as a timid and effeminate-looking young man, but during John Truman's later encounter with him in Chapter 9 he reveals himself to be a callous and greedy youth bent on the main chance. In keeping with this apparently divided identity, the sophomore is modeled on Melville's two younger brothers-in-law, Lemuel Shaw, Jr. (1828–1884) and Samuel Shaw (1833–1915), both of them Harvard-educated and trained as lawyers like their father. The use of two models would suit the sophomore's change in character from Chapter 5 to Chapter 9, for Samuel Shaw was a sensitive, sweet-tempered young man while his older brother Lemuel was a supercilious, class-bound product of Boston privilege. Both half-brothers of Melville's wife were visitors while on school vacations to the Melville household in New York in 1848; Melville would also have seen both during his regular visits to his wife's family in Boston. Lemuel Shaw, Jr., had just completed his sophomore year of college when Melville married Elizabeth in the summer of 1847; Samuel completed his sophomore year in the summer of 1851.

Samuel's visit to the Melvilles in the summer of 1851 in fact came at a critical time in Melville's literary career, the juncture between the completion of *Moby-Dick* and the inception of *Pierre.* As Leon Howard writes of this visit,

> young Sam Shaw, who had just finished his second year at Harvard, brought more energy into the Melville household than Herman liked. He arrived on July 22 for two weeks and was joined by his cousin Samuel Savage at the end of the first week. Elizabeth enjoyed their stay and was willing to "let them do just as they please and take care of themselves" [*Log* 1:419]; but Herman undertook to wear down their spirits by walking them up a mountain on August 2, and for months afterwards his favorite derogatory adjective was "sophomorean." (180–81)

Melville's granddaughter also describes Sam as "Sophomorean," at the same time singling him out for praise as the most sympathetic of Melville's young in-laws (Metcalf, 154). Nevertheless, Sam Shaw's visit in the summer of 1851 apparently stamped him in Melville's imagination as a paradigmatic sophomore and in *The Confidence-Man* Melville used him, along with his less sympathetic older brother, for a satiric version of an affluent young collegian. Doubtless, Melville's encounters with the two intellectually immature but socially privileged Harvard students in his wife's family aroused ambivalent feelings in the author for whom whaling took the place of Harvard or Yale.

Unable to respond either to John Ringman's attack on the pessimism of Tacitus or his ambiguous appeal to "confidence," the sophomore of Chapter 5 simply withdraws from the scene in embarrassment. While the brevity of this scene and the sophomore's inarticulateness here limit analysis, the sophomore's epicene identity and diffident behavior suggest aspects of Sam's personality.[19] (Like his older brother Lemuel, Jr., Sam was a life-long bachelor.) Melville's December 1846 purchase of *The Recreation: A Gift Book for Young Readers* during his courtship of Elizabeth Shaw was probably a Christmas gift for her brother Sam (Howard, 105), in which case it would serve as a prototype for Ringman's volume of Akenside. Ringman speaks to the sophomore of "confidence in my kind" and makes a pitch for "fraternal confidence," both of which remarks are likely puns on the displaced family connection here.[20]

The reappearance of the sophomore in Chapter 9 effectuates a shift in models from the sensitive Sam to his more snobbish older brother Lemuel, Jr., the "often supercilious Lemuel" as Melville's granddaughter calls him (Metcalf, 158). The most conspicuous example of Lemuel, Jr.'s superciliousness is his consistently negative attitude to his brother-in-law's literary works. An indication of this can be found in the letter he wrote his parents from London on May 9, 1852, describing his visit to Melville's English publisher, Bentley, during his "grand tour" of that year:

> I saw his assistant & had some conversation about Herman's books & was sorry to hear that Mr. Bentley is unwilling to take Herman's new work [i.e., *Pierre*] on the terms Herman wishes. I was told what I knew before that he is losing the prestige of his name which he gained by his first books, by writing so many books that nobody can read. I wish very much he could be persuaded to leave off writing books for a few years, & that is what his friends here say. (*C*, 224)

Four years later, Lemuel wrote his brother Sam on July 15, 1856, telling him of Melville's new book and expressing much the same judgment of his brother-in-law's fiction: "Herman writes that he has sold the western half of his farm at Pittsfield—upon pretty good terms—I believe he is now preparing another book [i.e., *The Confidence-Man*] for the press; . . . I know nothing about it; but I have no great confidence in the success of his productions" (Metcalf, 154). But perhaps the most glaring example of Lemuel, Jr.'s unsympathetic attitude to his brother-in-law's literary productions is another letter of April 27, 1857 to Sam:

> A new book by Herman called "The Confidence Man" has recently been published. I have not yet read it; but have looked at it & dipped into it, & fear it belongs [to] that horribly uninteresting class of nonsensical books he is given to writing—where there are pages of crude theory & speculation to every line of narrative—& interspersed with strained and ineffectual attempts to be humorous. I wish he could or would do better. (*Log*, 2:574)

The action of Chapter 9 covertly satirizes Lemuel Shaw, Jr.'s lack of "confidence" in the success of Melville's literary productions. For in Truman's mock outrage at the "fiction of depression" that lowered his company's stock, Melville is expressing a displaced version of his own frustrations at his unreceptive audience, as exemplified by the attitude of this hostile critic in his own immediate family. We may also notice the persistent references John Truman makes to the "unfortunate man" (John Ringman) whom the sophomore had encountered earlier in Chapter 5 but whose plight the sophomore now dismisses in favor of business matters. As the sophomore remarks:

> "And, I say now, I happen to have a superfluity in my pocket, and I'll just—"
>
> "—Act the part of a brother to that unfortunate man?"
>
> "Let the unfortunate man be his own brother. What are you dragging him in for all the time?" (*CM*, 49)

Such a dismissive attitude toward a "brother" is no doubt a reflection of Lemuel, Jr.'s similar attitude toward his literary brother-in-law. John Truman's last reference to the "unfortunate man" elicits the most brutal remark of the sophomore, who now claims that if he should happen to meet the unfortunate man again he "will send for the steward, and have him and his misfortunes consigned overboard."

The sophomore evinces a sharp business sense in relation to Truman's coal company stock as well as Truman's real estate speculation in the "New Jerusalem." The sophomore's behavior here suggests Lemuel, Jr.'s precocious business instincts. While still a student at Harvard, for example, Lemuel, Jr., wrote on April 26, 1849, to his cousin Samuel Savage, who had gone to seek his fortune in Guatemala:

> I was surprised that you seemed to think that I should advise you to settle in Guatemala. I think that that would be a great mistake. But if by submitting to live there for a few years, say six years, you can get $20,000, you could then come home only 28 years old, and with the means of going into business here, and of procuring "the comforts of a social home, and of living amongst your kindred and friends" which you say you wish. I do see the necessity of investing all your earnings in that country, if you cannot do any better, get your property into the form of gold and wait for an opportunity to bring or send it to this country, and although by this it lies idle for some time, it is better than sinking it in real estate there, which cannot be profitable for many years, if it ever can. (quoted in Kennedy and Kennedy, 8)

The sophomore's savvy dismissal of Truman's midwestern real estate in Chapter 9 thus matches Lemuel Shaw, Jr.'s apparent familiarity with Central American real estate values.

During the summer of 1851—the same summer a visiting Sam Shaw struck Melville as the incarnation of everything "sophomoric"—Lemuel Shaw, Jr., was traveling through the Midwest. On this excursion he journeyed by steamer through the Great Lakes to Chicago, and would have continued down the Mississippi River to Saint Louis but changed plans at the last minute out of fear of disease.[21] He spent the rest of his trip traveling through Ohio and on the Ohio River, visiting Louisville and Mammoth Cave before returning to Boston by early September. As in the case of both his sister and father, Lemuel, Jr.'s western peregrinations may have facilitated the process of Melville's imagining his brother-in-law as a passenger on the *Fidèle*. Significantly, when given the chance to invest in the "New Jerusalem," the sophomore responds: " 'Hardly think I should read my title clear, as the law students say.' " Lemuel was just such a law student while on his western travels, gaining his degree from Harvard a year later.[22]

Other details of the sophomore's behavior in Chapter 9 mimic Lemuel,

Jr.'s personality. For example, the sophomore evinces a taste for cigars and other creature comforts: " 'Sitting on my sofa after a champagne dinner, smoking my plantation cigar, if a gloomy fellow come to me—what a bore!' " Lemuel, Jr., had a similar taste for lounging with a cigar, writing his brother Sam from London on May 14, 1852: "Simpson's Cigar Divan & Dining Room are places you have heard of, that I have been in. I quite like the Divan. You pay a shilling & they give you a cigar & cup of good coffee & the principal thing a comfortable place to sit down, and read the magazines & papers of which they have a very large & good supply" (Lemuel Shaw Papers II, Massachusetts Historical Society). Lemuel's "grand tour," from which this letter dates, lasted from the spring of 1852 through the summer of 1853 and included an extended stay in England followed by a tour of the Continent and the Mediterranean. The fact that Melville was struggling to maintain his reputation at this time after the disastrous reception of *Pierre* may have contributed to his animosity toward the leisured brother-in-law who wanted him to stop writing "nonsensical books."

While we may savor the joke Melville played on Lemuel, Jr., by modeling a character after him in *The Confidence-Man,* there was perhaps less provocation for satirizing his other brother-in-law, Sam, even if the sophomore of Chapter 5 is clearly more of a fool than a knave. A final historical irony here appears in the fact that Lemuel, Jr.'s premature death from apoplexy in 1884 provided Melville and his wife with a large bequest from his estate; so Lemuel, Jr., did eventually act the part of a charitable "brother" to his brother-in-law, thereby contributing to Melville's final literary efflorescence in the writing of *Billy Budd.*[23]

THE SICK MAN, THOMAS FRY

In the second quarter of the novel, the Confidence Man encounters a series of characters from a lower social stratum than in the first quarter. Two of these characters are modeled on friends of Melville's youth in Albany, one of whom was also a relative. The first individual approached by the herb doctor, the "sick man" of Chapter 16, is based on Melville's second cousin, Augustus Platt Van Schaick (1822–1847). Melville was related to this Albany cousin through his maternal grandmother, Catherine Van Schaick. Slightly younger than Melville, Augustus Van Schaick was a graduate of the Rensselaer Polytechnical Institute, an engineer on the Erie Canal and the Troy and Schenectady Railroad, and a writer of literary bagatelles. By the mid-1840s he was in declining health (probably owing to tuberculosis) and undertook a recuperative voyage to Rio de Janeiro in early 1847; he died on the return voyage that September (*C,* 89, 91). In late April 1847, Melville sent his cousin, then in Southern latitudes, a copy of the recently published *Omoo* along with a letter that attempted to cheer him up:

> When I was last in Lansingburgh Cousin Maria read me a considerable portion of one of your last letters & I was much pleased to see that you had by no means lost that pleasantry of humor you had when here—From this I infer that you are not quite cast-down & indeed I think you have no reason to be, seeing that the beautiful climate of Rio must reinvigorate you and make you a robust fellow after all. That this will prove to be the case is my sincere & fervent wish. If you will take the advice of one who loves you you will keep up a valiant heart—Nil Desperandum—so as to come back to us again & send a challenge across the water to fight Bendigo for the Champion's Belt of all England. (*C*, 91)

Melville's sending a copy of the exuberant *Omoo* to Van Schaick may in fact have provided a biographical prototype for the herb doctor's offering the sick man his herbal remedy, the *Omni*-Balsamic Reinvigorator. (In his letter above, Melville noted that the beautiful climate of Rio should *reinvigorate* his cousin.) Similarly, Melville's attempt to inspire confidence in his terminally ill cousin suggests a basis for the herb doctor's jaunty insistence on the efficacy of his all-natural remedy.

In another letter the following June, Melville asked Van Schaick, "What think you of tropical climes My Dear Augustus? But you are a little too far South (on the very border indeed of the South Temperate Zone) to feel the full genial warmth of the Torrid Zone" (*C*, 93). Like the invalid Van Schaick, the sick man is first introduced as "an unparticipating man, visited, but not warmed, by the sun—a plant whose hour seems over, while buds are blowing and seeds are astir" (*CM*, 77). Moreover, the extended lecture by the herb doctor on the medical follies of "chemical practitioners" suggests a connection with Augustus Van Schaick's scientific education, while the herb doctor's inadvertently callous remark to the sick man ("it may so be that I shall never see you again") corresponds to the fact that Melville never saw his cousin after he sailed to Rio.

A final biographical aspect of the herb doctor's encounter with the sick man is perhaps more important as an oblique allusion to Melville's own literary career than as a fictive reminder of his deceased Albany cousin; the allusion here is to *White-Jacket*, which contains an extended account of a nautical visit to Rio de Janeiro and so may have been associated with the memory of Van Schaick. The herb doctor ends his encounter with the sick man in Chapter 16 by warning the sick man against "certain contrivers" who have been counterfeiting his medicine. We may compare this warning with the fact that in the summer of 1850 Melville was the victim of a Southern imposter assuming his name and collecting orders for his books, especially his most recent work, *White-Jacket* (*Log*, 1:377–78; Reeves). The herb doctor tells the sick man to hold the paper wrapper of his medicine up to the light and to look for a water mark reading "confidence," an operation with a likely parodic relation to the title page or "jacket" of Melville's fifth novel.[24]

The model for the crippled "soldier of fortune," Thomas Fry, whose story exposes the imperfect operations of the nation's legal system, is Melville's adolescent friend Eli James Murdock Fly (1817–1854). Slightly older than Melville and a friend of his brother Gansevoort as well, Fly was an apprentice in Peter Gansevoort's Albany law firm in the later 1830s. In 1839 Melville and Fly traded visits between Lansingburgh and East Greenbush where the impoverished Fly family lived, and in the summer of 1840 they traveled together to Galena, Illinois, to visit Melville's uncle. After they returned East that November, Melville shipped out on a whaler while Fly remained in New York to look for work in the law; in 1842–1843 Fly worked for a time in Gansevoort Melville's law office. His lack of success in his career is evident in a letter he wrote to Melville's uncle, Peter Gansevoort, in January 1843 while seeking assistance for the job of commissioner of deeds in New York, where he had been living "in trouble & in want" (*Log,* 1:162). Fly's former employer curtly rebuffed his entreaties, but Fly wrote again in January 1844, complaining, "I have struggled very hard here in New York, General, and I am very poor; an appointment of this kind would be of great assistance to me" (*Log,* 1:178). The following April Fly moved to Rhinebeck, New York, to start a law practice, where he apparently met with greater success (*C,* 570–71). At some point, however, Fly became ill with what would appear to be a form of tuberculosis; and though he eventually got married, he died in Boston in January 1854 (*C,* 182–83). It is not known how much contact Melville had with Fly in the later 1840s, but he provided assistance to his friend in the late winter of 1851. Thus, in a March 26, 1851 letter to Evert Duyckinck, Melville asked that Duyckinck send Fly's subscription to the *Literary World* to Brattleboro, Vermont, and mentioned that Fly, whom Melville reports as having "long been a confirmed invalid," was now on his way to Brattleboro (probably to seek Dr. Wesselhoeft's celebrated water cure there). Melville accompanied Fly on this trip as far as Springfield (*C,* 182–83). In February 1852, Melville wrote Duyckinck to cancel his and Fly's subscription to the *Literary World* (*C,* 222–23), after which time Fly apparently drops out of Melville's life until his death two years later.

The most obvious parallel between Thomas Fry and James Fly is that both are invalids who bear near-identical surnames. (The name "Thomas Fry" causes the herb doctor to inquire whether the unjustly imprisoned Fry is related to Elizabeth Gurney Fry, the English prison reformer.) Moreover, if the soldier of fortune's alms-seeking on the *Fidèle* recalls the western jaunt of Melville and his friend in 1840 and their return via the Mississippi River, Fry's description of his unhealthy cell in the Tombs was probably inspired by the first leg of their trip west via the Erie Canal. As Fry describes his imprisonment, " 'Well, souse I went into a wet cell, like a canal-boat splash-

ing into the lock; locked up in pickle, d'ye see? against the time of the trial' " (*CM,* 96). James Fly's poverty in New York is also comparable to Thomas Fry's destitution, while Fly's professional connection with the law in New York might have served as the basis for Fry's revelation of the corruption of the legal system in that city. Finally, the herb doctor's medical care for Thomas Fry evokes Melville's assistance to his invalid friend during the winter of 1851. Indeed, Thomas Fry's concluding benediction to the herb
doctor (" 'You have borne with me like a good Christian' ") might be considered a fictionalized version of the invalid Fly's gratitude to his boyhood friend for this assistance.[25]

THE WOODEN-LEGGED MAN, THE INVALID TITAN

The "wooden-legged man" of Chapters 3 and 6 and the "invalid Titan" of Chapter 17 represent two of the most outspoken opponents of the Confidence Man in the first half of the novel. Because of this similarity and because both are derived, in part, from Melville's two Revolutionary grandfathers, Thomas Melvill, Sr., and Peter Gansevoort, they may be usefully examined in conjunction.[26] The wooden-legged man represents a heavily displaced image of Melville's paternal grandfather, Thomas Melvill, Sr. (1751–1832). Born in Boston and orphaned at the age of ten (he eventually inherited a substantial fortune from his merchant father), Thomas studied for the ministry at Princeton. Following a trip to his ancestral Scotland he became caught up in Revolutionary politics in Boston. A participant in the Boston Tea Party, he served as a captain and then a major in an artillery regiment during the first years of the Revolutionary War. Based on his war service, he was appointed naval officer for the Port of Boston in 1787 and then made surveyor and inspector of revenue for the District of Boston and Charleston by President Washington in 1789. His position in the Boston custom house was endangered in 1820–1821 by the legal and financial embarrassments of his son Thomas, Jr., in Pittsfield, but his position was secured at this time with the timely intervention of Daniel Webster. As Allan Melvill wrote his father in April 1822, "no Officer deserves to stand higher with the Government & his fellow Citizens than yourself, your integrity, vigilance & capacity are proverbial, no Man can impeach them with impunity" (*Log,* 1:10). However, in April 1829 Thomas was unexpectedly ejected from his custom house post by Jackson's new spoils system, a gratuitous insult to a Revolutionary patriot that earned the enmity of Melville's father to the new populist president. (Young Herman visited his grandfather in Boston in the summers of 1827 and 1829, his second visit coinciding with the scandal over his grandfather's firing by the federal government.) Among his other civic duties, Thomas Melvill, Sr., was a director of the state bank, a delegate at the state constitutional convention, and an enthusiastic volunteer fire-fighter; he died the same year as his bankrupt son Allan, allegedly as a result of exposure during an evening of fire-fighting.

Just as the wooden-legged man acts as the civic watchdog on Melville's allegorical ship of state, Thomas Melvill, Sr., for most of his life acted as an inspector of revenue in the port of Boston. In fact, the wooden-legged man is introduced as "a limping, gimlet-eyed, sour-faced person—it may be some discharged custom-house officer, who, suddenly stripped of convenient means of support, had concluded to be avenged on government and humanity" (*CM,* 12). Several commentators have suggested that this act of ejectment bears a connection with Hawthorne's well-known case. Stanton Garner, on the other hand, relates it to the dismissal of Melville's cousin, Leonard Gansevoort, from the New York custom house in January 1854 (*Civil War World,* 12). The most likely source for this "discharged custom-house officer," however, is Thomas Melvill, Sr.'s unexpected ejectment from the Boston custom house in Melville's boyhood. Furthermore, Melville's paternal grandfather appears to have had a volatile temper like that of the wooden-legged man. At a meeting of the Bunker Hill Association on July 4, 1812, for example, he denounced the antiwar Federalists as "The Traitors in the United States; may they follow the example of *Judas,* and save the necessity of Judge, Jury, and Executioner" (quoted in Thomas, 240). And just as the wooden-legged man is obsessed with the legitimacy of the Confidence Man's charity operation, Thomas Melvill, Sr., was the target of what might be considered filial confidence games by his two sons, Allan and Thomas, Jr., both of whom relied on infusions of capital from their father and embroiled him in their struggles in New York and Pittsfield. As Allan Melvill wrote his father in April 1822, urging him to help discharge Thomas Melvill, Jr., from debtor's prison, "I still fear my dear Father that we can never repose confidence in him" (Leyda, 1).

The Confidence Man's other violent antagonist in the first half of the novel is a mournful-looking "invalid Titan" leading a young girl of mixed blood, both of whom board the *Fidèle* at a mysterious "houseless landing." This invalid Titan is derived in part from Melville's maternal grandfather, General Peter Gansevoort (1749–1812). Raymond Weaver has remarked that "the image of Peter Gansevoort was one of the most potent influences during Melville's most impressionable years" (39). Peter Gansevoort was best known for having commanded the defense of Fort Stanwix in the summer of 1777, an important victory in the early stages of the Revolutionary War: Peter held off an army of British and Indians that was thereby kept from joining Burgoyne, thus allowing for Burgoyne's defeat at Saratoga that same year. After the Revolution, Peter established a lucrative lumber business in an area north of Albany which eventually became the town of Gansevoort, New York. In 1788 the Confederation Congress appointed him to the position of Indian commissioner because of his extensive experiences in dealing with the Indians of New York State. Writing of a journey Peter made in 1790 to a New York tribe, Alice Kenney notes: "One unanticipated result of this trip—or perhaps of some similar but unrecorded one—was the establishment among the Seneca Indians of a family named 'Gansworth' who claim to this day to be descended from him" (141). During the latter part of his life, Peter was a prosperous timber merchant and Albany civic leader. He also retained various posts within the new nation's military establishment and was a brigadier general at his death just before the outbreak of the War of 1812.

The invalid Titan exhibits several traits that can be related to the figure of Peter Gansevoort. First, the Titan's mythic designation is appropriate for Melville's heroic Revolutionary grandfather, who was over six feet tall. (In *Pierre* Melville's hero meditates on the enormous stature of his Revolutionary grandfather [*P*, 29], a character also based on Peter Gansevoort.) Second, in an image suited to the defender of Fort Stanwix, the Titan walks with such a burdensome step that "shot seemed in his pockets." (Peter's refusal to surrender despite heavy British artillery saved the fort.) Third, the Titan assaults the herb doctor with his swamp-oak walking stick, an action suited to a celebrated military man like Melville's grandfather.[27] Fourth, the Titan is accompanied by a child of mixed blood, "not improbably his child, but evidently of alien maternity, perhaps Creole, or even Comanche." From her moccasins and beaded tassel-work blanket, her heritage is more likely Indian; hence, this child may be imaginatively derived from Peter's honorific "Gansworth" Indian family. Finally, the "houseless landing, scooped, as by a landslide, out of sombre forests" where the Titan emerges also might be related to the wild gorge on the Snock Kill River where Peter established his timber mills after the Revolution and where Melville had visited his uncle Herman, the inheritor of Peter's timber business (*Log*, 1:251).

Since Melville's grandfather had died seven years before he was born and thus existed for him only in imagination, Melville would seem to have also used this maternal uncle, Herman Gansevoort (1779–1862), as another model for the Titan. Melville had dedicated his second novel, *Omoo*, to this uncle, after whom he was named. Herman Gansevoort spent most of his life running his father's lumber business in Gansevoort, New York, but the business went bankrupt in the late 1840s and Herman was subsequently engaged in lawsuits over title to the family land in the early 1850s. In addition to these difficulties, the death of his wife in the fall of 1855 was a personal tragedy from which he never fully recovered. "For awhile he pottered around the house and the mills, but the rheumatism which had twisted his huge frame for years finally confined him to a sofa, where he lay from morning till night, often dozing, never complaining" (Kenney, 246). Melville had in fact visited his uncle in October 1855 while Herman's wife Catherine was dying (*Log*, 2:509). The invalid Titan on the *Fidèle* would thus seem to incorporate a displaced image of this Gansevoort patriarch, whose incapacitating bereavement could be a source for the Titan's incommunicable grief, bowed posture, and violent rage at the herb doctor's inflated claims for his medicine. Significantly, it is the herb doctor's claim to be able to cure the grief felt for a lost spouse that elicits the Titan's blow.

WILLIAM CREAM

The biographical model for William Cream, the *Fidèle*'s barber, can be found in Melville's most "worldly" close relation, his maternal uncle Peter Gansevoort (1789–1876). (This Peter Gansevoort should not be confused with Melville's maternal grandfather of the same name.) Lawyer, politician, businessman, and philanthropist, Peter was a consummate man of affairs and civic leader in Albany from his debut as a lawyer in 1811 until shortly before the Civil War.[28] Alice Kenney has described some of Peter's many professional activities during the 1830s when as state assemblyman and then senator he was allied with Van Buren's Democratic Albany Regency:

> Peter's most substantial legislative contribution was on committees, such as one to study poor laws and insane asylums, for which purpose he visited insane asylums in several states. His most important assignment was the busy committee on banks, to which in 1830 and again in 1831 thirty-two new banks petitioned for charters and seven or eight existing banks for renewals. This committee was very sensitive politically, since no bank could operate without a charter and charters were often granted or withheld as political favors.
>
> In 1832, Peter was elected to the New York State Senate. There he also did most of his work on committees, including state prisons, incorporation of cities and villages, public health, militia, public buildings, asylums for insane paupers, and for three years "literature," which covered all of the state's various activities in support of education. . . .
>
> While Peter was involved in the state government, he was nevertheless still fundamentally concerned with the community of Albany. He remained active in its nonpolitical civic affairs, serving as a bank director, a trustee of schools and charitable foundations, an organizer of civic banquets and other public ceremonials, and even as chairman of a committee to erect a mausoleum for DeWitt Clinton in newly developed Clinton Square. (158–59)

As a business advisor and investor in family enterprises, Peter was largely responsible for keeping the Melville family solvent from the 1820s to the 1840s. Thus, during the 1820s, Peter invested in Allan Melvill's importing business and facilitated loans to his brother-in-law from Albany banks. At a critical juncture in 1827, Peter loaned his needy brother-in-law $10,000 for a "confidential" investment in a "blind" business partnership with two other dry goods jobbers. As a "silent partner" in the firm, Allan could thereby endorse the notes of his own business venture. The investment proved to be a lucrative one, but Allan's finances were undone by one particularly insistent creditor in early 1830 (Gilman, 41). Following Allan's bankruptcy that year, Peter helped his brother-in-law get started in the Albany branch of a New York fur business and lent him another $2,000 in October 1831 to start a company of his own. When Allan died in early 1832, Peter helped young Gansevoort Melville to continue his father's fur business, into which all of Maria Melville's remaining capital was invested. After the Panic of 1837 wiped out Gansevoort's fur company, Peter was saddled with a $20,000 debt as the endorser of one of its notes, while Maria Melville was obliged to sign a $50,000 bond to the New York State Bank. Thereafter, Peter did what he could to assist the Melvilles, but because of financial difficulties of his own, was unable to make any contributions to his sister's family other than small donations at times of particular need.

As a child, Herman had spent several summer vacations in Albany with his bachelor uncle and grandmother. (His father Allan once called him Peter's protégé [*Log* 1:29].) After Allan Melvill's death, Peter got Herman his first job at the New York State Bank where Peter was a director. Peter thus acted as de facto head of the Melville family and surrogate father to Herman throughout the 1830s, during which time Herman undoubtedly felt like a "charity case" to his wealthier uncle. Indicative of this state of affairs was a letter Peter wrote his sister on October 18, 1839:

> I rec'd a few minutes since, my dear Maria, your letter by my nephew Herman. Most deeply do I sympathize in your situation and think not Maria, that I have at any time been without the most painful feelings on your account—My inability to contribute, a fixed sum for your support has arisen from the same cause by which you have been reduced—I am at this moment pressed on the Corning note, which was discounted for you after Gansevoort's failure, & which I am unable to pay, without great sacrifice—& the large debt due by you to the State Bank, the payment of which I was obliged to guaranty, remains unpaid— (*Log*, 1:96–97)

In late 1837 Peter had encouraged Melville to persevere in his teaching job in Pittsfield, which ultimately failed to yield any salary. Peter's attempt two years later to get Herman a job on the newly developed Erie Canal failed, despite Herman's efforts to train himself for a position as surveyor. Only Melville's going to sea in early 1841 put an end to his professional impasse, despite his being connected by birth with one of the leading families in Albany.

Although the barber's first appearance in *The Confidence-Man* provides limited grounds for comparison, the few hints of his biographical model may be listed as follows. First, just as Herman and Peter Gansevoort were kin (Herman's older brother bore Peter's surname), the man in *cream* colors and the barber, William *Cream,* share a comparable denomination. Second, the barber is described as "crusty-looking," a characterization that accords with Peter's occasionally irascible temper (*Log,* 1:85, 91, 162). Third, the barber's shop is placed in a setting suggestive of some "Constantinople arcade or bazaar, where more than one trade is plied," an image perhaps recalling Peter Gansevoort's Albany office building, Stanwix Hall, which combined upper rooms for professional and social activities, shops at street level, and a restaurant in the basement. Opened in 1833, the Hall was famous for an enormous tin dome of an exotic, Ottoman-like magnificence (Kenney, 200–201).

A more extensive correlation between the barber and Peter Gansevoort occurs, however, when the cosmopolitan is "shaved" by the barber in Chapters 42 and 43 of the novel, for this scene is directly based on family history from the late 1820s. Here Melville is covertly mocking his uncle for his assumed role as an agent of charity for the Melville family during Melville's youth. Thus the debate between the barber and the cosmopolitan mirrors Allan Melvill's "confidential" 1827 agreement with Peter Gansevoort for a loan of $10,000 for his "blind trust." The cosmopolitan now mimics the importunate role played by Melville's father, while the barber represents Peter Gansevoort as Allan Melvill's dupe. As Melville no doubt recognized from a reading of family correspondence, it was at this time that Allan Melvill preceded his son into the realm of the literary "confidence man." On February 10, 1827, Allan wrote to Peter introducing a new business arrangement:

> The new project, to which you so anxiously allude, has not been cherished in vain, but has progressed in all respects beyond my hopes & in conformity to my views, & is now so far matured, that it will go into full operation on the 1st of March next, with as many advantages & good prospects as ever dawned upon a similar establishment—it is entirely a *confidential Connexion* with Persons combining every qualification but money . . . but the whole project, promising as it is, on which myself, & those dear ones around me both now & hereafter depend, will be forever blasted in the bud, *without seasonable & adequate assistance,* in fact, I have already pledged myself to advance Ten Thousand Dollars as a Capital during three years. . . . Therefore as you value my present welfare & future existence, disappoint me not I beseech you, in an emergency fraught with all that is personally dear to me in life, & which ever involves the present & ultimate happiness of my Family—if you do, which kind heaven in mercy avert, I shall know not whither in this World to turn for succor in the very crisis of my fate, & all, all, may be lost to me forever. (*Log,* 1:29)

Peter Gansevoort was lured into the scheme, unenthusiastically advancing his brother-in-law $5,000 in response to this letter and a further $5,000 not long thereafter. Allan thereupon told Peter that he wanted to hold onto $5,000 for three years instead of the six months originally stipulated (Allan was able to pay $5,000 back after six months by means of another loan from his father; the other $5,000 was lost in Allan's financial woes after 1830 and debited against his wife's inheritance [Kenney, 178–79, 197].) Only a year later, on February 22, 1828, did Allan Melvill finally tell his brother-in-law the object of his investment: "I make known to you as a Friend & Brother that I have formed a *confidential* connexion with the highly respectable general Commission House of Messrs L P De Luze & Co in the Dry Good branch of their Business of a nature at once safe pleasant & encouraging" (*Log,* 1:32).

The smooth-tongued cosmopolitan's fooling of the barber for the price of a "shave" reenacts Allan Melvill's inadvertent bilking of his brother-in-law in his "confidential" business arrangement. Thus the cosmopolitan at first refuses to put in writing his verbal agreement with the barber: " 'I won't put it in black and white. It were a reflection upon our joint honor. I will take your word and you shall take mine.' " This refusal parallels Allan Melvill's desire not to have a written agreement with Peter Gansevoort after Peter's loan of $10,000. As Allan wrote his brother-in-law on March 10, 1828, such an agreement would show a "want of confidence" in their "uncommon friendship" (quoted in Rogin, 252).[29] The cosmopolitan, however, does eventually agree to draw up a contract in which the barber pledges to take down his "No Trust" sign and trust mankind, in exchange for the cosmopolitan's pledge to make good any loss that might result from this policy. (The contract here may recall the fact that Peter was one of Albany's leading lawyers.) Moreover, just as the agreement between the cosmopolitan and barber is dated April 1, 18—, Allan Melvill's "confidential" agreement with Peter Gansevoort was reached on the same date in 1827. On March 30 Allan Melvill wrote Peter a letter of melodramatic appeal:

> I have to request in the most *urgent manner,* as equally involving my personal honour & the welfare of my Family, that you would favor me by *return of mail* with your Note to my Order at six months from 31st March, for Five Thousand Dollars, to enable me to fulfill my engagements to *the concern,* on which depends all my present hopes & future prospects—I cannot be more explicit, but assure you on the sacred faith of a Brother, that you shall in all events be secured, & know everything to your entire satisfaction when we meet— . . . as you esteem me, & *love our dear Maria,* do not I conjure you as a friend & Brother, disappoint me, in the *utmost need* . . . or *all will be lost even to my honour,* & I hereby pledge myself never to request your responsibility for an additional sum. (*Log,* 1:31)

In the face of such pleading Peter acquiesced, and on April 1, 1827, he sent Allan a note for $5,000, the final half of the $10,000 he would sink into his brother-in-law's "confidential" scheme. This "confidential" April Fools' Day transaction is in fact echoed in an exchange that occurs after the barber and the cosmopolitan have signed their agreement, and the barber goes on to ask for a security deposit:

> "You speak of cash, barber; pray in what connection?"
> "In a nearer one, sir," answered the barber, less blandly, "than I thought the man with the sweet voice stood, who wanted me to trust him once for a shave, on the score of being a sort of thirteenth cousin."
> "Indeed, and what did you say to him?"
> "I said, 'Thank you, sir, but I don't see the connection.' "
> "How could you so unsweetly answer one with a sweet voice?"
> "Because, I recalled what the son of Sirach says in the True Book: 'An enemy speaketh sweetly with his lips;' and so I did what the son of Sirach advises in such cases: 'I believed not his many words.' " (*CM*, 236)

The barber thereupon asks for a fifty dollar security deposit; as we have noted, Peter Gansevoort's April 1 investment in Allan Melvill's scheme was $5,000. In effect, the conversational exchange above indirectly alludes to Peter Gansevoort's loan to his sweet-voiced "cousin" Allan Melvill, whose letters attest a well-developed skill in pleading an ostensibly worthy cause. Allan Melvill was, of course, a closer relation than a "thirteenth cousin," but from Allan's bad luck in business, it might appear that he was worthy of such a designation. Significantly, the barber's citation from Ecclesiasticus provides the lead-in to the encounter between the cosmopolitan and the old man at the end of the novel, the old man being derived from Melville's father, as we will soon discover.

Other incidental features here add to the underlying connection between the barber and Melville's uncle. In reply to the cosmopolitan's request for the removal of his "No Trust" sign, for example, the barber notes that he "lost a great deal, off and on, before putting that up." Peter Gansevoort might well have made this claim as a result of his charity to the Melville family. The barber's seemingly final reason for not extending credit to his customers ("Sir, you must excuse me. I have a family") is also possibly significant in terms of Peter Gansevoort's personal history, for in 1833 a middle-aged Peter married nineteen-year-old Mary Sanford, daughter of a wealthy lawyer and politician from Long Island. (The couple had two children, Henry, born in 1835, and Catherine, born in 1838; Mary died of tuberculosis in 1841 and two years later Peter married Susan Lansing of Albany.) Finally, the barber's last remarks about the cosmopolitan are in keeping with Peter Gansevoort's occasional inability to understand the behavior of his writer nephew: "the worthy barber always spoke of his queer customer as the man-charmer—as certain East Indians are called snake-charmers—and all his friends united in thinking him QUITE AN ORIGINAL" (*CM*, 237).[30]

Additional confirmation of Melville's use of his uncle as the biographical model for the barber is provided by a passage in *Redburn*. At the end of that novel, when Wellingborough Redburn demands payment for his services on the *Highlander* from Captain Riga, the captain mocks Redburn's earlier social pretensions: " '*you*, too, are the son of a wealthy French importer; and—let me think—was not your great-uncle a barber?' " (*R*, 306). Whereupon Captain Riga proceeds to "shave" Redburn's salary down to nothing, the final bitter lesson of Redburn's nautical initiation. Given the semiautobiographical status of Melville's hero in *Redburn*, if we change "great-uncle" in this passage (probably based on Melville's distinguished Revolutionary relation, Leonard Gansevoort) to "uncle," this scene in *Redburn* is a likely germ of Peter Gansevoort's comic metamorphosis into the *Fidèle*'s barber.

Melville's caricature of his uncle was certainly unjustified in terms of Peter Gansevoort's life-long dedication to his sister's family, but it nevertheless conforms to a pattern in his last novel of covert satirical attacks on father figures and paternal surrogates. It is useful to note that Melville's relationship to Peter Gansevoort, as obliquely dramatized in *The Confidence-Man*, is comparable to Hawthorne's early dependence on *his* mother's brother, Robert Manning, during boyhood and adolescence—a relationship that Gloria Erlich views as influencing a series of subversive characterizations of older males in Hawthorne's fiction. The next character to appear in Melville's novel traces this same psychological phenomenon back to its source in the biological father, now conflated with another uncle and surrogate father figure.[31]

THE OLD MAN, THE JUVENILE PEDDLER

Like the man in cream colors at the beginning of the novel, "the clean, comely, old man" at the end is a figure of radical innocence, the senescent equivalent to the mute's mock Christ. We have already seen that the old man parodies a traditional apocalyptic image of God the Father; yet he also bears a complex relationship to a pair of earthly fathers. For the old man embodies a fictionalized version of Allan Melvill (1782–1832), combined with features of Allan's older brother Thomas (1776–1845), another important surrogate father figure to Melville after his own father's untimely death at the age of forty-nine. The portrait that emerges is a devastating indictment of both his father's and uncle's moral derelictions, and the perceived obsolescence of their religious faith; yet it is a portrait tinged by a residual, if ambivalent, affection. Melville portrays here the satiric dethronement of the father in a belated act of filial revenge—a psychological and theological act of aggression with oedipal and agnostic implications.[32]

Brief biographies of Thomas and Allan Melvill will provide the necessary basis for our analysis.[33] An importer of fine dress goods from France and a commission merchant during his son Herman's childhood, Allan Melvill provided his family with a comfortable life while struggling amidst the competitive pressures of the New York commercial world. However, Allan's unexpected inability to pay a creditor in 1830 led to bankruptcy and removal from New York to Albany, his wife's home base. After struggling to reestablish himself in business there as a fur dealer, his affairs took another turn for the worse, and he contracted a fever in December 1831 after crossing the frozen Hudson River on foot while returning to Albany from a business trip to New York. Allan took to his bed in early January, and as his fever grew worse he lost his sanity, becoming a raving "maniac" according to his appalled older brother (*Log,* 1:52). Allan Melvill died shortly before midnight on January 28, 1832. At his death, his debt to his father amounted to $22,000—a sum that effectively consumed all of his share of his father's estate—while his debt to his wife was $4,000, which amount was debited against his wife's inheritance from her mother's unsettled estate (Gilman, 61). Over and above this legacy of debt, however, Allan Melville's sudden death initiated a process of unresolved mourning in his son, resulting in a profound ambivalence toward the father whose "betrayal" by dying left Melville a legacy of doubt and disinheritance.

Melville's first recorded encounter with Thomas Melvill, Jr., occurred when he accompanied his father on a visit to his uncle in Pittsfield in August 1831 (*Log,* 1:48). Thomas had arrived in Pittsfield in 1812 after spending sixteen years (1795–1811) as a banker and speculator in revolutionary France where he associated with distinguished individuals (Joel Barlow, Lafayette) and engaged in at least one shady operation: in 1797 he acted as the agent negotiating payment of bribes from the English government to the ruling French Directory. In 1802 he married a Frenchwoman, Françoise Fleury, with whom he had four surviving children; when his first wife died in 1814, Thomas married Mary Hobart a year later and fathered eight more children. During the War of 1812 he had assumed the rank of major and presided over a military cantonment in Pittsfield, but later faced charges of profiteering from his wartime post. In all, Thomas Melvill, Jr., spent twenty-five years as a farmer in Pittsfield where, despite agricultural awards and civic responsibilities, he was barely able to provide for his large family and was repeatedly jailed for debt, including stints in 1819, 1821, and 1835. During the 1830s he vacillated between Whig and Democratic parties, took an active interest in politics, and in 1836 wrote a series of articles for the Democratic *Pittsfield Sun* under the name "Ben Austin" which attacked lawyers, political opponents, imprisonment for debt, and the unjustifiable actions of banks during the speculative mania of the mid-1830s.

After his father's death, Melville went to Pittsfield for summer vacations in 1832, 1833, and 1836, joining his numerous cousins as well as his uncle's second wife in their spacious old family mansion—a place the Melville family would consider a haven from their struggles in Albany during this period. Beginning in June 1837, Melville again spent several months helping to run his uncle's farm when Thomas was in the process of reestablishing his family in Galena, Illinois. Melville later drew on these experiences for his affectionate, elegiac memoir of his uncle written for the second volume of his friend J.E.A. Smith's *History of Pittsfield, Massachusetts* (1876).[34]

In 1836 Thomas lost his animal stock owing to a severe winter, and the following fall his turnip crop was destroyed by an early frost—events that led him to contemplate a move west for a new start. So in 1837, at the behest of Hezekiah Gear, an old wartime associate who had prospered on the frontier, Melville's uncle led his family to Galena, Illinois, a frontier town based on lead mining and situated close to the Mississippi River. Here Thomas assumed duties as the manager of his friend Gear's general store and became a member of the local chamber of commerce, a notary public, and the head of a "General Agency Office" for the transaction of various commercial dealings, including the acknowledgment of deeds and depositions for the states of Massachusetts and Maine. And here Melville as a young man visited his uncle during the summer of 1840 on a western job hunt with his friend James Fly, as previously noted.[35]

During this visit Melville no doubt became familiar with the exotic, heterogeneous, and commercially active world of the Mississippi River where he would set his last published novel. Moreover, based on his apparent acquaintance with the Falls of Saint Anthony at Minneapolis, which he described in a discarded early chapter of *The Confidence-Man,* as well as his general familiarity with Mississippi scenery between St. Louis and Cairo, it is fairly certain that Melville took trips up and down the river on the many steamboats plying the Mississippi near Galena.[36] Thus it is fitting that the last chapter of *The Confidence-Man* should incorporate an image of the uncle who had originally introduced Melville to the novel's Mississippi setting. What Melville didn't know during his visit but must have learned some time thereafter was the fact that his uncle Thomas was systematically stealing from Hezekiah Gear's general store in order to augment his own income. This fact emerged about 1841 and darkened Thomas's last years in Galena, leaving an aura of scandal about his name. Gear could have sent Thomas to jail for the rest of his life, but since he was such a close associate (the families were close as well) and the money was irrecoverable, Gear contented himself with a largely symbolic banishment.[37]

In Chapter 45 of *The Confidence-Man* Melville has depicted both his uncle Thomas's patriarchal image and his moral failings in a scene that may have been based on an excursion the two made on the Mississippi River during the summer of 1840. Since Melville has left no direct record of his visit to his uncle in 1840, we must turn to his later portrait of Thomas in the *History of Pittsfield* for corroboration of detail here. Writing three decades after Thomas's death, Melville misremembered the date of his longest visit to his uncle's farm, but he nevertheless captured a vivid image of his romantic-looking uncle:

> In 1836, circumstances made me for the greater portion of a year an inmate of my uncle's family, and an active assistant upon the farm. He was then gray-headed, but not wrinkled; of a pleasing complexion; but little, if any, bowed in figure; and preserving evident traces of the prepossessing good looks of his youth. His manners were mild and kindly, with a faded brocade of old French breeding, which—contrasted with his surroundings at the time—impressed me as not a little interesting, nor wholly without a touch of pathos. . . .
>
> By the late October fire, on the great hearth of the capacious kitchen of the old farm-mansion, I remember to have seen him frequently sitting just before early bed-time, gazing into the embers, while his face plainly expressed to a sympathetic observer, that his heart—thawed to the core under the influence of the genial flame—carried him far away over the ocean to the gay Boulevards. (J.E.A. Smith, 399–400)

Melville's memory of his uncle as a rural patriarch may be compared with the initial description of the old man:

> Keeping his lone vigils beneath his lone lamp, which lighted his book on the table, sat a clean, comely, old man, his head snowy as the marble. . . . From his hale look of greenness in winter, and his hands ingrained with the tan, less, apparently, of the present summer, than of accumulated ones past, the old man seemed a well-to-do farmer, happily dismissed, after a thrifty life of activity, from the fields to the fireside—one of those who, at three-score-and-ten, are fresh-hearted as at fifteen; to whom seclusion gives a boon more blessed than knowledge, and at last sends them to heaven untainted by the world, because ignorant of it. (*CM,* 241)

Both descriptions emphasize a blessed mellowness of old age, the fruit of an agricultural existence, capped by a privileged place by the fireside; both portray a salubrious and attractive individual. And if Thomas, despite a "thrifty life of activity," was not quite a "well-to-do farmer," he had all the appearance of being one, including broad acreage and a beautiful old family mansion (now operating as the headquarters of the Pittsfield Country Club).

While there would seem to be a disparity between the old man's apparent provinciality and Thomas Melvill, Jr.'s Parisian past, the scene with the old man nevertheless contains several passing allusions to French culture. Thus the juvenile peddler is initially termed a "*marchand,* as the polite French might have called him"; Thomas might have called him so, for according to his nephew, Thomas possessed "the faded brocade of old French breeding." Furthermore, the peddler's counterfeit detector alludes to "the figure of Napoleon outlined by the tree"; Thomas's career as a banker in France was virtually coterminous with the French dictator's rise and fall.[38] (Thomas named his third child Napoleon; born in France in 1808, he died in April 1814 shortly after his French mother and infant brother [Sealts, *Melville's Reading,* no. 12].) Another French association in this scene is suggested by the cosmopolitan's ironic assurance of a providential "Committee of Safety" watching over him and the old man. The most famous committee of safety was, of course, the nine-member French Committee of Public Safety (1793–1795) at the center of the Revolutionary "Terror," which acted as a virtual dispensary of death sentences.

In the final chapter of *The Confidence-Man,* Melville would seem to be blending memories of his uncle in Pittsfield with his later view of him in Galena in 1840. Indeed, a concrete memory of that visit stands out in the initial characterization in which the old man's hands are described as "ingrained with the tan, less, apparently, of the present summer, than of accumulated ones past." Mention of the *present summer* is an easily overlooked incongruity, for *The Confidence-Man,* as we can hardly forget, is set on April 1. Melville doubtless mentioned "summer" here because the memory of his uncle during the summer of 1840 obtruded on his description of a character physically modeled on Thomas Melvill, Jr.

In the last chapter of the novel Melville is also surreptitiously mocking his uncle, for this scene directly recalls his uncle's life in Galena, particularly his uncle's unconvicted crime of stealing from a friend. Oblique reference to his uncle's theft occurs during the old man's encounter first with the cosmopolitan and then later with the peddler. Early in their conversation the cosmopolitan reads the old man the extended passage from Ecclesiasticus which the barber had earlier quoted:

> " 'With much communication he will tempt thee; he will smile upon thee, and speak thee fair, and say What wantest thou? If thou be for his profit he will use thee; he will make thee bare, and will not be sorry for it. Observe and take good heed. When thou hearest these things, awake in thy sleep.' "
>
> "Who's that describing the confidence-man?" here came from the berth again. (*CM,* 242)

The underlying message here not only concerns a formal recognition of the Confidence Man's identity, but is also a private biographical reference to

Thomas Melvill, Jr.'s depredations on his close friend and benefactor, Hezekiah Gear. That the old man discovers the text is from the Apocrypha relieves him of his anxiety over the disquieting wisdom of the Son of Sirach, but the implicit biographical irony here is further drawn out by the cosmopolitan as he meditates on the distressing implications of the "apocryphal" text. Pondering the chilling implications of the passage, the cosmopolitan shares his distress with the old man: " 'Take heed of thy friends;' not, observe, thy seeming friends, thy hypocritical friends, thy false friends, but thy *friends,* thy real friends—that is to say, not the truest friend in the world is to be implicitly trusted. Can Rochefoucault equal that?" (*CM* 243). Melville's awareness of his uncle's betrayal of Hezekiah Gear—the man who had established Thomas and his family in Galena—is the buried biographical fact behind the cosmopolitan's incredulity over the "wisdom" of the Son of Sirach.

The juvenile peddler's sale of a "traveller's patent lock" to the old man contains another covert allusion to his uncle's thievery in Galena, as found in a passage previously quoted in another context:

> "Look now, sir," standing the thing up on the table, "supposing this little door is your state-room door; well," opening it, "you go in for the night; you close your door behind you—thus. Now, is all safe?"
>
> "I suppose so, child," said the old man.
>
> "Of course it is, my fine fellow," said the cosmopolitan.
>
> "All safe. Well. Now, about two o'clock in the morning, say, a soft-handed gentleman comes softly and tries the knob here—thus; in creeps my soft-handed gentleman; and hey, presto! how comes on the soft cash?"
>
> "I see, I see, child," said the old man; "your fine gentleman is a fine thief, and there's no lock to your little door to keep him out"; with which words he peered at it more closely than before.
>
> "Well, now," again showing his white teeth, "well, now, some of you old folks are knowing 'uns, sure enough; but now comes the great invention," producing a small steel contrivance, very simple but ingenious, and which, being clapped on the inside of the little door, secured it as with a bolt. (*CM,* 245)

The old man is a "knowing 'un" here because Melville knew that his uncle was guilty of a theft comparable to that described by the peddler. As the peddler earlier noted, " 'your fine gentleman is a fine thief and there's no lock to keep him out' "—an observation especially pertinent if the "fine gentleman," like Thomas Melvill, Jr., was the trusted manager of the premises!

The peddler's gift to the old man of a counterfeit detector also probably has a covert relation to Melvill's uncle, for Thomas almost certainly had to deal with problematic bank notes as part of his commercial affairs in Galena. As mentioned earlier, he had in fact written about the nation's currency problems in 1836 at the height of Jacksonian "wildcat" banking, at which time he chastised banks for the overcirculation of small notes and warned about the disastrous consequences of speculative overexpansion.[39] The old man's uncertainty over his Mississippi bank bill thus continues the pointed private satire directed at Melville's uncle, whose financial expertise contrasted with his spendthrift, impecunious life. Finally, the old man's simple faith in providence, which is implicitly undermined throughout the last chapter, is also consistent with Thomas Melvill's devout (Episcopalian) religious beliefs (Gilman, 66).

The last chapter of *The Confidence-Man,* then, is filled with buried allusions to Thomas Melvill, Jr.'s personal history, as well as to Melville's trip to visit his uncle in Galena in 1840.[40] The scene with the old man actually reverses the circumstances of Melville's visit, at which time Melville was the naive nephew and his uncle the undetected "confidence man." Melville is here engaging in a multilayered private joke at the expense of his uncle, a flawed father-figure whose betrayal of a friend and benefactor must have added one more disturbing ambiguity to Melville's troubled moral universe. But Thomas Melvill, Jr., is not the sole target here, for Melville's father Allan, a more pervasive influence in Melville's fiction than his uncle, is equally in the dock in the last chapter of *The Confidence-Man* and provides the source for a supplemental range of allusions. Indeed, by examining Melville's "absent father" in fiction and then in fact, we may see that the old man represents an ironic consummation of Melville's fictionalized image of the father, as patterned on his own biological parent.

As Robert Lee Carothers has demonstrated, the search for the father is a pervasive theme in Melville's fiction. Reference to the narrator's or protagonist's fatherless state begins in *Redburn,* continues as an important theme in *Moby-Dick,* and receives its most sustained and explosive dramatization in *Pierre.* Thereafter, several of the works of short fiction, as well as *Israel Potter, Clarel,* and *Billy Budd,* all present protagonists who are orphans or *isolatoes* in quest of a missing father figure. In *The Confidence-Man,* the episode involving the old man represents another variation on the theme of the "absent father" and as such demonstrates formal continuities with Melville's explorations of the same theme in his earlier fiction. *Redburn* and *Pierre* are Melville's most significant portraits of the absent father and, for our purposes, two key texts for understanding the appearance of the displaced father in *The Confidence-Man.*

In *Redburn,* Wellingborough Redburn describes his deceased father in idealized terms: "I always thought him a marvelous being, infinitely purer and greater than I was, who could not by any possibility do wrong, or say an untruth" (*R,* 34). The first chapter of *Redburn* is a nostalgic evocation of Walter Redburn's benignant presence, which his son associates with the

European, and especially French, culture that the father knew as an importer. This is a lost and bitterly regretted world to Redburn, who is forced through poverty to ship on the *Highlander* as a "boy," the lowest grade of common seaman. Redburn's extended stay in Liverpool is also marked by his homage to a city associated with his father's former presence, as indicated by Redburn's attempted use of the guidebook to Liverpool once belonging to his father. But as Redburn soon discovers, the guidebook is long outdated, a fact that tarnishes the formerly pristine image of his father's world:

> It was a sad, a solemn, and a most melancholy thought. The book on which I had so much relied; the book in the old morocco cover; the book with the cocked-hat corners; the book full of fine old family associations; the book with seventeen plates, executed in the highest style of art; this precious book was next to useless. Yes, the thing that had guided the father, could not guide the son. And I sat on a shop step, and gave loose to meditation.
>
> Here, now, oh Wellingborough, thought I, learn a lesson, and never forget it. This world, my boy, is a moving world; . . . Guide-books, Wellingborough, are the least reliable books in all literature; and nearly all literature, in one sense, is made up of guide-books. Old ones tell us the ways our fathers went, through the thoroughfares and courts of old; but how few of those former places can their posterity trace, amid avenues of modern erections; to how few is the old guide-book now a clew! Every age makes its own guide-books, and the old ones are used for waste paper. But there is one Holy Guide-Book, Wellingborough, that will never lead you astray, if you but follow it aright; and some noble monuments that remain, though the pyramids crumble. (*R*, 157)

Redburn's meditations on the obsolescence of his father's guidebook provide a critical gloss on the last chapter of *The Confidence-Man,* which recreates the episode of the guidebook by means of the juvenile peddler's "counterfeit detector"—a riddling, ambiguous "guidebook" that befuddles the fatherly old man, just as Redburn was befuddled by his father's "prosy old guidebook."[41] Moreover, Redburn's reliance on the "one Holy Guide-Book" that will never lead him astray is a consolatory myth that is later exploded, along with the image of the perfect father, in the cosmopolitan's encounter with the old man. In this scene, we may see Melville reenacting the symbolic encounter of father and son in *Redburn,* but now with a pervading sense of irony at the father's naive faith and the Bible's seeming irrelevance to modern times:

> "Nor is this the only time," continued the other [the cosmopolitan], "that I have observed these public Bibles in boats and hotels. All much

> like this—old without, and new within. True, this aptly typifies that internal freshness, the best mark of truth, however ancient; but then, it speaks not so well as could be wished for the good book's esteem in the minds of the traveling public. I may err, but it seems to me that if more confidence was put in it by the traveling public, it would hardly be so."
>
> With an expression very unlike that with which he had bent over the Detector, the old man sat meditating upon his companion's remarks a while; and, at last, with a rapt look, said: "And yet, of all people, the traveling public most need to put trust in that guardianship which is made known in this book."
>
> "True, true," thoughtfully assented the other.
>
> "And one would think they would want to, and be glad, to," continued the old man kindling; "for, in all our wanderings through this vale, how pleasant, not less than obligatory, to feel that we need start at no wild alarms, provide for no wild perils; trusting in that Power which is alike able and willing to protect us when we cannot ourselves." (*CM,* 249–50)

While there is an element of pathos in this exchange on the efficacy of God's providence, as there was earlier in Redburn's disillusionment with his paternal guide, the cosmopolitan's implied refutations of the old man's faith in a higher "Power" indicate that Melville's fictional search for the father has been ironically attained. Redburn's "prosy old guidebook" and the juvenile peddler's counterfeit detector thus represent analogous texts designed to highlight the foolish credulity of the son in *Redburn* and the father in *The Confidence-Man.* And if the cosmopolitan now calls the old man's quest for confidence a "wild goose chase," Redburn's attempt to find his father's ghost in Liverpool might be given a similar designation.

Melville's other work most strongly marked by the ghost of Allan Melvill, *Pierre,* also contributes to an understanding of the biographical subtext of the last chapter of *The Confidence-Man.* To the enthusiastically pious Pierre, his father is a supremely virtuous man:

> When Pierre was twelve years old, his father had died, leaving behind him, in the general voice of the world, a marked reputation as a gentleman and a Christian; in the heart of his wife, a green memory of many healthy days of unclouded and joyful wedded life, and in the inmost soul of Pierre, the impression of a bodily form of rare manly beauty and benignity, only rivaled by the supposed perfect mold in which his virtuous heart had been cast. Of pensive evenings, by the wide winter fire, or in summer, in the southern piazza, when that mystical night-silence so peculiar to the country would summon up in the minds of Pierre and his mother, long trains of the images of the

past; leading all that spiritual procession, majestically and holily walked the venerated form of the departed husband and father. (*P*, 68–69)

We find here the same twofold emphasis on physical attractiveness and spiritual purity used to describe the old man in *The Confidence-Man*. Thus Pierre's father has a "bodily form of rare manly beauty and benignity"; the *Fidèle*'s patriarch is characterized as a "clean" and "comely" old man. Pierre's father is associated with the "green memory of many healthy days"; the old man shows a "hale look of greenness in winter." Pierre and his mother reimagine the father and husband during "pensive evenings, by the wide winter fire"; the old man is also associated with the fireside.

In another related passage, Pierre's reverent image of his father is again comparable to the image of the old man in *The Confidence-Man:*

> Made one green bower of at last, by such successive votive offerings of his being; this shrine seemed, and was indeed, a place for the celebration of a chastened joy, rather than for any melancholy rites. But though thus mantled, and tangled with garlands, this shrine was of marble—a niched pillar, deemed solid and eternal, and from whose top radiated all those innumerable sculptured scrolls and branches, which supported the entire one-pillared temple of his moral life; as in some beautiful gothic oratories, one central pillar, trunk-like, upholds the roof. In this shrine, in this niche of this pillar, stood the perfect marble form of his departed father; without blemish, unclouded, snow-white, and serene; Pierre's fond personification of perfect human goodness and virtue. Before this shrine, Pierre poured out the fullness of all young life's most reverential thoughts and beliefs. Not to God had Pierre ever gone in his heart, unless by ascending the steps of that shrine, and so making it the vestibule of his abstractest religion. (*P*, 68)

Pierre's father, "unclouded, snow-white, and serene," similarly evokes the image of the old man, "his head snowy as the marble." Moreover, the elaborate description of the marble shrine dedicated to his father in Pierre's imagination is analogous to the marble table at which the old man sits reading the *Fidèle*'s Bible, from which are reflected the rays of the cabin's biblically inscribed "solar lamp."

Pierre's dilemma consists of reconciling his idealized image of his father with the possibility—indeed the seeming reality—that he was the reverse of virtuous and pure, the father of an illegitimate daughter. By the same token, the displaced image of the father in *The Confidence-Man* loses an implied perfection during the old man's encounter with the cosmopolitan; like Pierre's father's descent from his pedestal into a miasma of sexual sin, the old man's imputed odor of sanctity is dissipated by a final whiff of the chamber pot. And while Pierre destroys the tainted image of the father by burning his portrait, the old man is merely led off into the darkness with an ineffectual "life preserver" in hand. The ending of *The Confidence-Man* is thus a parody of Pierre's patricidal actions, an annihilation of the father's spirit that supersedes Pierre's melodramatic renunciation of parental ties. Moreover, Melville has reversed the position of father and son in *Pierre,* for now it is the displaced father who is the "fool of fate" while the son is cast as a radically ambiguous god-man, Frank Goodman.

Pierre thus provides a critical gloss on the appearance of the old man at the end of *The Confidence-Man* and suggests how this figure provides the novel's anti-Christian theme with its satirical climax. For Pierre, the father represents the earthly image of the deity—who is, in turn, the hypostatized image of the father. With the unexpected collapse of the paternal image, the duplicate god is destroyed.[42] In *The Confidence-Man*—which takes place in the seemingly nihilistic, joke-ridden world where *Pierre* leaves off—the old man ironically confirms the obsolescence of the traditional image of the deity: since both God and the father have been violently dethroned, both their images survive as foolish relics of an exploded psychological construct or "fond personification"—in other words, defrocked confidence men. The cosmopolitan's testing of the old man's knowledge of the Bible confirms the disjunction of paternal image and divine creed. Indeed, the "apocryphal" text cited from Ecclesiasticus casts doubt on the authority of canonic scripture while showing the possibly superior wisdom of such uncanonic "apocrypha" as the words of Jesus, Son of Sirach—himself a potential theological impostor with a loaded first name.[43]

From our discussion of *Redburn* and *Pierre,* it is evident that a kind of terminal solution to the problem of the absent father in both Melville's life and literary art is being attempted in *The Confidence-Man* by means of a series of symbolic reversals in the status of father and son.[44] But we needn't rely exclusively on literary evidence here, for Melville has encoded specific biographical details of the father in the portrait of the old man—details that complement those biographical allusions noted earlier in reference to Melville's uncle. It should be noted that much of the covert satire directed toward his uncle is equally appropriate for his father. Indeed, the scene with the juvenile peddler might equally evoke the ghost of Allan Melvill, whose financial vicissitudes, bankruptcy, and death left a legacy of radical "distrust" in the mind of his son Herman.

Yet if Melville is indirectly reproaching his father for his financial failings here, the father's religious beliefs are also covertly under attack in this scene. As William Gilman remarks, "Melville's intimate knowledge of the Scriptures and his lifelong concern with the problems of the Christian religion began with his father's reverence for the Bible" (24). Allan Melvill told his young nephew Guert Gansevoort in October 1824: "neglect not the *Bible,* regard it as *your polar star*, its religious precepts & moral doctrines are alike pure & sublime, & equally inculcate obedience, patriotism, fortitude, & temperance" (*Log*, 1:19). The image of the old man reading the Bible at the end of *The Confidence-Man* thus evokes Allan Melvill's devotion to Holy Writ, while the cosmopolitan's effort to sabotage the old man's confidence in the Bible represents Melville's covert revenge on his father's faith in a merciful and providential divine parent, the product of Allan Melvill's liberal Unitarian beliefs. As Allan wrote to his brother-in-law Peter Gansevoort in 1828, "My humble yet ardent confidence, in the constant protection, & eventual bounty of our almighty Parent, has been strong & unwavering, this alone could have sustained me in a fearful & protracted struggle which would otherwise have overwhelmed the boldest spirit & the stoutest heart, & will I trust still enable me to meet every future emergency with composure & fortitude—" (*Log*, 1:33). Allan's obituary in the *Boston Daily Advertiser and Patriot* on February 3, 1832 noted:

> By the warmth of his affections, the purity of his principles, the undeviating integrity of his conduct, combined with great vigor of mind, and firmness and perseverance of purpose, and more especially of that equanimity arising from a firm confidence in the hopes and promises of another and better life, Mr. Melvill's character was such, as on no ordinary degree, to conciliate the affections, and to command the unshaken confidence of all those with whom he was associated, in business, in friendship, or in the nearer and more tender relations of domestic life. (quoted in Murray, Myerson, and Taylor, 2–3)

For Allan's son, such an assurance of "confidence" in a divine protector was no doubt crushingly ironic in view of the father's bankruptcy, insanity, and death. Moreover, Allan Melvill's "integrity" was a pious illusion in view of his business improprieties and failures. From its initial, unsettling text from the Apocrypha to its final depiction of a providential "stool," the last chapter of *The Confidence-Man* constitutes Melville's bitter retort to both the illusion of Christian providence and the flaws in his father's character. Consequently, the cosmopolitan's question of how to construe the words of the Son of Sirach hints that the father's faith was a flawed credulity toward an unreliable divinity, the mirror image of the son's own disillusioned view of the father.

Another implicit irony here is that the words of the Son of Sirach may have been partly inspired by Allan's Melvill's reading of the Bible on his deathbed. Three weeks before his death and a few days before he lost his reason, Allan Melvill marked in the family Bible Psalm 55, an anguished text lamenting an act of betrayal by a close associate. After her husband's death, Maria Melville wrote in the margin: "This chapter was mark'd a few days before my dear *Allan* by reason of severe suffering was depriv'd of his Intellect. God moves in a misterious way" (*Log,* 1:51). Psalm 55 reads, in part:

> My heart is sore pained within me: and the terrors of death are fallen upon me.
>
> Fearfulness and trembling are come upon me, and horror hath overwhelmed me. . . .
>
> Wickedness is in the midst thereof; deceit and guile depart not from her streets.
>
> For it was not an enemy that reproached me; then I could have borne it: neither was it he that hated me that did magnify himself against me; then I would have hid myself from him:
>
> But it was thou, a man mine equal, my guide, and mine acquaintance.
>
> We took sweet counsel together, and walked unto the house of God in company. . . .
>
> Evening and morning, and at noon, will I pray, and cry aloud: and he shall hear my voice. . . .
>
> He hath put forth his hands against such as be at peace with him: he hath broken his covenant.
>
> The words of his mouth were smoother than butter, but war was in his heart: his words were softer than oil, yet were they drawn swords. (4–5, 11–14, 17, 20–21)[45]

Many of the sentiments above parallel the excerpts from Ecclesiasticus quoted by the cosmopolitan; indeed, verse 21 above epitomizes the barber's original quote to the cosmopolitan, "an enemy speaketh sweetly with his lips." Allan Melvill may have felt betrayed by a business associate before his death, or he may have succumbed to vengeful feelings against the competitive business milieu that destroyed him. Whatever the explanation, his son probably adduced the Psalm as a final testament from his father, ambiguously suggesting both betrayal of, and by, the father.

The probability of Melville's reference here to his father's reading of the Bible during his last illness is heightened by the fact that Allan Melvill's deranged state on his deathbed is obliquely alluded to in the encounter between the juvenile peddler and the old man. First, the juvenile peddler refers to the efficacy of his "patent lock" which will preoccupy a thief trying to break it until he loses his reason: " 'let that soft-handed gentleman come now a' softly trying this little knob here, and let him keep a' trying till he finds his head as soft as his hand.' " (A "soft head" denotes both foolishness and, in the medical terminology of the day, derangement due to "softening of the brain.") Then, just before the peddler leaves, another significant exchange occurs between the cosmopolitan, the peddler, and the old man:

> "Sell you a money belt sir?" turning to the cosmopolitan.
>
> "Excuse me, my fine fellow, but I never use that sort of thing; my money I carry loose."
>
> "Loose bait ain't bad," said the boy, "look a lie and find the truth; don't care about a Counterfeit Detector, do ye? or is the wind East, d'ye think?"
>
> "Child," said the old man in some concern, "you mustn't sit up any longer, it affects your mind; there, go away, go to bed."
>
> "If I had some people's brains to lie on, I would," said the boy, "but planks is hard, you know." (*CM,* 246–47)

Apart from showing a mysterious professional connivance between the peddler and the cosmopolitan, this passage also underlines the apparent senility or "soft head" of the old man. Earlier in the scene, the juvenile peddler had hinted that the old man merited a child's rattle, like those he once sold at the Cincinnati fair. Significantly, Melville's father died close to midnight, the time depicted here. Moreover, the juvenile peddler would seem to be about Melville's age—eleven—when his father died. In this case, the peddler would represent Melville's mythologized boyhood self, permanently "disinherited" by this event.

The probability of this association is heightened by other covert autobiographical details here. Upon selling the old man the "traveler's patent lock," for example, the juvenile peddler pockets the change with "the phlegm of an old banker." Immediately after his father's death—indeed as a result of that event—Melville started working as a juvenile clerk in the New York State Bank in Albany. Equally telling is the ceremonial leave-taking of the juvenile peddler: "and then with a flourish of his hat—which, like the rest of his tatters, was, thanks to hard times, a belonging beyond his years, though not beyond his experience, being a grown man's cast-off beaver—turned, and with the air of a young Caffre, quitted the place" (*CM,* 247). Allan Melvill's original business in Albany consisted of the manufacture of fur caps. The juvenile peddler's precocious maturity parallels Melville's own premature paternal inheritance, paradigmatically represented by Allan Melvill's beaverskin headgear. Moreover, the juvenile peddler as "Caffre" is seemingly yet another allusion to Melville's outcast "Ishmaelite" identity, which informs much of his fiction and had its autobiographical basis in the father's early death.[46]

Finally, on a psychological level, we find in this scene a likely example of that ambivalence to the departed which is typical of unresolved mourning. This state involves simultaneous blaming of the deceased for abandonment and a fabrication of an idealized image of them in order to rescue them from blame. The mourner typically redirects unacceptable hostility to the deceased against the self. In keeping with this psychological paradigm, the old man in *The Confidence-Man* evokes an idealized image of the deceased father. The boy peddler at once projects a state of parental abandonment and, in his shabbiness and poverty, incorporates the mourner's (Melville's) deflection of blame against the father onto the self. The subversive treatment of the (anonymous) father in the novel also suggests the latent aggression that accompanies chronic mourning. The fact that twenty-five years after his father's tragic death Melville is dramatizing this event at the end of his last published novel suggests its centrality to his psychic and creative life.

The last chapter of *The Confidence-Man* thus re-creates the life and death of the father, as the juvenile peddler evokes Melville at the age of his father's death and the old man evokes an image of Allan Melvill at the age he would have been if still alive, in his mid-seventies. (The setting of the novel on April 1 is also not far from Allan Melvill's birthday on April 7.) Melville is enacting a ghostly drama referring back to the death of the father at the verge of the son's adolescence, and the burden of mourning he carried within him. We have previously noted the figure of Hermes as a mythical type for the peddler; Hermes's role as boundary god, patron of thieves, and conductor of the dead thus suits the peddler's role as "guide" to the ghost of the father.[47]

The old man's identity, then, is a composite of Allan and Thomas Melvill, Jr., blended into an archetypal paternal figure whose representation is rich in covert biography. If the idyllic memories of his uncle in Pittsfield and Galena inform the salubrious outward qualities of the old man, his uncle's unconvicted crime of theft provides much of the surface irony in the scene. Yet on a deeper level, the darker memories of his father's bankruptcy and death inform the old man's identity as the problematic father figure frequently encountered in Melville's writings. Both uncle and father were probably intimately related in Melville's mind, the father's older brother being the visible link to the father after the father's death. So when the cosmopolitan "kindly" leads the old man off to his stateroom ("kindly" here is a likely pun on the covert family relationship), Melville is fictively laying to rest the ghost of his father in an ambivalent act of veneration and vengeance toward his fallen paternal confidence men, Allan and Thomas Melvill, Jr.[48]

6

Biographical Models: Literary Brethren

In the preceding chapter, we have seen that—in addition to self-caricature—much of Melville's covert biographical satire in *The Confidence-Man* is keyed to models derived from his immediate and extended family, especially a series of father figures and paternal surrogates. A supplementary range of models, to be examined in this chapter, derives from Melville's literary brethren whose caricatures constitute a satirical critique of some of America's leading contemporary men of letters. As previously noted, three of these models—Emerson, Thoreau, and Poe—have already been identified, although they merit reexamination for further evidence of the sources and focus of Melville's satire. New to criticism of the novel is Melville's fictive transformation of his most important literary friends, Evert Duyckinck and Nathaniel Hawthorne. This chapter, then, examines the novel's covert and overt literary satire as Melville inducts his fellow writers into a representative world of fools and knaves.

HENRY ROBERTS

Henry Roberts, the country merchant, is the most visible gull on the *Fidèle* in the first quarter of the novel. A pervasive network of biographical details indicates that the country merchant is modeled on Evert Duyckinck (1816–1878), Melville's New York friend and literary mentor. Author, editor, anthologist, and literary nationalist on behalf of "Young America" (the movement named by Duyckinck's close friend Cornelius Mathews), Duyckinck played an important role in the development of American literature in the 1840s and 1850s.[1] The son of a Manhattan bookseller, Duyckinck inherited a modest competence that facilitated his choice of letters as a profession after originally training for the law. Following trips to the Midwest and then Europe in the later 1830s, Duyckinck began a career as a literary journalist in New York. As an editor at Wiley and Putnam in the mid-1840s, Duyckinck helped launch Melville as a writer with the publication of *Typee* in the "Library of American Books." He subsequently became a valued friend whom Melville saw frequently after moving to New York City in 1847. Melville was a regular visitor to Duyckinck's nearby residence at 20 Clinton Place (East 8th Street) where he drew on Duyckinck's well-stocked library and occasionally socialized with fellow literati over his host's punch bowl. As editor of the *Literary World* from February through April 1847 and from October 1848 through December 1853 (assisted by his younger brother George, who also served as business manager), Duyckinck produced an informative literary weekly that provided a critical sounding board during Melville's maturation as an artist—one to which Melville himself contributed as an occasional book reviewer.

The friendship, however, was gradually undermined by Melville's development in the direction of literary "metaphysics" and religious skepticism, in contrast to Duyckinck's moralistic critical doctrines and staunch Episcopalianism. For though fond of "Rabelaisian" humor and sociability, Duyckinck took his Christianity very seriously: he was a vestryman at his New York church, a writer for the Sunday School Union, and a friend to Episcopalian bishops. He also tended toward the high-church side of his faith in its current polarization over Puseyism. According to his ministerial eulogist, Duyckinck was "a hater of gloom and bigotry, but a lover of religion, rejoicing in an earnest sermon, an impressive worship, and apparently always ready to join devoutly in the Holy Communion" (Osgood, 6).[2]

Relations between Melville and Duyckinck began to go sour after the publication of *Moby-Dick* in November 1851, when Duyckinck in his *Literary World* review found reason for alarm at Melville's questioning of the religious proprieties. Duyckinck compounded the criticism by republishing the review in *Holden's Dollar Magazine,* a mass-market publication that he edited between April and December 1851. Not long thereafter, Melville was in New York in early January 1852 with the manuscript of *Pierre,* and some dramatic falling out with Duyckinck occurred at this time, almost certainly because of Duyckinck's mixed review of *Moby-Dick* as well as Duyckinck's conceivably shocked reaction to the moral enormities of *Pierre.* (It is likely but not proven that Melville showed the manuscript to Duyckinck at this time.) Partly in response to his rupture with Duyckinck, Melville wrote into the latter part of *Pierre* a scathing satire of Duyckinck's "Young America" movement in literature, and on February 14, 1852—Valentine's Day—Melville curtly canceled his subscription to Duyckinck's publication, thereby formalizing the break that had occurred the previous month (*C,* 222–23). Relations between the two reached a nadir with the appearance of *Pierre* in August 1852, a book in which the *Literary World* found only "incoherences of thought, in infelicities of language" and compared to a stagnant pool, "too muddy, foul, and corrupt."[3] The review said nothing about the fact that in *Pierre* Melville had included Duyckinck in his satire on the New York literary scene by caricaturing his friend as the aggressive editor of the *Captain Kidd* review (presumably Melville's retaliation for Duyckinck's critical protest against Ishmael's "piratical running down of creeds and opinions" in *Moby-Dick*).

Duyckinck's *Literary World* stopped publication at the end of 1853, and besides editing an Episcopalian magazine, *The Churchman,* Duyckinck spent the next two years engaged with his brother preparing their comprehensive *Cyclopaedia of American Literature*. By the time Melville was writing *The Confidence-Man,* relations with Duyckinck had apparently been interrupted for several years, although Duyckinck remained friends with Melville's sister Augusta and his brother Allan in New York. Their friendship, however, was back on its old footing when Melville spent a lively evening with Duyckinck in early October 1856 on his way through New York to Europe and the Holy Land. Hence some kind of reconciliation must have occurred before this date.[4] Following this restoration of relations, Melville's friendship with Duyckinck lasted uninterruptedly until Duyckinck's death in 1878 and was facilitated when Melville in 1863 moved back to New York from Pittsfield.

In his *Literati Papers* (1846), Edgar Allan Poe sketched a portrait of Duyckinck at the time that Melville first became acquainted with him. The portrait suggests a basis for Melville's later caricature of his friend in *The Confidence-Man:*

> In character he is remarkable, distinguished for the *bonhomie* of his manner, his simplicity and single-mindedness, his active beneficence, his hatred of wrong done even to an enemy, and especially for an almost Quixotic fidelity to his friends [i.e., the egregious Cornelius Mathews]. He seems in perpetual good humor with all things, and I have no doubt that in his secret heart he is an optimist.
>
> In person he is equally simple as in character—the one is a *pendent* of the other. . . . The forehead, phrenologically, is a good one; eyes and hair light; the whole expression of the face that of serenity and benevolence, contributing to give an idea of youthfulness. . . . His dress, also, is in full keeping with his character, scrupulously neat but plain, and conveying an instantaneous conviction of the gentleman. (*Complete Works,* 15:60–61)

A more probing evaluation of Duyckinck as a literary critic by Daniel Wells reveals the negative consequences of his characteristic optimism, serenity, and benevolence:

> Ironically, his sense of the spirit of the age was the best and the worst of Evert Duyckinck as a critic. His intense nationalism, democratic ambience, and critical acumen led him to determine with remarkable

> accuracy the American writers making the most lasting contribution to American letters. But this same confidence in American institutions and optimism about the democratic man, together with orthodox religious and philosophical opinions, brought about a blindness to the implications of American optimism that became the leading theme of the greatest American writers. (360)[5]

Henry Roberts in *The Confidence-Man* satirically embodies Melville's accumulated resentment toward his sometime literary friend and benefactor. For in the representation of Henry Roberts, Melville traces the evolution of his relationship with Duyckinck from 1846 to 1852, recapitulated in Roberts' successive encounters with three guises of the Confidence Man as Black Guinea, John Ringman, and John Truman. The sequence begins when Henry Roberts drops his card in front of Black Guinea in Chapter 3. As previously noted, Black Guinea incorporates a caricature of Melville as Ishmaelite outlaw and author of *Typee.* Melville became acquainted with Duyckinck in early 1846 in connection with the publication of *Typee;* Henry Roberts' dropping of his card in front of Black Guinea duplicates this event.

After encountering Guinea, Roberts goes in search of a list of men whom Guinea has named as guarantors of his authenticity. The subject of Guinea's reliability recalls the well-known dispute in 1846 concerning the veracity of *Typee,* which had been published by Wiley and Putnam as an authentic travel narrative. Duyckinck himself had expressed a "spice of civil skepticism" over the events narrated in *Typee* (*C,* 50). The veracity of *Typee* was vindicated by the unexpected appearance of Melville's companion Toby in the summer of 1846 to confirm Melville's visit to the Typee valley. As Melville wrote to Duyckinck in early July, "What will the politely incredulous Mr Duyckinck now say to the true Toby's having turned up in Buffalo. . . . Give ear then, oh ye of little faith" (*C,* 50). Melville caricatures his early dependence on Duyckinck with Black Guinea's list of sponsors: Guinea makes Roberts run a fool's errand as Melville pays his literary sponsor back in kind for Duyckinck's early doubts about his reliability.[6]

The Roberts–Duyckinck connection continues throughout Roberts' subsequent encounters with John Ringman and John Truman. In Chapter 4, the Confidence Man introduces himself as John Ringman and reminds Roberts of a previous acquaintance some six years back. Roberts claims not to remember Ringman, but he gives him money after Ringman describes himself as a fellow Freemason down on his luck; Ringman returns the favor with a stock tip concerning the Black Rapids Coal Company. In this scene John Ringman approaches the merchant using the classic confidence trick of pretended acquaintance employed by the "Original Confidence Man" whose reappearance in Albany in the spring of 1855 provided the catalyst for Melville's novel. As Johannes Bergmann has shown, Ringman's appeal to the merchant based on shared Masonic membership is derived from the ploy of

"Samuel Willis" while operating in Albany, as reported in the local press ("Original Confidence Man," 571–73). This was the same "Original Confidence Man" who had become a celebrity (then known as "William Thompson") in the summer of 1849 in New York and about whom Duyckinck had published an article in the *Literary World* on August 18. Composed largely of an extract from the New York *Merchant's Ledger,* the article (as earlier noted) viewed the swindles of the "Confidence Man" in a positive light because they proved that some men still retained their humanity and so were capable of being fooled. Here again was unmistakable evidence of Duyckinck's "optimism," and the fact that these views originated in a newspaper devoted to *merchants* may have influenced Duyckinck's later fictional induction into the fraternity. In any event, Melville's association of one of the ploys of the "Original Confidence Man" with the merchant is clearly derived from Duyckinck's original interest in this criminal celebrity.

John Ringman claims he met Roberts at the offices of "Brade Brothers" while he was traveling for a "Philadelphia house." This imaginary meeting suggests a parody of the Christian communion in which Duyckinck so readily partook. ("Brade" here is probably wordplay on "bread.") An emphasis on "bread" in fact pervades Ringman's reminiscence of his supposed visit to Roberts' house, where the topics of discussion involved, according to Ringman, " 'the urn, and what I said about Werter's Charlotte, and the bread and butter, and that capital story you told of the large loaf.' " In addition, the references to Ringman's affiliation with a "Philadelphia House," an "urn," and the suicidal Werther are probably related to the fact that Melville first consolidated his friendship with Duyckinck in the latter part of June 1846 while in the process of picking up the remains of his deceased brother Gansevoort in New York (*Log,* 2:915; *C,* 49). Ringman's allusion to Goethe's *Sorrows of Young Werther* is also a possible a reminder of Duyckinck's familiarity with the works of the German author.[7]

In keeping with John Ringman's biographical basis, the scene here also obliquely touches on the writing and reception of *Mardi.* For *Mardi* is the implicit text when Ringman introduces his stock tip and so initiates an allegory of Melville's literary reputation in terms of the stock market. Thus Ringman's reference to the "panic contrived by artful alarmists" recalls the mixed critical reception and popular failure of *Mardi.* It also recalls Melville's earlier comments to Duyckinck concerning *Mardi.* On February 2, 1850, Melville sent his friend a copy of the English edition of *Mardi* along with a letter in which he compared it to an aloe plant that might flower "a hundred years hence or not flower at all, which is more likely by far" and then imagined Duyckinck's huge library as a "refuge to a work, which almost everywhere else has been driven forth like a wild, mystic Mormon into shelterless exile" (*C,* 154). Ringman's prediction that the Black Rapids stock will rebound in the future has a parallel in the restoration of Melville's reputation with *Redburn* and *White-Jacket.* In this scene Melville is satirizing the vicissitudes of his early career as well as his friend's participation in the growing commercialization of the literary profession in the late 1840s.[8]

The merchant's encounter with John Truman in Chapters 10 through 13 represents a re-creation of the Melville–Duyckinck relationship in the early 1850s. As we have noted, John Truman of the Black Rapids Coal Company caricatures Melville as the author of his grand literary "blasphemies," *Moby-Dick* and *Pierre*. Thus when John Truman sells coal company stock to Henry Roberts, Melville is covertly retaliating against Duyckinck's condemnation of the heresies found in both books. To compound the personal satire here, the scene also has a source in biographical fact, for in 1850 George Duyckinck—who acted as manager of the inherited resources he shared with his older brother—invested $10,000 in stock of the Pennsylvania Coal Company & Wyoming Coal Association (Mize, 16n).

The prolonged encounter between John Truman and the merchant begins as the two watch a quartet of card players. (Duyckinck and Melville had been fellow whist players in New York [*Log*, 1:273; *C*, 104].) The merchant with good reason believes that some cardsharping is taking place, but Truman blithely announces, " 'A fresh and liberal construction would teach us to regard those four players—indeed, this cabin-full of players—as playing at games in which every player plays fair, and not a player but shall win' " (*CM*, 55). With this expression of mindless optimism, Melville begins a process of ironically inverting the philosophical positions of Duyckinck and himself, as incorporated into Truman's stock scam. In particular, Melville retaliates against his friend's outraged dismissal of *Pierre* by making Roberts an investor in a "diabolical" enterprise symbolized by the book Truman carries. Melville plays with this conceit in the following passage, in which Truman manipulates the merchant's credulity:

> "This transfer-book now," holding it up so as to bring the lettering in sight, "how do you know that it may not be a bogus one? And I, being personally a stranger to you, how can you have confidence in me?"
>
> "Because," knowingly smiled the good merchant, "if you were other than I have confidence that you are, hardly would you challenge distrust that way."
>
> "But you have not examined my book."
>
> "What need to, if already I believe that it is what it is lettered to be?"
>
> "But you had better. It might suggest doubts."
>
> "Doubts, may be, it might suggest, but not knowledge; for how, by examining the book, should I think I knew any more than I now think I do; since, if it be the true book, I think it so already; and since if it be otherwise, then I have never seen the true one, and don't know what that ought to look like."

"Your logic I will not criticize, but your confidence I admire, and earnestly, too, jocose as was the method I took to draw it out. Enough, we will go to yonder table, and if there be any business which, either in my private or official capacity, I can help you do, pray command me." (*CM,* 56–57)

The "doubts" here suggest the philosophical skepticism arising from Melville's most subversive literary productions. Yet this exchange would also seem to satirically re-create the scene of Melville and Duyckinck's split in early 1852, when Melville apparently clashed with Duyckinck over Duyckinck's *Moby-Dick* review as well as Melville's new novel. The merchant's eagerness to believe in the veracity of Truman's book would thus represent an ironic reversal of Duyckinck's faulting of Melville's skepticism in *Moby-Dick* and his apparent alarm over the impieties of *Pierre.* Truman effectively suggests that the "true book" (with obvious biblical implications) is merely a book whose truth is in the eye of the beholder.

This scene would also seem to derive in part from Melville's reading of Montaigne, a copy of whose work he purchased in early 1848 when he was in the process of expanding his philosophical and literary horizons by borrowing books from Duyckinck's library. As Montaigne argues at the end of his skeptical manifesto, "The Apology for Raimond Sebonde," in the Charles Cotton translation that Melville read (Sealts, *Melville's Reading,* no. 366):

> Our fancy does not apply itself to things that are foreign, but is conceived by the mediation of the senses, and the senses do not comprehend a foreign subject, but only their own passions; so that fancy and appearance are no part of the subject, but only of the passion and sufferance of the sense; which passion and subject are several things; wherefore, whoever judges by appearances, judges by another thing than the subject. And to say that the passions of the senses convey to the soul the quality of external subjects by resemblance: how can the soul and understanding be assured of this resemblance, having of itself no communication with the external subjects? as they who never knew Socrates cannot, when they see his portrait, say it is like him. (2:483)

If we substitute Truman's ledger for Socrates (Montaigne is actually echoing an argument in Plato's *Meno*), we have a similar paradigm for the unreliability of the senses. Montaigne thus provided support for Melville's dramatization of a skeptical epistemology that mocked his friend's reluctance to acknowledge the dark side of "truth," including the possibility that we may never know what "truth" is.[9]

After the merchant buys stock from Truman, the two sit for some time discussing the apparently gratuitous sufferings of three passengers on the

Fidèle: the miser, Black Guinea, and John Ringman. Truman's denial of Guinea's misery here may have been partly suggested by Duyckinck's conservative stance on the slavery issue, as befitted a man who was an enemy of "sectionalism" in literature and a friend of the South Carolina romancer, William Gilmore Simms. Duyckinck's views on the slavery issue can be examined in conjunction with the publication of *Uncle Tom's Cabin* in 1852, for the *Literary World* strongly criticized the novel's depiction of the peculiar institution first in an article entitled " 'Colored' Views" and then, after its remarkable success, in a later article entitled "The Uncle Tom Epidemic."[10] Balked in his attempts at identifying human misery in Guinea, the merchant relates the history of John Ringman and his wife Goneril. This recital is also appropriate to a character modeled on Duyckinck since Goneril is partly modeled on Fanny Kemble Butler, concerning whom Melville had written to Duyckinck from Boston in February 1849. (The caricature is fully discussed in Chapter 7.) With a name that evokes Melville and Duyckinck's shared interest in Shakespeare, the story of "Goneril" is an absurdist lampoon of the middle-class moral order that Duyckinck represented and mercilessly parodies Duyckinck's orthodox faith.[11]

The climax of the encounter between the merchant and John Truman occurs when the merchant is warned against "the emotional unreserve of his natural heart," only to make a "mad disclosure" after a few sips of champagne.[12] As we have remarked earlier, the merchant now confesses, " 'Ah, wine is good, and confidence is good; but can wine or confidence percolate down through all the stony strata of hard considerations, and drop warmly and ruddily into the cold cave of truth?' " This confession mimics elements from the review of *Pierre* in the *Literary World* (August 21, 1852), for during this scene Melville is parodying Duyckinck's indignation against his friend's scandalous novel by making Roberts a convert to *Pierre*'s dark truths. As the *Literary World* complained, "Mr. Melville's chapter on 'Chronometricals and Horologicals,' if it has any meaning at all, simply means that virtue and religion are only for gods and not to be attempted by man. But ordinary novel readers will never unkennel this loathsome suggestion. The stagnant pool at the bottom of which it lies, is not too deep for their penetration, but too muddy, foul, and corrupt. If truth is hid in a well, falsehood lies in a quagmire" (Higgins and Parker, 42). We may compare the "stagnant pool" or "quagmire" of falsehood here with Roberts' "cold cave" of truth.[13] The conclusion to the *Literary World*'s review of *Pierre* also provided potential ammunition for Melville's caricature of his friend as the victim of a bizarre transformation:

> The author of "Pierre; or the Ambiguities;" the writer of a mystic romance, in which are conjured up unreal nightmare-conceptions, a confused phantasmagoria of distorted fancies and conceits, ghostly abstractions and fitful shadows, is certainly but a spectre of the substantial

> author of "Omoo" and "Typee," the jovial and hearty narrator of the traveller's tale of incident and adventure. By what *diablerie,* hocus-pocus, or thimble-rigging, "now you see it now you don't" process, the transformation has been effected, we are not skilled in necromancy to detect. (Higgins and Parker, 43)[14]

After his embarrassing lapse of "confidence," the merchant exits from the scene, "mortified at having been tempted by his own honest goodness, accidentally stimulated into making mad disclosures—to himself as to another—of the queer, unaccountable caprices of his natural heart" (*CM,* 68). Such a lesson of human inconsistency recalls a remark Melville made to Duyckinck in a letter of February 12, 1851: "We are all queer customers, Mr Duyckinck, you, I, & every body else in the world. So if I here seem queer to you, be sure, I am not alone in my queerness, tho' it present itself at a different port, perhaps, from other people, since everyone has his own distinct peculiarity" (*C,* 180). Melville was writing to refuse Duyckinck's request to be daguerreotyped and to contribute to *Holden's Dollar Magazine,* which Duyckinck was then editing. Melville's uneasiness over his friend's accommodation to the commercial values of the literary marketplace was no doubt confirmed by this disagreement, which subsequently contributed to his animus against Duyckinck in both *Pierre* and *The Confidence-Man.* Indeed, just as Duyckinck was briefly caricatured in *Pierre* as the predatory editor of the *Captain Kidd Monthly,* so the merchant's surname, "Roberts," is probably wordplay on "robber." ("Henry" was the name of the second of Duyckinck's three sons and also of his brother-in-law, Henry Panton.)

Melville's satirical use of Duyckinck in the novel he brought to New York in the fall of 1856 was richly appropriate in the context of Melville's lively meeting with Duyckinck that October 1. Brimming with off-color and irreverent anecdotes, Melville now compounded a grand literary hoax by involving Duyckinck in "an orgie of indecency and blasphemy" comparable to the scenes in his latest novel where Duyckinck played a significant part. As Duyckinck wrote in his journal at this time:

> Herman Melville passed the evening with me—fresh from his mountain charged to the muzzle with his sailor metaphysics and jargon of things unknowable. But a good stirring evening—ploughing deep and bringing to the surface some rich fruits of thought and experience—Melville instanced old Burton as atheistical—in the exquisite irony of his passages on some scared matters; cited a good story from the Decameron the *Enchantment* of the husband in the tree; a story from Judge Edmonds of a prayer meeting of female convicts at Sing which the Judge was invited to witness and agreed to, provided he was in-

> troduced where he could not be seen. It was an orgie of indecency and blasphemy. (*Log,* 2:523)

Melville left the manuscript of *The Confidence-Man* with his brother Allan in New York when he departed on his trip to Europe and the Holy Land, but Duyckinck apparently did not read it at this time, for on March 31, 1857, the day before publication, Duyckinck wrote his brother George: "Allan Melville has just this moment sent me Herman's 'Confidence Man.' It is a grand subject for a satirist like Voltaire or Swift—and being a kind of original American idea might be made to evolve a picture of our life and manners. We shall see what the sea dog philosophy of Typee makes of it" (*Log,* 2:563). Although Duyckinck accurately placed Melville's novel in its literary tradition, his reference to his friend's "sea dog philosophy" and "Typee" sobriquet were further indications of his annoying fatuity. Needless to say, his remarks here are fraught with a rich dramatic irony. Beyond this tantalizing notation, we do not know what Duyckinck may have thought of the novel or whether he recognized any of the satire directed against himself. If he did, it did not stop him from continuing his friendship with Melville over the next two decades.[15]

Melville's use of his friend Duyckinck as the model for the merchant, then, anatomizes the evolution of their relationship from 1846 to 1852, when the publication of *Moby-Dick* and *Pierre* catalyzed their latent differences. Subsumed within the satire is Melville's resentment at Duyckinck's initially condescending attitude toward his literary protégé, their differing views about the nature of truth in fiction, their opposing responses to the expanding literary marketplace, and most important, their antithetical positions of religious orthodoxy and doubt. Melville indirectly comments on Duyckinck's failure to understand him when, just before the merchant buys his stock, John Truman remarks: " 'But, doubtless, there are plenty who know our Company, whom our Company does not know; in the same way that one may know an individual and yet be unknown to him' " (*CM,* 56). Following a period of silence between the merchant and Truman, the narrator also comments on friendship in a manner that may recall the long hiatus in relations between Melville and Duyckinck: "A kind of social superstition, to suppose that to be truly friendly one must be saying friendly words all the time, any more than be doing friendly deeds continually. True friendliness, like true religion, being in a sort independent of works" (*CM,* 58). While we may read this on the surface as a prediction of Melville's restored friendship with Duyckinck, it is also a telling indictment of Duyckinck's orthodox faith, which inhibited him from aiding or understanding his friend at a crisis in that friend's career. A final irony here may be that Melville's caricature purged his residual ire toward Duyckinck and thus smoothed the way to renewed relations.

PITCH

Pitch, the Missouri bachelor, would seem to be the only major character in the novel without an identifiable biographical model. More than one critic has suggested that Pitch bears a resemblance to James Fenimore Cooper (1789–1851); but none has mustered the evidence to prove the connection, nor has there been any attempt to relate Pitch to any of Cooper's characters.[16] To be sure, Pitch's frontier identity evokes aspects of Cooper's fictional world, and there are some loose parallels between Pitch's oppositional role in the novel and Cooper's last phase as social critic. Furthermore, a caricature of Cooper might have been the logical way to introduce Melville's satirical review of his literary contemporaries in the second half of *The Confidence-Man*. Cooper was clearly an important presence for any antebellum American novelist, and Melville was aware of his debt to the "founder" of the tradition. Writing in December 1851 to Rufus Griswold in response to an invitation to attend a ceremony commemorating Cooper's recent death, Melville noted that he never met the novelist but that Cooper was among the earliest authors he had read; Cooper had exercised an "awakening power" on his mind. Melville also decried the attacks on Cooper in the latter part of his career and concluded by saying that "he possessed no slightest weaknesses, but those, which are only noticeable as the almost infallible indices of pervading greatness. He was a great, robust-souled man, all whose merits are not even yet fully appreciated" (*C*, 216).[17]

The evidence supporting a connection between Pitch and Cooper may be summarized as follows. As a character possibly influenced by Cooper's most famous fictional creation, Pitch in his gruff manner and frontier dress is a kind of misanthropic Natty Bumppo; indeed, Natty ends his long life as a "Missouri bachelor" at the conclusion to *The Prairie*. (On the other hand, Pitch is a farmer, not a hunter like Natty; he is also a well-read frontier philosopher, not an uneducated "natural" like Cooper's illiterate hero.) As a possible caricature of Cooper himself, Pitch's irascibility suggests Cooper's antagonistic attitude to Jacksonian America dating from *Homeward Bound* and *Home As Found* (1837) and continuing through his attacks on democracy in *The Crater* (1847) and on the jury system in *The Ways of the Hour* (1850). Pitch's reference to the "torpedoes" sent to newspapers editors (*CM*, 109) may also recall Cooper's libel suits in the late 1830s and early 1840s against newspaper editors like Thurlow Weed. Pitch's equivocal position on the slavery issue (*CM*, 112–13) matches Cooper's equivocal remarks on slavery in *The American Democrat* (1838). Finally, Pitch's debating abilities suggest Cooper's frequent engagement in polemics throughout his career.

Yet for every similarity between Pitch and Cooper, there are important dissimilarities that make the direct use of Cooper or any of his characters here implausible. It is perhaps more useful to view Pitch as an exploded cliché of the backwoods philosopher based on popular stereotypes of the frontier created by Cooper, as well as those writers who followed in his literary wake.

CHARLIE NOBLE

The third quarter of *The Confidence-Man* is dominated by an encounter between Frank Goodman, the cosmopolitan, and Charlie Noble, a riverboat sharper. John Seelye has suggested that the encounter of Goodman and Noble was inspired by the friendship of Hawthorne and Melville during their joint residence in the Berkshires. Seelye asserts that "in the gulling conversation between the two confidence-men, Frank Goodman and Charlie Noble, Melville was commenting ironically upon his failure to establish an ideal communion of souls" with Hawthorne ("Ungraspable Phantom," 195). Seelye is correct in associating the scenes between Goodman and Noble as reflecting the friendship of Hawthorne and Melville. But in identifying Hawthorne as the model for Frank Goodman and Melville himself as the model for Charlie Noble, he has reversed the implied identities of Goodman and Noble, for it is in fact *Hawthorne* who is satirically transformed into the character of Charlie Noble, while it is Melville himself who plays the role of "cosmopolitan," as earlier noted. Melville's caricature of Hawthorne accordingly mirrors the history of their friendship and echoes a gamut of Hawthorne's and Melville's writings, including Melville's letters to his Berkshire neighbor. As a reflection of Melville's bitter disappointment in Hawthorne's character, the portrait that emerges represents Melville's skeptical, even scathing, reevaluation of his sometime "bosom friend."

The story of Melville's "discovery" of Hawthorne—the reading of *Mosses from an Old Manse* in July 1850, his first meeting with the author on August 5 at a celebrated literary picnic, and his pseudonymous review of Hawthorne's *Mosses* in two August numbers of Duyckinck's *Literary World*—is well-known and has rightly been recognized as marking an epoch in Melville's creative and personal life. The concurrent reading of Hawthorne's work and meeting him in person resulted in what may be called a literary conversion experience, changing the nature of *Moby-Dick* and providing a catalyst for Melville's fiction throughout the 1850's. Comparing Hawthorne to Shakespeare, Melville's *Mosses* review argued that Hawthorne was the living incarnation of a great American artist—a compelling if enigmatic prophet whose powers of enchantment and dark moral vision deserved national attention. It has generally been recognized that Melville's assertion of Hawthorne's genius was also a way of proclaiming his own creative mandate. Indeed, the *Mosses* review probably crystallized critical positions that in some respects were better suited to Melville than to Hawthorne. However, Melville's creative identification with Hawthorne was an act of profound homage to a fellow artist of comparable moral vision.[18]

Following this auspicious debut, Melville moved his family to Pittsfield from New York in October 1850, and Melville and Hawthorne traded visits and letters during the ensuing year, during which time Melville brought *Moby-Dick* to completion, while Hawthorne produced *The House of the Seven Gables* and a volume of children's stories. At some point late in the summer of 1851, however, Hawthorne decided to move from Lenox back to the Boston area and subsequently left the Berkshires with his family in late November 1851 just as *Moby-Dick,* dedicated to Hawthorne, was being published. Recent evidence shows that no alleged estrangement occurred before Hawthorne's departure, for cordial relations continued up until that time. Indeed, Melville's last letter to Hawthorne in Lenox, in response to Hawthorne's having "understood" *Moby-Dick,* clearly demonstrates Melville's intense intellectual and emotional attachment to his Berkshire friend, or what he called an "infinite fraternity of feeling" with Hawthorne.[19]

Thereafter, the friendship began to wane as the two writers' lives and reputations diverged, Hawthorne in the ascendant, Melville in the descendant. Distressed over the disappointing critical reception and mediocre sales of *Moby-Dick,* Melville had in the winter of 1852 finished work on *Pierre,* the publication of which the following August would result in critical and financial disaster. Hawthorne, on the other hand, was enjoying both popular and critical success with his two most recent novels, *The Scarlet Letter* and *The House of the Seven Gables,* and by the spring of 1852 had completed work on *The Blithedale Romance.* Newly installed in Concord, he had also agreed to write the presidential campaign biography that summer for his Bowdoin college friend, Franklin Pierce. He nevertheless found time in July to invite Melville for a visit to Concord and to send along a copy of the newly published *Blithedale.* Postponing any visit, Melville instead tried to interest his friend in the story of an abandoned Cape Cod wife, Agatha Robertson (misnamed Robinson by Melville), which Melville had picked up on a recent visit to Nantucket and Martha's Vineyard with his father-in-law. In a series of letters to Hawthorne that summer and fall, Melville began to formulate a pattern of symbolic imagery for the Agatha material while insisting that the story was peculiarly adapted to Hawthorne's talents (*C,* 231–42). Here was a belated attempt to renew the creative kinship Melville had earlier felt toward Hawthorne in the Berkshires.

Melville finally visited Hawthorne in Concord after more than a year's separation on December 2, 1852 (*Log,* 2:932). When Hawthorne now declined the use of the Agatha story, Melville himself employed it for the lost work he was unable to publish, *The Isle of the Cross,* the title of which was an adaptation of the Isles of Shoals which Hawthorne had visited with Franklin Pierce in September 1852 and suggested as the setting for the story. As a result of his services in helping his college friend attain the presidency, Hawthorne went on to receive the most lucrative of all consular appointments, Liverpool, which was officially confirmed in March 1853. In the spring of 1853 Melville's family tried to get Hawthorne to help sponsor an acceptable consular appointment for Melville, but without success. After Hawthorne's departure for England that summer, communication halted between the two, although enough fellow-feeling existed three years later for Melville to visit Hawthorne for several days in Liverpool in November 1856. Melville returned to Liverpool for another short visit in early May 1857, a few weeks after Hawthorne had signed (on March 20) Melville's contract for English publication of *The Confidence-Man.* (The novel had appeared there in early April.) With Melville's departure for America on May 5, the two never saw or spoke to each other again, as far as is known.[20]

In all, the Noble–Goodman encounter takes up eleven chapters in *The Confidence-Man.* But about half of this sequence, or five chapters, is taken up by the two interior fables recounted by Frank and Charlie. How do these interludes relate to the Melville–Hawthorne relationship as depicted in *The Confidence-Man*? The answer is that the Goodman–Noble encounter is bracketed between narratives that mirror the literary art of Melville and Hawthorne. The friendship begins with Noble's protracted account of Colonel Moredock in Chapters 25 through 28 and ends with Goodman's brief tale of Charlemont in Chapter 34—two stories that develop themes representative of their authorial originals, but as auditors, not narrators. Thus Charlie Noble's story of the Indian killer John Moredock is a Melvillean tale of monomania and murderous revenge with thematic ties to *Moby-Dick,* while Frank Goodman's story of Charlemont is analogous to several of Hawthorne's short stories and to an interpolated tale in *The Blithedale Romance.* (These two interior fables are more fully explicated in Chapter 7.)

This narrative device mirrors the evolution of the Melville–Hawthorne friendship, which began in the summer of 1850 during the composition of *Moby-Dick* and extended through the publication of *The Blithedale Romance* in the summer of 1852 and the correspondence concerning the Agatha story later that summer and fall. Melville has thus framed the Goodman–Noble encounter between two "yarns" that belatedly fulfill Melville's desire to share a creative production with Hawthorne, as illustrated by the "Agatha" letters. The reciprocity involved in the Agatha project is conveyed by the letter Melville wrote to Hawthorne not long after their meeting in early December 1852:

> The other day, at Concord, you expressed uncertainty concerning your undertaking the story of Agatha, and, in the end, you urged *me* to write it. I have decided to do so, and shall begin it immediately upon reaching home; and so far as in me lies, I shall endeavor to do justice to so interesting a story of reality. Will you therefore enclose the whole affair to me; and if anything of your own has occurred to you in your random thinking, won't you note it down for me on the same page with my memorandum? I wish I had come to this determination at

> Concord, for then we might have more fully and closely talked over the story, and so struck out new light. Make amends for this, though, as much as you conveniently can. With your permission I shall make use of "The Isle of Shoals," as far as the name goes at least. I shall also introduce the old Nantucket seaman, in the way I spoke to you about. I invoke your blessing upon my endeavors; and breathe a fair wind upon me. (*C*, 242)

Frank Goodman comments on the uniformity of sentiment between himself and Noble using a relevant trope: " 'You are a man after my own heart,' responded the cosmopolitan, with a candor which lost nothing by its calmness. 'Indeed,' he added, 'our sentiments agree so, that were they written in a book, whose was whose, few but the nicest critics might determine' " (*CM*, 158).

Not only do Goodman and Noble's sentiments appear to agree, but the two share comparable attire and mannerisms. Noble is decked out in "the unsuitableness of a violet vest, sending up sunset hues" to his countenance. The cosmopolitan is dressed in "a vesture barred with various hues, that of the cochineal predominating," and sports a "jaunty smoking-cap of regal purple." Noble exhibits a "warm air of florid cordiality"; Goodman's appearance makes "a florid show." Noble's first greeting of Goodman "with the bluff *abord* of the West" duplicates Goodman's similar greeting of Pitch a chapter earlier, when Goodman hailed the Missouri bachelor with "a cordial slap on the shoulder." A similar logic of mirrored identities governs the significance of Melville's use of names here: the name of his own persona is derived from Hawthorne's Puritans (e.g., "Young Goodman Brown"), while Hawthorne's persona carries a punning name derived from the sea, the setting of Melville's most characteristic fiction.[21] (Noble's middle name, "Arnold," however, reminds us of the famous traitor of the Revolutionary War, a covert warning against Noble's duplicity as well as Hawthorne's fickle loyalty.)

Both Goodman and Noble are depicted as genial Mississippi confidence men and "boon companions" whose easy friendship masks an underlying competition, namely, Noble's design to bilk Goodman by getting him "fuddled." Goodman and Noble's affable interchange of ideas over wine and cigars duplicates the sociality of Melville and Hawthorne during their meetings in Pittsfield and Lenox. As Hawthorne noted in a letter to George W. Curtis on April 29, 1851, Melville "is an admirable fellow, and has some excellent old port and sherry wine" (*Letters 1843–1853*, 425). Three months later, Hawthorne remarked of a meeting on Melville's birthday (August 1): "Melville and I had a talk about time and eternity, things of this world and of the next, and books, and publishers, and all possible and impossible matters, that lasted pretty deep into the night; and if the truth must be told, we smoked cigars even within the sacred precincts of the sitting-room"

(*American Notebooks*, 448). In like manner, Charlie Noble and Frank Goodman share a bottle of port wine, smoke cigars, and discuss authors (Shakespeare), publishers (the press), and a variety of other possible and impossible matters such as the advent of a universal "geniality."[22]

In his letters to Hawthorne, too, Melville advocated a bibulous style of sociability similar to that enjoyed by Goodman and Noble. In January 1851, for example, Melville wrote: "Hark—There is some excellent Montado Sherry awaiting you & some most potent Port. We will have mulled wine with wisdom, & buttered toast with story-telling & crack jokes & bottles from morning till night" (*C*, 176). In another letter on June 29, 1851, Melville took time out from his final labors on *Moby-Dick* to envision another such meeting: "When I am quite free of my present engagements, I am going to treat myself to a ride and a visit to you. Have ready a bottle of brandy, because I always feel like drinking that heroic drink when we talk ontological heroics together" (*C*, 196).

Melville may be indirectly alluding to his initial enthusiasm for Hawthorne when his persona, Goodman, "cigar in mouth, slowly raised the bottle, and brought it slowly to the light, looking at it steadfastly, as one might at a thermometer in August, to see not how low it was, but how high" (*CM*, 174), an action conceivably related to Melville's first meeting with Hawthorne and his laudatory *Mosses* review in August 1850. An oft-noted aspect of his *Mosses* review is that many of Melville's remarks on Hawthorne could equally apply to Melville himself. At the end of a famous letter to Hawthorne in November 1851, for example, Melville pretended to measure his creative endowment against Hawthorne's: "The divine magnet is in you, and my magnet responds. Which is the biggest? A foolish question—they are *One*" (*C*, 213). Frank Goodman similarly uses a "magnetic" trope when accepting Charlie Noble's invitation to drink after Noble has warbled an Anacreontic couplet in a cracked voice: " 'When mermaid songs move figure-heads, then may glory, gold, and women try their blandishments on me. But a good fellow, singing a good song, he woos forth my every spike, so that my whole hull, like a ship's, sailing by a magnetic rock, caves in with acquiescence' " (*CM*, 159).[23]

The Goodman–Noble encounter accordingly mirrors Melville's strong psychological identification with Hawthorne and the history of their friendship as recorded in Melville's letters to his friend; but it also draws on pivotal texts of each author. Melville's *Mosses* review provides a critical gloss on many of the salient features of the encounter between Noble and Goodman, for virtually every point Melville made in his essay on Hawthorne is satirically inverted in the portrait of Charlie Noble. A comparison of the *Mosses* review with illustrative examples from the Goodman–Noble encounter will demonstrate this connection.

At the beginning of his *Mosses* review, Melville announced, "A man of a deep and *noble* nature has seized me in this seclusion," a sentiment later echoed in the assertion that "if you travel away inland into his deep and *noble* nature, you will hear the far roar of his Niagara" (*PT,* 239, 249; emphasis added). Melville's review describes his feeling of possession by Hawthorne, a claim reinforced by reference to the magic of Hawthorne's literary personality. Melville quotes with approval Hawthorne's remark in "The Old Manse": "what better could be done for anybody, who came within our magic circle, than to throw the spell of a magic [Hawthorne had written "tranquil"] spirit over him?" (*PT,* 241). Significantly, Charlie Noble is first introduced "in the semicircular porch of a cabin, opening a recess from the deck, lit by a zoned lamp swung overhead, and sending its light vertically down, like the sun at noon" (*CM,* 139). At the end of their encounter, Goodman creates another "magic circle" around Noble after Noble has rejected Goodman's plea for a loan: "taking ten half-eagles from his pocket, [Goodman] stooped down, and laid them, one by one, in a circle round him; and, retiring a pace, waved his long tasseled pipe with the air of a necromancer, an air heightened by his costume, accompanying each wave with a solemn murmur of cabalistical words" (*CM,* 180). Goodman's encounter with Noble thus begins and ends within "magic circles," the first under the creative emblem of the golden sun, the second inside a mocking circle of gold coins.[24]

In his *Mosses* review, Melville praised Hawthorne as a writer for whom a comparison with Shakespeare was not inappropriate: "Now, I do not say that Nathaniel of Salem is greater than William of Avon, or as great. But the difference between the two men is by no means immeasurable. Not a very great deal more, and Nathaniel were verily William" (*PT,* 246). This is high praise indeed, and Melville must have significantly revised it in his mind when he came to write *The Confidence-Man.* As Frank Goodman notes, "Shakespeare has got to be a kind of deity. Prudent minds, having certain latent thoughts concerning him, will reserve them in a condition of lasting probation" (*CM,* 172). As part of his revised estimate, Melville effectively reaffirms Shakespeare's unique stature as a literary artist while employing two Shakespearean characters, Polonius and Autolycus, as moral touchstones for the interaction of Noble and Goodman.

In his *Mosses* review, Melville had also praised Hawthorne for his delicate humor: "What a mild moonlight of contemplative humor bathes that Old Manse!—the rich and rare distillment of a spicy and slowly-oozing heart. No rollicking rudeness, no gross fun fed on fat dinners, and bred in the lees of wine,—but a humor so spiritually gentle, so high, so deep, and yet so richly relishable, that it were hardly inappropriate in an angel" (*PT,* 241). In the chapter entitled "The Boon Companions," Goodman and Noble engage in a discussion of humor that exposes Noble's deficiency in this quality. Thus when both Charlie and Goodman see a pauper boy wearing grotesque-looking old boots, Noble callously laughs out loud while Goodman notes the boy's appearance with "quiet appreciation." The biographical source for this incident may have been Melville's attempt in the spring of 1851 to buy a pair of shoes for Julian Hawthorne.[25] More incriminating than this first case is Noble's laugh over the ancient Syracusan tyrant Phalaris, who according to Goodman engaged in the "practical punning" of beheading a subject on a "horseblock" merely for having a "horse-laugh." We may recall that Hawthorne had made fun of his own political "decapitation" in "The Custom-House." As with the comparison with Shakespeare, Melville is here inverting an originally overgenerous estimate of Hawthorne's "religion of mirth."

In his *Mosses* review, Melville described the proper mode of understanding Hawthorne's greatness as akin to the process of testing gold by means of a touchstone: "You cannot come to know greatness by inspecting it; there is no glimpse to be caught of it, except by intuition; you need not ring it, you but touch it, and you find it is gold" (*PT,* 244). In *The Confidence-Man,* Melville uses this same metaphor in the encounter between Goodman and Noble, but now with an ironic thrust, as Goodman remarks:

> "A moment since, we talked of Pizarro, gold, and Peru; no doubt, now, you remember that when the Spaniard first entered Atahalpa's treasure-chamber, and saw such profusion of plate stacked up, right and left, with the wantonness of old barrels in a brewer's yard, the needy fellow felt a twinge of misgiving, of want of confidence, as to the genuineness of an opulence so profuse. He went about rapping the shining vases with his knuckles. But it was all gold, pure gold, good gold, sterling gold, which how cheerfully would have been stamped such at Goldsmiths' Hall. And just so those needy minds, which, through their own insincerity, having no confidence in mankind, doubt lest the liberal geniality of this age be spurious. They are small Pizarros in their way—by the very princeliness of men's geniality stunned into distrust of it." (*CM,* 177)

No intuition is necessary to verify this profusion of pure gold, as Goodman outdoes Noble at the game of confidence-building. Underlying this reference to Incan treasure is the gold metaphor of Melville's initial judgment of Hawthorne.[26]

Melville in his *Mosses* review had described Hawthorne's tales and sketches in terms of apple imagery, echoing Hawthorne's own celebration of the apple trees in his "Old Manse" orchard: "For no less ripe than ruddy are the apples of the thoughts and fancies in this sweet Man of Mosses" (*PT,* 241). In the Goodman–Noble encounter, the two smoke cigars, putting their ashes into a pottery ash tray made to look like a ripe apple: "one [globe] in guise of an apple flushed with red and gold to the life, and, through a cleft at top, you saw it was hollow. This was for the ashes" (*CM,* 168). The apple here is a clay replica of the biblical Apples of Sodom: the glowing apple of friendship Hawthorne seemed to offer Melville turned out to be an ashy simulacrum.

Finally, one of the most revealing aspects of Melville's review of *Mosses* is his characterization of Hawthorne as a literary confidence man:

> The truth seems to be, that like many other geniuses, this Man of Mosses takes great delight in hoodwinking the world,—at least, with respect to himself. Personally, I doubt not, that he rather prefers to be generally esteemed but a so-so sort of author; being willing to reserve the thorough and acute appreciation of what he is, to that party most qualified to judge—that is, to himself. . . .
>
> But with whatever motive, playful or profound, Nathaniel Hawthorne has chosen to entitle his pieces in the manner he has, it is certain, that some of them are directly calculated to deceive—egregiously deceive, the superficial skimmer of pages. To be downright and candid once more, let me cheerfully say, that two of these titles did dolefully dupe no less an eagle-eyed reader than myself; and that, too, after I had been impressed with a sense of the great depth and breadth of this American man. (*PT,* 250–51)

If, according to Melville, Hawthorne's titles deceive the unwary reader, Charlie Noble's punning "title" may also fool the superficial reader of *The Confidence-Man.* Moreover, if Melville had in 1850 identified Hawthorne as a literary confidence man, in his last published novel he transformed him into a literal one.

From the evidence adduced above, it is evident that in his depiction of Charlie Noble, Melville was systematically inverting his appreciation of Hawthorne in the *Mosses* essay. Yet while this essay provided several implicit motifs for Frank Goodman's interaction with Charlie Noble, *The Blithedale Romance* represents another important source for Melville's caricature of Hawthorne. Critics have suggested Hawthorne's possible appropriation of his recent experience with Melville in the Berkshires to flesh out the relationship between Coverdale and Hollingsworth, in particular Coverdale's "betrayal" of Hollingsworth in order to remain free of Hollingsworth's obsession with the reform of criminals.[27] Melville's reading of *Blithedale* in the summer of 1852 did not have any immediately perceptible effect on his dealings with Hawthorne, as the Agatha letters show. However, the book would eventually serve as both a source and an analogue to Melville's last published novel: both works ironically undercut America's millennial and utopian ideologies; both draw on a theatrical metaphor of masquerade; both raise questions about the ability of fiction to mirror reality.[28]

Yet for our purposes the most important result of Melville's reading of his friend's novel was his use of one of *Blithedale*'s characters as a model for Charlie Noble: Professor Westervelt, professional mesmerist and diabolical necromancer. Westervelt's first appearance to Coverdale in the woods near Blithedale establishes his demonic character:

> In the excess of his delight, he opened his mouth wide, and disclosed a gold band around the upper part of his teeth; thereby making it apparent that every one of his grinders and incisors was a sham. This discovery affected me very oddly. I felt as if the whole man were a moral and physical humbug; his wonderful beauty of face, for aught I knew, might be removeable like a mask; and, tall and comely as his figure looked, he was perhaps but a wizened little elf, gray and decrepit, with nothing genuine about him, save the wicked expression of his grin. The fantasy of his spectral character so wrought upon me, together with the contagion of his strange mirth on my sympathies, that I soon began to laugh as loudly as himself. (*Blithedale Romance,* 95)

Like Westervelt, Charlie Noble is handsome at first view, but on closer acquaintance reveals himself to be an equivocal or even "spectral" character possessed of a conspicuous pair of false teeth:

> But, upon the whole, it could not be fairly said that his appearance was unprepossessing; indeed, to the congenial, it would have been doubtless not uncongenial; while to others, it could not fail to be at least curiously interesting, from the warm air of florid cordiality, contrasting itself with one knows not what kind of aguish sallowness of saving discretion lurking behind it. Ungracious critics might have thought that the manner flushed the man, something in the same fictitious way that the vest flushed the cheek. And though his teeth were singularly good, those same ungracious ones might have hinted that they were too good to be true; or rather, were not so good as they might be; since the best false teeth are those made with at least two or three blemishes, the more to look like life. (*CM,* 139–40)

The resemblance between Westervelt and Noble coveys a satirical indictment of Noble as a Gothic necromancer or devil figure whose personal beauty is a coverup for physical decrepitude.[29] As the negative qualifiers of his appearance suggest, he may even be a galvanized corpse or a hobgoblin in human form:

> A man neither tall nor stout, neither short nor gaunt; but with a body fitted, as by measure, to the service of his mind. For the rest, one less favored perhaps in his features than his clothes; and of these the beauty may have been less in the fit than the cut; to say nothing of the fineness of the nap, seeming out of keeping with something the reverse of fine

> in the skin; and the unsuitableness of a violet vest, sending up sunset hues to a countenance betokening a kind of bilious habit. (*CM,* 139)

Charlie Noble's physical vacuity may be compared to Melville's comments on Hawthorne's appearance in a letter to Duyckinck on February 12, 1851: "Still there is something lacking—a good deal lacking—in the plump sphericity of the man. What is that?—he doesn't patronize the butcher—he needs roast-beef, done rare" (*C,* 181). Evert Duyckinck had also called Hawthorne "a fine ghost in a case of iron" in a letter to his wife in August 1850 (Metcalf, 87). Significantly, Charlie Noble is constitutionally unable to drink wine or smoke cigars; his bizarre laugh is "a strange kind of cackle, meant to be a chirrup"; and his departure is necromantically arrested by Goodman's laying down of a magic circle of coins. Melville even plays on Noble's fictive origins in a conversational exchange between Noble and Goodman upon the arrival of the bottle of wine that Noble has ordered:

> This being set before the entertainer, he regarded it with affectionate interest, but seemed not to understand, or else to pretend not to, a handsome red label pasted on the bottle, bearing the capital letters, P.W.
>
> "P.W.," said he at last, perplexedly eying the pleasing poser, "now what does P.W. mean?"
>
> "Shouldn't wonder," said the cosmopolitan gravely, "if it stood for port wine. You called for port wine, didn't you?"
>
> "Why so it is, so it is!"
>
> "I find some little mysteries not very hard to clear up," said the other, quietly crossing his legs. (*CM,* 161)

The "handsome red label" here is likely a bow in the direction of Hawthorne's most famous romance. On the other hand, the cosmopolitan's ability to read the letters "P.W." on the wine label hints that he can read Noble's literary label—*P*rofessor *W*estervelt! Melville is also possibly drawing on the tavern scene in *Blithedale* in which Miles Coverdale drinks with Old Moody (*Blithedale Romance,* 180). Taken together, these allusions reveal that Melville has, paradoxically, assimilated Hawthorne's romance both as a creative model and as a vehicle of satire against its creator.[30]

In addition to Melville's use of *The Blithedale Romance* here, the portrayal of Charlie Noble includes a few covert allusions to Hawthorne's earlier two novels. For example, after Noble has railed against Polonius, whom he calls a "discreet, decorous, old dotard-of-state," Goodman attempts to defend the old courtier:

> "Now charity requires that such a figure—think of it how you will—should at least be treated with civility. Moreover, old age is ripeness, and I once heard say, 'Better ripe than raw.' "
>
> "But not better rotten than raw!" bringing down his hand with energy on the table.
>
> "Why, bless me," in mild surprise contemplating his heated comrade, "how you fly out against this unfortunate Polonius—a being that never was, nor will be. And yet, viewed in a Christian light," he added pensively, "I don't know that anger against this man of straw is a whit less wise than anger against a man of flesh. Madness, to be mad with anything."
>
> "That may be, or may not be," returned the other, a little testily, perhaps; "but I stick to what I said, that it is better to be raw than rotten. And what is to be feared on that head, may be known from this: that it is with the best of hearts as with the best of pears—a dangerous experiment to linger too long upon the scene. This did Polonius." (*CM,* 173)

In Chapter 18 of *The House of the Seven Gables* ("Governor Pyncheon"), Judge Pyncheon—a "discreet, decorous, old dotard-of-state" like Polonius—also lingers too long upon the scene, as the narrator derisively moralizes over his blood-stained corpse. (Noble's reference to "pears" may also recall the Judge's hobby of pomology.) In addition, Noble's derisive attitude toward Polonius may have another source in the preface to *The Scarlet Letter,* in which Hawthorne had noted of the older customs officials:

> Externally, the jollity of aged men has much in common with the mirth of children; the intellect, any more than a deep sense of humor, has little to do with the matter; it is, with both, a gleam that plays upon the surface, and imparts a sunny and cheery aspect alike to the green branch, and gray, mouldering trunk. In one case, however, it is real sunshine; in the other, it more resembles the phosphorescent glow of decaying wood. (*Scarlet Letter,* 15–16)

Charlie Noble remarks of Polonius: " 'The ribanded old dog is paralytic all down one side, and that the side of nobleness. His soul is gone out. Only nature's automatonism keeps him on his legs. As with some old trees, the bark survives the pith, and will still stand stiffly up, though but to rim round punk, so the body of old Polonius has outlived his soul' " (*CM,* 173). As the reference to "nobleness" makes clear, Noble's harsh critique of Polonius mirrors its moribund speaker; Melville thus deflects Hawthorne's images of natural decay back onto a caricature of their creator. (The "side of nobleness" is the left side, the side of the heart, which Melville apparently thought deficient in Hawthorne's own composition.)

In addition to these buried allusions to Hawthorne's writings, the satiric portrait of Charlie Noble also incorporates a number of biographical details that confirm Noble's identity as a caricature of Hawthorne. For example, in an allusion suggesting Hawthorne's critical attitude to his New England forbears, Noble at one point makes a denigrating remark about the Puritans:

> "I do hope now, my dear fellow," said the cosmopolitan with an air of bland protest, "that, in my presence at least, you will throw out nothing to the prejudice of the sons of the Puritans."
>
> "Hey-day and high times indeed," exclaimed the other, nettled, "sons of the Puritans forsooth! And who be Puritans, that I, an Alabamaian, must do them reverence? A set of sourly conceited old Malvolios, whom Shakespeare laughs his fill at in his comedies." (*CM*, 170)

Charlie Noble's Southern origin may puzzle us in terms of its possible connection with Hawthorne, but this regional association is apparently part of Melville's strategy of satirical inversion and displacement here. Moreover, just as Melville had signed his review of Hawthorne's *Mosses,* "A Virginian Spending July in Vermont," he may now be crediting Hawthorne with a comparable Southern origin, but from the rank Deep South instead of courtly Virginia. Melville is also conceivably lampooning Hawthorne for his close association with the presidential administration of his college friend Franklin Pierce, which was widely perceived as pro-Southern. If this is indeed the case, Frank Goodman's act of putting gold coins in a circle around Noble conveys Melville's belief that Hawthorne literally "sold out" with his biography of Pierce in exchange for the lucrative Liverpool consulship. Hawthorne had himself written in "The Custom-House" of his earlier government service in the Polk administration:

> It is sadly curious to observe how slight a taste of office suffices to infect a poor fellow with this singular disease. Uncle Sam's gold—meaning no disrespect to the worthy old gentleman—has, in this respect, a quality of enchantment like that of the Devil's wages. Whoever touches it should look well to himself, or he may find the bargain to go hard against him, involving, if not his soul, yet many of its better attributes; its sturdy force, its courage and constancy, its truth, its self-reliance, and all that gives the emphasis to manly character. (*Scarlet Letter,* 39)

Melville's feelings of betrayal by Hawthorne may have been aggravated by the fact that Hawthorne was unable to help *him* get a suitable consular appointment in the spring of 1853, even though Hawthorne was a presumed prime agent in the distribution of patronage under Pierce.[31] We do not know whether Melville mentioned his financial difficulties to Hawthorne during this period, but it is significant that Melville's last meeting with Hawthorne in Concord on December 2, 1852, occurred just a month after Melville missed his second semiannual interest payment ($92.25) on his $2,050 loan from Tertullus Stewart. Whatever the exact biographical connection here, Frank Goodman's manipulation of Charlie would seem to dramatize Melville's grievances over the contrast between his own foundering career and financial woes at this time, in contrast to the growing magnitude of Hawthorne's literary and financial success.[32]

Finally, a few other small details of the Goodman–Noble encounter that can be related to biographical evidence may be listed here. After Goodman has requested money from Noble, Noble springs to his feet and buttons up his coat, "as if hastily to depart upon a long journey" (*CM,* 179), an action possibly related to the fact that Hawthorne went on a comparable journey to take up his Liverpool consulship in July 1853. Similarly, Goodman comments on the remarkably life-like "act" that Noble performs in rejecting Goodman's plea for help: " 'You played your part better than I did mine; you played it, Charlie, to the life' " (*CM,* 181)—as did Hawthorne. Goodman at one point observes that Noble is "touchy," a characteristic suggestive of Hawthorne's hatred of being touched (Mellow, 379). Noble's shady-looking demeanor as a reflection of Hawthorne's physical appearance is also attested, for example, by Longfellow's brother-in-law, Tom Appleton, who in 1844 remarked that Hawthorne looked like a "boned pirate," or Henry James, Sr., who commented to Emerson after meeting Hawthorne at the Saturday Club in the early 1860s: "Hawthorne isn't a handsome man nor an engaging one any way personally: he had the look all the time to one who didn't know him of a rogue who suddenly finds himself in a company of detectives" (quoted in Mellow, 242, 540).

Useful corroboration for Charlie Noble as a caricature of Hawthorne can be found in other writings of Melville's in which Hawthorne served as a literary model. William Dillingham has demonstrated that Hawthorne provided the buried biographical impetus for "The Piazza," a sketch written in early 1856 that functions, in part, as another fictive summation of Melville's attitude to his former friend:

> If Melville were disappointed that Hawthorne did not turn out to be a demigod who opened his arms to him, he was also a little disgusted with himself . . . for expecting so much, for being such a dreamer, and, in effect, for making such a fool of himself. Nevertheless, the friendship died when Melville discovered that there was a Marianna deep within Hawthorne, for that made him just another man instead of the master he had hoped for. "The Piazza" reviews the whole relationship, Melville's weariness and need of a savior, his hope when he caught the glimmer of Hawthorne's brilliance, his attempt to get to know his new

> friend, his startling discovery of inner weakness and weariness there, and Hawthorne's death as his friend. (*Melville's Short Fiction,* 334–35)

Dillingham notes that the structure of the encounter between the narrator and Marianna is that of a man wearied by life and illness who encounters a young woman whose own pathological weariness "shocks" the narrator back into a semblance of spiritual health—a meeting of doubles with an abrupt termination, as in the Goodman–Noble encounter. "The Piazza," in effect, rehearses a disillusioning spiritual quest utilizing the same motifs of enchantment and disenchantment and implying some of the same negative conclusions about Hawthorne as those found in *The Confidence-Man.*

Furthermore, as Walter Bezanson points out, in *Clarel* Melville again drew on his knowledge of Hawthorne for the creation of Vine, a mysterious middle-aged American artist notable for his reticence (*Cl,* 593–604). The depiction of Vine actually duplicates some of the same elements found in the portrait of Charlie Noble, including an attempt at close spiritual communion between Clarel and Vine (like that between the cosmopolitan and Charlie Noble) and a climactic "exposure" scene of Vine's weaknesses (*Cl,* 286–87). Clarel's first view of Vine is significant for our purposes:

> But who is he uncovered seen,
> Profound in shadow of the tomb
> Reclined, with meditative mien
> Intent upon the tracery?
> A low wind waves his Lydian hair
> A funereal man, yet richly fair—
> Fair as the sabled violets be. (*Cl,* 88)

His name recalling Charlie Noble's wish that a "vine" be planted on his grave, Vine, like Noble, is a character of ambiguous personal appeal who is (literally) overshadowed by death; moreover, just as Noble wore a "violet vest," Vine is associated here with the flower violet ("shyness" in contemporary flower language). Vine, like Noble, is also associated with the testing of gold, for the black "Lydian stone" alluded to above was used to test the purity of gold. From a biographical perspective, then, we can affirm that "The Piazza," *The Confidence-Man,* and *Clarel* all obliquely dramatize the ebb tide of Melville's enthusiasm for Hawthorne and an obsessive ambivalence toward his lost friend. (Melville's "Monody"—almost certainly commemorating Hawthorne's death—indicates that Melville felt as much grief as bitterness and disillusionment over his failed friendship with Hawthorne.)

In his biography of his father, Julian Hawthorne has described Hawthorne's psychological makeup in terms that are directly relevant to Melville's caricature of Hawthorne in *The Confidence-Man:*

> Now Hawthorne, both by nature and by training, was of a disposition to throw himself imaginatively into the shoes (as the phrase is) of whatever person happened to be his companion. For the time being, he would seem to take their point of view and to speak their language; it was the result partly of a subtle sympathy and partly of a cold intellectual insight, which led him half consciously to reflect what he so clearly perceived. Thus, if he chatted with a group of rude sea-captains in the smoking-room of Mrs. Blodgett's [Liverpool] boarding-house, or joined a knot of boon companions in a Boston bar-room, or talked metaphysics with Herman Melville on the hills of Berkshire, he would aim to appear in each instance a man like as they were; he would have the air of being interested in their interests and viewing life by their standards. Of course, this was only apparent; the real man stood aloof and observant, and only showed himself as he was, in case of his prerogatives being invaded, or his actual liberty of thought and action being in any way infringed upon. But the consequence may sometimes have been that people were misled as to his absolute attitude. Seeing his congenial aspect towards their little round of habits and beliefs, they would leap to the conclusion that he was no more and no less than one of themselves; whereas they formed but a tiny arc in the great circle of his comprehension. This does not seem quite fair; there is a cold touch in it; it has the look of amusing one's self at others' expense or profiting by their follies. The drunkard who complains that his companion allows him to get drunk, but empties his own glass over his shoulder, generally finds some sympathy for his complaint. Literally, as well as figuratively, it might have been said that Hawthorne should "drink square," or keep out of the way. There is nothing, however, to prevent the most contracted mind from perceiving that to be a student of human nature is not the same as to be a spy upon it. Nor can Hawthorne be charged with deception,—with pretending to be that which he was not. (1:88–90)

Here is a virtual resumé of Melville's satirical critique of Hawthorne as Charlie Noble. Indeed, the description of Hawthorne's deceptive drinking habits bears an uncanny resemblance to what transpires during the Noble–Goodman encounter. Frank Goodman's keeping a cool head while Noble plies him with drink no doubt represents Melville's belated response to his retrospectively embarrassing intoxication with Hawthorne in 1850–1851. Based on Julian Hawthorne's attempt to exonerate his father of the charge of heartlessness or even treachery, we may gather that Melville was not the only one to feel betrayed by Hawthorne's chameleon-like nature, which Melville characterizes as Charlie Noble's "warm air of florid cordiality, contrasting itself with one knows not what kind of aguish sallowness of saving discretion lurking behind it." We can also perhaps understand why Melville may have felt both emotionally and intellectually deceived by Hawthorne, who seemingly profited by Melville's "folly" of idolizing him, only to find himself a "tiny arc in the great circle" of Hawthorne's life instead of an inmate in Hawthorne's elusive, innermost magic circle.[33]

We may conclude that the genesis of the character of Charlie Noble grew out of Melville's perception in his *Mosses* review of Hawthorne as a literary "confidence man." Thus Charlie Noble's shady associations continue Melville's homage to Hawthorne as a fellow devil's disciple whose art was at odds with the optimistic tenor of American life. On the other hand, Melville's adaptation of Hawthorne's artist-magician figure, Professor Westervelt, implies that Melville saw in Hawthorne a depersonalized "scientific" interest in violating the human soul, a product of Hawthorne's identity as an artist as well as his inheritance of the Puritan obsession with moral scrutiny. Yet if Charlie Noble represents a skeptical reevaluation of Melville's relationship with Hawthorne, there can be no doubt that it is also steeped in the bitterness of wounded affection; it caricatures the worst of Hawthorne just as Melville's *Mosses* review loudly proclaimed the best. Moreover, just as Evert Duyckinck's "betrayal" in 1852 led to Duyckinck's extended caricature as Henry Roberts, Hawthorne's failure to fully respond to Melville's friendship—or his failure to live up to Melville's ideal—during roughly the same period led to an equally virulent caricature. This consecutive falling out with his closest friends—the one, his professional mentor for the first half of his active literary career, the other, his dominant literary inspiration for the latter half—undoubtedly compounded the latent bitterness of Melville's satire. (Melville figuratively conveys this covert history of betrayal by obliquely casting Duyckinck/Roberts in the role of the fallible apostle Peter while Hawthorne/Noble assumes the more perfidious role of Judas.) In sum, the character of Charlie Noble demonstrates that the much-debated "estrangement" between Melville and Hawthorne was not the product of a dramatic falling-out, but was rather a cumulative phenomenon resulting from Melville's hindsight into Hawthorne's troubled personality, the consolidation of Hawthorne's reputation at the same time as his own rejection by readers, critics, and publishers, and Melville's realization that his version of Hawthorne was possibly a projection of his own spiritual, emotional, and creative needs.

We do not know what Hawthorne thought of Melville's last novel and whether he recognized Charlie Noble as a caricature of himself. While it would seem an act of extraordinary subterfuge for Melville to involve Hawthorne in the actual publication of the novel, Melville could have considered the portrait sufficiently displaced to preclude discovery; or he might have felt "purged" of the novel's subversive content, as when he wrote Hawthorne concerning *Moby-Dick,* "I have written a wicked book, and feel spotless as the lamb" (*C,* 212); or he could have considered it the consummate (or desperate) act of one literary confidence man to another. Whatever Melville felt is impossible to determine, but it is not the least irony of Melville's meeting with Hawthorne in November 1856 that Hawthorne at this time wrote a moving tribute to Melville that contained a profound insight into Melville's character, at the same time that Melville had just completed a telling fictive caricature of *his* erstwhile friend, one containing an equally astute if more unflattering insight into Hawthorne's character.[34]

There is black humor in this, as there is in the fact that Hawthorne himself had twenty years earlier written an essay on April Fools' Day for the *American Magazine of Useful and Entertaining Knowledge:*

> It is a curious fact, that the custom of making April Fools prevails in the most widely separated regions of the globe. . . . It is desirable to have the privilege of saying, on one day in the year—what we perhaps think, every day—that our acquaintances are fools. But the false refinement of the present age has occasioned the rites of the holyday to fall somewhat into desuetude. It is not unreasonable to conjecture, that this child's play, as it has now become, was, when originally instituted, a vehicle of the strongest satire which mankind could wreak upon itself. (Turner, *Hawthorne as Editor,* 106–107)

After cataloguing a list of potential April fools in his survey of this useful institution, Hawthorne concluded by invoking a universal sphere of human folly: "And now let the whole world, discerning its own nonsense, and humbug, and charlatanism, and how in all things, or most, it is both a deceiver and deceived—let it point its innumerable fingers, and shout in its own ear—Oh, World, you April Fool!" (Turner, *Hawthorne as Editor,* 108). That Hawthorne was deeply implicated in Melville's literary version of the project outlined above would seem an act of poetic justice.[35]

MARK WINSOME, THE CRAZY BEGGAR

The identification of the mystic, Mark Winsome, as a caricature of Emerson has long been accepted in criticism of the novel.[36] However, a critical review of this identification that takes additional evidence into account will provide a sharper focus than has heretofore been possible. Melville's attendance at a lecture by Emerson on "Mind and Manners in the Nineteenth-Century" in Boston on February 5, 1849 effectively began his long-term, ambivalent reaction to Emerson's personality and thought. So much is evident in Melville's report of this firsthand encounter to his friend Duyckinck in New York. Claiming not to "oscillate in Emerson's rainbow," Melville nevertheless thought that Emerson was "more than a brilliant fellow" and "an uncommon man" chiefly because he was a fearless thought-diver:

> Swear he is a humbug—then is he no common humbug. . . . I was very agreeably disappointed in Mr Emerson. I had heard of him as full of transcendentalisms, myths & oracular gibberish. . . . To my surprise I found him quite intelligible, tho' to say truth, they told me that that night he was unusually plain.—Now, there is a something about every man elevated above mediocrity, which is, for the most part, instinctively perceptible. This I see in Mr Emerson. And frankly, for the sake of argument, let us call him a fool;—then had I rather be a fool than a wise man.—I love all men who *dive*. (*C*, 121)

Yet despite his admiration, Melville still imputed to Emerson an obtuse egotism, or "the insinuation, that had he lived in those days when the world was made, he might have offered some valuable suggestions" (*C*, 121). Melville also acknowledged the accuracy of Duyckinck's complaint about the unsociability of Emerson's nature, which was "above munching a plain cake in company of jolly fellows, & swiging off his ale like you and me" (*C*, 122); but he facetiously made this into a problem of anatomy: "Ah, my dear sir, that's his misfortune, not his fault. His belly, sir, is in his chest, & his brains descend down into his neck, & offer an obstacle to a draught of ale or a mouthful of cake" (*C*, 122). (Photographs of Emerson's columnar neck and diminutive chest suggest a physical basis for Melville's anatomical caricature.)[37]

After this first direct exposure to Emerson the lecturer in early 1849, Melville's subsequent acquaintance with Emerson's writings is not documented beyond his reading of some unidentified essays at Hawthorne's house in Lenox in early September 1850 (*Log*, 2:925). Nevertheless, his extensive familiarity with Emerson's thought can be seen in the skeptical, or even scathing, allusions to transcendentalist doctrine in *Moby-Dick, Pierre,* and such short fiction as "Cock-A-Doodle-Doo!" and the first half of "Poor Man's Pudding and Rich Man's Crumbs." While these fictionalized criticisms respond to different aspects of Emerson's thought, only in *The Confidence-Man* do we find Melville including a direct representation of Emerson's person in a character whose talk is a pastiche of pseudo-Emersonian pronouncements and whose behavior is keyed to Melville's criticisms of 1849.

Thus, as an embodiment of Emersonian egotism, Winsome oracularly descants on mystical matters to the cosmopolitan and then goes on to introduce Egbert as a "reflection" of his philosophy; whereupon the narrator wryly notes, "Though portions of this harangue may, perhaps, in the phraseology seem self-complaisant, yet no trace of self-complacency was perceptible in the speaker's manner" (*CM*, 198). Winsome also demonstrates a physical incapacity for conviviality by refusing Goodman's offer of wine, "due to constitution as much as morality." Even Melville's praise for Emerson in 1849 is satirically inverted in the character of Winsome, for Emerson's penchant for thought-diving now appears as mere floating on an inland waterway. As Winsome remarks, " 'Advance into knowledge is just like advance upon the grand Erie canal, where, from the character of the country, change of level is inevitable; you are locked up and locked down with perpetual inconsistencies, and yet all the time you get on' " (*CM,* 193).

Winsome's blithe acceptance of his own inconsistency here is confirmed by the conjunction of spiritual and materialistic elements in his character when first introduced: "Toning the whole man, was one-knows-not-what of shrewdness and mythiness, strangely jumbled; in that way, he seemed a kind of cross between a Yankee peddler and a Tartar priest, though it seemed as if, at a pinch, the first would not in all probability play second fiddle to the last" (*CM,* 189). Winsome's concluding words to Goodman in fact constitute a rationale for uniting mysticism and the marketplace, " 'for any philosophy that, being in operation contradictory to the ways of the world, tends to produce a character at odds with it, such a philosophy must necessary be but a cheat and a dream' " (*CM,* 198). Like Plotinus Plinlimmon, his Emersonian precursor in *Pierre,* who adduced a formula for reconciling heavenly ("chronological") and earthly ("horological") values in a "virtuous expediency," Winsome conjoins a canny materialism with a mystical idealism, a mixture that may be said to characterize Emerson's thought.[38]

In his first book, under the heading of "Discipline," Emerson had in fact expatiated on the beneficial lessons of the marketplace: "Debt, grinding debt, whose iron face the widow, the orphan, and the sons of genius fear and hate;—debt, which consumes so much time, which so cripples and disheartens a great spirit with cares that seem so base, is a preceptor whose lessons cannot be foregone, and is needed most by those who suffer from it most" (*Nature,* 24). "Prudence" and parts of other essays in his first two collections would inculcate comparable lessons. In a similar vein, "Power," "Wealth," and "Economy" were delivered as lectures in New York in early 1852, just when Melville was learning the bitter lessons of the marketplace from the reception and sales of *Moby-Dick*—lessons that in turn contributed to the virulent satire in the latter part of *Pierre.* In effect, while Emerson was calmly preaching the higher wisdom of economic law, Melville was discovering to his detriment that his most profound creations did *not* translate into success in the literary marketplace. Here perhaps was the heart of Melville's bitterness against Emerson's heartless reconciliation of God and Mammon.[39]

There has been some disagreement about which of Emerson's works contributed most of the character of Winsome, a problem compounded by the fact that Emerson's essays often contain similar-sounding conceptual ingredients. However, from the number of unmistakable echoes and the fact that it is generally recognized as Emerson's most concentrated formulation of his philosophy, we may conclude that *Nature* is Melville's chief satirical sourcebook (as Egbert Oliver originally argued), although a few likely allusions to some of Emerson's other works also contribute to the portrait.[40] The two main points in *Nature* that Melville is satirically highlighting are Emerson's Neoplatonic equation of beauty, goodness, and truth, and his insistence that the physical universe can be interpreted according to recognizable signs or emblems. Melville uses the first point to show up Emerson's naive nonrecognition of evil and the second to demonstrate the fact that the universe is more radically ambiguous than Emerson acknowledged. Melville is thus attacking Emerson for his solutions to the problem of evil and the related problem of knowledge—the two horns of Melville's own persistent religious and epistemological dilemmas.

Melville's starting point for his critique is the third chapter of *Nature,* entitled "Beauty." At the beginning of their encounter, Goodman's expressions of conviviality and hospitality strike Winsome as "beautiful conceits," leading him to remark to Goodman: " 'yours, sir, if I mistake not, must be a beautiful soul—one full of all love and truth; for where beauty is, there must those be' " (*CM,* 190). In this assertion, Winsome is echoing basic Neoplatonic and transcendentalist doctrine, as found, for example, in Emerson's concluding remarks in "Beauty": "Beauty, in its largest and profoundest sense, is one expression for the universe. God is the all-fair. Truth, and goodness, and beauty, are but different faces of the same All" (*Nature,* 17). Hearing Winsome's equation of love and truth with beauty, Goodman launches into a praise of the rattlesnake, effectuating a *reductio ad absurdum* of Winsome's idealism: " 'Yes, with you and Schiller, I am pleased to believe that beauty is at bottom incompatible with ill, and therefore am so eccentric as to have confidence in the latent benignity of that beautiful creature, the rattle-snake, whose lithe neck and burnished maze of tawny gold, as he sleekly curls aloft in the sun, who on the prairie can behold without wonder?' " (*CM,* 190). Not the least irony of this "beautiful" image, which echoes Milton's description of Satan's temptation of Eve, is that the rattlesnake is ready to strike the wondering observer! Emerson had in fact begun his chapter on "Beauty" with an insistence that all the forms of nature are equally beautiful:

> And as the eye is the best composer, so light is the first of painters. There is no object so foul that intense light will not make beautiful. And the stimulus it affords to the sense, and a sort of infinitude which it hath, like space and time, make all matter gay. Even the corpse has its own beauty. But beside the general grace diffused over nature, almost all the individual forms are agreeable to the eye, as is proved by our endless imitations of some of them, as the acorn, the grape, the pine-cone, the wheat-ear, the egg, the wings and forms of most birds, the lion's claw, the serpent, the butterfly, sea-shells, flames, clouds, buds, leaves, and the forms of many trees, as the palm. (*Nature,* 12–13)

Goodman's rattlesnake example recalls the beautiful serpent on Emerson's list, which the intense light of the sun makes agreeable to the eye.

Observing Goodman's imitation of the rattlesnake "with little surprise," Winsome goes on to ask whether its beauty isn't such as to make Goodman feel like becoming a snake himself:

> "When charmed by the beauty of that viper, did it never occur to you to change personalities with him? to feel what it was to be a snake? to glide unsuspected in the grass? to sting, to kill at a touch; your whole beautiful body an iridescent scabbard of death? In short, did the wish never occur to you to feel yourself exempt from knowledge, and conscience, and revel for a while in the care-free, joyous life of a perfectly instinctive, unscrupulous, and irresponsible creature?" (*CM,* 190)

(Significantly, the Emersonian "rainbow" in which Melville originally refused to oscillate is now Winsome's "iridescent scabbard of death.") Winsome's pantheistic union with the "viper" effectively parodies Emerson's famous "transparent eye-ball" passage in the first chapter of *Nature,* in which Emerson described the spiritual rejuvenation available in the "woods," where "a man casts off his years, as the snake his slough" (*Nature,* 10). Melville's satirical point in Winsome's identification with the rattlesnake is that Emerson's conception of nature blithely discounts the malignancy found in nature's dark half; and as Ishmael argued in "The Masthead," any intuitive identification with the pantheistic (or Neoplatonic) oneness of nature is as much an invitation to partake of death as it is of life. The other point deriving from Melville's satirical critique of *Nature* here is that Emerson's mystical "I-eye" rigorously excludes the rest of humanity, who are potentially only "a trifle and a disturbance." Thus when replying to the "infantile intellectuality" of Winsome's suggestion that he too be a snake, Goodman disavows the desire because then " 'there would be no such thing as being genial with men—men would be afraid of me, and then I should be a very lonesome and miserable rattle-snake' " (*CM,* 191).[41]

Goodman's trust in the "latent benignity" of the rattlesnake, then, is consistent with the tenets of Emerson's moral idealism and his well-known dismissal of the existence of evil, as in this assertion in his "Divinity School Address": "Good is positive. Evil is merely privative, not absolute. It is like cold, which is the privation of heat" (*Nature,* 78).[42] Goodman, pursuing his hypothesis to its logical end, enjoins a discussion of moral accountability that demonstrates the ethical problems of an Emersonian universe. In Chapter 5 of *Nature* ("Discipline"), Emerson claimed: "The moral law lies at the center of nature and radiates to the circumference. . . . The moral influence of nature upon every individual is that amount of truth which it illustrates to him. Who can estimate this?" (*Nature,* 26–27). Yet if nature seems to teach the murderous law of the jungle, should man follow this same "law"? Goodman raises such an issue when asking whether Winsome wouldn't agree, " 'that would be no symmetrical view of the universe which should maintain that, while to man it is forbidden to kill, without judicial cause, his fellow, yet the rattle-snake has an implied permit of unaccountability to murder any creature it takes capricious umbrage at—man included?' " (*CM,* 192). Goodman breaks off his investigation as "no genial talk" at this point because he has led the discussion through an incisive critique of Emerson's attempt to adduce a positive moral law from an amoral or malign nature.

A related critique of *Nature* that Melville invokes here is Emerson's insistence that nature is a text that can be read like a book. Melville's critique emerges from Winsome's assertion that the rattlesnake's rattle inculcates a "beautiful lesson," namely, that nature "labels" its creatures so that those bitten by a rattlesnake are at fault for ignoring the auditory warning label. At the beginning of *Nature,* Emerson had confidently announced: "Undoubtedly, we have no questions to ask which are unanswerable. We must trust the perfection of the creation so far, as to believe that whatever curiosity the order of things has awakened in our minds, the order of things can satisfy. Every man's condition is a solution in hieroglyphic to those inquiries he would put" (*Nature,* 1). At the end of the section on "Language," Emerson similarly wrote: "A life in harmony with nature, the love of truth and of virtue, will purge the eyes to understand her text. By degrees we may come to know the primitive sense of the permanent objects of nature, so that the world shall be to us an open book, and every form significant of its hidden life and final cause" (*Nature,* 23). The discourse of Winsome and Goodman is, in part, a comic refutation of Emerson's confidence in mankind's ability to read the book of nature, including the book of human nature. For the dramatic impetus behind the scene between Goodman and Winsome arises from Winsome's attempt to affix a "label" onto Charlie Noble, but the label keeps falling off.

Winsome begins by indulging in some mystical obfuscation that echoes the conclusion to *Nature:* " 'What are you? What am I? Nobody knows who anybody is. The data which life furnishes toward forming a true estimate of any being, are as insufficient to that end as in geometry one side given would be to determine the triangle' " (*CM,* 193).[43] When Goodman points out the inconsistency between this doctrine of "triangles" and that of "labels," Winsome cites his Erie Canal analogy to demonstrate that knowledge is only to be gained by being inconsistent. In answer to Goodman's renewed request for Noble's "label," Winsome produces an Egyptian word specified by a dash (presumably an Emersonian "solution in hieroglyphic"). When Goodman asks for a gloss, Winsome cites a definition from the Neoplatonic philosopher Proclus, again indicated by a dash. Not unexpectedly, Goodman requests the "favor" of an explanation, but Winsome claims ignorance of the meaning of "favor" as used by Goodman and mystically invokes a previous incarnation as the stoic Arrian to explain his ignorance of this word "in the current language of that former time" (the word "favor" is evidently "Greek" to him). Finally, after Winsome cites his mysterious Egyptian word again, Goodman himself makes fun of Winsome's impenetrability by punning on Winsome's claim that Noble is a "Mississippi operator," blithely misinterpreting "operator" to mean a doctor. All of this comedy of linguistic errors constitutes a rebuttal of Emerson's confident belief that the book of nature offers obvious lessons or "labels" that can be read in a reliable manner by Emersonian man.[44]

Winsome's persistent attempts to warn Goodman about Noble's shady character contain an added satirical dimension when we consider their underlying biographical models, and the association Hawthorne and Emerson may have had in Melville's mind. Melville would have learned in the preface to *Mosses from an Old Manse* that a few years before Hawthorne's first residence in Concord in the 1840s, Emerson wrote *Nature* at the Manse (which was built by Emerson's grandfather). The philosophical incompatibility of Hawthorne's Calvinism and Emerson's transcendental idealism is possibly a displaced biographical element in Winsome's antipathy to Noble.[45] But a more direct biographical source for the Noble–Winsome antagonism can be found in a passage in "The Old Manse" describing Hawthorne's relationship with Emerson during his stay in Concord:

> For myself, there had been epochs in my life, when I, too, might have asked of this prophet the master-word, that should solve me the riddle of the universe; but now, being happy, I felt as if there were no question to be put, and therefore admired Emerson as a poet of deep beauty and austere tenderness, but sought nothing from him as a philosopher. It was good, nevertheless, to meet him in the wood-paths, or sometimes in our avenue, with that pure, intellectual gleam diffused about his presence, like the garment of a shining-one; and he so quiet, so simple, so without pretension, encountering each man alive as if expecting to receive more than he could impart. And, in truth, the heart of many an ordinary man had, perchance, inscriptions which he could not read. (*Mosses*, 31)

Mark Winsome's comically belabored attempt to read Charlie Noble's "label" parallels Hawthorne's skeptical assessment of his Concord neighbor.

The "pure, intellectual gleam" that Hawthorne imputes to Emerson is a salient feature in Mark Winsome, who has a "pellucid blue eye," sits "purely and coldly radiant as a prism," defines a "favor" as " 'a bridal favor I understand, a knot of white ribands, a very beautiful type of the purity of true marriage,' " and drinks ice water, "its very coldness, as with some is the case, proving not entirely uncongenial." Melville is here describing a "coldness" Emerson acknowledged was part of his own nature. The representative test of Winsome's frigid nature occurs during the appearance of the crazy beggar toward the end of Winsome's encounter with the cosmopolitan. But here we must pause to examine the beggar as a caricature of Edgar Allan Poe.

Harrison Hayford has comprehensively demonstrated that Poe provided the model for the crazy beggar who seeks to interest Winsome and Goodman in his "rhapsodical tract." Even without a detailed review of the biographical evidence, however, there are a number of fairly overt allusions in the beggar's characterization to suggest Poe. Thus the peddler's sudden appearance while Winsome–Emerson is discoursing on the sublimity of death and mummies is an appropriate way to introduce the author of "Some Words with a Mummy" and other tales of the "grotesque and arabesque"; it may also be related to Poe's own premature death in October 1849, the same year as Melville's first encounter with Emerson. The initial description of the beggar provides a representative image of Poe in this connection: "Though ragged and dirty, there was about him no touch of vulgarity; for, by nature, his manner was not unrefined, his frame slender, and appeared the more so from the broad, untanned frontlet of his brow, tangled over with a disheveled mass of raven curls, throwing a still deeper tinge upon a complexion like that of a shriveled berry" (*CM,* 194–95). Here is Poe the decayed Southern aristocrat and sickly alcoholic, possessing the broad intellectual brow of Romantic "genius" overshadowed by unruly "raven" hair. The beggar's "ragged and dirty" clothes, however, are uncharacteristic of Poe's usual semi-respectable attire; but they would be appropriate for an evocation of Poe on his way to his squalid death in Baltimore, which makes Winsome's rejection of the beggar a re-creation of the failure of charity within the literary establishment that was alleged to have hastened Poe's end. It is also an implicit refutation of Melville's hope, expressed in his *Mosses* essay, for a mutually supportive plurality of geniuses in American literature (*PT,* 252–53).

The Confidence-Man was no doubt a suitable forum for the cameo appearance of a specialist in literary hoaxes, masquerades, and comic deviltry. In "Diddling Considered as One of the Exact Sciences," Poe had in fact anatomized the techniques of the contemporary confidence man before he was officially christened. There is no record of Melville and Poe ever meeting, but Melville clearly knew Poe's work and his notorious reputation; Evert Duyckinck, Poe's editor and supporter, would have provided information here. Moreover, Melville doubtless knew Poe's rhapsodic and apocalyptic *Eureka*—the prototype of the beggar's "rhapsodical tract"—which was given in lecture form as "The Universe" in New York on February 3, 1848, and published by Putnam (to little critical notice and a fourteen dollar advance) later that June, a time when Melville was himself exploring the universe of *Mardi.* Melville did not attend Poe's lecture, but he no doubt heard about it from his friend Duyckinck. As Perry Miller writes, "Evert Duyckinck, the patron if not quite the admirer of the author, told [his brother] George that Poe's performance was 'full of a ludicrous display of scientific phrase—a mountainous piece of absurdity for a popular lecture and moreover an introduction to his projected magazine—the Stylus: for which it was to furnish funds.' Duyckinck says that Poe succeeded only in driving people from the room" (*Raven and Whale,* 228).[46]

But the purpose of introducing the shade of Poe at this point is not primarily a joke at Poe's expense but rather a means of testing Winsome's charity in the same way that the silent pauper boy, and then Goodman himself, had earlier tested Charlie Noble's. Winsome inevitably fails the test when he judges the crazy beggar a fraud, thereby overlooking the fact that his theatrical madness is a tragicomic reflection of Winsome's own manufactured mysticism. As Goodman notes after a quick perusal, the beggar's "addled dream of glory" is "quite in the transcendental vein."[47] From Goodman's own more kindly treatment of the beggar, we may assume that Melville's sympathies were with the shade of Poe, whose rejection by Winsome—a repetition of Goodman's rejection by Noble—would seem to duplicate Melville's own experience in the literary marketplace, as Joel Porte notes:

> Thus Melville is suggesting that Emerson is Transcendental only north-north-west; when the wind blows from State Street, he knows how to hang onto his coins. Of course, Melville's interview is imaginary; and he is hardly fair to Emerson by insinuating that the latter was a pennypinching hypocrite. But by 1857 Melville's bitterness over his own failed career was sufficiently strong so that he felt compelled to let his audience know, however cryptically, that in the literary world there decidedly were haves and have-nots. Genius was going a-begging, and he and Poe were brothers in dispossession. (*Representative Man,* 267)

The scene here may also remind us of the factional war Poe fought in the mid-1840s against the Transcendentalists and other assorted voices from the Boston "frog pond." Poe had first indicated his estimate of Emerson in his series on "Autography" in *Graham's Magazine* (January 1842): "Mr. Ralph Emerson belongs to a class of gentlemen with whom we have no patience whatever—the mystics for mysticism's sake. Quintilian mentions a pedant who taught obscurity, and who once said to a pupil 'this is excellent, for I do not understand it myself.' How the good man would have chuckled over Mr. E!" (*Complete Works,* 15:260). A similar criticism was repeated in a posthumously published essay in *Graham's* (January 1850), entitled "About Critics and Criticism," in which Poe characterized the literary style of Emerson and his school as "an assumption of airs or *tricks* which have no basis in reason or common sense. The quips, quirks, and curt oracularities of the

Emersons, Alcots [*sic*] and Fullers, are simply Lily's Euphuisms revived" (*Complete Works,* 13:195). Mark Winsome is similarly exposed as a mystical performer of transcendental "tricks" whose outrage over the beggar's simulated madness combines Winsome's habitual solipsism with the canny perception of unauthorized intellectual competition. Goodman's telling reply to Winsome's dismissal of the beggar as a fraud (" 'invidious critics might object the same to some one or two strolling magi of these days' ") is a palpable hit at Winsome's mystical-theatrical flair, a burlesque of Emerson's oracular performances on the lecture circuit. It is relevant to note that Emerson was crisscrossing the country in the early and mid-1850s, having first ventured into the Mississippi and Ohio valleys in the spring of 1850 (von Frank, Ch. 7). Melville might well conceive that Emerson's mystical-material synthesis was helping to promote a self-reliant or selfish individualism nationwide. Indeed, Mary Kupiec Cayton has examined the relationship between Emerson and his midwestern audiences at this time, concluding that "Emerson's presence and message became implicated in the expansion of the commercial culture that sponsored his visits" (614–15). Such would explain the aggressive exaggerations that Melville uses to deflate Winsome–Emerson's pretensions to spreading his mystical "gospel," with its implicit inversions of the Sermon on the Mount. In the ensuing sequence with Winsome's "practical disciple," Egbert, we see the transcendental ethics of this counterfeit Christ put into practice by a mock St. Paul.

EGBERT

The question of how closely Egbert is modeled on Henry David Thoreau has remained something of a moot point in criticism of the novel largely because the resemblance does not appear as salient as that of Winsome–Emerson. Nevertheless, additional evidence only confirms the supposition that Egbert is an authentic Thoreauvian caricature who mimics Thoreau's person, his writings, and his status as a transcendental "disciple" of Emerson. Melville would have learned much about Thoreau from conversations with Hawthorne and Duyckinck, as well as from his reading of *A Week on the Concord and Merrimack Rivers* and *Walden.*[48] Melville's visit to Hawthorne in Concord on December 2, 1852 may also have included an exposure to—or at least talk about—Thoreau, which would explain the accuracy of Melville's presentation of the physical characteristics of Thoreau as Egbert. These include a "neuter sort" of countenance, a commercial-looking "sharp nose and shaved chin," and a rigidly erect body "like one of those wire men from a toy snuff-box," the latter characterization evoking Thoreau's small, erect stature, while also functioning as a visual pun on the principle of "self-reliance."

Egbert's introduction as Winsome–Emerson's "practical disciple" closely accords with contemporary views of the Emerson–Thoreau relationship. As

Walter Harding writes, "It is amusing how far some went in accusing Thoreau of imitating his neighbor. Lowell, visiting Concord, wrote a friend that Thoreau so imitated Emerson's tone and manner that with his eyes shut he wouldn't know them apart" (66). The young F. B. Sanborn thought him "a sort of pocket edition of Emerson" (quoted in Harding, 353). Emerson's own journal notations demonstrate his sense of Thoreau's imitativeness: "In reading [Thoreau], I find the same thought, the same spirit that is in me." Indeed, "Thoreau gives me, in flesh and blood and pertinacious Saxon belief, my own ethics. He is far more real, and daily practically obeying them, than I" (quoted in Harding, 66, 303–304). Melville could hardly have known it, but Winsome's words introducing Egbert are almost an exact echo of Emerson: " 'You, Egbert, by simply setting forth your practice, can do more to enlighten one as to my theory, than I myself can by mere speech. Indeed, it is by you that I myself best understand myself' " (*CM,* 197–98).

As a naturalist, surveyor, carpenter, handyman, and pencil manufacturer, Thoreau was clearly more "practical" than his mentor. Egbert's status as a "practical poet in the West India trade" has nevertheless remained a stumbling block for those critics who cannot reconcile it with Thoreau's antipathy to the "curse of trade" (as he phrased it in *Walden*). Yet Egbert's business affiliation is no doubt partly based on Thoreau's own business persona in *Walden*. Leonard Neufeldt has in fact demonstrated how closely *Walden* resembles the young men's guides and success manuals of the era: "The protracted labor on *Walden* secured its success, made 'success unexpected in common hours' its theme, and increasingly identified enterprising young men eager for success as its internalized readers. As such, *Walden* presented itself as a success manual, a guidebook for devotes of success in a culture of enterprise" (66).[49] Thoreau's whole first chapter was, after all, a lesson in "Economy" in which his experiment in living was figuratively described as a business venture:

> I determined to go into business at once, and not wait to acquire the usual capital, using such slender means as I had already got. My purpose in going to Walden Pond was not to live cheaply nor to live dearly there, but to transact some private business with the fewest obstacles; to be hindered from accomplishing which for want of a little common sense, a little enterprise and business talent, appeared not so sad as foolish.
>
> I have always endeavored to acquire strict business habits; they are indispensable to every man. If your trade is with the Celestial Empire, then some small counting house on the coast, in some Salem harbor, will be fixture enough. You will export such articles as the country affords, purely native products, much ice and pine timber and a little granite, always in native bottoms. These will be good ventures. (*Walden,* 19–20)

Thoreau's famous credo in "Where I Lived and What I Lived For" also mimics the habits of the Yankee trader: "to cut a broad swath and shave close, to drive life into a corner, and reduce it to its lowest terms, and, if it proved to be mean, why then to get the whole and genuine meanness out of it, and publish its meanness to the world" (*Walden,* 91). From a selective reading of *Walden,* Melville probably considered Thoreau a "practical poet" suited for the commercial milieu he used as a figurative standard of conduct in his writings.

Yet whatever oblique references to *Walden* there may be here, the more overt target of Melville's satirical critique of Thoreau is (as Egbert Oliver first indicated) his essay on Friendship incorporated into "Wednesday" of *A Week on the Concord and Merrimack Rivers.* In this essay, Melville no doubt found Thoreau's frigid idealisms so close to those found in Emerson's own essay on Friendship that the uniformity of master's and disciple's remarks suggested a combined attack on both this transcendental Christ figure and his mock St. Paul. Whether denominated charity or brotherly love, Paul's *agape* of I Corinthians 13 was a central tenet of Christ's new brotherhood of man. Egbert, on the other hand, teaches a forbidding version of *agape* that sees friendship or brotherly love as an impossibly exalted relation not to be soiled by the everyday needs of living human beings. Melville's indignation at this aspect of Emersonian philosophy culminates in the cosmopolitan's dismissal of Egbert after a searching examination of what might be called the Transcendentalists' pseudo-*agape;* Egbert–Thoreau thus acts as a "pocket edition" of the gospel of Winsome–Emerson.[50]

Following Emerson's example, Thoreau's essay is founded on the notion that true friendship is an ideal construct that cannot exist in flesh and blood, and thus is above all worldly considerations such as lending your friend assistance in times of need. This notion is in fact diametrically opposed to the notion of Christian "charity," and Frank Goodman sets up his hypothetical case to test Egbert's charity with such considerations in mind. The hypothetical "Frank" will be " 'a common man, with no more philosophy than to know that when I am comfortably warm I don't feel cold, and when I have the ague I shake' " (*CM,* 201). In other words, "Frank" will play Everyman, and "Charlie" will be his bosom friend who, when solicited for a loan, will adduce Mark Winsome's philosophy of friendship. "The Hypothetical Friends" dramatizes this solicitation, the crux of which is stated by Charlie early in the debate: " 'I give away money, but never loan it; and of course the man who calls himself my friend is above receiving alms. The negotiation of a loan is a business transaction. And I will transact no business with a friend. What a friend is, he is socially and intellectually; and I rate social and intellectual friendship too high to degrade it on either side into a pecuniary make-shift' " (*CM,* 202–203).

This policy is directly derived from Thoreau's "Friendship," for in Thoreau's view the true friend is above material considerations:

> To say that a man is your Friend, means commonly no more than this, that he is not your enemy. Most contemplate only what would be the accidental and trifling advantages of Friendship, as that the Friend can assist in time of need, by his substance, or his influence, or his counsel. . . . We do not wish for Friends to feed and clothe our bodies,—neighbors are kind enough for that,—but to do the like office to our spirits. For this few are rich enough, however well dispose they may be. (*A Week,* 266)

The true friend also scorns the notion of Christian charity:

> Friendship is not so kind as is imagined; it has not much human blood in it, but consists with a certain disregard for men and their erections, the Christian duties and humanities. . . . When the friend comes out of his heathenism and superstition, and breaks his idols, being converted by the precepts of a newer testament; when he forgets his mythology, and treats his friend like a Christian, or as he can afford; then Friendship ceases to be friendship, and becomes charity; that principle which established the almshouse is now beginning with its charity at home, and establishing an almshouse and pauper relations there. (*A Week,* 275–76)

"Charlie's" argument is in fact an elaborate excuse not to lend his friend money based on Thoreau's anti-Christian, transcendental distinction between the higher and lower friends, the one pure and the other tainted by charity or expediency. Thus "Charlie" points out the fact that loans involve strict financial arrangements that can't be termed friendly because of the possible enmity latent in infringement of the terms of the loan. When "Frank" suggests that some of these terms be waived, "Charlie" claims that any kind of loan is a violation of the pact between the higher friends and goes on to cite his " 'sublime master, who, in his Essay on Friendship, says so nobly, that if he want a terrestrial convenience, not to his friend celestial (or friend social and intellectual) would he go; no: for his terrestrial convenience, to his friend terrestrial (or humbler business-friend), he goes' " (*CM,* 204). The reference to Emerson's "Friendship" is patent:

> Why should we desecrate noble and beautiful souls by intruding on them? Why insist on rash personal relations with your friend? Why go to his house, or know his mother and brother and sisters? Why be visited by him at your own? Are these things material to our covenant? Leave this touching and clawing. Let him be to me a spirit. A message, a thought, a sincerity, a glance from him, I want, but not news, nor pottage. I can get politics, and chat, and neighborly conveniences, from cheaper companions. Should not the society of my friend be to

> me poetic, pure, universal, and great as nature itself? Ought I to feel that our tie is profane in comparison with yonder bar of cloud that sleeps on the horizon, or that clump of waving grass that divides the brook? (*Essays: First Series,* 123)

Faced with Winsome–Emerson's official doctrine of friendship, "Frank" tries to find an argument or appeal that will allow him to remain a friend and still qualify for a loan. But such appeals are of no avail, for the needier "Frank" becomes in his pleas, the more dismissive and cruel "Charlie" becomes, the opposite of that exaltation of the needy stated in the Sermon on the Mount and confirmed in I Corinthians. To "Frank's" cry for help, "Charlie" only notes, " 'How foolish a cry, when to implore help, is itself the proof of undesert of it' " (*CM,* 206). In all his remarks, "Charlie" is armed with his master's prudential philosophy, a pseudo-*agape* that doesn't even honor the Golden Rule. For when "Frank" poses the case of "Charlie" himself needing a loan at some point, "Charlie" rejects such a case, citing this time not the authority of Winsome but the homiletic example of China Aster.

It should be noted that in Egbert's transformation into "Charlie" during this scene, Melville is also possibly evoking the long-term friendship of Thoreau and Hawthorne which began during Hawthorne's Old Manse period. Despite some reservations, Hawthorne clearly admired the young naturalist and social critic.[51] As Hawthorne wrote to Duyckinck in 1845, Thoreau "is the most unmalleable fellow alive—the most tedious, tiresome, and intolerable—the narrowest and most notional—and yet, true as all this is, he has great qualities of intellect and character" (*Letters 1843–1853,* 106). Having read *A Week* at roughly the same time he met Hawthorne in the summer of 1850, Melville no doubt discussed its author during Hawthorne's residence in the Berkshires. According to a literary memoirist, Hawthorne referred to his visit to Melville at Arrowhead in March 1851 as "A Week on a Work-Bench in a Barn" (*Log,* 1:407). (The two had spent much of their time together in Melville's barn.) Melville's disappointment over the demise of his friendship with Hawthorne no doubt included an ironic appreciation (or even jealousy) of the fact that the "unmalleable" Thoreau may have ultimately been closer to Hawthorne than the man who proclaimed his genius to the world and dedicated his greatest novel to him. Consequently, Egbert's assumption of the character of "Charlie" and his discussion with Frank on the subject of friendship constitute a displaced exploration of Melville's failed friendship with Hawthorne. From this perspective, Goodman's dismissal of "Charlie" would represent a belated revenge on Hawthorne's emotional frigidity wherein Melville's original "infinite fraternity of feeling" is vindicated against the pseudo-*agape* of his Concord contemporaries.

Melville's caricature of Thoreau in the person of Egbert does not accord well with our contemporary view of Thoreau as a pioneering naturalist, ecologist, and social critic, but it should not be forgotten that Thoreau in his time often elicited harsh criticism as a perverse and forbidding character. Even as close a friend as Ellery Channing could in 1853 pen a scathing portrait:

> Behold H D T, he who believed in simplicity, he who has gone steadily along over the rough places and the thorns, in order to crucify and to kill out the human virtues, to render himself a Spartan. Each social faculty in which all others delight, he mortifies. Behold the victim of mortification. On him neither beauty nor goodness; you have him there, eminently chaste and abstinent, and at the same time dry as husks. His abstinence and his chastities have made him only doubly repulsive to his kind. (quoted in Harding, 306)

Melville's judgment is substantially the same, for Egbert is impossibly "chaste and abstinent" in his ideals of friendship, and equally repulsive to his kind, as the cosmopolitan's dismissal indicates.[52]

Melville's indictment of Emerson and Thoreau in the persons of Winsome and his disciple Egbert represents the most transparent personal satirical attack in the novel. Melville is implying that, based on certain key texts, Emerson and Thoreau are heartless New England skinflints whose resistance to charity and absence of sympathy are gross deficiencies in both their idealizing philosophies and Puritan temperaments. Melville is writing as a champion of the heart, a spiritual New Yorker repulsed by the frigid intellectualisms of transcendental New England. So we find repeated allusions to cold, chill, and ice in the scenes featuring these two characters, climaxed by the cosmopolitan's final ironic charity to Egbert: " 'And here, take this shilling, and at the first wood-landing buy yourself a few chips to warm the frozen natures of you and your philosopher by' " (*CM*, 223). In view of this climax of revulsion, it is appropriate that Winsome and Egbert bring to an end Melville's satire on his literary contemporaries as he turns once more to family members for models in the final sequence of the novel.[53]

In this and the previous chapter, we have seen that virtually all of the major characters of *The Confidence-Man* are based on biographical models. This finding runs counter to long-standing critical belief that *The Confidence-Man* is an exception to Melville's general reliance on his own experiences as the raw material for much of his fiction. It must be acknowledged, however, that most of the biographical subtext in *The Confidence-Man* is hidden from the reader. Melville is thus avoiding the notorious "personal" element of satire, which during the eighteenth century was frequently criticized as symptomatic of the spitefulness of the writer of satire. Yet many commentators recognized that the remedial, corrective mission of satire—its justification in most defenses—seemed to mandate a license to attack knaves and fools by name, or under a transparent pseudonym.[54] On the other hand, satirists have traditionally disguised their full meanings under various layers of allegory and indirection, as Melville is doing here. Moreover, both the intimately personal nature of much of his biographical satire in *The Confidence-Man* and the demands of aesthetic distance must have also played a role in Melville's obliquity of method in the novel—a distance that Melville had failed to maintain in *Pierre* and then had paid the price in popularity for doing so.

7

Interior Fables: Misanthropes and Philanthropists

In the last two chapters we have explored the covert biographical dimension of Melville's satire. We now turn to the subject of the novel's four so-called interior fables—the stories of Goneril, John Moredock, Charlemont, and China Aster—which function as representative fictions mirroring the larger satirical universe of the narrative. As a portrait gallery of Theophrastan "characters," the four fables thematically operate as antithetical moral exempla, thereby figuring the traditional rhetorical division of satire into *vituperatio* and *laus,* blame and praise. Two of them originating with the Confidence Man and two with characters bearing the name "Charlie" (Egbert is in the role of "Charlie" when he narrates the story of China Aster), the fables reinforce the novel's pervasive network of binary oppositions and moral polarities. Indeed, as we will see in this chapter, the protagonists of the first two stories are typologically associated with Satan, and the protagonists of the second two with Christ. The fables accordingly mirror the novel's division of the world into knaves and fools, victimizers and victims, misanthropes and philanthropists.

One particular aspect of the fables that has drawn repeated comment is their oblique manner of narration, for in three out of four stories the narrator deflects responsibility for the story onto another source.[1] While some critics have considered this fact a symptom of Melville's skeptical epistemology in the novel, it actually constitutes a well-known literary strategy, for as Hershel Parker remarks, "the pretense of telling a story in a more formal style is a literary convention, just as much as an author's dissociating himself from his material is. The influences on Melville's practices stretch back at least as far as the eighteenth-century convention of treating the presumed author as a mere editor" ("Use of Evidence," 122). Moreover, while they implicitly parody the sensational and sentimental tendencies of antebellum popular literature, the fables also continue the covert biographical satire we have already seen operating throughout the novel, thereby adding new features to Melville's caricatures of Duyckinck, Hawthorne, Emerson, and Thoreau. A critical examination of the interior fables within their biographical, historical, and theological frames of reference will demonstrate the multiplicity of Melville's satirical strategies and targets here.

GONERIL

Ostensibly told as a sentimental tearjerker, the novel's first interior fable, the story of Goneril in Chapter 12, may remind us of a well-known subgenre of satire against women. Indeed, the narrator's allusion to the Roman stoic Thrasea at the beginning of the story evokes the era that produced one of the most notorious examples of this tradition, Juvenal's Sixth. However, the more explicit literary context for the story of Goneril is, as her name implies, Shakespearean. Goneril is a modern burlesque of the feminine "mystery of iniquity" and sexual perversity that contributes to the dark moral backdrop of *King Lear*. Yet the story of Goneril is patently no Shakespearean tragedy of cosmic proportions but is instead a domestic black comedy in which the female villain is synthesized out of a well-known contemporary actress and a legendary she-devil.

Egbert Oliver first suggested Melville's use of Fanny Kemble (1809–1893) as a model for Goneril.[2] A member of a famous theatrical family, Kemble had prematurely retired from the stage in 1834 to marry a wealthy Philadelphian, Pierce Butler, the descendant of a prominent Georgia family of slaveholders and himself the owner of a Georgia plantation. After over a decade of marital strife, the couple was finally divorced in 1849, thereby ending a legal battle that was avidly covered by the national press.[3] In February 1849, at the height of the Kemble–Butler divorce scandal, Melville while visiting Boston had heard Fanny Kemble perform one of her readings of Shakespeare which she undertook to support herself at this time. As he somewhat indelicately reported to Duyckinck, "She makes a glorious Lady Macbeth, but her Desdemona seems like a boarding school miss.—She's so unfemininely masculine that had she not, on unimpeachable authority, borne children, I should be curious to learn the result of a surgical examination of her person in private. The Lord help Butler—not the poet—I marvel not he seeks being amputated off from his matrimonial half" (*C*, 119–20). Melville may have later come in contact with Kemble during his residence in Pittsfield, for she resided in Lenox part-time after her divorce and was an acquaintance there of the Hawthornes. Melville almost certainly heard of Kemble's activities in the area, for she became a local item of gossip partly owing to her adoption of masculine attire for her favorite sports of riding, fishing, and archery.

Whatever the exact extent of Melville's personal acquaintance with Kemble, his letter to Duyckinck contains the germ of his later fictional portrait of Goneril based on an exposure to Kemble as a Shakespearean interpreter at the height of her divorce scandal. This is confirmed by the fact that Melville's fictional guise for this phase of his career, John Ringman, originally tells the story of Goneril to Henry Roberts in Chapter 4 of the novel. Melville's judgment that Kemble excelled as Lady Macbeth no doubt facilitated her transformation into another example of Shakespeare's imperiously "phallic" women. This well-known Shakespearean interpreter probably figured as the same feminine type in Melville's imagination.

Evidence of the physical caricature of Fanny Kemble in the character of Goneril is fairly extensive. Thus Goneril's cheeks exhibit "a certain hardness and bakedness, like that of the glazed colors on stone-ware"; Kemble had what was described as a "muddy" complexion. Goneril is "in person lithe and straight, too straight, indeed, for a woman"; Kemble had been drilled in posture as a girl by a member of the British Guards. Goneril's "Indian" identity and rude health recall Kemble's love of outdoor sports like riding and archery. Finally, just as Melville had expressed doubts about Kemble's sexual identity in his letter to Duyckinck, the narrator conveys a doubtful impression of Goneril's femininity: "Her Indian figure was not without its impairing effect on her bust, while her mouth would have been pretty but for a trace of moustache. Upon the whole, aided by the resources of the toilet, her appearance at distance was such, that some might have thought her, if anything, rather beautiful, though of a style of beauty rather peculiar and cactus-like." The last image probably subsumes a pun on Goneril's ambiguous sexuality (cacti are "prickly"). The characterization of her vindictive behavior also has a phallic suggestiveness: "Like an icicle-dagger, Goneril at once stabbed and froze."

Not only is Goneril a "phallic" woman, as Melville perceived Fanny Kemble to be, but she is also an outspoken one: "In a large sense she possessed the virtue of independence of mind. Goneril held it flattery to hint praise even of the absent, and even if merited; but honesty, to fling people's imputed faults into their faces." A number of individuals noted Fanny Kemble's uncompromisingly judgmental nature. Even to an admirer, Charles Sumner, she was "peculiar, bold, masculine and unaccommodating" (quoted in Furnas, *Fanny Kemble,* 357). At the beginning of her marriage, Kemble had published the record of her American tour, *Journal of a Young Actress* (1835), which contained unflattering remarks on a number of individuals and invidious comments on the American scene.[4] Not long after his divorce, Pierce Butler wrote of his former wife: "There are two strongly marked features in her character—great energy of will, and a decided preference for her own judgment and opinions over those of every other person. Hence arose that sense of imagined oppression of which she so constantly complained, and which led her to offer a perverse opposition, not only on points of importance, but on matters comparatively insignificant, and to exhibit nonconformity and an unyielding spirit in everything" (*Statement,*

12–13). The tumultuous private history of the Kemble–Butler marriage had become public knowledge when Fanny published a widely reprinted *Narrative* (1847) outlining her version of the events leading to her final flight to England in 1845; Pierce Butler responded with his own *Statement* (1850), which attempted to vindicate his conduct and demonstrate the distortions in Fanny's *Narrative.* While they are more malicious than Fanny Kemble's actions, Goneril's attempts to slander and destroy her husband nevertheless suggest Kemble's outspoken campaign against Pierce Butler during the last stage of their marriage in 1844–1845 and then after Butler sued for divorce two years later. Significantly, at the conclusion of his *Statement,* Butler cast himself as the victim of an "evil touch" akin to Goneril's: "My divorce leaves me with but a single object worth pursuing, the vindication of my conduct as a husband and a father from the elaborated tissues of accusations which, I presume, she placed upon record on the exulting expectation that it would thus be made, like a shirt of Nessus, to stick to me forever" (188).

The circumstances of Goneril's fight with her husband recall some, but not all, aspects of the Kemble–Butler divorce proceedings. Like John Ringman, Pierce Butler kept his marital difficulties secret until his patience was exhausted; and like Ringman, who tries to protect his daughter from the baleful influence of his wife, Pierce Butler sought to shield his two daughters from their mother's erratic behavior. As in the legal contest between Ringman and Goneril, which Goneril pursues "at the suggestion of some woman's rights women," Fanny Kemble's divorce became a feminist cause célèbre enlisted in the incipient women's rights movement. On the other hand, unlike the story of Goneril, it was the husband, Pierce Butler, who initiated his divorce suit and gained custody of the children; neither were charges of derangement involved in Butler's contest with his wife (which suggests something of Melville's own marital history), nor was Fanny Kemble ever accused of sexual misconduct (this being a rumor associated with Butler himself), nor was Butler financially ruined by his divorce. Melville has selectively recast Fanny Kemble's history in order to satirize her overweening "phallic" nature and her well-publicized attack on male headship of the family. Apparently deficient in traditional feminine virtues, Fanny Kemble offended Melville's essentially chivalrous view of women; she was a Duessa, not a Una.[5]

Whatever the merits of this judgment, we need not charge Melville with the viciousness he is burlesquing in Goneril's character because Goneril is a serio-comic monster who, in significant respects, transcends her historical model. Melville's Goneril is so marginally human that the suspicion arises that she may actually be some kind of devil in human form. And the unrecognized underlying joke here stems from the fact that Goneril is in fact modeled on a certified she-devil, Lilith, the legendary first wife of Adam, whose conflict with her spouse led her to assume the identity of a demon and become the wife of the devil. In his portrait of Goneril, Melville has synthesized the basic core of this legendary material, including Lilith's quarrel with, and divorce from, her husband Adam, her position as satanic associate or "devil's dam," her role as lethal seductress of young men, and her penchant for preying on young children.[6]

A central element uniting Goneril and Lilith involves their shared marital difficulties, as Maximilian Rudwin notes:

> Talmudic tradition has it that Lilith was created simultaneously with Adam, both being joined together at the back, for it is written "male and female created He them, and called their name Adam." (Gen. i.27.) In this condition they constantly quarreled and tore at each other. Then the Lord repented that he had fashioned them in this way and separated them into two independent bodies; but even thus they would not live in peace. A mismated pair from the very start, their incompatibility of temperament was too great for peace. Their views differed considerably on the all-important question of the headship of the family. Lilith was the first woman to challenge masculine supremacy. This *Mater malorum* is said to have started the fight for equal rights for women by contesting her husband's claim to be the head of the family. (96)

Like Lilith and Adam, Goneril and her husband are a mismatched pair who quarrel and eventually divorce because of Goneril's pathological behavior and refusal to submit to her husband's authority. Seen in this light, Melville's dovetailing of the characters of Fanny Kemble and Lilith was an understandable gesture. Lilith was also a figure of sexual perversity, a femme fatale who seduced and snuffed out the lives of young men: "In Eastern tradition, Lilith, as princess of the succubi, is primarily a seductress of young men" (Rudwin, 101). Goneril similarly demonstrates her lubricity by giving "mysterious touches" to "comely young men." Lilith was equally notorious for her evil influence on young children: "In Talmudic tradition Lilith is primarily a demoness who selects small children as her special victims. . . . The hatred of Lilith for the children of men is, according to an old Jewish belief, the result of her jealousy of the mother of mankind, who replaced her in the affections of Adam and thus robbed her of the joys of motherhood" (Rudwin, 95). True to her legendary archetype, Goneril consummates her perversity by making a victim of her own daughter: "after all that had happened, the devil of jealousy entered her, a calm, clayey, cakey devil, for none other could possess her, and the object of that deranged jealousy, her own child, a little girl of seven, her father's consolation and pet."

From her close association with the figure of Lilith, it becomes apparent that Goneril is a female demon whose ties with humanity are tenuous, as her characterization at one point implies:

> Lithe though she was, she loved supineness, but upon occasion could endure like a stoic. She was taciturn, too. From early morning till about three o'clock in the afternoon she would seldom speak—it taking that time to thaw her, by all accounts, into but talking terms with humanity. During the interval she did little but look, and keep looking out of her large, metallic eyes, which her enemies called cold as a cuttlefish's, but which by her were esteemed gazelle-like; for Goneril was not without vanity. (*CM,* 61)

The implication here is that with her cold-blooded nature, Goneril not only shows "suspiciously serpentine traits" (Ramsey, " 'Touching' Scenes," 39), but is virtually identical with a snake. For like the serpent in Eden condemned by God to go on its belly and eat "dust" all the days of its life (Genesis 3:14), Goneril loves "supineness" and has a taste for sucking on "little dried sticks of blue clay." Commentators who cite the peculiarities of Southern "clay-eaters" here miss the subversive allusion to Genesis. Goneril's ophidian identity accords with one variant of the Lilith legend that cast her as the serpent in Eden seducing Adam and Eve in revenge for her displacement from Paradise, a scenario dramatized in Dante Gabriel Rossetti's contemporaneous poem, "Eden Bower." Goneril is in fact both snake-like in her vindictiveness and toad-like in her ability to give the "evil touch." Her hair, "worn in close short curls all round her head," also suggests the image of the snake-haired Medusa.

The virtual congruence of the snake-like Lilith and the monstrously behaved Goneril effectively answers the query posed by the narrator at the beginning of her story, "whether the human form be, in all cases, conclusive evidence of humanity." What appears to be merely a rhetorical question turns out to be a hint that in Goneril's case the human form is emphatically *not* a guarantee of humanity. And once we call the narrator's bluff, we discover that Goneril is in fact the perfect bride for the Adam-like Ringman, as well as for the Confidence Man in his mock-diabolic machinations in the first half of the novel. By the same token, the name of Goneril's husband, Ringman, is eminently suitable for one who has conjured up a devil for a wife, just as Goneril's "mysterious touches" are the sexual equivalent of the Confidence Man's uncanny ability to put the "touch" on the merchant (Porte, *Romance in America,* 164).

The irony of this performance is similarly illustrated by the discussion between Truman and Roberts after the story is told, during which Truman attempts to downplay Goneril's diabolism by denying any disturbing content to her story. Yet the subversive implication here is that such apologetics are, quite literally, a joke since all of Truman's pious jargon is a mere cover-up for Goneril's reptilian she-deviltry. The success of the fraud can be seen in the fact that Goneril's true nature goes completely unrecognized by the merchant. When we factor in the merchant's biographical model, it becomes apparent that the story of Goneril is a satirical afterpiece to Melville's fictionalized attack on his friend Duyckinck's optimistic faith.

It should be noted that the story of Goneril also constitutes a concentrated parody of contemporary popular culture, for Melville is performing here a virtuosic burlesque of the antebellum sentimental tradition. Mary Jean Northcutt provides a useful guide to Melville's deft handling of sentimental convention:

> Superficially, the story is a faultless example of a sentimental tale: it contains the requisite widow (in this case widower), orphan, villainous deed, and unmerited, patiently borne suffering. And like most sentimental novels of the time, the story is unerringly "domestic"—concerning marriage, family, and children. It remains only for Henry Roberts to put the final touch to the pattern by passing over money to the Man with the Weed and thereby affirming the sentimentalist belief that virtue will ultimately be rewarded both spiritually and monetarily. (128)

Melville's manipulation of his sentimental tale into a grotesque parody is followed by a similar manipulation of the tale's overly pat moral, thereby revealing the duplicitous nature of the sentimental ethos: "Roberts may be said to represent the 'pitying' surface of sentimentalism while [Truman], by his asseverations of the ultimate benignity of Providence, blatantly points out the callousness underlying the tradition" (Northcutt, 131). Although Ringman is ultimately vindicated by the unexpected demise of his "monstrous" wife, Melville demonstrates the absurdity of the sentimental tradition by making Goneril a burlesque embodiment of evil incarnate and then having John Truman argue that this disguised "devil's dam" was not so black as she was painted!

It goes without saying that Melville's parody of sentimental conventions in "Goneril" also involves self-parody of Melville's own "romance" conventions.[7] We have already observed that Goneril shares many features with *Mardi*'s equivalent Lilith-figure, Annatoo; she might also claim kinship with Pierre's poisonous sister-wife, Isabel. A burlesque *reductio ad absurdum* of the dark lady of romance, Goneril is a dangerous sexual being, her name and mysterious "touches" hinting at venereal disease and her noxious behavior evoking a host of *belles dames sans merci* of nineteenth-century Romanticism.

JOHN MOREDOCK

While the story of Goneril represents a bizarre "mystery of iniquity" in a domestic setting, Charlie Noble's story of John Moredock the Indian-hater focuses on a similar phenomenon on the nation's frontier. Moreover, while the story of Goneril exemplifies a sentimental disposition to discount the existence of evil, the story of John Moredock exemplifies an antithetical tendency to become pathologically obsessed with it. Divided into an analysis of the mythical figure of the Indian-hater *par excellence* and the historical John Moredock, the sequence is a "tall tale" of murderous misanthropy told by Noble while appropriating the identity of James Hall (1793–1868), author of the multiple fictional and nonfictional accounts of Indian-hating that helped create a cultural stereotype.[8]

The ostensible pretext for Noble's story is his initial observation to Goodman that Pitch "ain't quite so good a fellow at bottom" as Moredock because Pitch's misanthropy is too all-encompassing. By implication, Noble's story portrays a more concentrated form of misanthropy by showing an individual who focuses his hatred on a single race. Noble's ensuing tale in effect represents a bridge between the opposing worlds of the first and second halves of the novel, for it paradoxically illustrates both the seeming necessity and dire moral consequences of living according to a policy of radical mistrust. As Elizabeth Foster remarks, "In the large framework of the novel, the tale of the Indian-hater stands as the rooftree, being the culminating argument for skepticism and the forecast of a world without charity" (xci).

A prolonged critical controversy has focused on the question of whether John Moredock is represented as a hero or a villain, or even as an absurdist, serio-comic fabrication. The difficulty here stems partly from the ambiguous tone of the Indian-hating sequence and partly from the problematic intersection of allegorical and historicist modes of interpretation. Critics of an allegorical persuasion, who interpret the Confidence Man as the devil, are predisposed to consider Moredock an heroic opponent of the evil epitomized by the savage red men in the tale. Critics of an historicist persuasion, on the other hand, generally view Moredock as a deluded killer who typifies the nation's long history of injustices to the Indian. To complicate the issue, a third possibility has been suggested based on the assumption that the whole Indian-hating sequence is an improbable frontier fable with a fraudulent or unfathomable hero, in which case its meaning appears to collapse into an absurdist joke or an insoluble riddle.[9]

As an ambiguous dramatization of diametrically opposing values, the Indian-hating chapters occupy a parallel position in *The Confidence-Man* as Plinlimmon's pamphlet does in *Pierre,* both being labyrinthine ethical interludes that function as both crux and hoax. Yet despite the involutions of irony and narrative authority in this sequence, the seemingly antithetical interpretations of the Indian-hater are potentially reconcilable once we come to grips with Melville's belief in the ultimate interdependence of good and evil, for Moredock is potentially *both* hero *and* villain, while the comic absurdity found here also conveys Melville's belief in the potential void at the heart of (human) nature. The Indian-hating sequence in fact typifies a central ethical dilemma poised by the novel, that is, the conflict of absolute versus relative values: If evil exists as an absolute entity, then the Indian-hater is a hero. If, on the other hand, evil is a relative phenomenon, then the Indian-hater is a misguided killer. The ambiguity of this sequence is thus consonant with the paradoxical moral norm found throughout Melville's novel and, in turn, representative of the open-ended ethical inquiry often illustrated by satire. Furthermore, many of the story's textual complexities can be unraveled by using the biographical, social, and theological frames of reference we have been tracing throughout the novel.

On a biographical level, we should recall that Charlie Noble and Frank Goodman are displaced representatives of Hawthorne and Melville. From this perspective, the Moredock story grows out of both authors' obsession with the problem of evil as well as Melville's assimilation of Hawthorne's creative example. As noted earlier, Charlie Noble's narrative may be considered Melville's reformulation of his earlier epic hero Ahab in the fictionalized voice of the writer who provided the catalyst for his creation. Indeed, the career of the Indian-hater *par excellence* sounds like a radically condensed version of Ahab's quest, for the Indian-hater acts upon " 'a calm, cloistered scheme of strategical, implacable, and lonesome vengeance' " (*CM,* 149–50). And like much else in the Noble–Hawthorne caricature, Melville's *Mosses* review constitutes a key text for understanding the biographical backdrop to the Indian-hating chapters. There Melville had expressed his fascination with Hawthorne's moral vision of "blackness," arguing that "this great power of blackness in him derives its force from its appeals to that Calvinistic sense of Innate Depravity and Original Sin, from whose visitations, in some shape or other, no deeply thinking mind is always and wholly free" (*PT,* 243).

That Hawthorne was indeed concerned with such problems is confirmed by the extended visit Hawthorne paid to Melville at Arrowhead in mid-March 1851, which may have provided a biographical prototype for the Indian-hating sequence. As Elizabeth Melville later reported of this visit, "the two men passed most of their time discussing the profoundest problems of human life, philosophy, and even of theology. Hawthorne seemed to be especially absorbed in the problems of necessity, moral freedom, and evil in nature" (quoted in Scharnhorst, 2).[10] It is precisely these problems, conveying both writers' Calvinistic belief in man's fallen nature, that provide a backdrop to the chapters on Indian-hating. Indeed, this interlude constitutes a dramatic rendition of Hawthornean "blackness," showing the Indian-hater as compelled to exterminate what he considers a manifestation of evil after experiencing the frontier equivalent of the Fall.

Moredock is thus another version of the principal literary and psychological character type that Hawthorne offered as a creative example to Melville, a type for whom an obsession with the existence of evil eventuates in a kind of diabolical possession. As Richard Slotkin remarks, "Hawthorne's tales reflect a Puritan image of the wilderness as the land of the terrible unconscious, in which the dark dreams of man impress themselves on reality with tragic consequences. The hunter becomes like the beast he hunts; the would-be destroyer of bestial sin himself degenerates into a Belial" (475). Richard Brodhead, on the other hand, has analyzed Melville's appropriation of this Hawthornean character type, whom Brodhead calls a "daimonic hero": "The mark of this figure, as Melville reconstructs him, is that he has passed through a radical reorganization of selfhood, a process at once of extreme intensification and extreme reduction" (*School of Hawthorne,* 35). What Melville found in James Hall's story of the Indian-hater, John Moredock, was just such a monomaniacal "daimonic" hero whose intensification and reduction of selfhood leads to a *reductio ad absurdum* of heroic assertion against evil. Charlie Noble's impersonation of James Hall on Indian-hating is thus grounded in this strategic overlap of explicit and implicit literary models.

Yet there were additional reasons for the conflation of one of Hall's "western" narratives with the use of Hawthorne as a satirical model here. In a letter of June 1851, for example, Melville depicted Hawthorne and himself as beleaguered literary *isolatoes* who formed "a chain of God's posts round the world," for "in the boundless, trackless, but still glorious wild wilderness through which these outposts run, the Indians do sorely abound, as well as the insignificant but still stinging mosquitoes" (*C,* 195). And in the *Mosses* essay, Melville not only transformed Hawthorne into a "western" author synonymous with American nature (*PT,* 249), but also associated Hawthorne's ability to insinuate "dark" truths about the human condition with Shakespeare's ability to do the same: "Through the mouths of the dark characters of Hamlet, Timon, Lear, and Iago, he craftily says, or sometimes insinuates the things, which we feel to be so terrifically true, that it were all but madness for any good man, in his own proper character, to utter, or even hint of them" (*PT,* 244). Charlie Noble's assimilation into the personality of James Hall during the Indian-hating sequence constitutes just such a self-protective gambit.[11]

On the other hand, despite the dark truths implied by the Indian-hating chapters, we find here a number of sensational elements that undermine its high seriousness, potentially transforming it into burlesque. Thus, when first hearing the name of John Moredock at the beginning of Noble's yarn, Frank Goodman offhandedly asks, " 'was he any way connected with the Moredocks of Moredock Hall, Northamptonshire, England?' " (*CM,* 140). The question implicitly evokes the mock-heroic figure of "More of More Hall" who vanquished the Dragon of Wantley in the well-known ballad of the same name (collected in Percy's *Reliques*) by kicking him in the posteriors.[12] Noble's delivery of Judge Hall's story is also punctuated with several incongruous anticlimaxes, such as Noble's failure to gain a view of the sleeping Moredock, Goodman's interruption of Noble's bloody story to refill his

Indian "calumet" (i.e., peace pipe), or Noble's rendition of Hall's pompous tobacco "toast" to the memory of Moredock. William Ramsey has identified a number of other deflationary "moot points" in Charlie Noble's adaptation of Hall's text, including the bogus solemnity of comparing the heroic backwoodsman to the lowly "'possum," the sham creation of a treacherous chief "Mocmohoc" (literally, a "mock Mohawk"), and the similarity of some of this narrative material to contemporary stage burlesques on Indian themes.

These equivocal and parodistic elements in the Indian-hating sequence might lead one to the conclusion that Melville is reversing an earlier judgment of Hawthorne's literary strategies, as described in his *Mosses* review: "But unlike Shakespeare, who was forced to the contrary course by circumstances, Hawthorne (either from simple disinclination, or else from inaptitude) refrains from all the popularizing noise and show of broad farce, and blood-besmeared tragedy" (*PT,* 245). It is in fact just such elements of "broad farce" and "blood-besmeared tragedy" that Charlie Noble adds to James Hall's sober-minded account of Colonel John Moredock in his adaptation of this material in *The Confidence-Man*. The transformation would seem to demonstrate the impracticability of Melville's program for national authorship advanced in the *Mosses* review, for there Melville had predicted that American literature was soon going to surpass the achievements of Shakespeare: "Believe me, my friends, that Shakespeares are this day being born on the banks of the Ohio." With his literary headquarters in Cincinnati, James Hall was by the mid-1850s apparently the only writer Melville might cite as a fulfillment of this prediction. The burlesque elements in the Indian-hating sequence thus implicitly ridicule Melville's own overconfident prediction of the westerly march of literary empire.

Critics have disagreed about whether Melville is attacking James Hall as an apologist for his culture's crime of Indian extermination, or merely using him as a mouthpiece that Melville manipulates for other satirical ends.[13] Yet Noble's transformation of the historical James Hall into a propagandistic Indian-hater is hardly to be taken as Melville's own verdict on this minor chronicler of the early nineteenth-century frontier. Moreover, any attempt to malign James Hall for his presumed Indian-hating must discount Hall's considerable sympathy for the Indian in his writings. On the other hand, Noble's sensationalized version of Hall's narrative typifies America's long historical addiction to tales of the "West," with their clearly demarcated heroes and villains, which later bore fruit in the popular genre of the "western." Hence, when at the beginning of his recital Charlie Noble describes James Hall as talking to the "press" about Indian-hating, the implication is either that Hall repeatedly reworked his story of Moredock (five different nonfictional and fictional versions in all) or that the contemporary press was eager to exploit such saleable copy.[14]

The central placement of the Indian-hating sequence in the novel is also no doubt related to the central role that the myth of the frontier has played in the evolution of American culture. Richard Slotkin has traced the beginnings of this myth in the cultural confrontation of white European and Indian peoples in the "wilderness" of the New World. He documents, among other things, the demonization of the Indian in Puritan sermons and histories, the religious significance of the captivity narrative, and the popularization of the legendary figure of Daniel Boone, the prototypical backwoodsman whose life was the focus for a host of regional and even international writers attempting to interpret the meaning of American civilization. Melville's representation of the figure of the Indian-hater evokes the long tradition Slotkin examines, including the Puritan view of the Indian as devil, the wilderness as an eschatological arena for vanquishing him, and the vogue of Boone narratives that celebrated the "western" character and helped generate the literary heroes of Hall, Cooper, Simms, Bird, and others.

Noble begins his recital with an anecdote of a near-encounter with Moredock while on a trip west as a boy with his father. Taking the opportunity to observe this legendary killer while he was sleeping in the cornloft of a cabin, Noble recounts his experience: " 'Not much light in the loft; but off, in the further corner, I saw what I took to be the wolf-skins, and on them a bundle of something, like a drift of leaves; and at one end, what seemed a moss-ball; . . . That bit of woodland scene was all I saw. No Colonel Moredock there, unless that moss-ball was his curly head, seen in back view' " (*CM,* 141). This elusive man of moss (the Hawthornean image is no doubt intentional) is apparently invisible except for the wilderness elements that constitute the backdrop to his campaign of revenge. Thus whatever moral phenomenon Moredock represents is presumably a "mystery of iniquity" subsumed within the demonized, Indian-ridden wilderness of the white imagination; he is, in short, the stuff of myth and legend.[15]

The Puritan legacy of the demonized savage is in fact the moral burden of the preamble to the Moredock story proper, the mythic characterization of the Indian-hater *par excellence.* In this account, the upbringing of a child on the frontier teaches it the histories of " 'Indian lying, Indian theft, Indian double-dealing, Indian fraud and perfidy, Indian want of conscience, Indian blood-thirstiness, Indian diabolism—histories which, though of wild woods, are almost as full of things unangelic as the Newgate Calendar or the Annals of Europe. In these Indian narratives and traditions the lad is thoroughly grounded' " (*CM,* 146). Once the grown-up Indian-hater *par excellence* receives some "signal outrage," he is launched on his career of vengeance and disappears into the wilderness: " 'Doubtless events, terrible ones, have happened, must have happened; but the powers that be in nature have taken order that they shall never become news' " (*CM,* 150). The Indian-hater *par excellence*'s fanatical pursuit of revenge into the wilderness thus leads to perpetual warfare and ultimate self-annihilation, a Hobbesian war of all against all; he is absorbed into the terrible void behind the face of nature which Ishmael imagined as conceived in fright.

One step removed from this "ideal" figure is John Moredock, a "diluted" Indian-hater, who combines a vocation of Indian killing with civilized life on the frontier. On a mythological level, however, both Moredock and the Indian-hater *par excellence* are united by their resemblance to the figure of Milton's Satan. In Melville's adaptation of this representative figure of revenge, both the ideal and real Indian-haters constitute satanic antiheroes whose hatred, instead of being directed at a demonized God, is devoted to exterminating a demonized race of man. And while neither the ideal not the historical Indian-hater is explicitly associated with Milton's Satan, they both embody Satan's heroic assertion of will, at the same time evoking the hero-villain of contemporary Gothic literature (Godwin, Radcliffe, Lewis, Shelley), a figure who often bore a distinctive resemblance to Milton's antihero.

Yet if the historical Indian-hater, Moredock, is a satanic figure in his ruthless assertion of will, he nevertheless starts his career as an American Adam. First introduced heading west to an Eden-like settlement on the banks of the Mississippi, Moredock discovers the existence of evil in the extermination of his whole family by renegade Indians, an event that represents a reenactment of the Fall. Moredock accordingly consumes the news of his family's murder like Adam eating the apple: " 'as the tidings were told him, after the first start he kept on eating, but slowly and deliberately, chewing the wild news with the wild meal, as if both together, turned to chyle, together should sinew him to his intent. From that meal he rose an Indian-hater' " (*CM,* 153). After this climatic moral awakening, Moredock's fate is seemingly fixed as he goes on to kill the twenty renegade Indians who were responsible for the murder of his family and then is compelled to make a career of killing. For as a "Leatherstocking nemesis," he is seemingly locked into a fatalistic pattern of imitating his demonized antagonists, inadvertently becoming their duplicate, as his characterization at times implies.

Another notable feature of the Moredock sequence is the religious status given to Indian-hating as a kind of demonic parody of Christianity, a religion of brotherly hatred. In the midst of his peroration on the Indian-hater *par excellence,* for example, Charlie Noble in the role of "Judge Hall" performs a mock catechism with an imaginary questioner who expresses doubts about the picture of Indian depravity found in the parable of "Mocmohoc." John Moredock's habit of killing Indians is also characterized as parodic Christian dogma: " 'Sins of commission in that kind may have been his, but none of omission' " (*CM,* 154). Noble ends his discourse on Moredock with the claim that because it renounces "the pomps and glories of the world," Indian-hating, " 'whatever may be thought of it in other respects, may be regarded as not wholly without the efficacy of a devout sentiment.' " The

Indian-hater's demonic inversion of Christianity is, in effect, a religion of misanthropy and a reversion to the Old Testament *lex talio.*[16]

While this religious dimension suggests the anti-Christian ambiance that distinguishes many of the characters in the second half of the novel and so serves as a kind of introductory leitmotif, it is inevitably overshadowed for many readers by the political aspects of the Indian-hating sequence. And as a number of critics have pointed out, this sequence blends an apparent celebration of the Indian-hater with an ironic evocation of the ruthless historical treatment of the Indian in this era of Indian Removal. The figure of the Indian-hater *par excellence* is in fact specifically invoked as the advanced guard of a "conquering civilization" that relies on men like Moredock to dispose of such savage impediments to continental expansion. Joyce Sparer Adler has shown that the story from the mouth of Noble *qua* Hall is an example of how an unwelcome historical truth, the displacement and extermination of the Indian, is strategically buried behind self-serving historical fiction: "The 'history' of Moredock the Indian-hater with its long introduction is Melville's demonstration of the fact that in the bulk of the recorded history of America's drive to the West, the Indian has not been judged like the white man whose crimes, as in this story, are rationalized and even revered" (116). As Adler notes, a number of passages in Noble's rendition of Hall show that the one-sided, negative view of Indian "nature" is undercut by authorial irony. For example, describing the genesis of the hatred felt by the backwoodsman for the Indian, Noble *qua* Hall goes on to qualify his remarks:

> " 'Still, all this is less advanced as truths of the Indians than as example of the backwoodsman's impression of them—in which the charitable may think he does them some injustice. Certain it is, the Indians themselves think so; quite unanimously, too. The Indians, indeed, protest against the backwoodsman's view of them; and some think that one cause of their returning his antipathy so sincerely as they do, is their moral indignation at being so libeled by him, as they really believe and say. But whether, on this or any point, the Indians should be permitted to testify for themselves, to the exclusion of other testimony, is a question that may be left to the Supreme Court.' " (*CM*, 146–47)

He goes on to cite the Christianized Indian's belief that "his race's portion by nature is total depravity" and that those Indians who depict their race as virtuous "are sometimes the arrantest horse-thieves and tomahawkers among them," ending with the tell-tale refrain, "So, at least, avers the backwoodsman." Such Swiftian indirections hint that the cultural indoctrination of the Indian-hater is propaganda, not history.[17]

Yet it would be a mistake to view the Indian-hating sequence in *The Confidence-Man* as directed at a sociopolitical target alone, for it exemplifies the complex melding of biographical, historical, and theological levels of significance we have seen at work throughout the novel.[18] By the same token, the moral anomaly of the Indian-hater typifies the moral mystery of man; for after Noble has completed his disquisition on Indian-hating, the cosmopolitan is ostensibly baffled by the seeming inconsistencies of Moredock's character: " 'That story strikes me with even more incredulity than wonder. To me some parts don't hang together. If the man of hate, how could John Moredock be also the man of love?' " (*CM,* 156). The question raises the recurrent theodicy issue that haunts the novel. We may assume that the cosmopolitan is only pretending a Socratic ignorance in his question here, as demonstrated by his subsequent theorizing about the possibility of such moral anomalies as the "genial misanthrope" and the "surly philanthropist." His own story of Charlemont also explores the seeming inconsistencies of human nature and the problem of misanthropy in a character antithetical to that of John Moredock.

CHARLEMONT

The briefest of the novel's four fables and the most unmediated in terms of narrative voice, the story of Charlemont, the "gentleman-madman," is recited in Chapter 34 by the cosmopolitan to Charlie Noble as a simple sentimental tale, in contrast to the elaborate indirection and sensationalism of Noble's performance. And if Noble's story of the Indian-hating John Moredock manipulated the literary and cultural stereotypes of the frontier, the story of Charlemont mimics another antebellum literary genre, the sentimental sketch of Washington Irving. A sensitive, warm-hearted bachelor whose financial reverses cause him to suddenly withdraw from St. Louis society in order to recoup his fortunes abroad, Charlemont is a literary descendant of the numerous tribe of "bachelors" fathered by the fluent pen of Geoffrey Crayon. In particular, Charlemont's experience of the emotional and spiritual costs of bankruptcy evokes a theme found in Irving's *Sketch Book* in such sketches as "Roscoe" and "The Wife."[19]

"Charlemont" also continues Melville's displaced exploration of his creative interaction with Hawthorne. We may note first the residual influence here of *The Blithedale Romance,* for just as "Charlie Noble" mimicked traits of Dr. Westervelt, "Charlemont" appropriates a few elements from Fauntleroy's story in Chapter 22 of *Blithedale.* Thus both "Charlemont" and "Fauntleroy" are told over wine by enigmatic "confidence men"; both feature wealthy characters from the Midwest; both involve unspecified financial ruin and the disappearance of each character to a distant city; both characters seek renewed happiness after prolonged obscurity. The psychological dimension of the character of Charlemont also evokes other, more complex Hawthorne characters, especially those, like the Reverend Hooper and

Goodman Brown, who are blighted by a morbid conviction of human sinfulness.

Not only are there literary parallels between "Charlemont" and Hawthorne's fiction, but there are also a number of biographical correspondences between Goodman's story and Melville's personal relationship to Hawthorne. Thus Hawthorne conceivably "betrayed" Melville by leaving the Berkshires; Charlemont mysteriously "cuts" his friends in St. Louis. Hawthorne went to the port of Liverpool to reestablish his finances; Charlemont goes to the port of Marseille to reestablish his. Melville once figured Hawthorne's personality as a volume entitled "Hawthorne: A Problem" (*C,* 185); Charlemont's behavior in abandoning and resuming his friendships seems an "enigma." Even the name "Charlemont" could be related to Melville's contact with Hawthorne in the Berkshires, for the town of Charlemont, Massachusetts, is located twenty-five miles northeast of Pittsfield, while Hawthorne's residence in Lenox was six miles south of Melville's Berkshire home.[20]

As suggested in Chapter 6 of this study, the opposition between the story of the Indian-hater and the story of the "gentleman-madman" embodies a displaced version of Melville's transition from the literary ethos of rebellion dramatized in *Moby-Dick* and *Pierre,* to one of submission, as exemplified by such figures of stoical endurance as Bartleby, Merrymusk, and Hunilla. Symptomatic of this transition was the story of Agatha Robertson that Melville offered to Hawthorne in 1852 and then used himself in his unpublished *Isle of the Cross.* The story of "Agatha" involved a Quaker woman of Falmouth, Massachusetts, who married a shipwrecked English sailor; after two years he deserted her when pregnant with their daughter and eventually made a second, bigamous marriage in Virginia where he prospered in business. Following a seventeen-year absence, he reappeared at the home of his first wife and daughter, offering them financial assistance. When his second wife subsequently died, he invited his original family to move with him to Missouri; when they refused, he moved there himself and made yet another bigamous marriage. As the lawyer in the case noted, "It was to me a most striking instance of long continued & uncomplaining submission to wrong and anguish on the part of a wife, w[hi]ch made her in my eyes a heroine" (*C,* 624). Her name derived from the Greek word for "good," Agatha, like Charlemont, exhibits a Christ-like suffering and forgiveness of personal betrayal.[21]

Like the Agatha story, Charlemont's history in fact offers a kind of secularized version of Christ's life, for both Charlemont and Christ experience a change of character at about the age of thirty; both sacrifice themselves for the redemption of human sinfulness; both commemorate the "mystery" of their sacrifice at a dinner party over wine; both act according to principles that seem "mad" to worldly usage. Charlemont's knowledge that he would be betrayed by his associates parallels Christ's similar knowledge; it also parallels the cosmopolitan's Christ-like foreknowledge of his betrayal by

Charlie Noble. In its implied theological frame, then, the story of Charlemont is a fictive version of the Atonement; it is in fact just the kind of story we might expect from the cosmopolitan in his role here as Christ at the Last Supper.[22]

It should be noted, however, that the religious implications of the story of "Charlemont" are buried beneath a veneer of sentimental pathos: the full force of the cosmopolitan's fable is only brought out after the story is finished, at which point it becomes apparent that the cosmopolitan is using "Charlemont" as a moral barometer in the failed redemption of Charlie Noble. Hence the cosmopolitan breezily discounts any explicit moral for "Charlemont" by claiming it to be an invented story told strictly for amusement. Yet the transparent irony of the cosmopolitan's claim is revealed by the self-evident similarities between Charlemont's experience and Charlie's recent behavior, as reflected in Charlie's uneasiness after the story is finished. Claiming that the wine has "played the deuce" with him (or vice versa), Charlie hastily exits, thereby presenting an obvious contrast to the Charlemont who fled his friends because of simulated, not genuine, misanthropy. Goodman's assertion that Charlie must be "losing his mind" to complain about the wine he ordered again evokes the antithetical example of the gentleman-madman.

In his examination of *The Confidence-Man* as a critique of liberal Protestantism, James Duban argues that "the story of Charlemont brings into focus still another phase of Melville's quarrel with liberal Christianity by showing that its whitewash of human nature degrades Christ's Agony on the Cross to a mission inspired by the delusions and 'dulcet error' of a Gentleman-Madman" (*Melville's Major Fiction,* 212). For John Wenke, on the other hand, the story of Charlemont makes thematic use of Shakespeare's *Timon of Athens* in order to draw attention to the necessity of dissimulation in social relations: "The lesson which Frank Goodman implies in his story of Charlemont is that identity and motive must be hidden behind a protecting mask; if one shows oneself too plainly to the world, one runs the risk of losing friends, pride, dignity, self-possession" ("No 'i' in Charlemont," 272).[23] Viewed as a fable either of innate depravity or of social role playing, Christian or classical archetypes, the story of Charlemont is an appropriate conclusion to the protracted debate between Goodman and Noble on the individual's need for society even though it is a matrix of human vices. The story also anticipates the moral burden of the last interior fable in which the cost of material failure in that society is not merely suffering, as in "Charlemont," but death.

CHINA ASTER

Taking place on a lower social stratum than that of Charlemont but involving a similar subject of financial ruin, Egbert's story of China Aster in Chapter 40 recounts the misfortunes of a struggling candle maker from

Marietta, Ohio. Aster accepts the offer of a $1,000 loan from his friend Orchis in order to expand his business from tallow to spermaceti candles, but is thereafter caught in a web of contractual obligations that eventually destroy him. With its didactic tone, heavy pathos, and appended moral, the story of China Aster constitutes a parody of a contemporary moral tract. Indeed, its title character bears the name of a juvenile annual published in Portland, Maine, from 1845 to 1851, as Robert Sattelmeyer and James Barbour have shown. (It has gone unremarked that the name similarly parodies that of John Jacob Astor, the richest man in America at his death in 1848.)

The cultural resonances of "China Aster" also reach back to the influential example of Benjamin Franklin. As a subversive rewriting of the Franklinian myth of success, the fable implies that trying to do good to the world is not a money-making enterprise, and that industry, frugality, and prudence (Franklin's cardinal virtues) do not assure one of success. Even the promise of future financial reward that motivates the entrepreneur can be a delusive dream: China Aster's dream of wealth features a lying angel named "Bright Future" who dispenses showers of dollars like a celestial slot machine. "China Aster" is, in short, a fable of failed entrepreneurial capitalism within a larger business culture of success.

While it is grounded in a cultural continuum of entrepreneurial enrichment and moral self-improvement, the immediate satirical context of "China Aster" is transcendentalist doctrine, namely, Egbert–Thoreau's exposition of the insuperable moral divide between business and friendship. The didacticism of "China Aster" ultimately situates transcendental morality in the tradition of Yankee shrewdness and smug Franklinian moralism. Thus Thoreau's opening chapter on "Economy" in *Walden* builds on frugal foundations laid by Poor Richard; and as Leonard Neufeldt has demonstrated, *Walden* is both a straightforward and a parodic "young man's guide," the popular nineteenth-century genre that provided formulas for success in the Franklinian tradition.[24]

Yet beyond its immediate transcendentalist context, "China Aster" is also predicated on other religious, sexual, and biographical frames of reference. In its religious dimension, China Aster's story constitutes a typological conflation of the martyrdoms of both Job and Christ. The resemblance to Job is most clearly seen in the fact that Aster's elderly advisors, Old Plain Talk and Old Prudence, are explicitly cast in the role of Job's comforters; and like their biblical prototypes they promote a conservative, obtuse moralism that fails to address Aster's true spiritual condition.[25] On the other hand, a more sustained typological resemblance exists between China Aster and Christ, including a covert allusion to the Nativity in Aster's name. (The infant Christ is the "star in the east" sought by the magi [Matt. 2:2].) Significantly, China Aster is first characterized as "one whose trade would seem a kind of subordinate branch of that parent craft and mystery of the hosts of heaven, to be the means, effectively or otherwise, of shedding some light through the darkness of a planet benighted" (*CM,* 208), a vocation comparable to Christ's mission to be a "light to lighten the gentiles" (Luke 2:32) and "the light of the world" (John 8:12). Moreover, the Sermon on the Mount provides an implicit rationale for China Aster's aspirations to improve his candle-making business: "Neither do men light a candle, and put it under a bushel, but on a candlestick; and it giveth light unto all that are in the house. / Let your light so shine before men, that they may see your good works, and glorify your Father, which is in heaven" (Matt. 5:15).

The relation between Aster and his friend Orchis also figures a covert sexual allegory that functions as a subversive subtext to the story's religious symbolism. Commentators have remarked that the name of China Aster's friend, Orchis, is not only a tropical flowering plant but is also the Greek word for testicle.[26] John Carlos Rowe provides a useful overview of some of the relevant sexual symbolism here:

> The names China Aster and Orchis refer respectively to the stars toward which man aspires and the earth into which the genitallike root of the orchird burrows. These names seem to support the philosophical critique of romantic idealism that is the ostensible subject of the tale, but we are reminded by various puns that "Orchis" also refers to the testicles and that the China Aster is a garden flower with large, perhaps inviting blooms. The tale certainly confirms this crude pun: Orchis does "screw" China Aster. In another sense, Orchis provides the semen/spermaceti that China Aster cannot make productive, suggesting in the crude banter of Mississippi rivermen a pun on philanthropy as a sort of buggery or otherwise infertile sexuality. Indeed, Orchis himself is ruined at the hands of the "Come-Outers," which may well argue for an allegory of onanism, or wasted, scattered seed. (116)

Yet China Aster is not only a starry idealist, for he is also (figuratively speaking) a spermaceti-producing phallus. And the apparent allegory of onanism here is in fact derived from the model of the spermatic economy we have seen operating elsewhere in the novel. "China Aster" accordingly parodies the perils of improper regulation of semen which haunted the antebellum male with fears for his success, his sanity, and even his life. As Barker-Benfield writes, "The way in which a man handled the intimate economic relation between mind and body was seen to be continuous with the way in which he handled money, specifically debt and expenditure. . . . That the young man should engage the world at all (and thus expose his interior economy to its dangerous vicissitudes) was due to his possession of penis and testicles. Appropriately, the easiest and most dangerous 'abuse' threatening a young man's energies was his ejaculation of sperm" (179).

In keeping with this cultural model, Orchis and Aster constitute symbolic male genitalia, while Aster's career dramatizes the dangers a man faces in "overspending" himself: China Aster fails in business, loses his mind, and dies, all because he unwisely accepted from his friend Orchis a $1,000 loan which, in the pat moral of the story, is said to be the "root" of the problem. The close relation between masturbation, debility, and money is accordingly revealed at a few key points in the story. When first pressing his loan on Aster, for example, Orchis remarks, " 'China Aster, I am afraid that, in leaning over into your vats here, this morning, you have spilled out your wisdom' " (*CM,* 209). Aster does indeed (figuratively) "spill" his wisdom when he succumbs to the lure of his twice-repeated dream of a smiling angel who, "holding a kind of cornucopia in her hand, hovered over him, pouring down showers of small gold dollars, thick as kernels of corn" (*CM,* 212). Dispensing the equivalent of manna from heaven, the angel calls herself "Bright Future" but her actions also mimic the phenomenon of nocturnal emission. China Aster thus serves as a type for all men who are unprepared for entrepreneurship in a business culture of ruthless competition and risk.

In its biographical context, the story of China Aster recalls various aspects of Melville's own professional career as well as that of his father. The biographical allegory of "China Aster" accordingly combines allusions to Melville's plight as a writer with his father's earlier failure in business, thus conflating the seemingly fated careers of both father and son in their struggles to improve their status in a developing market economy. As critics have noted, China Aster's acceptance of a $1,000 "friendly loan" directly mimics the $2,050 loan Melville accepted from his "friend" Tertullus D. Stewart in May 1851, which was due to mature in May 1856. "China Aster" represents Melville's fictionalized retelling of the galling history of this "friendly" loan, which Stewart had pressed on Melville despite Melville's reluctance to accept it (*C,* 291). China Aster's ambition to market spermaceti candles is no doubt related to the composition of *Moby-Dick,* the work Melville was finishing when he accepted Stewart's loan. Significantly, a month after he received this loan Melville described himself in comparable terms when he wrote Hawthorne that he was "now come to the inmost leaf of the bulb, and that shortly the flower must fall to the mould" (*C,* 193).

Furthermore, the choice China Aster faces between producing tallow candles and those of spermaceti effectively allegorizes Melville's conflict between the commercial popularity he established at the start of his career with *Typee, Omoo, Redburn,* and *White-Jacket,* and the unpopular products of his attempts at truth-telling, *Mardi, Moby-Dick,* and *Pierre.* Aster's third venture in spermaceti candles, like Melville's third venture in truth-telling, was "almost a total loss," while Aster's subsequent switch back to tallow candles suggests Melville's attempt to regain public favor with *Israel Potter.* Aster's borrowing of six hundred dollars from a "rich old farmer" also recalls Melville's $1,500 mortgage to the previous owner of Arrowhead, Dr. John

Brewster; Melville had defaulted on this debt for the first time in September 1855 (*C*, 291). Finally, Aster's use of funds due his wife from a "childless uncle" is a probable echo of Melville's reliance on his wife's family resources. As a displaced account of Melville's failing literary career and mounting financial problems when writing *The Confidence-Man,* Aster's demise suggests that the nation in which Melville hoped to fulfill a prophetic vocation as a writer preferred the darkness to the light.[27]

Yet the disappointments of Melville's literary career alone do not explain all the autobiographical elements of "China Aster," for the life of Melville's father informs the story's more tragic aspects. Aster's financial entanglement with friends, relatives, and other creditors in fact parallels Allan Melvill's comparable network of indebtedness. China Aster's late-night death due to exhaustion and exposure similarly recalls Allan Melvill's expiration from related causes. Melville may even be obliquely alluding to his father's deathbed markings of Psalm 55 in the "epitaph" which Aster wrote for himself and which is eventually inscribed on his tomb: "there was discovered, in China Aster's otherwise empty wallet, an epitaph, written, probably, in one of those disconsolate hours, attended with more or less mental aberration, perhaps, so frequent with him for some months prior to his end" (*CM*, 218). In "China Aster," then, Melville comments on his father's career, as he does again in the last chapter of the novel; but the filial piety suggested by Melville's assimilation of his father's fate to his own in the fable balances the paternal sabotage latent in the depiction of the old man.

"China Aster," in sum, provides a model for many of the socioeconomic changes in America that Melville is satirizing throughout *The Confidence-Man*. And uniting the various thematic levels of this last interior fable is its critique of a society governed by principles of market capitalism and laissez-faire. As a parable of the new economic order of antebellum America, "China Aster" dramatizes the human costs of an economy that glorified an entrepreneurial ideal of success and discounted the possibility of failure. Laissez-faire postulated that universal benefits would accrue from making the individual a free competitive agent, limited only by the sanctity of contracts. China Aster engages in this basic model of entrepreneurial self-improvement but misjudges the market for his product and subsequently goes down to defeat in a network of contractual obligations. Contrary to the theory that laissez-faire ultimately benefits society as a whole, the story of China Aster shows all characters either losing their money (Orchis and Aster), dying (Aster and his wife), or ending up in the poor house (Aster's children). Melville's parabolic incorporation of his father's as well as his own experience in the marketplace demonstrates that beneath the heavy pathos of the story is hidden the bitterness generated by personal experience.

We have seen, then, that the four interior fables in *The Confidence-Man* exemplify the novel's blending of biographical, historical, and theological frames of reference. The stories of Goneril and John Moredock offer contrasting civilized and savage settings, female and male anti-heroes; those of Charlemont and China Aster deal with members of upper and lower social classes and with the different costs of economic failure to each protagonist. Yet as moral exempla, the four fables offer two basic attitudes to experience, exemplified by the division within the fables of satanic and Christ-like archetypes. Goneril and Moredock, both associated with stereotypical "savages," are diabolic aggressors activated by ill-will and revenge; Charlemont and China Aster variously reenact the teachings and career of Christ. The first pair exemplifies a condition of dehumanized and murderous misanthropy; the second exemplifies a philanthropic but vulnerable charity. In these typologies of moral conduct there is seemingly no *via media*.

8

Interpolated Essays: Apologia and Ars Poetica

Whereas *The Confidence-Man*'s four interior fables offer antithetical examples of moral conduct, in keeping with the novel's dialectical design, its three interpolated essays—Chapters 14, 33, and 44—present digressive commentaries on the author's narrative strategies. The three essays, which recall comparable digressions in *Mardi* and *Pierre,* explore issues of consistency, realism, and originality in fictional characterization. With their tautological chapter titles and serio-comic tone, these essays have been compared to the essays or "proems" in Henry Fielding's *Joseph Andrews* and *Tom Jones.* Yet however much both their manner and matter seem to echo Fielding, as well as other eighteenth-century "self-conscious narrators" like those found in *The Tale of a Tub* or *Tristram Shandy,* the three interpolated essays in *The Confidence-Man* actually exemplify a well-known satirical convention. As Robert C. Elliott points out, "From the times of Horace, Persius, and Juvenal, down to Boileau, Swift, and Pope, and into our own day with men like Wyndham Lewis, the satirist has felt compelled to write an *apologia,* whether formal or informal, in verse or prose" (265). In short, just as the novel's interior fables constitute satirical "characters," the interpolated essays may be said to form a tripartite satirical "defense" or *apologia.*[1]

Furthermore, as Melville's attempt to legitimate both his literary methods and his moral character, the three interpolated essays combine their satirical *apologia* with a more general *ars poetica* that not only comments on the method of *The Confidence-Man* but also looks back on Melville's whole fictional oeuvre. Evoking the well-known critical dicta of Aristotle and Horace, Melville argues first that fiction must provide moral instruction through its truth to the complexities of human experience (*utile*); second, it must give pleasure to the reader through its imaginative heightening of reality (*dulcis*); and third, it effectuates a balance between creative originality (*poesis*) and a direct imitation of life (*mimesis*). Finally, each of the three essays also grows out of the personal and topical satire we have explored in previous chapters of this study. Thus Chapter 14 is aimed at Evert Duyckinck's criticisms of Melville's fiction, Chapter 33 responds to Hawthorne's prefaces to his romances, and Chapter 44 explores issues of originality in the context of both Melville's own literary career and the contemporary American quest for an "original" literary genius. In the following analysis, we explore both the explicit and implicit literary contexts of the interpolated essays.

The fictive occasion for the argument in Chapter 14 is the inconsistent behavior of Henry Roberts when, after having his confidence repeatedly bolstered by John Truman, he nevertheless makes a "mad disclosure" that mere "confidence" won't mitigate life's "hard considerations." The narrator argues that such inconsistency is actually true to human nature. Indeed, depicting human inconsistency and ambiguity may give the reader a more reliable guide to human nature than any simplified representation that caters to readers' desire for easy comprehension.

While the narrator's remarks on inconsistency explicitly affirm a basic thematic premise of the novel, that is, the moral ambiguity of human nature, the essay also has a specific topical inspiration, for it is grounded in Melville's troubled relations with his friend and literary mentor, Evert Duyckinck. Just as Melville's relationship with Evert Duyckinck provided the model for the extended encounter of the Confidence Man with Henry Roberts, the chapter of authorial commentary immediately following this encounter uses Duyckinck's critical doctrines as a touchstone for Melville's defense of his own literary methods. Duyckinck's *Literary World* reviews of *Moby-Dick* and *Pierre* provide the implicit source for the argument presented in Chapter 14. As the many surviving drafts of Chapter 14 show (*CM,* 413–68), Melville painstakingly thought out this belated reply to his friend's earlier critical comments on his fiction.

Chapter 14 in effect represents an answer to Duyckinck's critical indictment of Melville's philosophical and religious skepticism, as dramatized in his greatest fiction. With qualified praise, Duyckinck had called *Moby-Dick* "a most remarkable sea-dish—an intellectual chowder or romance, philosophy, natural history, fine writing, good feeling, bad sayings." Yet he could not help seeing many aspects of the character of Ishmael as alarmingly irreligious: "This piratical running down of creeds and opinions, the conceited indifferentism of Emerson, or the run-a-muck style of Carlyle is, we will not say dangerous in such cases, for there are various forces at work to meet more powerful onslaught, but it is out of place and uncomfortable. We do not like to see what, under any view, must be to the world the most sacred associations of life violated and defaced." Duyckinck concluded his review by calling Ishmael a successful embodiment of contradictory opinions, but nevertheless a flawed fictional character: "So much for the consistency of Ishmael—who, if it is the author's object to exhibit the painful contradictions of this self-dependent, self-torturing agency of a mind driven hither and thither as a flame in a whirlwind, is, in a degree, a successful embodiment of opinions, without securing from us, however, much admiration for the result" (Branch, *Critical Heritage,* 267–68).

Melville's defense of his representation of human inconsistency in Henry Roberts—and by extension *The Confidence-Man* as a whole—constitutes a belated response to Duyckinck's moralistic indictment of Ishmael, whose ability to balance conflicting philosophical claims is often considered an integral part of Melville's literary achievement in *Moby-Dick.* So in Chapter 14 the narrator begins by stressing the connection between the merchant's behavior and the charge of inconsistency, as though responding to an invisible critic:

> To some, it may raise a degree of surprise that one so full of confidence, as the merchant has throughout shown himself, up to the moment of his late sudden impulsiveness, should, in that instance, have betrayed such a depth of discontent. He may be thought inconsistent, and even so he is. But for this, is the author to be blamed? True, it may be urged that there is nothing a writer of fiction should more carefully see to, as there is nothing a sensible reader will more carefully look for, than that, in the depiction of any character, its consistency should be preserved. But this, though at first blush, seeming reasonable enough, may, upon a closer view, prove not so much so. For how does it couple with another requirement—equally insisted upon, perhaps—that, while to all fiction is allowed some play of invention, yet, fiction based on fact should never be contradictory to it; and is it not a fact, that, in real life, a consistent character is a *rara avis?* Which being so, the distaste of readers to the contrary sort in books, can hardly arise from any sense of their untrueness. It may rather be from perplexity as to understanding them. (*CM,* 69)

Invoking the merchant as his test case, Melville is arguing that people like Duyckinck adhere to critical canons that are untrue to that very "nature" which served as the ultimate touchstone for Duyckinck's notion of "verisimilitude," a key term in his critical vocabulary (Wells, 145–46).

We have already seen that the encounter between John Truman and Henry Roberts fictively rehearses Melville's falling out with Duyckinck over *Pierre.* Thus, in addition to answering Duyckinck's *Moby-Dick* review, the remarks in Chapter 14 refer to the quarrel over *Pierre.* Indeed, the argument here enacts Melville's retrospective vindication of the novel in the face of the critical hostility of his moralistic friend. Duyckinck's *Pierre* review in August 1852 repeatedly stressed Melville's unfaithfulness to truth and nature:

> Mr. Melville may have constructed his story upon some new theory of art to a knowledge of which we have not yet transcended; he evidently has not constructed it according to the established principles of the only theory accepted by us until assured of a better, of one more true and natural than truth and nature themselves, which are the germinal principles of all true art. . . . The combined power of New England transcendentalism and Spanish Jesuitical casuistry could not have more completely befogged nature and truth, than this confounded Pierre has done. It is needless to test minutely the truth and nature of each character. In a word, Pierre is a psychological curiosity, a moral and intellectual phenomenon; Isabel, a lusus naturae; Lucy, an incomprehensible woman; and the rest not of the earth nor, we may venture to state, of heaven. The object of the author, perhaps, has been, not to delineate life and character as they are or may possibly be, but as they are not and cannot be. We must receive the book, then, as an eccentricity of the imagination. (Higgins and Parker, 41–42)

To such a confident assurance of what constitutes truth and nature in the depiction of character, Melville opposes a more stringent test:

> But let nature, to the perplexity of the naturalists, produce her duck-billed beavers as she may, lesser authors, some may hold, have no business to be perplexing readers with duck-billed characters. Always, they should represent human nature not in obscurity, but transparency, which, indeed, is the practice with most novelists, and is, perhaps, in certain cases, someway felt to be a kind of honor rendered by them to their kind. But whether it involve honor or otherwise might be mooted, considering that, if these waters of human nature can be so readily seen through, it may be either that they are very pure or very shallow. Upon the whole, it might rather be thought, that he, who, in view of its inconsistences, says of human nature the same that, in view of its contrasts, is said of the divine nature, that it is past finding out, thereby evinces a better appreciation of it than he who, by always representing it in a clear light, leaves it to be inferred that he clearly knows all about it. (*CM,* 70)

Duyckinck had compared the meaning of *Pierre* to a "stagnant pool" and called for clarity; Melville now indicts his friend's limited critical acumen when gazing into the "waters of human nature." Furthermore, just as Montaigne is the likely source for the skeptical evaluation of John Ringman's "true book," the French essayist is referred to when the narrator remarks, "But if the acutest sage be often at his wits' ends to understand living character, shall those who are not sages expect to run and read character in those mere phantoms which flit along a page, like shadows along a wall?"

(*CM,* 69). The "acutest sage" here is no doubt Montaigne, whose essay entitled "Of the Inconstancy of Our Actions" constitutes a meditation on inconsistency in the same vein as Chapter 14, as Tom Quirk has pointed out ("Two Sources").[2]

In this chapter of authorial commentary, however, Melville is not just settling old scores with a critical mentor, for he is also indicting those writers of fiction who present human nature in "transparency," as well as those who create characters whose apparent complexities finally turn out to be an illusion; the latter class of writers "challenge astonishment at the tangled web of some character, and then raise admiration still greater at their satisfactory unraveling of it" (*CM,* 70). Melville is seemingly protesting against the very notion of a "denouement" in the traditional form of the novel, repeating an attack he had earlier made in *Pierre* in which he had caustically written of popular novels' "inverted attempts at systematizing eternally unsystematizable elements; their audacious, intermeddling impotency, in trying to unravel, and spread out, and classify, the more thin than gossamer threads which make up the complex web of life" (*P,* 141). In its sardonic reference to fiction that caters "to the understanding even of school misses," the argument in Chapter 14 of *The Confidence-Man* also recalls Melville's sarcastic attack in *Pierre* (Bks. XVII and XVIII) on the nation's overly effete literary establishment in this era of the "feminine fifties."

On the other hand, however much Melville's remarks here may appear to reflect a long-term "quarrel with fiction," as Nina Baym as termed it, they do not reflect an outright rejection of fiction as a vehicle of imaginative truth, but rather the novels that most of the public—and especially the female public—consumed in this era of the newly developed "best seller." As his ensuing remarks show, Melville adduces a traditional moral basis for his criticism of contemporary fiction when he posits the example of a "studious youth" who should be given a "true delineation" of human nature that will guide him at the threshold of life, in the same way that a reliable map will help a stranger navigate the crooked streets of Boston. Melville thus repeats the classical principle that literature should have an educative value, the Horatian *utile;* his subsequent claim that human nature is an unchanging object of study similarly implies a classical concept of mankind.

Situated between the cosmopolitan's magical transformation of Charlie Noble and his ensuing tale of Charlemont, Chapter 33 begins as an answer to an imaginary reader who might complain that the antics of the cosmopolitan are too "unreal." The narrator goes on to justify himself by claiming that he caters to the reader's need for distraction from a prosaic reality by presenting a version of nature that offers "more reality, than real life can show." His art is comparable to the drama, in which the audience sees individuals acting with an "unreserve unavailable in daily life."

Given the narrative placement of this essay near the end of the Noble–

Goodman encounter, it comes as no surprise that Hawthorne's prefaces to his first three romances provide an implicit rationale for Melville's digression here. Hence instead of parrying a critical attack from a friend as in Chapter 14, Melville is now endorsing a fellow artist's theory of fiction in order to answer the reader who may be put off by the novel's seemingly unrealistic mode of representation. Melville's invocation of the reader's willing suspension of disbelief in the depiction of the cosmopolitan thus reformulates Hawthorne's prefatory comments on his literary method.

In "The Custom House," Hawthorne compared his fiction to a "neutral territory, somewhere between the real world and fairy-land, where the Actual and Imaginary may meet, and each imbue itself with the nature of the other" (*Scarlet Letter,* 36). Distinguishing between a novel and romance in the preface to *The House of the Seven Gables,* Hawthorne wrote that the novel depicts the "probable and ordinary course of man's experience" while the romance is permitted a "certain latitude" in its mode of representation. However, the writer of a romance "will be wise, no doubt, to make a very moderate use of the privileges here stated, and, especially, to mingle the Marvellous rather as a slight, delicate, and evanescent flavor, than as any portion of the actual dish offered to the public" (*House,* 1). While echoing the substance of Hawthorne's literary request for a "neutral territory" or a "certain latitude" appropriate to the "romance," the argument in Chapter 33 of *The Confidence-Man* has a more immediate source in the plea made in the preface to *The Blithedale Romance.* Here Hawthorne had offered a theatrical analogy to justify his infringements of realistic norms of representation:

> In short, his present concern with the Socialist Community is merely to establish a theatre, a little removed from the highway of ordinary travel, where the creatures of his brain may play their phantasmagorical antics, without exposing them to too close a comparison with the actual events of real lives. In the old countries, with which Fiction has long been conversant, a certain conventional privilege seems to be awarded to the romancer; his work is not put exactly side by side with nature; and he is allowed a license with regard to every-day Probability, in view of the improved effects which he is bound to produce thereby. Among ourselves, on the contrary, there is as yet no such Faery Land, so like the real world, that, in a suitable remoteness, one cannot well tell the difference, but with an atmosphere of strange enchantment, beheld through which the inhabitants have a propriety of their own. This atmosphere is what the American romancer needs. In its absence, the beings of imagination are compelled to show themselves in the same category as actually living mortals; a necessity that generally renders the paint and pasteboard of their composition but too painfully discernible. (*Blithedale Romance,* 1–2)

Distancing himself like Hawthorne from the "severe fidelity to real life" required by some readers, the narrator of *The Confidence-Man* similarly seeks to please those who turn to fiction for both entertainment and a heightening of experience like that found in the drama:

> There is another class, and with this class we side, who sit down to a work of amusement tolerantly as they sit at a play, and with much the same expectations and feelings. They look that fancy shall evoke scenes different form those of the same old crowd round the custom-house counter, and same old dishes on the boarding-house table, with characters unlike those of the same old acquaintances they meet in the same old way every day in the same old street. And as, in real life, the proprieties will not allow people to act out themselves with that unreserve permitted to the stage; so, in books of fiction, they look not only for more entertainment, but, at bottom, even for more reality, than real life itself can show. Thus, though they want novelty, they want nature, too; but nature unfettered, exhilarated, in effect transformed. (*CM,* 182–83)

With nods in the direction of Hawthorne's preface to *The Scarlet Letter* ("the same old crowd round the custom-house counter") as well as the preface to *The House of the Seven Gables* ("the same old dishes on the boarding-house table"), Melville is thus reformulating the theatrical analogy of Hawthorne's *Blithedale* preface, but with a more assured sense of creative power than Hawthorne's diffident nature would allow. Both writers are nevertheless affirming a familiar tenet of literary Romanticism, that is, the imagination's ability to create a fictive reality that is more "real" than the world of appearances.

In short, Melville's remarks here reflect the situation of the American writer of "romance" who is attempting to validate an imaginative realm for his fiction.[3] Melville's claim that he is merely seeking to entertain his audience may also remind us of another classical requirement for the "poetic" art, the need to give pleasure (*dulce*). More than one critic has noticed that the claims on behalf of truth to nature in Chapter 14 seem inconsistent with those on behalf of nature "unfettered, exhilarated, in effect transformed," as described in Chapter 33. But rather than invalidating the argument in both chapters, or showing the bad faith of the narrator, the apparent inconsistency here arises from two different aspects of literary representation, an ethical one concerned with truth and an aesthetic one concerned with pleasure or beauty—in other words, the Horatian *utile* and *dulce*.

The immediate occasion for the interpolated essay in Chapter 44 is the barber's remark that the cosmopolitan is "QUITE AN ORIGINAL." After observing that education and experience inevitably reduce one's estimation of originality, the narrator goes on to qualify the presence of originality in most contemporary fictional characters as compared with Hamlet, Don Quixote, and Milton's Satan. Thus while a number of contemporary fictional characters may strike the reader as "novel, or singular, or striking, or all four at once," the original character "is like a revolving Drummond light, raying away from itself all round it." Only one such powerful character can inhabit a work of fiction. And even the truly original character cannot be produced in the author's imagination alone, for "all life is from the egg."

The narrator's remarks in Chapter 44 imply that the "original" character is one who partakes of both the moral mystery and revelatory luminescence of the divine. And while Chapter 44 implies that Melville's Confidence Man is indeed an attempt at such an "original" character, the argument here also constitutes a kind of "vanity of human wishes" for the writer who aspires to create this class of character according to Melville's demanding specifications. Significantly, the narrator's characterization of the novelist's *modus operandi* evokes both Melville's ironic method in *The Confidence-Man* as well as his discovery of the historical model for his protagonist in contemporary New York: "Every great town is a kind of man-show, where the novelist goes for his stock, just as the agriculturalist goes to the cattle-show for his. But in the one fair, new species of quadrupeds are hardly more rare, than in the other are new species of characters—that is, original ones." While this assertion hints at an allusion to Bunyan's Vanity Fair, used by Thackeray in his 1848 novel of the same name, Chapter 44 may also have a contemporary topical source in a November 1853 article in *Putnam's* magazine on Charles Dickens' phenomenal ability to create "original" characters, as most recently seen in *Bleak House* (Quirk, "Two Sources").

Yet whatever the immediate topical inspiration for Chapter 44, it implicitly emerges out of Melville's own prolonged meditation on the process of literary creation, and the expression of individuality and originality that were the hallmark of the romantic writer. The excursus on originality thus has a source in Melville's own aspirations as a writer who once sought to become the messiah of American literature but who was now a prophet in the wilderness. In 1850, we recall, Melville thought he had found *the* original American genius in Nathaniel Hawthorne, and he commemorated the event in his *Mosses* essay. Based on this discovery, and fortified by his own growing literary ambitions, Melville on this occasion championed a uniquely original American literature, noting of his country's writers: "It is true, that but few of them as yet have evinced that decided originality which merits great praise. . . . But it is better to fail in originality, then to succeed in imitation" (*PT,* 247). This claim, however, was brusquely retracted two years later in *Pierre,* when Melville wrote: "The world is forever babbling of originality; but there never yet was an original man, in the sense intended by the world; the first man himself—who according to the Rabbins was also the first author—not being original; the only original author being God" (*P,* 259).

The narrator's qualified remarks on "originality" in Chapter 44 of *The Confidence-Man* thus stand halfway between the alternating celebration and denigration of the concept in Melville's earlier writings.[4]

Significantly, Melville's choice of three original characters in Chapter 44 involves no work of American literature—again, a reversal of the outspoken literary nationalism found in the *Mosses* review. Instead, Melville chose characters from three great works of seventeenth-century drama, fiction, and poetry—Hamlet, Don Quixote, and Milton's Satan—who are said to act as high-powered lights radiating through their fictive worlds like suns at the center of a planetary system. In this sense, these characters are comparable to the Confidence Man as a satirical agent who illuminates the moral darkness around him. Moreover, each of the three may be considered as typifying one aspect of the Confidence Man's composite moral identity of vengeful knave (Satan), holy fool (Don Quixote) and trickster-like "original genius" (Hamlet).

Finally, in addition to commenting on *The Confidence-Man*'s general satiric method, Melville's image of the Drummond light—and indeed much of the argument in this chapter—also forms part of a debate relating to classic and romantic theories of literary creation. On the one hand, a classical notion of *mimesis* is apparent in the narrator's insistence that an artist must always go to nature for his subject, for "all life is from the egg." On the other hand, the characterization of Hamlet, Don Quixote, and Milton's Satan evokes a conventional symbol of the romantic artist, the lamp. The god-like nature of the romantic creator is also evident in the imaginative act that creates an original character, "so that, in certain minds, there follows upon the adequate conception of such a character, an effect, in its way, akin to that which in Genesis attends upon the beginning of things." The act of creation is the same for the human and the divine author, the one creating the literary, the other the cosmic *theatrum mundi*. In this concluding theoretical discussion, Melville balances the claims of *mimesis* and *poesis* in the genesis of great works of art while indirectly affirming the exalted vocation of the artist.

Epilogue

Melville completed composition of *The Confidence-Man* some time in the summer of 1856, for his sister Augusta was busy preparing a copy of the novel in the middle of July (*Log*, 2:517). In August Melville took a much-needed vacation, visiting his uncles in Gansevoort and Albany, and spending time with his brother Allan on Lake George. Allan would go on to handle the legal details of Melville's contract for *The Confidence-Man* with his new publisher, Dix, Edwards & Co., and then oversee publication of the novel while Melville was on his extended tour of Europe and the Levant. For some time during that summer, Melville's family decided that Melville's health required a long vocation from his writing. As Judge Shaw wrote to his son Sam on September 1, 1856:

> I suppose you have been informed by some of the family, how very ill, Herman has been. It is manifest to me from Elizabeth's letters, that she has felt great anxiety about him. When he is deeply engaged in one of his literary works, he confines him[self] to hard study many hours in the day, with little or no exercise, & this specially in winter for a great many days together. He probably thus overworks himself & brings on severe nervous affections. He has been advised strongly to break off this labor for some time, & take a voyage or a journey, & endeavor to recruit. (*Log*, 2:521)

In accordance with this plan, Melville went to New York in late September and spent the next few days socializing with Evert Duyckinck and others while getting ready for his trip, which began on October 11.

Although Melville's trip was planned as a recuperative journey to restore his health, the nine-month excursion may have been equally important as a species of spiritual pilgrimage. Indeed, Hawthorne's account of his meeting with Melville in Liverpool that November reveals Melville's despair over his loss of religious faith, specifically his inability to believe in a spiritual afterlife:

> Melville, as he always does, began to reason of Providence and futurity, and of everything that lies beyond human ken, and informed me that he had "pretty much made up his mind to be annihilated;" but still he does not seem to rest in that anticipation; and, I think, will never rest until he gets hold of a definite belief. It is strange how he persists—and has persisted ever since I knew him, and probably long before—in wandering to and fro over these deserts, as dismal and monotonous as the sand hills amid which we were sitting. He can neither believe, nor be comfortable in his unbelief; and he is too honest and courageous not to try to do one or the other. If he were a religious man, he would be one of the most truly religious and reverential; he has a very high and noble nature, and better worth immortality than most of us. (*Log*, 2:529)

Given Melville's obsession at this point with loss of faith in a personal immortality, it is not surprising that we find repeated signs of this preoccupation in the laconic and sometimes cryptic notations he made in his journal. In Constantinople that December, for example, upon seeing the area where Constantine's soldiers had fought and died now devoted to agriculture, he parodied St. Paul (I Cor. 15) in commenting, "sowed in corruption & raised in potatoes" (*J*, 62). (Melville was so taken with Paul's famous formula that he would use it again several weeks later when remarking on a Roman tomb with olive trees growing out of it: "sown in corruption, raised in olives" [*J*, 111]; and in another related entry he noted: "Tomb on 'Appian'—sown in corruption, raised in grapes" [*J*, 159].) Yet it is apparent that his flippant dismissal of personal immortality masked a deeper despair. One prominent indication of this was Melville's response to the emotional agony of the widow at an Armenian funeral in Constantinople:

> Saw a burial. Armenian. Juggling & incantations of the priests—making signs &c.—Nearby, saw a woman over a new grave—no grass on it yet. Such abandonment of misery! Called to the dead, put her head down as close to it as possible; as if calling down a hatchway or cellar; besought—"Why don't you speak to me? My God! It is I!—Ah, speak—but one word!—All deaf. So much for consolation.—This woman & her cries haunt me horribly. (*J*, 62)

In Egypt in early January the pyramids stimulated him into one of his most outspoken comments on the malevolence and inscrutability of the Old Testament deity: "It was in these pyramids that was conceived the idea of Jehovah. Terrible mixture of the cunning and awful" (*J*, 75). This disillusioned observation was confirmed by his view of the stony landscape of Judea later that month, the sight of which led him to make the ironic query: "Is the desolation of the land the result of the fatal embrace of the Deity? Hapless are the favorites of heaven" (*J*, 91). In the same vein, Melville noted the unsettling feeling of being cheated in Jerusalem, where Christianity was seemingly made into a marketable commodity (*J*, 85); and seeing the "Beautiful Gate" in that city, now walled up by the city's Ottoman overlords, he remarked that it "seems expressive of the finality of Christianity, as if this was the last religion of the world—no other, possible" (*J*, 86). Such comments reaffirmed the skeptical views he had been dramatizing a few months before in his most recent novel, and particularly in its last chapter.

Given his mock enactment of the Second Coming in that novel and in that last chapter, it is not surprising to find Melville commenting on American millenarians preparing for this event in the Holy Land. According to Pauline doctrine (Romans 11), the conversion and return of the Jews to their homeland was a catalyst or precondition for Christ's Second Advent. Melville found several Americans in Joppa who were ostensibly preparing the way for Christ's return through missionary work and agricultural instruction among the Jews, but in the meantime suffering much deprivation and discouragement. In particular, Melville recorded his conversation with a Deacon Dickson from Groton, Massachusetts (John Steinbeck's great-grandfather); in 1853 Dickson had sold his farm in America and moved with his family to Palestine. Melville's wry description of this encounter is in the satirical, dramatic mode of his most recent novel:

> *H.M.* "Have you settled here permanently, Mr Dickson?"
>
> *Mr D.* "Permanently settled on the soil of Zion, Sir." with a kind of dogged emphasis.
>
> *Mrs. D.* (as if she dreaded her husband's getting on his hobby, & was pained by it)—"The walking is a little muddy, aint it?"—(This to Mr. S. [i.e., Mr. Saunders, a Seventh-Day Adventist missionary])
>
> *H.M. to Mr. D.* "Have you any Jews working with you?"
>
> *Mr D.* No. Can't afford to hire them. Do my own work, with my son. Besides, the Jews are lazy & dont like work.
>
> *H.M.* "And do you not think that a hindrance to making farmers of them?"
>
> *Mr D.* "That's it. The Gentile Christians must teach them better. The fact is the fullness of Time has come. The Gentile Christians must prepare the way.
>
> *Mrs D.* (to me) "Sir, is there in America a good deal of talk about Mr D's efforts here?
>
> *Mr D.* Yes, do they believe basicaly in the restoration of the Jews?

> *H.M.* I can't really answer that.
>
> *Mrs D.* I suppose most people believe the prophecys to that effect in a figurative sense—dont they?
>
> *HM.* Not unlikely. &c &c &c. (*J*, 93–94)

Melville's final comment on Dickson's project: "The whole thing is half melancholy, half farcical—like the rest of the world" (*J*, 94).

In contrast to his wry depiction of this American millenarian, Melville himself was more inclined to despair when he had earlier passed by the island of Patmos on which St. John experienced his famous Revelation. He coasted this bleak island the first time on his way south from Constantinople to Egypt, at which time he commented: "Patmos, too, not remote; another disenchanting isle. . . . to look upon the bleak yellow of Patmos, who would ever think that a god had been there[?]" (*J*, 71–72). But the full expression of Melville's spiritual predicament was only revealed upon his return past the island a few weeks later, after he had visited the Holy Land and was on his way to Italy:

> Patmos is pretty high, & peculiarly barren looking. No inhabitants.—Was here again afflicted with the great curse of modern travel—skepticism. Could no more realize that St: John had ever had revelations here, than when off Juan Fernandez, could believe in Robinson Crusoe according to De Foe. When my eye rested on arid height, spirit partook of the barrenness.—Heartily wish Niebuhr & Strauss to the dogs.—The deuce take their penetration & acumen. They have robbed us of the bloom. If they have undeceived any one—no thanks to them. (*J*, 97)

It may seem extraordinarily ironic to find Melville confessing an inability to believe in the existence of St. John or his Revelation when he had just satirically refigured the Apocalypse in his most recent novel. Moreover, his complaint that the German historian Barthold Niebuhr and the theologian David Strauss had destroyed Christianity in their historicizing and mythicizing treatment of sacred subjects appears incongruous in view of Melville's own imaginative manipulation of Christian history in *The Confidence-Man.* But Melville is merely expressing his personal frustration arising out of the conflict between the skepticism he shared with some of his European contemporaries, and his own residual impulse toward religious faith.

Melville's tour subsequently took him to Italy for about two months (mid-February to mid-April), where he immersed himself in that country's rich heritage of classical, Renaissance, and Baroque art, an experience that would contribute to his developing interest in art and aesthetics. Like a number of his contemporaries, Melville was reacting to the apparent exhaustion of Christianity by turning to the "religion" of art. In the meantime, some of the comments in his travel journal continued to reflect his divided mood of skepticism and despair over the waning of his religious faith. The skepticism can be seen in his characterization of the amusing scapegrace he hired as a guide in Venice: "Antonio good character for Con. Man[.] Did not want to die. Heaven. You believe dat? I go dere, see how I like it first" (*J*, 120). However, Melville's reaction to Leonardo's *Last Supper* in Milan was perhaps more characteristic of the generally somber mood of his travels: "Significance of the Last Supper. The joys of the banquet soon depart. One shall betray me, one of you—man so false—the glow of sociality so evanescent, selfishness so lasting" (*J*, 121). As we have seen, Melville had dramatized the same belief in the latter half of *The Confidence-Man.*

Back in Liverpool in preparation for his return to America, Melville saw Hawthorne for the last time (*J*, 129). As earlier noted, Hawthorne had helped get *The Confidence-Man* published in England a few weeks before Melville passed through in early May: the English edition, published by Longman, Brown, Green, Longmans & Roberts, came out near the beginning of April. When Melville returned home to America on May 20, 1857, *The Confidence-Man* had already been published on April 1; but by the end of the month, his publishers, Dix & Edwards, had gone bankrupt, thereby carrying the April Fools' Day motif in the novel to unexpected and disheartening lengths. Only three substantial reviews of the novel appeared in America at this time, as compared with nine long British reviews in the leading papers and journals, several of them quite favorable. As Hugh Hetherington remarks, "one cannot help suggesting that the British journalists were more sophisticated connoisseurs of satire" (264). Representative of the more positive British response was the anonymous reviewer for the July 1857 issue of the *Westminister and Foreign Quarterly Review,* who accurately perceived the contemporary historical dimension of Melville's satire but was apparently unaware of its larger religious dimensions:

> We are not among those who have faith in Herman Melville's South Pacific travels so much as in his strength of imagination. *The Confidence-Man* shows him in a new character—that of a satirist, and a very keen, somewhat bitter observer. His hero, like Mr. Melville in his earlier works, asks confidence of everybody under different masks of mendicancy, and is, on the whole, pretty successful. The scene is on board an American steamboat—that epitome of the American world—and a variety of characters are hustled on the stage to bring out the Confidence-Man's peculiarities. . . . Money is of course the great test of confidence, or credit in its place. Money and credit follow the Confidence-Man through all his transformations—misers find it impossible to resist him. It required close knowledge of the world, and of the

> Yankee world, to write such a book and make the satire acute and telling, and the scenes not too improbable for the faith given to fiction. Perhaps the moral is the gullibility of the great Republic, when taken on its own tack. At all events, it is a wide enough moral to have numerous applications, and sends minor shafts to right and left. (Branch, *Critical Heritage,* 385)

Contrary to this praise for Melville's intimate knowledge of American life, his own local paper, the *Berkshire County Eagle* (edited by his friend J.E.A. Smith), claimed, "We need not say to those who have read the book that as a picture of American society, it is *slightly* distorted" (*Log,* 2:580). In America generally, the critical response was either perfunctory, puzzled, or else annoyed by the novel's obscurity; even the more positive comments did not penetrate very deeply into the book's overall significance.[1]

Whatever the reviewers in either England or America thought of the book, few readers in both countries actually bought it. In America, where sales figures have not survived, the demise of Melville's publisher only four weeks after publication left the novel in a commercial limbo from which it never emerged. In September 1857 Melville was unable to purchase the stereotype plates of the novel even at a discount, and the plates were probably destroyed (*C,* 311–16). In England by June 1857, 343 out of 1,000 copies printed had been sold. Two years later, the total sold had reached only 386, while 516 copies had been "wasted" (i.e., sold as scrap paper) and the publisher had lost over £20 on the book (*CM,* 317). Inasmuch as he had gone through a similar commercial debacle with *Pierre* and had not made an adequate income from his writing in half a decade, Melville was prepared by the summer of 1857 to give up trying to make a living writing fiction (*Log,* 2:580). Like a number of other writers of the era, he would try the lecture platform for a livelihood. And so like his own cosmopolitan, Melville assumed the role of perambulant citizen of the world, discoursing on "Statues in Rome," "The South Seas," and "Traveling" over the next three years while quietly beginning a new, noncommercial writing career as a poet. In the meantime, his last published work of fiction virtually disappeared from view. Despite its immediate topical relevance, Melville's satire would have to await a later age for an audience.

But if *The Confidence-Man,* and indeed Melville himself, effectively disappeared from public view, the moral and metaphysical tendencies of his last novel prophetically anticipated the work of the leading writers of the next generation. Although more firmly committed to providing entertainment for his culture, Mark Twain was a successor to Melville as moral jester and increasingly bitter critic of both a malign cosmos and a "damned human race." Indeed, if *Life on the Mississippi, Huckleberry Finn,* and the various versions of *The Mysterious Stranger* were somehow imaginatively synthesized, they might create a narrative approximating *The Confidence-Man.*[2]

Still another brave desponder, Henry Adams, would in his later writings such as the *Education* envision an apocalyptic finale to the progressive-minded, outwardly prosperous nineteenth century. And Henry James, who produced an early novel entitled *Confidence* (1879), would strike a note comparable to that found in Melville's novel when he portentously asked at the end of his record of a visit to America early in the twentieth century, *The American Scene* (1907): "What *was* preliminary confidence, where it had to reckon so with the minimum of any finished appearance? How, when people were like that, did any one trust any one enough to begin, or understand any one enough to go on, or keep the peace with any one enough to survive?" (426).

The Confidence-Man also prefigures in both theme and form a number of trends in modern fiction, including the mythic method embraced by literary Modernism. Like Melville's novel, Joyce's *Ulysses* constitutes a dawn-to-midnight microcosmic epic incorporating a mythic search for the father and employing characters modeled on the author's family, friends, and literary contemporaries. Robert Alter, on the other hand, has traced Melville's philosophical vision in the novel to Conrad, Kafka, and Beckett, while R.W.B. Lewis has demonstrated how *The Confidence-Man*'s apocalyptic framework prefigures related narratives by West, Ellison, Barth, and Pynchon. Finally, as John Wenke reminds us, *The Confidence-Man* "anticipates those modern writers who see the form of the novel primarily as a complex, teasing, self-referential puzzle, a mystifying letter to oneself, a cunning exercise in aesthetic detachment designed to keep the gentle reader amused, but at a careful distance" ("No 'i' in Charlemont," 275). Although sown in the corruption of American ideals and Christian metaphysics, Melville's last published novel has clearly arisen in spirit to fertilize the imaginations of a saving remnant of contemporary readers and writers.

Notes

CHAPTER 1

1. The history of the appearance of the "Original Confidence Man" is fully chronicled in Bergmann, "Original Confidence Man" (quotations are from pages 563, 564, and 566). The "Historical Note" in *CM,* 276–94, provides a useful overview of the genesis of the novel.

2. On the historical and literary prototypes of the "Original Confidence Man," see Bergmann, "Original Confidence Man: Development," Chs. 1–3; Seelye, "Introduction"; Blair, *Confidence Man,* Ch. 1; and Halttunen, Chs. 1–2. On the confidence man as a characteristic figure in American literature, see the studies of Kuhlmann, Wadlington, Lindberg, and Lenz.

3. For a standard survey of American millennialism, see Tuveson, *Redeemer Nation.* (Tuveson, 34, substitutes the terms "millenarian" and "millennialist" for the more traditional "premillennial" and "postmillennial.") On the interplay of pre- and postmillennialism during the nineteenth century, see Moorhead. On William Miller and his movement, see Numbers and Butler; see also Gaustad. It should be noted that Miller's prediction of the Second Coming for some time between March 1843 and March 1844—which has been estimated to have gained about 50,000 converts with perhaps a million who were vaguely "expectant"—was officially disconfirmed on October 22, 1844, the final revised date. Melville undoubtedly knew of Miller's movement since he returned home from his four years in the Pacific in mid-October 1844 and was discharged in Boston (*Log,* 1:186; *C,* 27, 565–71). Here he might have observed the Millennial Tabernacle built by the Millerites to prepare for their apocalyptic ascension. Furthermore, Melville's return home to his family in Lansingburgh, New York, later that month exactly coincided with the expected Second Coming of Christ. See Hershel Parker, "Biography," 31.

4. For a more detailed summary of Melville's personal life leading up to the composition of his last novel, see the "Historical Note" in *CM,* 255–76; see also Howard, 226–37, and Foster, xx–xxxii.

5. On the themes and methods of Melville's short fiction, see Fisher and Dillingham, *Melville's Short Fiction*. For a discussion of *Israel Potter* in relation to *The Confidence-Man*, see John McWilliams, 189–200.

6. Griffith provides an insightful analysis of Melville's religious thought and the genesis of his skepticism. For a brief overview, see Braswell. Thompson provides a one-sided, overstated account of Melville's "quarrel" with the deity, but provides important analyses of the Christian symbolism of Melville's fiction. For other informative surveys of Melville's religious thought in comparative context, see Baritz, Ch. 6; Frederick, Ch. 3; and Carter, 176–95.

7. Melville's first explicit treatment of the theodicy issue occurs in Chapter 135 of *Mardi*. Traditionally, there are five ways to explain the problem of evil posed by theodicy: first, there is no god; second, god is malevolent, or else a malevolent deity exists alongside a good deity (dualism); third, human beings are guilty of original sin and hence deserving of evil; fourth, suffering is educative; fifth, suffering is temporary. For an overview of theodicy as a theological issue, see Hick.

8. On Melville's sources for the "ship of fools" motif in Brandt and his imitators in late medieval and Renaissance literature, see Rosenberry, "Ship of Fools."

9. Bryant, *Melville & Repose*, 234–38, has documented the textual links between the various guises of the Confidence Man in the first half of the novel, as well as the manner in which his interlocutors in the second half are united by traits that characterize the Confidence Man in the first half.

10. It should be noted that Shroeder anticipated Lewis in pointing out some of the apocalyptic imagery of the last chapter of Melville's novel, suggesting that "Melville's book of the Apocalypse . . . is more closely allied to the vision of Pope's *Dunciad* than to that of John's Revelation" (312). Over the last three decades, several other critics have variously interpreted the significance of the novel's apocalyptic structure and symbolism. Thus Combs argues that "*The Confidence-Man* is, in fact, a complex allegory creating a kind of looking-glass world, a world where the unfolding of Christian history is inverted and subverted. The 'vision' of the novel culminates in an apocalypse which invokes but does not share the assurance of those events prophesied in the book of Revelation. As a false prophet or anti-christ, the confidence man effects an ironic mimicry of Christ's ministry" (12). For Schultz, the novel is "a parodic anatomy based upon the mythology of the Biblical account of the Apostasy and framed by the First and Second Comings of Christ" (241). Melville "is asking whether the Panglossian answer of faith that there will be final justice or that the ultimate order of reality is providential may not itself be a cheat, a trick worthy a cosmic confidence man" (259). May argues that the seven guises of the Confidence Man after the mute (*not* a guise of the Confidence Man in his reading) are based on the fact that seven "is an apocalyptic symbol of completion. The appearances of the confidence man, moreover, represent the last loosing of Satan, the classic Christian sign of the imminent end of the world. In showing mankind either immune to or a victim of the wiles of his loosed Satan, Melville doubts the very possibility of the ideal of charity among men" (61–62). Ketterer concludes that Melville's use of apocalyptic symbolism reveals his "perception of the reality of a Satanic universe" (*New Worlds*, 295). Karcher, *Shadow*, Ch. 7, argues that Melville's fictive enactment of the Second Coming constitutes a judgment on American's "national sin" of slavery. Following the lead of Franklin, Mani claims that *The Confidence-Man* dramatizes a conjunction of biblical and Hindu eschatology: "In his portrayal of the euphoric

belief of contemporary society that the kingdom of God has finally arrived in America, Melville draws not only upon the Christian Apocalypse for his image of Antichrist's false millennium but also upon the Hindu tradition of Vishnu and the Buddhist Void or *Nirvana*" (274). The analysis offered in the present study alternately confirms, amplifies, augments, or dissents from the claims of these critics, while it offers a comprehensive new appraisal of the novel's apocalyptic symbolism.

11. For a discussion of "The Celestial Railroad" and other related sketches from Hawthorne's *Mosses from an Old Manse* as examples of "satirical apocalypse," see Cook, "New Heavens." For a discussion of the larger mythic meaning of apocalypse, see May, Ch. 1. For a useful collection of essays on the genesis of Judeo-Christian apocalypse and its later influence on both English and American literature and culture, see Patrides and Wittreich.

12. For speculations on the source and significance of Manco Capac in the novel, see Tuveson, "Creed," and Eberwein. For a study of the mythical origins of April Fools' Day celebrations and their possible influence on *The Confidence-Man,* see Franklin, *Wake of the Gods,* 168–74. It should be noted that immediate calendrical circumstances may have also helped inspire the April Fools' Day setting of Melville's last published novel. Lane points out that Palm Sunday in 1855 occurred on April 1, possibly reminding Melville of the religious origins of April fooling (or the foolish origins of Christianity). In addition, Melville's provocative sexual allegory, "The Paradise of Bachelors and the Tartarus of Maids," was published in the April 1, 1855 issue of *Harper's* magazine. That Melville was preoccupied by the idea of April fooling at this time is also shown by his inclusion of an April Fools' Day joke in "I and My Chimney," written in the spring of 1855 (*PT,* 496).

13. For an informative overview of the challenges to traditional faith in nineteenth-century America, see James Turner, Chs. 3–9. On the interdependence of science and religion in the first half of the nineteenth century, see Hovenkamp.

CHAPTER 2

1. Much early criticism of the novel recognized its genre as satire but considered it an artistic failure. Thus according to Freeman, "Melville's satire in *The Confidence-Man* fails completely" (141). For Mumford, "When one regards *The Confidence Man* in its true light, not as a novel, but as a companion to *Gulliver's Travels,* its whole aspect changes: its turbid, tedious, meandering quality remains: but there are rapids of dangerous and exhilarating satire" (174). For Matthiessen, Melville "was too bitter, too distressed personally, to keep his satire under control, and so there is no progression to his theme" (411). For Brooks, "The opaqueness of this laborious satire, which Melville half-heartedly meant to continue, resulted from his obvious inability to draw characters any longer that were vivid enough to support the burden of thought" (168). For Arvin, "*The Confidence-Man* is not a great allegorical satire because it is not a living narrative" (249). For Mason, "the bemused fascination with which Melville's affronted sensibility looked at the spectacle of his commercialised continent was utterly alien to the detachment necessary to the satiric temper" (205). Analysis of *The Confidence-Man* as a successful satirical fiction began with the work of Chase and Foster in the 1950s. Better equipped to understand the novel following the appearance of Foster's annotated Hendricks House edition in 1954, some critics

offered more positive assessments—or at least continued recognition—of its satire. Thus Rosenberry remarked that "no other American book has so trenchantly satirized the national character—indeed, human nature in general—through the basic figures of our comic folklore" (*Comic Spirit,* 178). For James E. Miller, "Meaning in *The Confidence-Man* exits on three interlocking levels—the realistic western narrative, the symbolic American satire, and the universal allegory. Reading the book on one level only, many critics have condemned it for failure to achieve something it did not attempt" (175). For Dubler, "the book's genre . . . is satire" (309). For Humphreys, the novel's "total effect is less of gloom than of a shifting satiric fantasy of which the keynote is entertainment" (110). For Hillway, "*The Confidence-Man* hammers at human weakness with a savage but anguished satire. In essence the book amounts to a psychological analysis of human character, the allegorical spotlight centering on its moral ambiguities" (120). During the 1970s two critics in particular persuasively argued that the novel was satirical in form: Wilmes situated *The Confidence-Man* in the evolution of Melville's use of the "satirical mode" throughout his fiction; Kern showed that the novel qualifies as Menippean satire (or "anatomy" according to Frye's system of classification). It should be noted, however, that over the last three decades many critics have denied or ignored *The Confidence-Man*'s status as satire or else identified it as belonging to some other literary mode or genre. Thus Mitchell argues that "while there may be localized satirical elements in the novel, it seems doubtful that a book which lacks embodied precepts can be a satire" (29–30); both Leon Seltzer, 26, and Alvin Seltzer, 76, offer a similar caveat. Foster, xcii, Seelye, *Ironic Diagram,* 117–30, Blackburn, 158–77, and Wicks, 125–34, all classify it as a picaresque fiction. Schultz, 228–41, considers it a synthesis of picaresque and anatomy. Sten calls it a proto-existential "new novel." For Buell, it is a "carefully-constructed muddle" ("Last Word," 20). For Ramsey, it is a "metaphysical excursion in the catalogue mode" ("*Confidence-Man,*" 19). Bryant, "Melville's Problem Novel," argues that *The Confidence-Man* is ambiguously positioned between didactic and mimetic modes. For David Reynolds, "The novel is less a social satire or metaphysical treatise than it is a study of the creation of fictions, of the supremacy of style over content" (558). For Grenberg, "The narrative in *The Confidence-Man* is unarguably uncertain and 'incomplete'—a collocation of broken threads and loose ends" (180). Significantly, two recent essays suggesting new approaches to the novel's peculiarities of form also fail to mention its satirical basis; see Kearns and Dolan. For discussions of *The Confidence-Man* specifically as a work of comic fiction, see Rosenberry, *Comic Spirit,* Chs. 10–12; Hauck, *Cheerful Nihilism,* 112–30; Mushabac, 131–42; and Bryant, *Melville & Repose,* Chs. 12 and 13.

2. On the theory of satire, see Frye, 223–39, 308–14; Kernan, *Cankered Muse,* Ch. 1, and *Plot of Satire,* Ch. 1; Rosenheim, Ch. 1; Paulson, 3–20; Guilhamet, Ch. 1; and Test, Ch. 1. For a recent revisionary critique of some traditional views of satire, see Griffin.

3. Foster, xciv–v, early remarked on the heterogeneous nature of the novel's literary borrowings. More recently, Ramsey has emphasized the proliferation of forms in the novel: "If there are numerous borrowings from a variety of genres in *The Confidence-Man,* none of them predominates in this blend of stage farce, pantomime, minstrelsy, parody, picaresque, Socratic dialogue, and biblical myth" ("*Confidence-Man,*" 335). Yet as Guilhamet writes, "The design of satire brings together a generic mixture while ensuring that no genre represented will be a completed pattern" (141).

4. Schultz and Blackburn offer the most compelling cases for the novel as picaresque: Schultz, 229–35, analyzes it as a generic hybrid of picaresque and anatomy; Blackburn, 158–77, views the novel as a picaresque fiction with God as its cosmic picaro. On Sterne and the novel, see Rosenberry, *Comic Spirit,* 146–48. For other comments on the eighteenth-century philosophical background of the novel, see Tuveson, "Creed."

5. See Kernan for further discussion of satiric plot, which he characterizes as driven by the "energies of dullness" and intensification rather than development. See also Bloom and Bloom, Ch. 2, and Griffin, Ch. 4. Foster notes that "*The Confidence-Man,* in appearance without form or pattern or progression, is in reality as formal as a fugue" (xci). Several critics, however, have judged *The Confidence-Man* as formally flawed or incomplete. For Stone, the novel is simply "unfinished" (233). Based on the novel's last sentence as well as suggestive notations in Melville's journal during his 1856–1857 trip to Europe and the Levant, Horsford argues that the novel was uncompleted since Melville was planning to write a sequel. Hoffman writes of the novel's overall "failure of form" (*Form and Fable,* 310). In two speculative genetic studies, "*Confidence-Man*" and "Genesis," Branch attempts to show that the novel is a disparate patchwork of narrative fragments. For a critique of Branch's analysis, see Parker, "Use of Evidence."

6. Randolph points out that "an innumerable variety of purely rhetorical devices is employed to give point, compactness, speed, climax, contrast, surprise, and a score more of the special effects so necessary to good satire" (373). A number of critics have commented on the language, style and wordplay in the novel. Lewis notes the "self-erasing" quality of the prose ("Confidence Man," 64–66). Tichi argues that the language of the novel exemplifies the "debasement" of language in antebellum America. Blair remarks that the novel's frequent puns "unite in compact verbal play the conflicting interpretations of characters and events which constitute the essential ambiguity of the whole" ("Puns and Equivocations," 91). Ramsey, " 'Touching' Scenes," calls attention to the range of meanings associated with the words "touch" and "touching" in the novel.

7. Other critics have variously commented on the ambiguity of Melville's satirical norm. According to Cawelti, "We are left in the air with no way of resolving two mutually exclusive possibilities" (83). For Wadlington, "The hero's vantage point of perfect confidence allows a caustic view of everything he comes into contact with, and yet it is apparent that it is not itself the real norm but is also undercut" (146). For Agnew, "*The Confidence-Man* points in two directions at once: backward, toward an ancient tradition of corrective criticism, and at the same time forward, toward the modernist's stance of indeterminacy" (201). For Palmeri, "The need for trust between people as a precondition for society, although paradoxically there is no ground for such trust, thus comes to constitute the absent center of value in *The Confidence-Man,* comparable to the need for an interior moral judgment in *The Tale of a Tub*" (98). On the other hand, some critics adduce a positive norm from the novel. According to Dubler, "In this novel the implied standard is one of goodness, decency, and righteousness. This is the standard against which are measured the depicted foibles and crimes. Within the context of the book's dialectic movement, the 'good' is the underdeveloped synthesis, undeveloped not because it is non-existent, but because it falls outside the scope of the author's literal intention, which is to depict various forms of evil" (309). For Drew, "while two interpretations of the book are

formally possible one of them [i.e., charity as an ideal] is consistently presented as slightly superior" (439). For Schultz, "What is left in the dialectic of *The Confidence-Man* is a common sense ethic that rejects either extreme of an unthinking philanthropy or an unfeeling misanthropy" (273). Finally, John McWilliams notes that "It is misleading to conclude . . . that *The Confidence-Man* is a satire without a controlling system of authorical values. Melville recognizes that the 'unshackled democratic spirit of Christianity' has been thoroughly betrayed in contemporary life, and he suggests no means for restoring it; nonetheless, that standard remains the one by which the *Fidèle* is judged and found wanting" (197).

8. On Erasmus's use of the figure of Folly, see Test, 212–13. On Swift's vision of "satiric truth" in man's limitless capacity for error, see Rosenheim, Ch. 4. Describing a series of "phases" of satire across a spectrum of comedy at one end and tragedy at the other, Frye, 126–39, suggests a relativistic, sliding scale of satiric norms from social convention to cosmic absurdity. On twentieth-century American comic apocalypses, see Lewis, "Days of Wrath." On the larger tradition of apocalypse in American fiction, see May.

9. Randolph notes that "the Satirist utilizes miniature dramas, sententious proverbs and quotable maxims, compressed beast fables (often reduced to animal metaphors), brief sermons, sharp debates, series of vignettes, swiftly sketched but painstakingly built up satiric 'characters' or portraits, figure-processions, little fictions and apologues, visions, apostrophes and invocations to abstractions—anything and everything to push his argument forward to its philosophical and psychological conclusions in much the same manner as events might push action forward to a dénouement in drama or fiction" (373). On the melding of satire and drama in Melville's novel, see also Dubler.

10. On the structural principles of comic form and the development of European comedy, see Frye, 165–86.

11. See Kernan, *Cankered Muse,* Chs. 2 and 3, for the figure of the satyr-satirist, and Ch. 4 for the development of "comical satire." On the origins of satire in the ritual curse, see Elliott, Chs. 1 and 2; for an examination of the motif of the "satirist-satirized" in the protagonists of *Timon of Athens, The Misanthrope,* and *Gulliver's Travels,* see Elliott, Ch. 4.

12. Hartman has argued for *Volpone* as a possible source for *The Confidence-Man,* but the parallels are not numerous enough to make a credible case. Mushabac, 139–40, briefly suggests *Every Man Out of His Humor* as a possible Jonsonian model but without drawing attention to the figure of the satirist-satirized found therein.

13. On the influence of Shakespearean drama on the novel, see Howard, 229–31; Long, Ch. 7; and Quirk, *Melville's Confidence Man,* 82–89. Howard adduces Jacques and Touchstone as the Confidence Man's Shakespearean models; Long considers Autolycus and Feste the principal prototypes.

14. Trimpi, "Harlequin-Confidence-Man," argues that the Confidence Man is actually based on the figure of Harlequin; the mute is thus Harlequin playing the role of Pierrot. Trimpi ambitiously attempts to fit the whole of *The Confidence-Man* into a dramatic model derived from commedia dell'arte and its successor tradition of pantomime. Yet Trimpi's fixed theatrical model is not convincing; moreover, all her "masks" are in fact ultimately related to the stereotyped characters of Greco-Roman New Comedy who have shaped European comedy for the last two thousand years.

Trimpi does, however, recognize various levels of satire in the novel, but she subordinates these to her theatrical paradigm.

15. Toll, Ch. 2, describes the rise of minstrel entertainment to national popularity starting in the mid-1840s. Identifying Guinea as a version of Tambo, Ramsey argues that "By linking his characters to acting and minstrelsy, Melville hints early in the story that what follows has as much to do with stage burlesque as with conventional prose fiction. . . . In a fiction dominated by dialogue and verbal wit instead of character description and story line, the imposters and their victims comprise a large, comic and heterogeneous olio, or a random series of speciality acts" ("*Confidence-Man*," 123, 125).

16. See Reynolds, 551–60, for an appraisal of the novel in the context of humorous writings of the 1850s. He concludes that "the humorous use of popular fads and movements throughout the novel shows Melville manipulating contemporary cultural phenomena with the bitter irony of the urban humorists" (555). Ramsey, "Barnum's Man," notes that the transformation of Black Guinea into John Ringman between Chapters 3 and 4 of the novel suggests an 1850 Barnum hoax that featured a Negro who gradually made himself white with the help of a certain medicinal "weed." (He was actually a black albino who washed off fake pigment.)

17. On Melville's skeptical epistemology in the novel, see especially Dryden, Ch. 5, and Roundy. On *The Confidence-Man* and the grotesque, see Dale Jones. On the novel and the absurd, see Leon Seltzer. Both Agnew, 195–203, and Chai, 88–99, postulate Melville's use of the *theatrum mundi* metaphor. On the novel's representation of the problem of indeterminacy and human identity, see in particular Bell, 231–45; Kemper; Bellis, "Confidence Man" and *No Mysteries,* 167–87; and Van Cromphout.

CHAPTER 3

1. As Tanner remarks, "To appreciate what Melville is doing in his extraordinary novel, it is really essential to try to see it in its historical context—that is, as being very specifically concerned with matters and phenomena generated in and by the conditions of American society, or lack of it, in the first half of the nineteenth century when the euphoria of Independence had not yet been sobered by the Civil War. Of course the novel touches on matters of universal importance and concern, but some of these universal problems first began to emerge in their modern form in the America of this time" (xiii). Two New Historicist studies have focused on the novel in relation to the development of a national market economy in the Jacksonian era, but they have not contextualized it within a detailed historical framework of the 1850s: Rogin, 236–54, reads the novel as a dramatization of the nation's new "depersonalized" marketplace and Melville's father's earlier failure in this market; Dimock, Ch. 6, posits the influence of the market as an economic model of selfhood, or what she somewhat opaquely calls "personified accounting." For other general overviews of the novel's historical and social contexts, see the introductions by Seelye, Tanner, and Matterson in their editions of the novel.

2. Melville's first-hand knowledge of the world of the Mississippi riverboat and the Southwestern frontier was gathered during his trip to visit his uncle in Galena, Illinois, in the summer of 1840. From the evidence of his fiction, he and his friend

James Fly traveled west via the Erie Canal and Great Lakes and returned via the Mississippi and Ohio rivers. See Howard, 31–37; Gilman, 151–53; Nichol; Tanselle; and Garner, "Picaresque Career". For a brief overview of the novel's "western" sources, see the "Historical Note" in *CM*, 280–82. Fussell, 303–26, analyzes *The Confidence-Man* in the context of the difference between true and false images of the western "frontier." Seelye, " 'Wicked River,' " points out Melville's probable use of Timothy Flint's writings on the Mississippi for his discarded introductory "River" chapter of the novel. On the latter, see "Manuscript Fragments" in *CM*, 490–99, and "Melville's 'River' Source" in *CM*, 511–18. Possible "local color" inspiration might have been provided by William T. Porter's weekly journal of sport and belles lettres, *The Spirit of the Times* (1831–1861), the chief forum for antebellum Southwestern humor. This journal was full of anecdotes, sketches, and stories (including those by James Hall), many of them set in the Old Southwest on or near the Mississippi River. Lenz, 117–37, examines *The Confidence-Man* in the context of the Southwestern humorists. Bergmann, "Original Confidence Man: Development," Ch. 3, provides an informative survey of the types and ploys of antebellum Southwestern confidence artists, as reflected in contemporary exposés by the reformed gambler, Jonathan Green. Sumner, comparing the image of the West presented in *Mardi* and *The Confidence-Man*, finds it "irredeemably corrupt and evil" (49) in the latter novel.

3. On corruption in New York City in the early 1850s, see Spann, Chs. 11–15. On corruption nationwide during the same period, see Summers, Chs. 1–10. On industrial development in the 1840s and 1850s, see Cochran and Miller, Ch. 4. On gambling in antebellum America, see Bergmann, cited in Note 2 above. Quirk, *Melville's Confidence-Man*, 36–37, comments on the implied association of gambling and investing in the encounter between Truman and Roberts.

4. As Shepherd remarks, "Roberts' skeptical outburst is not something piped through him; rather, it comes from his own deepest, but formerly unawakened sense of reality and a mysterious evil at the core of things which his seemingly rational beliefs do not encompass" (186). In another analysis of the merchant's encounter with Truman, Duban argues that the novel's "epistemological assumptions exploit the rhetoric of moral certainty, first to undermine the moral argument against Calvinism by pointing out the ambiguities surrounding the perception of truth—and then to enmesh in a web of theological skepticism those persons aboard the *Fidèle* who refuse to acknowledge the genuineness of whatever evidence exists for recognizing human iniquity" (*Melville's Major Fiction*, 199–200).

5. On the widespread adulteration of alcoholic beverages in antebellum America, see Furnas, *Demon Rum*, 74–75. Rorabaugh argues that heavy drinking in the first half of the nineteenth century—the basis for the concurrent rise of the temperance movement—was related to the economics of grain distribution and the anxieties generated by the rapid pace of socioeconomic change. He notes that the design of many steamboats at this time encouraged drinking: "Of all forms of public transportation, only the steamboat focused so much attention on the bar. In part, this design reflected the owners' hopes for high profits from liquor sales; some boats were little more than floating saloons. More important is the fact that the steamboat was conceived at a time when drinking was central to American society. Boat designs that stressed bars conformed to a cultural imperative" (18). For a detailed historical account of the rise of the temperance movement in nineteenth-century America, see

Tyrrell. For a popular social history of the same movement, see Furnas, *Demon Rum,* Chs. 1–8.

6. A similar comic conflation of alcoholic and supernatural "spirits" can be found in a current farce on temperance hotels entitled *Departed Spirits: or, The Temperance Hoax.* See Furnas, *Demon Rum,* 149. On the covert meaning of "Charlie Noble," see Franklin, *The Confidence-Man,* 228n. Karcher, "Philanthropy," examines *The Confidence-Man* in relation to Orestes Brownson's satire on the contemporary spiritualist craze, *The Spirit Rapper,* as well as Hawthorne's use of spiritualism in *The Blithedale Romance.*

7. The discussion here actually re-creates an eighteenth-century debate over the nature of wit and humor. Thus Noble's callous laugh exemplifies Hobbes's theory of humor as a feeling of "sudden glory" of superiority over an object of ridicule, whereas Goodman's more restrained sense of humor throughout this scene recalls the "amiable humor" of sympathetic identification, as found in the writings of Addison, Steele, Fielding, and Sterne. On this development, see Tave. For another discussion of the dynamics of humor in the Goodman–Noble encounter, see Bryant, *Melville & Repose,* 250–51, 258–61.

8. Wright, *Bible,* 153–57, first noticed the parody of Proverbs 23 in Noble's panegyric to the "press." Furnas points out that temperance speeches and sermons "came to include both the most severe Scriptural strictures on wine and a florid tribute to Water" (*Demon Rum,* 72–73). Noble's pun on "press" also suggests a possible relation to the New York wine merchant Frederic S. Cozzens' pamphlet publication, *Cozzens' Wine Press: A Vinous, Vivacious Monthly* (1854–1861), which offered stories, articles, and poetry celebrating wine and its consumption. (A minor Knickerbocker writer, Cozzens published his *Sparrowgrass Papers* in 1856.)

9. The heartwood of an American tree (*Haematoxylon Campechianum*), "logwood" was once used in the manufacture of red dye. "The alleged use of logwood in colouring spurious or adulterated port wine was at one time a frequent subject of jocular allusion" (*OED*). Oliver Wendell Holmes used the same joke in his "Autocrat of the Breakfast Table" series in 1857. See Furnas, *Demon Rum,* 73–74.

10. Karcher's ambitious argument is bolstered by a wealth of historical data, but there is reason to doubt the validity of her thesis, including the claim that "The central issue of the chapter in which Guinea plays the role of a crippled black beggar is whether the passengers—and the readers—who encounter him evidence any fellow feeling for the Negro. This issue is equally central to the succeeding chapters in which, under the guises of the man with the weed, the man in gray, and the Black Rapids man, 'Guinea' follows up the passengers who have seemingly befriended him and unmasks their racism" (*Shadow,* 195–96). What the Confidence Man "unmasks" in each character is not so much Karcher's insistent "racism," as it is human selfishness and moral depravity in general. Thus Karcher's attempt to make the agent for the Black Rapids Coal Company a peddler of stock in "the industrial analogue of the southern slave system" (*Shadow,* 211–12) misdirects Melville's satire from its target in the corruptions of the antebellum stock market to an industrial red herring. Karcher's claim that the Black Rapids Coal Company includes an indictment of the use of slaves in Southern coal mining in Virginia overlooks the fact that most coal mining at this time was done in Pennsylvania. See Taylor 38–40, 170, 233, 387. (As I demonstrate in Chapter 6, the immediate inspiration for this company was in fact Evert Duyckinck's 1850 investment in the Pennsylvania Coal Company and Wyo-

ming Coal Association.) By the same token, Karcher's attempt to slur the merchant as exhibiting "a racism so deep-seated that it determines his every response to other human beings according to whether he perceives them as black or white" (*Shadow,* 211) again provides the wrong context in which to judge him. The fact that slavery is not touched upon in the second half of the novel, especially in the long conversation of the cosmopolitan and Charlie Noble, an "Alabamaian," also weakens Karcher's argument. For these and other reasons, it is evident that Karcher's interpretation misdirects Melville's perception of "blackness" from a relevant moral and metaphysical to a largely irrelevant racial context.

11. For an illustration of the pervasiveness of this idea, compare Aunt Chloe's remark to Mrs. Shelby in *Uncle Tom's Cabin:* " 'Now, Missis, do jist look at dem beautiful white hands o' yourn, with long fingers, and all a sparkling with rings, like my white lilies when de dew's on 'em; and look at my great black stumpin hands. Now, don't ye think dat de Lord must have meant *me* to make de pie-crust, and you to stay in de parlor?' " (37). For Karcher, on the other hand, Melville's image of the gentleman keeping his hands clean symbolizes "the myth of the kind master, maintained by blaming all the abuses of the slave system on the brutish overseer and the low-born slave trader, and by projecting onto the slave the vices the master could not acknowledge in himself" (*Shadow,* 232).

12. On the evangelical faith and "benevolent empire" of antebellum America, see Tyler; Timothy Smith; Perry Miller, *Life,* Bk. 1; Nye, Chs. 2 and 8; Walters; and Abzug.

13. Nye, 383–99, surveys developments in higher education at this time, including conflicts over curricular reform that focused on the need for a more practical, even vocational, emphasis in college education. He notes that Greek-letter fraternities "began to appear in New England and New York colleges in the fifties. By midcentury there were fraternities in all major universities and most small colleges, introducing to the campuses a kind of sophisticated social life that administrators did not quite know how to handle" (396–97).

14. In a history of the New York police, Richardson remarks that the Tombs "served as the station house for the Sixth Ward police in addition to being a prison and court. The Sixth Ward, in which the Five Points was located, consistently had the highest number of arrests, the highest number of absentees, and the most requests for lodgings. Captain Matthew Brennan reported that sewerage constantly seeped in and that no one could possibly stay there in wet weather. According to Dr. A. S. Jones, the physician of the Police Department, 'More miserable, unhealthy, and horrible dungeons cannot well be conceived of.' The Tombs was built on the site of a swamp, the Collect, and it was not surprising that many policemen in the district were prostrated from pulmonary diseases" (60–61).

15. Miller, *Jacksonian Aristocracy,* Ch. 6, surveys the increasing social and economic pressures on independent artisans like Thomas Fry during the 1840s and 1850s as industrialization enriched the few and created a growing urban proletariat composed of immigrants, laborers, and the destitute. For a survey of the plight of the poor in New York City during this period, see Spann, Chs. 4–7 and 10.

16. See James Harvey Young for a full account of nineteenth-century patent medicines; on the advertisement of remedies, see Chs. 8 and 11; on contemporary criticisms of patent medicines, see 67–74. Richard Dean Smith, 144–61, has glossed the ailments of the herb doctor's patients and the nature of the herb doctor's remedies

in the context of contemporary medical science, but without taking into account the patent medicine industry, the basis for Melville's satire here.

17. James Harvey Young notes of patent medicine marketing: "Signs and symbols abounded from the religious realm. Besides angels, Eve also appeared, picking fruit in a garden. The Good Samaritan had a career that spanned the centuries. Nostrums were marketed bearing such names as Balm of Gilead, Paradise Oil, Resurrection Pills, and 666 (see Revelation 13:18)" (186).

18. For a study of the problems young men faced in finding suitable employment and moral guidance in mid-nineteenth-century America, see Horlick. The P.I.O. man's attempt to place a "boy" helper with Pitch resembles in some respects the philanthropic work of Charles Loring Brace in New York City in the 1850s. In 1853 Brace founded the Children's Aid Society to benefit abandoned, abused, and delinquent children; some of these children he relocated to the supposed healthy environment of western farms through a "placing out" system. See Spann, 267–73; Walters, 199–200. As Walters notes, however, "The plan neither succeeded in 'draining the City of vagrant Children,' as he hoped, nor served as much of a solution to the problems of poverty and juvenile crime" (200).

19. On contemporary scientific use of analogical reasoning, see Daniels, Ch. 9. On the interdependence of science and religion during this period, see also Hovenkamp. Grenberg, 184–89, discusses some of the philosophical issues at stake in Pitch's encounter with the Confidence Man.

20. Pitch as Melville's ethical ideal is perhaps most effectively stated by Bowen, 411–19. See also Seelye, *Ironic Diagram,* 127–28. For Karcher, on the other hand, Pitch is ideologically contaminated by contact with slavery: Pitch's long argument with the P.I.O. man "is about the impact slavery has on the nation that sanctions it, on the master who profits from it, and on the slave who endures it" (*Shadow,* 255). Bryant, *Melville & Repose,* 245–50, sees Pitch as a type of "false misanthrope."

21. See Quirk, *Melville's Confidence Man,* 39–44, for a more extensive discussion of the resemblances between Noble, Winsome, and Egbert.

22. For a discussion of money in Jacksonian and antebellum America, see Galbraith, Chs. 7 and 8. For an overview of the financial institutions and economic developments of this era, see Taylor, Chs. 14 and 15. Besides counterfeiting, the chaotic currency of the pre-Civil War era created other opportunities for exploitation, as Taylor points out: "Merchants and manufacturers at times suffered serious loss because of having to accept depreciated or doubtful paper. Undoubtedly, also, the inconvenience of a nonuniform currency added to their cost of doing business. However, business was customarily able to pass on these losses to employees or customers and, at least in some cases, actually to enlarge its earnings by currency manipulation. Workmen repeatedly complained that their wages were seriously reduced because employers forced them to accept depreciated paper at its face value. Merchants, constantly making money transactions and therefore much better informed than their customers as to the market value of bank notes, often picked up an additional profit because of such knowledge" (329–30).

23. Quirk, *Melville's Confidence Man,* 141–46, provides a guide to the verbal innuendos of the conversation between the barber and the cosmopolitan, but he mistakenly calls the contemporary broker a "pandering retailer akin to a Yankee peddler" and thus overlooks some of the wider cultural implications of the debate. He has also found the likely literary source for the scene with the barber in the November

1855 *Harpers Monthly Magazine,* which carried Melville's story "Jimmy Rose." See Quirk, *Melville's Confidence Man,* 163–65. Sewell discusses the debate between the barber and the cosmopolitan in the context of contemporary arguments that Christianity and business could be harmonized.

24. See Hunter, Chs. 6 and 13, for a detailed examination of western steamboat accidents and the movement for government regulation: "Part of the price to be paid for the great benefits of steam navigation, the West was soon to learn, was a succession of disasters in kind and scale unprecedented in the peacetime experience of this region. . . . Only a frontier massacre could match the sudden terror, the mass slaughter, the torture, and the lurid destruction attending the many steamboat accidents" (270). Steamboating in the West was in fact more dangerous compared to the rest of the country: "Between 1830 and 1850 twice as many steamboat explosions occurred on the western rivers as in the remainder of the country, with a loss of three times as many lives, although western steamboats during this period comprised less than half of the steamboat tonnage of the entire country. In the years after 1850 there was an even greater concentration upon the western rivers of losses from steamboat explosions" (291).

25. On the cultural anxieties generated by rapid technological advances during this era, see Douglas T. Miller, *Birth of Modern America,* Ch. 3. In an attempt to relate Melville's life preserver/chamber pot joke to a contemporary source, Duban and Scheick point out that the invention of a steamboat life preserver using a large "metallic air vessel" under a seat or stool was announced in the New York *Christian Inquirer* on August 14, 1852, but apparently was never patented. Melville's life preserver joke here, however, should be seen in a more general historical context: "Life preservers of one kind or another were introduced by 1840 on some steamboats and later [i.e., in 1852] were required by law but, judged by reports of accidents, they played a negligible role" (Hunter, 280n).

26. Miles explains the currency problem in Mississippi at this time: "The speculative mania of the middle eighteen-thirties was not confined to the Southwest, but was prevalent in varying degrees throughout the nation. But in no state were its effects felt so profoundly as in Mississippi. Consequently, when the 'Flush Times' ended, as they did abruptly with the panic of 1837, no state experienced more disastrous financial reverses. . . . By the middle eighteen-forties all banks had ceased operations in the state; in fact, resentment against such institutions was so intense that no further banks were chartered in antebellum Mississippi. A constitutional amendment to deny the legislature power to charter such institutions was presented to the electorate in 1847, but it did not receive an absolute majority of those voting in the general election of that year and thus failed of adoption. Thereafter until the Civil War Mississippians generally relied for their paper currency upon bank notes issued by institutions chartered by other states, while commission merchants and brokers performed many of the services earlier rendered by the banks" (130, 157).

27. In his historical gloss on the peddler's counterfeit detector, Weissbuch notes that "The counterfeit detector serves to reflect all the nineteenth-century mundane interest and falsity which Melville satirically condemned in his book" (18). For a survey of the history of counterfeiting in America, see Glaser.

28. On the "spermatic economy," see Barker-Benfield, Ch. 15. Todd was Congregational minister in Pittsfield, Massachusetts, from 1842 to 1873 and so was probably a familiar figure to Melville in the 1850s. He may even have helped inspire

Melville's story, "The Lightning-Rod Man." See Philip Young, Ch. 4. As young men, Melville's two brothers, Gansevoort and Allan, owned Todd's *Index Rerum* and *Student's Manual,* respectively (Sealts, *Melville's Reading,* nos. 526a and 527).

CHAPTER 4

1. As noted, critics have debated whether *The Confidence-Man* qualifies as an allegory and what allegorical modes it employs. Thus for Mushabac, it is "neither . . . allegorical nor allegorically satirical" (139). For Lindberg, "the novel is not a philosophical dialogue or an allegory" (19). Quirk claims that the novel's "ambiguous title character possessed a dramatic flexibility that permitted his creator to explore through him a wideranging suggestiveness too complex for simple allegory" (*Melville's Confidence Man,* 61). For Bryant, "the non-fulfillment of Black Guinea's list leads to an arrhythmic, asymmetric, and incomplete fiction, one that is at best a problematic allegory" (*Melville & Repose,* 235). Rosenberry, on the other hand, asserts that *The Confidence-Man* is a "*dynamic allegory,* generating its meaning out of the moral flux of role-playing characters" (*Melville,* 52). Barney, Ch. 5, argues that the novel is a Romantic allegory exemplifying a shift from traditional social and cosmic hierarchy to individual imagination. Chai, 88–99, affirms that the novel illustrates a movement from symbolism back to allegory in Melville's fiction. Among critics who have attempted to find a paradigm for the progression of the Confidence man's guises, Foster, lv–lvi, associates them with the Sermon on the Mount and I Corinthians 13; Franklin, *Wake of the Gods,* 174–87, traces them to Hindu mythology; Browner associates them with various seventeenth- and eighteenth-century philosophers; McHaney derives them from the metamorphoses of Milton's Satan; and Quirk, *Melville's Confidence Man,* 61–73, adduces them from St. Paul's list of Christian vocations in I Corinthians 12:28. For a discussion of the structure of the novel in relation to the Pauline virtues, see Blair, *Confidence Man,* 37–45.

2. Barney points out that "The beginning and end of *The Confidence-Man* establish its typological structure. . . . As in the *Psychomachia, Piers Plowman,* and Book One of the *Fairie Queene,* we find a beginning which recalls *the* beginning, narrations of experiences, and an end which recalls the apocalypse" (145–46). Bryant similarly notes that "The novel's first half is an Old Testament that supplies the type of the confidence man; the second, New Testament half, the antitype" (*Melville & Repose,* 236). For Reed, on the other hand, "*The Confidence-Man* is neither parody nor satire of Scripture . . . but a novelization of the Old and New Testaments, a project that both recapitulates earlier forms of a novelistic critique of literature and defies the traditional assurances of the novel itself" (210). For a discussion of Melville as a typological symbolist, see Brumm, Ch. 8. On Melville and the Bible generally, see Foster and Heidmann.

3. For another discussion of allusions to the biblical apocalypse in the first chapter of *The Confidence-Man,* see Karcher, *Shadow,* 186–89. See also my note on the text, "From 'Myth' to 'Mystery,' " for an emendation of the word "myth" in the fourth paragraph of the novel—a well-known textual crux—to "mystery," a correction that slightly augments the apocalyptic ambience of the first chapter.

4. For a useful tabulation of critical opinion on the Confidence Man's symbolic identity, see Madison. (Madison's findings are discussed in the "Historical Note" in

CM, 342–43.) According to Madison's calculation, among 101 critics writing between 1922 and 1980, sixteen consider the Confidence Man unknowable or ambiguous, sixteen as the devil, two as Christ, four as God, four as a trickster god, six as both God and the devil, and ten as a man; twenty-four don't discuss his symbolic identity while nineteen associate him with some other identity. In theory, virtually all of these critical positions are acceptable. The challenge is to find the interpretive model—that is, Melville's skepticism in conjunction with his alternative answers to the theodicy question—that will encompass them all.

5. James E. Miller, Jr., remarks that the identification of the mute as a type of Christ "is suggested by innumerable symbolic clues, not the least of which is the final position by the stairs leading upward: the way to heaven, salvation, is through Christ" (177). On the image of the farmer surveying his snow-covered March fields, see Dante, *Inferno,* Canto XXIV, 1–15. See also the Gospel of John, in which Jesus indicates to his disciples that the divine "harvest" is imminent: "Lift up your eyes, and look on the fields; for they are white already to harvest" (John 4:35).

6. Combs, 30–31, first pointed out the biblical source for this scene, adducing somewhat different parallels than my own. It should be noted that Thomas Fry's use of crutches and his sardonic "diabolical" personality also ally him with the tradition of *The Devil on Two Sticks,* the English title of Le Sage's *Le Diable Boiteux* (1707), a widely imitated novel that featured the legendary crippled devil Asmodeus as a satirical commentator who was able to see into the private lives of the inhabitants of Seville. (On this novel and its imitations, see Rudwin, 90–93; see also the reference to Asmodeus in *CM,* 89.) A contemporary example of the genre was Harrison Gray Buchanan's *Asmodeus; or, Legends of New York* (1848). In *The Confidence-Man* Thomas Fry performs an Asmodeus-like exposure of the "mysteries" of criminal justice in New York City.

7. Trimpi, "Harlequin-Confidence-Man," 173, has also noted the herb doctor's parody of transubstantiation and the historical fragmentation of Protestant faiths.

8. Combs, 87, remarks that the auburn-haired man's scribbling with his cane here evokes Christ's writing on the ground when confronted with Jews who wanted to stone the woman taken in adultery (John 8:1–11). Heidmann adds that the effect of the comparison "is to contrast the auburn-haired man's censoriousness with Jesus's unwillingness to judge, itself frequently a New Testament virtue" (204).

9. On the Confidence Man and Milton's Satan, see Blair, *Confidence Man,* 27–31; Quirk, *Melville's Confidence Man,* 76–82; and Horth. Horth claims that it is the "sustained element of irony, far more than all of the allusions and hints of the demonic in the text, that links [the Confidence Man] directly with the demonic tradition" (143). For an informative analysis of Melville's annotations of his recently recovered edition of Milton, see Grey.

10. Rosenberry, "Ship of Fools," notes that the "Devil's Joke" here probably draws on the figure of Cock Lorell, king of the gypsies in Elizabethan popular literature and lore, who was reputed to dwell in the "Devil's Hole" in Derbyshire. Jonson employs this tradition in his masque, *The Gipsies Metamorphosed,* in which Cock Lorell's residence is denominated the "Devil's Arse." Franklin, *The Confidence Man,* 179n, points out Melville's parody of Dickens's *Martin Chuzzlewit* in the depiction of a disease-ridden Cairo; Martin becomes a cook for the inn-keeper at Cairo while his servant Mark Tapley recovers from fever and ague. Nichol, 622, draws

attention to the existence of a rock formation above Cairo dubbed the "Devil's Oven."

11. In the most comprehensive argument that the Confidence Man is a figure of divine inscrutability, Magaw writes: "As the microcosmic symbol of the God of the macrocosm, the Confidence-Man in all his guises remains forever an enigma, a visible object whose masks are many layers deep—each layer consisting of just another appearance, another illusion, that man himself has attributed to his concept of God" (86). Irwin similarly argues that the novel "raises the question of whether the countless gods worshiped by mankind throughout its history, those idealized objects of human confidence, are individual deities or simply masks (Janus, Osiris, Dionysus, Christ) of a single deity; indeed, he raises the question so that he can raise at the same time the possibility that the multiplication of these gods with their contradictory natures reveals their true origin as idealized projections of the inconsistent human self" (322).

12. Critical estimates of the cosmopolitan are mixed. Keyser goes so far as to argue that he is *not* a guise of the Confidence Man; he is instead an individual who effectively balances knowledge of man's evil with the need for sociability and charity. Adducing a wide array of New Testament parallels, Bruner argues that the cosmopolitan is a disguised incarnation of Christ and thus performs an unambiguously redemptive mission. Quirk, *Melville's Confidence Man*, 89–101, asserts that the cosmopolitan's beneficent qualities were largely determined by his reading of *Don Quixote* during composition of the novel; the cosmopolitan is thus a version of Cervantes' idealistic knight. Other critics, however, find the cosmopolitan's identity more equivocal. Thus for Flibbert, "On the surface, the cosmopolitan is the voice of the people; beneath the surface, he is the devil's advocate" (148). For Kuhlmann, "The cosmopolitan, then, combines the gracious immunity of a traveling god and the warm sociability of the devil as gentleman" (119). For Wenke, "The change from con man to good man, while incidentally an embrace of Christian principles, appears actually to derive from the limitations imposed on the Confidence Man by his most difficult interlocutors, Charlie Noble, Mark Winsome, and Egbert" ("Melville's Masquerade," 237–38).

13. For a standard modern account of Dionysus, see Otto. Irwin, 337–42, demonstrates that the interaction of Frank Goodman and Charlie Noble subsumes an interplay of Dionysian and Apollonian archetypes, but he doesn't extend this Dionysian element to Goodman's identity as a whole. It is pertinent to note that after *The Confidence-Man* Melville continued to explore Dionysian motifs and characters in his writing. In Part 3 of *Clarel,* for example, the pilgrims enact a bacchic revel at the monastery of Mar Saba (*Cl,* 298–318). And in two late prose sketches concerning the "Marquis de Grandvin," Melville created another cosmopolitan, Dionysian persona. Finally, in some of his late poetry he continued to explore Dionysian themes. See Stein, *Poetry,* Chs. 11 and 12.

14. The sudden appearance of the cosmopolitan in Chapter 24 and his ensuing encounter with Pitch would seem to play on specific features of the Athenian festival of Dionysus in the early spring, the Anthesteria, which commemorated the blossoming of flowers. On the first day of this three-day festival, new wine was tasted and offered at the shrine of Dionysus in the Marshes; on the second, an actor masked as Dionysus was carried in procession in a ship through Athens; the last day was a time when the dead were thought to roam the city and citizens smeared the doors of their

houses with pitch to ward them off. In a possibly parodic scenario, Melville's Dionysian cosmopolitan arrives on the *Fidèle* from the swampy domain of Cairo and has his first encounter with a character named Pitch, whose suspicions about the cosmopolitan stem from the death and disease-ridden town from which he has emerged. Moreover, just as the Anthesteria was a festival of flowers, the cosmopolitan at one point suggests to Pitch a joint trip to London, where he plans to stay on "Primrose Hill," which Pitch will stay at Covent Garden, the London flower market.

15. Bruner, 58 ff., adduces detailed evidence of the cosmopolitan's possible associations with Christ here: Goodman's maroon slippers recall the dried blood on the feet of Christ; his pipe, as a peace pipe, evokes Christ's role as prince of peace; his praise of wine suggests Christ's mystical "vine teaching" in John 15; in his encounter with Pitch the cosmopolitan attempts to enact Christ's first miracle at Cana—turning the water-loving Pitch into a wine lover—and also plays the role of divine conciliator (II Cor. 5:19). For Reed, on the other hand, "the Cosmopolitan is a figure not of Christ but of Paul, not the Son of Man who announces that the Kingdom of God is at hand but the Apostle who writes of the transformation of the Old Law into the New" (208).

16. Ramsey notes that "the barber and Goodman sign a written agreement, which amounts to a parody of the New Covenant between God and man, as earned in the Crucifixion of Christ" ("*Confidence-Man,*" 324). Bruner, 248 ff., notices the crucifixion motif of this scene and sees the cosmopolitan's role here as imitating Christ's judgment of the sheep and the goats (Matt. 25:32–33). In particular, she associates the cosmopolitan's remark to the barber, " 'Why now, if you go through life gritting your teeth in that fashion, what a comfortless time you will have' " (*CM,* 228) with Christ's judgment on the unrighteous: "there shall be weeping and gnashing of teeth" (Matt. 25:30). She also relates the cosmopolitan's muteness while being shaved (*CM,* 234) to Isaiah's description of the man of sorrows: "He was oppressed and he was afflicted, yet he opened not his mouth: he is brought as a Lamb to the slaughter, and as a sheep before her shearers is dumb, so he openeth not his mouth" (53:7). For other comments on the religious symbolism of the scene between the barber and the cosmopolitan, see Stein, "Melville's *The Confidence-Man.*"

17. Principal commentators on the apocalyptic symbolism of the last chapter include Shroeder, 309–12; Foster, lxxxiv–lxxxvii; Hoffman, *Form and Fable,* 307–10; Schultz, 241–59; Dryden, 184–88; May, 67–69; Ketterer, *New Worlds,* 293–95; Karcher, *Shadow,* 191–93; and Mani, 265–69.

18. Foster, 363n, first pointed out the biblical source of the "horned altar," but she did not suggest a source for the image of the robed man beyond calling him a symbol of the New Testament. Hoffman, *Form and Fable,* 309, identifies the robed man as St. John but gives no reason for doing so. May's interpretation of the robed man is closest to my own: "Considered alone, the reference to the robed man with the halo could be almost any Christian saint (Rev. 6:9–11), but together with the horned altar (Rev. 8:3, 9:13) it almost certainly refers to the popular but traditional association of the John of Revelation with St. John the apostle and evangelist" (67). Karcher identifies the robed man as an emblem of Christ, the "altar" of the New Testament (*Shadow,* 192). On Melville's source for the solar lamp in Rabelais' *Fifth Book,* see Cook, "Rabelais' Solar Lamp."

19. Stein, "Melville's *The Confidence-Man,*" 49, first noted that the old man was a type of the Ancient of Days. The resemblance was confirmed by Ramsey, "*Confi-*

dence-Man," 325, but has not otherwise been acknowledged in the critical literature. Earlier commentators have adduced related allegorical identities for the old man. Thus for Richard Chase, "At the immediate cultural level the old man has clear affinities with Uncle Sam; yet in the larger symbolism of Melville's universe, he is the Old God and Father of all the planets sitting at his death-white table at the center of the universe" (205). For Hoffman, "the old man, the ultimate dupe in this Masquerade, is America grown old in ignorance of evil" (308).

20. Theodore Parker noted in his controversial discourse, "The Transient and Permanent in Christianity" (1841): "Modern criticism is fast breaking to pieces this idol which men have made out of the scriptures. It has shown that here are the most different works thrown together; that their authors, wise as they sometimes were, pious as we feel their spirit to have been, had only that inspiration which is common to other men equally pious and wise; that they were by no means infallible, but were mistaken in facts or in reasoning—uttered predictions which time has not fulfilled; men who in some measure partook of the darkness and limited notions of their age, and were not always above its mistakes or its corruptions" (quoted in Jerry Wayne Brown, 158). On the development of the higher criticism in America, see Brown; see also Hovenkamp, Ch. 4.

21. Schultz first pointed out the peddler's resemblance to the cosmic Christ depicted in Revelation 19, noting that "Just as the image of Antichrist is coalesced with that of Christ in the figure of the Cosmopolitan, so in the figure of the boy are merged the Divine and the diabolical" (259). For Combs, "The boy is doubly Christlike, for he is not only a scapegoat, but a sample of suffering, displaced, and rejected humanity" (88). Bruner, 303, associates the peddler with Antichrist and notes that his selling a lock against the ultimate thief in the night—death—is a cruel hoax. For Ketterer, the peddler "may be Anti-Christ. His appearance betokens Hell and fiery destruction" (*New Worlds,* 293–94). For Karcher, the peddler symbolizes "both the 'fiery trial' that was to test Christ's followers (I Peter 4:12) and the final conflagration" (*Shadow,* 192).

22. See Dryden, 192–94. Dryden adduces the *Homeric Hymn* to Hermes as Melville's source here; he also remarks that the conspiratorial relationship of the peddler and the cosmopolitan recalls the compact between Apollo and the infant Hermes after Apollo proves that Hermes has stolen his sacred cattle. The final image of the peddler, who "scraped back his hard foot on the woven flowers of the carpet, much as a mischievous steer in May scrapes back his horny hoof in the pasture" (*CM,* 247), may even covertly parody this event, for Hermes stole Apollo's cattle by driving them *backwards* from their grazing place.

23. For Ramsey, "The old man's actions finally dramatize that the search for wisdom, like the search for Guinea's 'ge'mmen,' is a fool's errand, a circular journey in which one returns to the starting-point holding nothing" ("*Confidence-Man,*" 333–34). For Gaudino, "In this closing scene, we see the whole process of reading and writing assailed. The written text itself appears unreliable; the Bible which supposedly teaches truth contradicts its own truths and offers truths that seem too naive to be accepted, and the pamphlet creates, rather than solves, the problem of detecting counterfeiting" (136).

24. Irwin notes that "the ending of *The Confidence-Man* seems to be a bitter parody of the conclusion of *Moby-Dick* and the notion of the writing self's survival in the written self of the work. Each book ends with the image of a life preserver.

. . . The chamber pot life preserver ('a brown stool') suggests that the symbolic partial object by which the self seeks to survive the body's death is not seminal but fecal, not the seed of a new birth but poisonous waste" (346–47).

CHAPTER 5

1. See Oliver, "Melville's Picture" and "Melville's Goneril"; Hayford, "Poe." The Emerson and Poe identifications have been almost universally accepted, while those of Thoreau and Fanny Kemble have been somewhat less securely established.

2. Trimpi's theory was first set forth in an article, "Melville's Confidence Men," which attempted to show that the characters of John Ringman, the man in gray, and the P.I.O. man were modeled on William Cullen Bryant, Theodore Parker, and Horace Greeley, respectively. Her book extends these identifications to include Benjamin Lundy, the "slavery issue," Thurlow Weed, Charles Sumner, and Henry Ward Beecher as models of other guises of the Confidence Man, and a wide range of historical figures from Stephen Douglas to Supreme Court Justice John McLean as models for his interlocutors. Rather than argue each of Trimpi's identifications, in what follows I will simply demonstrate more viable alternatives. While Melville was no doubt aware of some of the shifting political alignments of the 1850s, he clearly did not have the detailed knowledge or partisan political interests alleged by Trimpi. Her study, moreover, suffers from at least three fundamental weaknesses: first, it is incompatible with most other criticism of the novel; second, there is no evidence that Melville knew anything about most of Trimpi's suggested models; and third, Trimpi's interpretation of the novel makes it into an impenetrable biographical dictionary, not a work of literature. Trimpi's identifications have generally not gained currency in criticism of the novel, although Matterson incorporates them into his introduction to the recent Penguin edition of the novel. In *Melville's Confidence Men,* Ch. 3, and "Daumier's Robert Macaire," Trimpi also tries to link *The Confidence-Man* to contemporary political cartoons and graphic arts, but the resemblances here are again merely coincidental.

3. For Mumford, "The Confidence Man may be considered as Melville's own masquerade; his own bitter plea for support, money, confidence" (175). For Porte, "That Melville, the committed romancer who praised Hawthorne so extravagantly for his unrelievedly dark view of human existence, should body himself forth as an attractively persuasive, fantastically clever, perfidious exponent of the opposite view—herein lies the essential diabolism and infinite trickiness of *The Confidence-Man*" (*Romance in America,* 160). According to Kuhlmann, "For Melville, another easily wounded 'misanthropic philanthropist,' the confidence man offered a needed protection, a mirrored shield, the ultimate mask from behind which an embittered author could address his country" (122). For Flibbert, "*The Confidence-Man* is an ironic portrait of the artist succeeding as a con artist, adopting the angles and stratagems of a business-oriented culture in order to reap its rewards" (154). Finally, for Dillingham, "Melville is fantasizing about himself in the role of an extraordinary man in complete control of himself and thus in command of great insight and power" (*Melville's Later Novels,* 300). See also the psychoanalytic readings of the novel by Edwin Haviland Miller and Barry Chabot; both comment on the author's identification with his con man hero.

4. For a discussion of Melville's role as Christian reformer at this stage of his career, see Braswell, *Melville's Religious Thought,* 41–52. On *White-Jacket* and war, see Adler, Ch. 3.

5. As Fisher remarks, "Melville, no less than Joyce, was concerned with the moral and spiritual paralysis of his time and place, and the fifteen stories which he wrote in the space of a few years—after the major undertakings of *Moby-Dick* (1851) and *Pierre* (1852)—like the fifteen stories of *Dubliners,* explore a series of social, intellectual and spiritual crises" (xi).

6. See Bryant, "Citizens" and *Melville & Repose,* 122–27. Bryant, "Nowhere a Stranger" and *Melville & Repose,* 119–22, has also proposed that Melville's portrait of the cosmopolitan possibly draws on the figure of Vincent Nolte as portrayed in a review of Nolte's autobiography, "Fifty Years in Both Hemispheres," published in the September 1854 *Putnam's.* An international businessman of German extraction, Nolte exemplified some of the more equivocal associations of "cosmopolitanism" during this era. Lang and Lease, "Melville's Cosmopolitan," have associated Melville's cosmopolitan with Bayard Taylor, pointing out that several travel articles by Taylor and reviews of his work were featured in *Putnam's* in 1854 and 1855 opposite Melville's own contributions. Taylor was one of Melville's New York acquaintances and author of half a dozen popular travelogues by the mid-1850s; Melville facetiously alluded to Taylor's literary success in conversation with Evert Duyckinck in October 1856 (*Log,* 2:523).

7. Matthiessen long ago put Melville's remark in its proper perspective: "What harried Melville was the same debate between faith and doubt that aged Clough so young, that determined the temper of Arnold's 'Obermann' and 'The Grand Chartreuse,' and that became one of the most pervasive elements in Victorian poetry. For Melville to give up idealism for materialism, to accept the doctrine of the annihilation of the soul at death, would be a hard decision; and as Hawthorne suggests, he never really made it" (490–91).

8. According to Franklin, "The story of Pierre, the hero of *The Ambiguities,* is the story of a Christian youth, who, by trying to become symbolically and ethically a new Christ, becomes symbolically and ethically a pagan god; who, in trying to be a savior, becomes the destroyer of all that he tries to save" (*Wake of the Gods,* 99).

9. The analysis offered here of Melville's father-in-law as the gentleman's biographical model draws on my earlier version of this identification; see Cook, "Melville's Man." On Shaw's life and judicial career, see Frederic Chase and Levy. On his character as a father, see Cohen and Yannella, 164–84. Thomas explores Shaw's judicial ideology in relation to "Benito Cereno," "Bartleby," and *Billy Budd.* For a more recent exploration of legal themes in Melville's fiction that also postulates Melville's ambivalent relationship to his father-in-law's legal authority, see Weiner. Norris has argued that the gentleman with gold sleeve-buttons is modeled on Abbott Lawrence (1792–1855), an eminent New England industrialist and leading "Cotton Whig" whom Melville met in 1849 during his trip to England where Lawrence was United States ambassador (*J,* 22–24, 29, 308–10). Norris suggests that the oblique culpability of Melville's gentleman is patterned on Lawrence's dependence on Southern cotton to run his looms in Lawrence and Lowell, Massachusetts; the gentleman's charity derives from the well-known charitable activities of Abbott Lawrence as well as those of his brother Amos. Although there are some suggestive resemblances between the gentleman with gold sleeve-buttons and Abbott Lawrence, the Shaw con-

nection offers more convincing parallels and is more in keeping with Melville's satirical methods throughout *The Confidence-Man*. Furthermore, any satirical attack on Abbott Lawrence by 1856 would be vitiated by the fact that he was now dead, while most of the Cotton Whigs had been converted to antislavery sentiment by mid-1854 following passage of the Kansas-Nebraska Act and the controversial Burns rendition at that time.

10. Theodore Parker's two diatribes on Sims' rendition, which give an indication of the widespread popular reaction to the case, emphasize this point at length. See "The Chief Sins of the People" in *Sins and Safeguards,* 1–48, and "The Boston Kidnapping" in *Slave Power,* 316–85. These two discourses are the most outstanding among Parker's many references to *Sims.* The first was preached two days before Sims' final rendition early on April 12, 1851, while the second was delivered a year later to commemorate the event. On the "Shadrach" case, see Levy, 87–91.

11. Shaw was prepared to carry out Latimer's rendition based on the original 1793 Fugitive Slave Law, but owing to abolitionist pressure, Latimer's owner agreed to sell him for $400 and he was given his freedom. As a result of *Latimer,* Massachusetts passed its stringent Personal Liberty Law, which forbade the state from allowing its jails to be used in federal rendition cases. See Levy, 78–85.

12. Dana's remarks on Shaw during the earlier Shadrach rendition of February 1851 are also relevant here: Shaw's willingness to remand fugitive slaves "shows how deeply seated, so as to affect, unconsciously I doubt not, good men like him, is this selfish hunkerism of the property interest on the slave question" (Lucid, 2:413).

13. In "The Boston Kidnapping," Theodore Parker wrote of two fugitive slaves who fled Boston for England in the fall of 1851: "William and Ellen Craft were at the 'World's Fair,' specimens of American manufactures, the working-tools of the South; a proof of the democracy of the American State; part of the 'outward evidences' of the Christianity of the American Church. . . . America did not compete very well with the European States in articles sent to the Fair. A 'reaping machine' was the most quotable thing; then a 'Greek slave' [by Hiram Powers] in marble; next an American slave in flesh and blood. America was the only contributor of slaves; she had the monopoly of the article; it is the great export of Virginia,—it was right to exhibit a specimen at the World's Fair" (*Slave Power,* 345).

14. In the midst of this trip, Shaw wrote his wife on July 8 from Chicago that he was "strongly inclined to visit Mr. Henshaw's place at Rock River & then to go to Galena, & then down the Mississippi" (quoted in Puett, 35). This itinerary, requiring protracted and exhausting stage and boat travel, was apparently not followed: Shaw and his daughter took the Great Lakes route both to and (probably) from Chicago, where his oldest son, John Oakes, was then living.

15. Shaw may have dipped into Melville's last published novel but there is no record of what he thought of it. In a letter of April 17, 1857 to his son Sam, Shaw remarked of the novel, "I have it but have not yet read it" (quoted in Foster, xxvi).

16. For an overview of Shaw's financial support of Melville and his wife, see *C,* 672–74. It is relevant to note that the fatherly relation of Shaw and Melville as obliquely dramatized in Chapter 7 of *The Confidence-Man* is comparable to the relation that earlier obtained between Shaw and Melville's older brother Gansevoort. Gansevoort wrote Shaw in early 1841 at the start of his legal career: "From my Father's early death it has been my misfortune that I have had no adviser of mature age, experience & knowledge of the world in whose purity of motive and soundness

of judgment, I could place confidence—Am I too sanguine in hoping that that void, in matters of importance, will now be supplied by my Father's early friend—who on more intimate acquaintance will, I trust, be disposed to feel himself justified in transferring that confidence and affection to his son—To merit this adds another to the many incentives to virtuous & vigorous action which I now possess" (*Log,* 1:114).

17. A selection of Elizabeth Shaw Melville's letters from her early married life can be found in Metcalf, Ch. 3. Puett provides a sympathetic study of Melville's wife and the valuable assistance she gave to her husband's literary productions.

18. The charitable lady may also owe something to Elizabeth Melville's appearance at the fancy dress picnic given by the neighboring Morewoods on September 7, 1855. As the *Berkshire Eagle* on September 14 punningly reported, "Mrs. H[erman] M[elville] as Cypherina Donothing, in a costume of cyphers was no cypher, and although continually adding up cyphers to get at a sum of cyphers, found naught to amuse her; and was one of the most successful characters of the day, although she did nothing well" (*Log,* 2:507). Apparently bedecked with zeroes, Elizabeth's oddly unflattering character resembles in certain respects the characterization of the charitable lady, for the latter wears a "twilight dress, neither dawn nor dark," while her twenty dollars is "an inconsiderable sum" to the man in gray, who had earlier lamented her lack of confidence: " 'Nay, nay, you have none—none at all. Pardon, I see it. No confidence. Fool, fond fool that I am to seek it!' " (*CM,* 44). Melville may well have been the mind behind his wife's costume—Edwin Haviland Miller, 270–71, agrees on different grounds—since it would seem to derive from Ecclesiastes, a biblical text Melville knew well: "that which is wanting cannot be numbered" (Eccles. 1:15). This proverb, appearing in the Vulgate as "*stultorum infinitus est numerus*" ("infinite is the number of fools"), was a late medieval and Renaissance commonplace on the subject of folly.

19. Sam was something of a "mommy's boy" and was more inclined to write his mother than his father, the reverse of his older brother Lemuel. As an example of his refined sensibilities, Sam wrote to his mother from London on June 5, 1856: "It would give me so much pleasure if you were only here to enjoy some of these sights with me, such as the Meeting of the Charity Children in St. Paul's today, where the whole space under the dome and much more beside is surrounded by these children ranged tier above tier on temporary benches. The effect of their all singing together is sublime" (Metcalf, 155).

20. The Northwestern–Newberry edition of the novel prints "fraternal" here, instead of the "paternal" in the original edition. For the rationale of this correction, see "Discussions of Adopted Readings" in *CM,* 378.

21. Explaining his change in his itinerary, he wrote his father on August 10, 1851: "I then expected [in a previous letter] to go to St. Louis by way of the canal and Illinois River—but on inquiry I found that there would be some danger of cholera, and very considerable danger of taking fever and ague, if I went by that route, and also that I should have to travel alone. I therefore changed my plans and am now on my way to Cincinnati via Detroit and Sandusky" (Lemuel Shaw Papers I, Massachusetts Historical Society).

22. Lemuel, Jr.'s earlier visit to his brother-in-law in New York City from late January to early February 1848 during Lemuel's junior year at Harvard may also have influenced Melville's depiction of the sophomore here. During this visit, Melville took "Lem" to the top of Trinity Church steeple in downtown Manhattan as well as

uptown to see the new Aquaduct bridge over the Haarlem River that brought Croton reservoir water to New York City at this time. See Metcalf, 52. Perhaps not coincidentally, when John Truman tries to interest the sophomore in the layout of the "New Jerusalem" on the Mississippi, he mentions the existence of a "perpetual fountain" there; the sophomore, on the other hand, asks about the existence of "water lots." The sophomore's expressed liking for "prosperous" and "comfortable" fellows also evokes Lemuel, Jr.'s round of parties and entertainments while in New York City, including a "masked ball" to which he went in "old French court dress" (Metcalf, 51).

23. At his death, Lemuel, Jr.'s estate was valued at $323,450, of which Elizabeth's share was $37,949; $33,516 was paid to her during Melville's lifetime. See Charvat, 199. In justice to Lemuel, Jr., it should be noted that he could occasionally be sympathetic to his brother-in-law, as evidenced by the dinner party he and his father threw for Melville on May 27, 1857 shortly after Melville's return from his trip abroad. See Howard, 255; *Log,* 2:579. With *The Confidence-Man* in mind, it is amusing to note that while in London in June 1856, Sam Shaw complained to his mother of the many charity seekers there who seemingly outdid John Ringman in ingenuity: "Indeed people practice every imaginable device to obtain money from passersby. There are men that chalk pictures on the sidewalk in colored chalks, innumerable blind people with dogs, ballad singers, men without arms or legs, Crimean soldiers, and others whose only business is to sit on steps and look as haggard and ghastly as they can, some of them are frightful" (Metcalf, 155).

24. One other piece of evidence linking the sick man to Melville's cousin deserves mention. The herb doctor concludes his dialogue with the sick man by quoting the physician Iapus's claim in the *Aeneid* that his cure of Aeneas's wound was the result of Venus's divine power (*Aeneid,* Book 3, 427–29). In keeping with other such wordplay in the novel, this allusion may contain a covert reference to *Augustus* Van Schaick, for it is well known that Vergil identified the hero of the *Aeneid* with the Emperor Augustus, Aeneas's alleged descendent, for whom the poem was written.

25. Melville had earlier used his friend Fly as a model for Charlie Millthorpe in *Pierre.* See Murray, *Pierre,* 487–88n. The two characters are in fact roughly comparable: Millthorpe, an impecunious lawyer, is a "transcendental" optimist; "Happy Tom" is a victim of the law who assumes a pose of optimism in order to beg for coins. Thomas, 192–99, associates Thomas Fry's hard luck story with Melville's experience in the literary marketplace. He finds an historical analogue to Fry's tale in a Boston murder case early in the century that involved both Melville's paternal grandfather and his father-in-law.

26. On Thomas Melvill, Sr.'s life, see Weaver, 40–43; Gilman, 38–39; and Garner, "Allan Melvill." While not explicitly identifying him as a character model, Rogin, 237, compares the wooden-legged man to Thomas Melvill, Sr. On Peter Gansevoort's life, see Kenney, 89–144.

27. This action is comparable to that of Pierre Glendinning's Revolutionary grandfather—also derived from Peter Gansevoort—who "annihilated two Indian savages by making reciprocal bludgeons of their heads" (*P,* 29–30).

28. Peter's official positions included judge advocate general (1819–1821), member of Governor Clinton's military staff, member of the State Assembly (1830–1831), state senator (1833–1836), and first judge of the County Court of Albany (1843–1847). For Peter Gansevoort's life, see *Log;* Gilman; and Kenney, *passim.* On his

politics, see Parker, "Melville and Politics," 9–15, 38–50. On his strict character as a father, see Cohen and Yannella, 154–63.

29. Rogin notes the resemblance between Allan Melvill's disclaimer and the cosmopolitan's policy here but does not suggest that the barber and the cosmopolitan have biographical models.

30. See, for example, the letter Peter wrote to his sister on October 9, 1852 complaining that Herman failed to call on Alfred Billings Street, a mediocre poet and neighbor of his uncle's in Albany, who was visiting Pittsfield at this time: "Oh Herman, Herman, Herman truly thou art an 'Ambiguity' " (*Log,* 1:461). Two more possible connections between the barber and Peter Gansevoort may be remarked. First, the barber's procedure of preparing his lather "as if it were a mug of new ale" may recall the original basis of the Gansevoort family fortune in Albany, the brewery business. See Kenney, 22–31. Second, the barber's name, "William Cream," is possibly related to William of *Orange,* whose Dutch principality gave Albany its original name, Fort Orange. Peter's consciousness of his Albany Dutch ancestry was strong: At a public dinner on July 27, 1827 honoring a visiting dignitary from the Netherlands, Peter toasted, "The House of Orange—illustrious for the heroes and statesmen which have adorned its annals" (quoted in Parker, "Melville and Politics," 14).

31. A relevant historical irony here is that twenty years after *The Confidence-Man* was written, Peter's gift of $1,200 allowed Melville to publish his book-length poem *Clarel* in 1876. Peter's investment in Allan Melvill's "confidential" scheme was thus repeated nearly half a century later in Peter's donation of a smaller but comparable sum for Melville's own unprofitable literary exploration of a lost theological confidence. Although Peter died before the publication of *Clarel,* he may have read—or at least tried to read—*The Confidence-Man.* Stone writes: "When, in the autumn of 1947, I read Peter Gansevoort's copy of *The Confidence-Man* in the New York Public Library the last pages were uncut" (229n). Did Peter stop reading out of lack of interest, or because he recognized his nephew's embarrassing use of family history? Whichever was the case, Herman was still an "ambiguity."

32. Edwin Haviland Miller argues that "the brazen handling on the part of the Confidence-Man and the boy would appear to be an enactment of the oedipal drama, even to the suggested besmearing of the paternal figure. If, as we have conjectured, the Confidence-Man frequently speaks for Herman Melville, the old man's pious platitudes are reminiscent of Allan Melvill's" (281). Noting that the scene here occurs at the same hour as Allan Melvill's death, Miller concludes that "*The Confidence-Man* was . . . the bitter retaliation of a son upon the paternal Confidence Man." Although marred by heavy-handed psychologizing and inadequate evidence, Miller's brief analysis constitutes the closest any critic has come to a direct link between the old man and Allan Melvill. For a relevant study of the effect of Melville's unresolved mourning for his father on his fiction through *Pierre,* see Tolchin. For an analysis of comparable psychological dynamics in the writings of Hawthorne, see Crews.

33. Allan Melvill's life is chronicled in Weaver, 49–60, 63–68; Gilman, 1–61; *Log,* 1:3–52; Edwin Haviland Miller, 56–72; and Cohen and Yannella, 123–36, 146–53. On Thomas Melvill's life, see Sealts, "Ghost"; Parker, "Melville and Politics," 50–74; Garner, "Picaresque Career"; and Philip Young, 27–38.

34. The original, longer text of the memoir, with Melville's erratic spelling and punctuation, is available in Sealts, "Thomas Melvill, Jr."

35. For discussions of Melville's trip to Galena and the condition of this frontier town in 1840, see Tanselle and Garner, "Picaresque Career," *Extracts,* No. 62.

36. As Garner notes, "For a young man considering the advantages of seeking his fortunes along the frontier it would have been prudent for him to see as much of it as possible, and so he may have embarked on such an excursion with Fly and one or more of his relatives" ("Picaresque Career," *Extracts,* No. 62, 7).

37. Concerning Melville's knowledge of these events, Garner remarks, "It is not too much to conclude that the scandal surrounding his uncle must have come to Melville's attention" ("Picaresque Career," *Extracts,* No. 62, 10). This would have come from Thomas's widow Mary or his son Robert, both of whom were back in Pittsfield in the late 1840s, running the family mansion as a boarding house; Melville stayed with them for summer vacations in 1848 and 1850 (*Log,* 1:280, 378).

38. See Melville's original memoir of his uncle: "By the hearth fire above mentioned, he often at my request, described some of those martial displays and spectacles of state which he had witnessed in Paris in the time of the first Napoleon. But I was too young & ignorant then, to derive the full benefit from his pictorial recollections" (Sealts, "Thomas Melvill, Jr.," 215).

39. See Thomas's articles as "Ben Austin" in the *Pittsfield Sun,* January 7 and 28, and February 4 and 25, 1836 (the latter two noted in Parker, "Melville and Politics," 64–65). Thomas's pseudonym refers to the self-styled tribune of the people of Massachusetts, Benjamin Austin (1752–1820) who, as "Honestus," led a crusade for legal reform in 1786 and thereafter acted as the gadfly of New England Federalism. Thomas's articles make interesting reading both as a prophecy of the Panic of 1837 and as an indicator of the private context of Melville's satire on his uncle. Thomas's article of February 4 is especially relevant here: "So long as our present statutes in relation to banks and banking remain in force, so long as banks continue to be uncontrolable, . . . so long as they can transact business with but little other capital than promissory notes, so long will our Legislature be importuned for new banks, charters will be granted, and bank capital extended, until the whole system will end as did the famous Mississippi speculation of Mr. Law, and the south sea bubble. A more appalling catastrophe can hardly be imagined." In the portrait of the old man, Melville subverts his uncle's financial acumen using a parallel example from Mississippi banking history.

40. We may note another possible reference relating to Thomas Melvill, Jr.'s life in Galena at this time. During the summer of 1840, the presidential race between Harrison and Van Buren was in full swing. Partly because recent German and Irish immigrants controlled the local Democratic party, Thomas came out for the Whig candidate, Harrison; Whig campaign emblems of log cabin and hard cider were deployed here, as elsewhere in the nation. See Garner, "Picaresque Career, *Extracts,* No. 62, 6. It is probably no coincidence that in the last chapter of *The Confidence-Man* a passenger with a thick Irish brogue tells the old man to go to bed, while the juvenile peddler carries a strange "toy" possibly recalling the miniature log cabins carried in procession during this campaign.

41. The peddler's counterfeit detector indirectly evokes Walter Redburn's library of European guides, which Redburn describes with a close attention to textual decor (especially title-page vignettes) similar to that demanded by the peddler's pamphlet (*R,* 141). Furthermore, the counterfeit detector's instructions to look for "the figure

of a goose, very small indeed, all but microscopic," may recall Allan Melvill's marital connection with Maria *Gans*evoort, whose surname derived from the Dutch word for goose (a goose was in fact featured on the family crest).

42. As Murray remarks, "Melville intimates—again anticipating the findings of depth psychology—that the image of God was generated out of early idealizations of the father. . . . Pierre's reaction, which includes the threat that he will give himself up 'to be a railing atheist,' shows, among other things, that his trust in God depended on the substantiality of his relationship with his father" (*Pierre,* xlv–xlvii).

43. In the Bible with Apocrypha that he acquired in March 1850 (Sealts, *Melville's Reading,* no. 62), Melville wrote of *The Wisdom of Jesus the Son of Sirach, or Ecclesiasticus:* "This admirable book seems partly Mosaic & partly Platonic in its tone. Who wrote it I know not. Some one to whom both Plato & Moses stood for godfather" (*Log,* 1:370).

44. Further confirmation for the appearance of the father at the end of *The Confidence-Man* is provided by *Israel Potter,* which contains an analogous encounter with the absent father in its final chapter. For a relevant discussion of fathers and sons in *Israel Potter,* see Watson, "Melville's *Israel Potter.*"

45. Allan Melvill marked verses 4 and 5 and put large brackets around verses 11–14; he also double scored next to verse 16 ("As for me, I will call upon God; and the LORD shall save me"), bracketed verse 22 ("Cast thy burden upon the LORD, and he shall sustain thee: he shall never suffer the righteous to be moved") and underlined the last phrase of verse 23 ("but I will trust in thee"). Melville almost certainly was familiar with these last markings by his father in the family Bible (Sealts, *Melville's Reading,* no. 60), which were then glossed by Maria Melvill for all her children to see. The Bible has few other annotations; Psalm 55 is located near the center of the Bible where it might have lain open.

46. This "Caffre" also might recall the youthful black boy Pip, a character whose interaction with Ahab at the end of *Moby-Dick* is comparable to that of the juvenile peddler and old man at the end of *The Confidence-Man.* Tolchin claims that "In Ahab's relationship with Pip, Melville toys with the anger of his own memory of being abandoned by his father" (135).

47. As Melville probably knew, the name Hermes was derived from ancient milestones, later formed into apotropaic, ithyphallic "herms"; this suggests a continuity with the stone and sexual symbolism of *Pierre.* Like the figure of Enceladus at the end of *Pierre,* the juvenile peddler is a mythological figure of filial disinheritance and revolt; unlike Enceladus, the peddler is successful in his covert attack on the father.

48. For this psychological process, Melville had good company in his friend Hawthorne, for as Crews has demonstrated, Hawthorne's writings exemplify the "practice of denigrating fathers *in absentia*" (104), while his plots "depict with incredible fidelity the results of unresolved Oedipal conflict. After establishing . . . that this conflict is re-enacted everywhere in Hawthorne's fiction, we can appreciate the intense malice behind his treatment of literal and symbolic fathers—a malice which often meets with no justification on moral grounds" (262). Melville certainly had more justification for his anger towards his real and surrogate fathers, but this is subsumed in *The Confidence-Man* beneath a complex irony that destroys the authority of the father with devastating, if darkly comic, effect.

CHAPTER 6

1. On Duyckinck's life and career, see Osgood; Stafford; Mize; Perry Miller, *Raven and Whale;* Wells; Roche; Yannella, "Writing the '*Other* Way' "; and Greenspan. The "Historical Note" in *CM,* 257–76, provides a concise review of Melville's relations with Duyckinck from 1846 through 1852; Melville's caricature of his friend as Henry Roberts confirms the claim that "So many elements in *The Confidence-Man* touch on Melville's connection with Duyckinck as to suggest that in this last of his published fictional works he was, among other matters, reappraising his New York years" (*CM,* 258). It should be noted that Duyckinck traveled to St. Louis in the summer of 1837; hence the presence in *The Confidence-Man* of a character modeled on him riding a Mississippi steamboat had biographical precedent. See McDermott, 60–62, for the July 12, 1837 letter that Duyckinck in St. Louis wrote to his friend William Alfred Jones in New York, commenting on some of the romantic distortions that Washington Irving had introduced into his recently published *Tour of the Prairies* (1835).

2. As Perry Miller notes, "Duyckinck was a devout Episcopalian, leaning . . . to the high-church party. A vestryman in St. Thomas's, a friend of Bishops Wainright and Hawks, he wrote for the Sunday School Union. He once told Mrs. Kirkland that he could not live except 'under the shelter of the church' " (*Raven and Whale,* 73).

3. The full review is reprinted in Higgins and Parker, 40–43; for a detailed account of the circumstances surrounding the break between Melville and Duyckinck in early 1852, see 9–18. See also the "Historical Note" in *MD,* 689–98.

4. In his *Reminiscences,* Richard Lathers—Allan Melville's brother-in-law and a friend of Melville's—locates Melville at one of Duyckinck's "Saturday night supper parties" during Thackeray's "Four Georges" lecture tour in the fall and winter of 1855–1856: "Here, in the company of such kindred spirits as Dr. J. W. Francis, Rev. Dr. Hawks, the poet Fitz Greene Halleck, the comedian Hackett, the novelist Herman Melville, and the poet and traveler Bayard Taylor, the genial nature of Thackeray fairly radiated cheer" (51). Since Thackeray spent most of November lecturing in New York and only stopped there briefly in early January and again in early April amidst engagements around the country, it seems likely that this gathering, if actually occurred, must have taken place some time in November. Garner, who discusses Melville's friendship with Lathers during the Civil War, characterizes Lathers's *Reminiscences* as "sometimes woefully inaccurate" (*Civil War World,* 459n). Such would seem the case with the guest list of this hypothetical supper party.

5. Wells similarly notes that Melville's quest for metaphysical and psychological depth in *Moby-Dick* and *Pierre* offended Duyckinck "because the probings on this level seemed to be an incursion on God's territory . . . Evert's increased distress at Melville's abnormal heroes must be seen not as evidence that Evert's shallowness prevented him from detecting their meaning and value, but conversely that his comprehension of their meaning conflicted with his orthodox religious views, posed a moral threat to readers, and constituted an abandonment in the artistic sense of the traditional novel of manners whose wholesomeness, humanity, and reverence for beauty from Fielding to Thackeray in England and from Irving through Cooper in America were the essences of the Anglo-American tradition" (150–51). For other

comments on Duyckinck's critical limitations and a list of his references to Melville in the *Literary World,* see Buford Jones.

6. On the critical reception of *Typee,* including the debate about its veracity, see Hetherington, Ch. 2, and Branch, *Critical Heritage,* 3–12, 53–89. Significantly, one English review considered *Typee* an April Fools' Day joke, much to Melville's annoyance (*C,* 86). Melville's exasperation with the skeptical reception of *Typee* found vent elsewhere in his correspondence at this time (*C,* 38, 65). Perry Miller, *Raven and Whale,* Ch. 3, discusses the importance of Melville's reliability in Duyckinck's literary campaign on behalf of Young America; Miller also analyzes Melville's attack on Duyckinck in the "Young America" chapters of *Pierre,* remarking that "Melville goes back in agony over the success of *Typee* and works off his long-concealed resentment against the sublime condescension of Young America" (*Raven and Whale,* 306–307).

7. Duyckinck, who knew German, had included Goethe's *Autobiography* and *Wilhelm Meister* in the Library of Choice Reading for Wiley and Putnam. Duyckinck also published Thackeray's poetic parody of *Werther,* "Sorrows of Werther," in the *Literary World,* December 10, 1853. Foster, 301–302n, notes that the poem was later reprinted in a review of Thackeray's poetry in the December 1855 *Putnam's,* the same issue that carried the last installment of "Benito Cereno."

8. On the critical reception of *Mardi, Redburn,* and *White-Jacket,* see Hetherington, Chs. 4–6, and Branch, *Critical Heritage,* 13–24, 139–236. Stafford comments on Duyckinck's advocacy of the aggressive marketing of authors, as expressed in an 1845 *Democratic Review* article entitled, "On Writing for the Magazines": "He pointed out clearly the parallel between literary wares and any other kind of merchandise and between the author and merchant; and he defended the author and the publisher from the criticism of those who were somewhat horrified at the darkening of the fair name of literature and genius by commercialization" (14).

9. As Bell remarks, "If 'truth' was a fiction and nothing was truer than fiction, then *nothing,* quite literally, *was* the truth. It is small wonder that Evert Duyckinck attacked *Moby-Dick* for its 'piratical running down of creeds and opinions' " (145).

10. See the *Literary World* reviews of April 24 and December 4, 1852. While acknowledging Stowe's command of melodrama and humorous touches in the April review, Duyckinck nevertheless took strong issue with the accuracy of the novel's depiction of slavery and claimed that it was "capable of producing infinite mischief." Another article entitled "Log Cabin Literature" (October 23, 1852) commented on the "negro mania" that had resulted since the publication of Stowe's novel, with authors blackening their faces like minstrel performers. A summary of Duyckinck's reaction to the *Uncle Tom's Cabin* controversy can be found in Wells, 203–10. On Duyckinck and Simms, see Roche, Ch. 3.

11. It is also possible that the story of Goneril obliquely touches on a family scandal that occurred in August 1848 involving Duyckinck's seventeen-year-old sister-in-law, Cassy Panton, and his married friend, William Alfred Jones, a literary associate since their days at Columbia College and a member, with Cornelius Mathews, of Duyckinck's inner circle in the 1840s. On vacation with the Jones family on Long Island, a sexually precocious Cassy engaged in a heated flirtation with Jones (whose wife was significantly older than he). When Jones refrained from actually possessing her, a scene ensued and she returned to her brother-in-law in New York

claiming that she had been preyed upon by a vile seducer. Despite Jones's attempt at an explanation, a morally inflexible Duyckinck banished Jones from his life in perpetuity. For the details of this murky affair, see Perry Miller, *Raven and Whale,* 231–37. Perhaps not coincidentally, the merchant's story of Goneril tells of a similarly depraved female nature, whose sexual provocations lead to moral scapegoating, scandal, and perpetual exile for Ringman. The merchant's inability to fathom Goneril's depravity is thus a potential burlesque of Duyckinck's inability to imagine sexual culpability in his sister-in-law—another instance of Duyckinck's imaginative limitations.

12. Truman's consumption of champagne with Roberts may be compared with the fact that Duyckinck had given Melville a dozen bottles of champagne as a gift for entertaining him in Pittsfield in August 1850 (*C,* 168, 603). For Melville's recurrent complaints to Duyckinck that a writer can never be totally "frank" with his readers, see Melville's letters of March 3 and December 14, 1849 (*C,* 122, 149).

13. The "cold cave" here also suggests a derivation from a Berkshire natural curiosity explored by Duyckinck, Melville, and others during the picnic of August 5, 1850 at which Melville first met Hawthorne. In a letter to his wife, Duyckinck wrote of "the Icy Glen, a break in one of the hills of tumbled huge, damp, mossy rocks in whose recesses ice is said to be found all the year round" (Metcalf, 82).

14. We may note that Duyckinck was also distressed by the same "morbid" tendency in Hawthorne as evidenced by the publication of *The Blithedale Romance.* On August 28, 1852, one week after the denunciation of *Pierre* in the *Literary World,* Duyckinck reprinted a review of *Blithedale* from the *London Atlas* entitled "False Tendencies in American Literature," an attack on Hawthorne's—and by implication, Melville's—latest examples of morbid psychological fiction. For a survey of Duyckinck's long-term, generally supportive relationship with Hawthorne, see Roche, Ch. 4.

15. In his copy of the novel, Duyckinck marked a passage from Chapter 33: "so precious to man is the approbation of his kind, that to rest, though but under an imaginary censure applied to but a work of imagination, is no easy thing" (*Log,* 2: 564). The notation demonstrates that he was at least partially aware of the autobiographical basis of the novel. In this connection it is instructive to cite Duyckinck's comments on satire as a literary medium in America. Writing in an 1847 diary in response to the demise of the satirical weekly, *Yankee Doodle,* edited by his friend Cornelius Mathews, Duyckinck noted: "There are besides essential differences between a publication of the class of Punch in England and this country. In the former there are institutions and classes to satirize, here there are only individuals and individuals resent what classes must endure. There are subjects enough here for satire but they are not permanent—before you catch them they have changed" (Yanella and Yanella, 242). It should be noted that a decade previous to Melville's caricature of his friend, Charles F. Briggs ("Harry Franco") had satirized Duyckinck and Mathews as "Tibbings" and "Jasper Ferocious" in his picaresque tale of New York life, *The Trippings of Tom Pepper* (1847, 1850), the first volume of which Melville owned (Sealts, *Melville's Reading,* no. 86a). For a discussion of this caricature, see Perry Miller, *Raven and Whale,* 177–83. Yannella, "Writing," convincingly argues that Melville used Duyckinck as the model for "Standard" and Cornelius Mathews for "Hautbois" in his 1854 story "The Fiddler." Wells, 169–79, makes a case for the

Duyckinck–Melville relationship as a model for the narrator and Bartleby in "Bartleby, the Scrivener."

16. Fussell first suggested that Pitch represented a caricature of Cooper, "or, more subtly stated, the spirit of Cooper reaffirming itself through Melville" (314n). Franklin, *The Confidence-Man,* 154–55n, and John Seelye, "Ungraspable Phantom," 439, also suggest in passing a connection between Pitch and Cooper. Wright, "Confidence Men," posits a resemblance between Melville's title character and Cooper's Jacksonian vulgarian, Steadfast Dodge of *Homeward Bound.*

17. Melville had briefly and benignly reviewed Cooper's *Sea Lions* and *Red Rover* for the *Literary World* (April 28, 1849 and March 16, 1850). While writing *Israel Potter,* he had also drawn on Cooper's *History of the Navy of the United States of America* for information on John Paul Jones and his Revolutionary naval battles. On Melville's use of Cooper's *History,* see the "Historical Note" in *IP,* 194–95, 198–200.

18. An indispensable collection of essays and annotated bibliography on the Melville–Hawthorne relationship is available in Wilson, *Hawthorne and Melville.* The pioneering study of this relationship is by Hayford, "Hawthorne and Melville." The best compilation of primary sources is in Metcalf, Chs. 6–9. In the ensuing discussion I rely on biographical studies of Hawthorne by Julian Hawthorne, Edwin Haviland Miller, Mellow, Arlin Turner, and Erlich. On the formal continuities between the two writers, see Bell, Ch. 6, and Brodhead, *Hawthorne, Melville.* Brodhead, *School of Hawthorne,* Ch. 1, also points out Melville's appropriation of the figure of the "daimonic hero" from Hawthorne. Fisher, Ch. 1, provides an informative analysis of Melville's literary strategies in the *Mosses* review. Edwin Haviland Miller, 19–36, narrates the events surrounding Melville's first encounter with Hawthorne and makes the friendship a keynote of his biography. For contemporary accounts of the literary festivities of August 1850, see Duyckinck's letters to his wife in Metcalf, 79–87, and the three *Literary World* articles by Cornelius Mathews entitled "Several Days in Berkshire," appearing in the August 21, 31 and September 7, 1850 issues.

19. Examining the recently discovered papers of Melville's sister Augusta, Wilson, "Melville at Arrowhead," demonstrates that sociable relations continued until the eve of Hawthorne's departure; hence no alleged "estrangement," and certainly no mythical homoerotic "overture" had transpired. Seelye, "Ungraspable Phantom," Edwin Haviland Miller, and Watson, "Estrangement," all argue that homosexuality played a part in Melville's response to Hawthorne, as evidenced by characters and episodes in Melville's fiction and poetry. In this writer's opinion, the theory of Melville's alleged homosexual attraction to Hawthorne is misleading for at least four reasons: first, it displaces the psychology of the creator back onto the creature; second, it takes inadequate account of the Christian symbolism of spiritual communion that pervaded Melville's attitude to Hawthorne; third, it takes insufficient notice of the personal "magnetism" that Hawthorne exerted on others besides Melville; and finally, it ignores the fact that Melville's relation to Hawthorne involved the same ambivalent impulses of reverence and revolt that typified Melville's quest for God: Hawthorne was, in effect, a literary God who failed. For an incisive discussion of Melville's quest for "fraternity" with Hawthorne, see Wilson Carey McWilliams, 354–58.

20. In 1947 Melville's grandniece, Agnes Morewood, recorded a Melville family legend that Hawthorne sent Melville a Christmas card in 1857 with remarks on the novel (*Log,* 2:579; *C,* 658–59). This may be the same as an unidentified "note" from

Hawthorne about *The Confidence-Man* that was apparently burned along with other family papers by Melville's niece, Maria Melville Morewood. See the "Historical Note" and "Manuscript Fragments" in *CM,* 315, 404.

21. Compare Emerson on "Friendship": "In the last analysis, love is only the reflection of a man's own worthiness from other men. Men have sometimes exchanged names with their friends, as if they would signify that in their friend each loved his own soul" (*Essays: First Series,* 125). Melville's use of names here may also be compared with the fact that Hawthorne was given the pseudonym "Noble Melancholy" and Melville that of "New Neptune" in Cornelius Mathews' *Literary World* account of the literary socializing of August 1850; see Note 18 above.

22. Just as Frank Goodman is masquerading in cosmopolitan costume, Melville on his thirty-second birthday was masquerading as a Spanish cavalier. As Hawthorne recorded in his journal, while he was engaged in reading the papers in Lenox, "a cavalier on horseback came along the road, and saluted me in Spanish; to which I replied by touching my hat, and went on with the newspaper. But the cavalier renewing his salutation, I regarded him more attentively, and saw that it was Herman Melville!" (*American Notebooks,* 447–48).

23. Goodman's consulting of a thermometer during this scene may be compared with the fact that Melville was given a thermometer by his friend Evert Duyckinck in August 1851 as a gift for entertaining him at Arrowhead that month (*C,* 204). Goodman's ensuing analysis of the "genial misanthrope" and the "surly philanthropist" also suggests a relation to some of Melville's comments to Hawthorne in his letters, for example: "It seems an inconsistency to assert unconditional democracy in all things, and yet confess a dislike to all mankind—in the mass. But not so.—but its an endless sermon, no more of it" (*C,* 191). By the same token, Charlie Noble's earlier assertion, "Now the bridge that has carried me so well over, shall I not praise it?" (*CM,* 158), may pun on the name of Hawthorne's close friend and mentor, Horatio Bridge.

24. Hirsch discusses the ambiguous interplay of white (theurgic) and black (goetic) magic in the novel in relation to the evolution of Melville's poetics of fiction and the critical doctrines announced in the *Mosses* review. The fact that Charlie Noble is a caricature of Hawthorne lends her argument an interesting new dimension. The same is true of Irwin's exploration of the mythic background to the Goodman–Noble encounter in the interplay of Dionysian and Apollonian archetypes.

25. See Melville's April 1851 letter to Hawthorne (*C,* 185). The different reactions of Charlie and Frank are additionally ironic when we consider Hawthorne's authorship of several volumes of children's stories, including *A Wonder Book for Girls and Boys,* which he wrote in Lenox. Melville may also be drawing on Hawthorne's occasional manifestations of child-like malice, as can be seen in some of the incidents and attitudes described in "Twenty Days with Julian and Little Bunny" (July–August 1851) in the *American Notebooks.* For example, a poor neighbor boy is described as "this odious little urchin" (441).

26. Given the fact that Melville is mocking his earlier enthusiastic endorsement of Hawthorne's genius throughout this encounter, the image of the cheerful stamping of gold at "Goldsmiths' Hall" here is a likely pun referring back to another point in the *Mosses* review. After criticizing Washington Irving for being an American imitator of a "foreign model," Melville asserted: "Let us believe it, then, once for all, that there is no hope for us in these smooth pleasing writers that know their powers.

Without malice, but to speak the plain fact, they but furnish an appendix to Goldsmith, and other English authors. And we want no American Goldsmiths" (*PT,* 248). Seen in this light, Frank Goodman's celebration of geniality as a species of gold would seem to contain a hint that Hawthorne is, after all, another smooth, pleasing writer in the "Goldsmith" mold. (Significantly, in his *Mosses* review Melville had noted that the title of "Young Goodman Brown" had made him expect it to be a "simple little tale" like Goldsmith's "Goody Two Shoes.")

27. See Murray, *Pierre,* lxxvi–lxxix; Watson, "Estrangement," 390–92; and Mellow, 400. As Lueders notes, "The relationship of Coverdale and Hollingsworth, of Plinlimmon and Pierre, is the relationship of Hawthorne and Melville all over again. It is the successful, compromising, rational intellect versus the emotional, ideal-seeking failure. Each relationship is, on the surface, free of animosity or hostility, yet the differences set the men apart and plague their consciences" (146).

28. See McIntire for a full comparative study of both novels. See also Brodhead, *Hawthorne, Melville,* 186–93, for a relevant discussion comparing *Blithedale* with *Pierre.*

29. Coverdale's first glimpse of Westervelt reveals a similar combination of refinement and coarseness. See *Blithedale Romance,* 91–92. Kemper, 35n, briefly notes the resemblance between Westervelt and Noble without comment.

30. In the portrait of Charlie Noble, Melville was also drawing on a pair of motifs he had used earlier in nearly contiguous chapters of *White-Jacket,* the comic-diabolical grotesque (Chs. 61–63), and the phenomenon of the double (Ch. 59). In *Pierre,* too, the fickle friendship of Glen Stanly with Pierre resembles Noble's fickle boon companionship with Goodman, in contrast to Pierre's more benign friendship with "Charlie" Millthorpe.

31. Julian Hawthorne includes a relevant discussion of this delicate juncture in his father's career: "In other words, he foresaw that he would be accused of acting the part of a vulgar office-seeker,—of aiding Pierce only in order that Pierce might be the better able to aid him, and of apostatizing from his real political convictions in order to put money in his purse. It is true that he might have avoided the worst part of this reproach by declining the office which Pierce afterwards tendered to him; but, as it happened, he did not decline, but accepted it. We are forced to conclude, therefore, that he either bartered truth and honor for a few thousand dollars and a glimpse of Europe; or else that, being conscious of his own honesty and rectitude of purpose, he regarded with his customary indifference the angry accusations of his opponents. As for the present biographer, his only care will be to afford each reader the fullest liberty to decide the matter according to his private prejudices and prepossessions. Argument on such a subject is futile" (1:463–64). For a detailed account of the attempt to get Melville a consular appointment at this time, see Hayford and Davis, 173–83. Whatever Melville's perception of the matter, Hawthorne was unable to help his friend simply because the competition was stiff and the Pierce administration rewarded office-seekers according to political expediency, not personal merit. For an account of the corruption that the spoils system generated in the early 1850s, see Summers, Ch. 1.

32. Hershel Parker, "*Isle,*" provides a useful overview of Melville's financial and professional difficulties at this point. Already in June 1851 Melville wrote Hawthorne after noting the popularity of Hawthorne's books in New York: "So upon the whole, I say to myself, this N.H. is in the ascendant. My dear Sir, they begin to patronize"

(*C,* 193). A year later, he noticed the same phenomenon during his trip to Nantucket: "My Dear Hawthorne:—This name of '*Hawthorne*' seems to be ubiquitous. I have been on something of a tour lately, and it has saluted me vocally & typographically in all sorts of places & in all sorts of ways" (*C,* 230). Brodhead, *School of Hawthorne,* Ch. 3, describes Hawthorne's establishment as a "classic" during the 1850s by means of aggressive marketing by his publishers, Ticknor and Fields.

33. Sophia Hawthorne has indicated the kind of impersonal attraction Hawthorne exerted on Melville (and others) in a letter to her older sister, Elizabeth, on October 2, 1851: "Nothing pleases me better than to sit & hear this growing man dash his tumultuous waves of thought up against Mr Hawthorne's great, genial, comprehending silences—out of the profound of which a wonderful smile, or one powerful word sends back the foam & fury into a peaceful booming, calm—or perchance not into a calm—but a murmuring expostulation—for there is never a 'mush of concession' in him. Yet such a love & reverence & admiration for Mr Hawthorne as is really beautiful to witness—& without doing anything on his own part, except merely *being,* it is astonishing how people make him their innermost Father Confessor. Is it not?" (Metcalf, 106). The similarity of Emerson's to Melville's experience of Hawthorne is also noteworthy. After attending Hawthorne's funeral in 1864, Emerson commented: "It would have been a happiness, doubtless to both of us, to have come into habits of unreserved intercourse. It was easy to talk with him,—there were no barriers,—only, he said so little, that I talked too much, and stopped only because, as he gave no indications, I feared to exceed" (quoted in Arlin Turner, *Nathaniel Hawthorne,* 394).

34. The dramatic irony latent in some of Hawthorne's remarks at this time is uncanny. Thus, after exculpating himself any fault in not being able to help Melville get a consular appointment, Hawthorne wrote of his meeting with Melville: "we soon found ourselves on pretty much our former terms of sociability and *confidence*"; he concluded with the assertion that Melville "has a very high and *noble* nature, and better worth immortality than most of us" (*Log,* 2:527, 529; emphasis added). In justice to both writers, Melville's truest and most generous tribute to Hawthorne occurs at the end of his letter of late November, 1851: "I shall leave the world, I feel, with more satisfaction for having come to know you. Knowing you persuades me more than the Bible of our immortality" (*C,* 213).

35. It is interesting to discover that an exactly contemporaneous account of the relations between two literary "boon companions" appears in Dickens's *The Lazy Tour of Two Idle Apprentices* (1857). In this fictionalized travelogue Dickens appears as "Francis Goodchild," while his close friend Wilkie Collins appears as "Thomas Idle" (shades of Francis Goodman and Charlie Noble!). Dramatizing the antithetical natures of Dickens and Collins, this minor novella exemplifies a writer's preoccupation with his shadow self comparable to that found in *The Confidence-Man.* We may note, finally, the general parallel between Melville's shifting attitude toward Hawthorne as a writer and the evolution of Henry James's divided attitude toward him. See the detailed exegesis in Brodhead, *School of Hawthorne,* Chs. 7–9.

36. As previously noted, Oliver first convincingly identified Winsome as a caricature of Emerson and Egbert as Thoreau. Of the Emerson caricature, he asserted that "The argument of the mystic in practically every point comes from *Nature*—by suggestion, by association of ideas, by direct condensation, or by distorted synopsis" ("Melville's Picture," 65). Foster, lxxiii–lxxxii, confirmed Oliver's identification of

Winsome as Emerson but argued that Melville drew not on *Nature,* but on a wide range of Emerson's other essays; she also hypothesized that Egbert was not modeled on Thoreau but was instead a fictional projection of Emersonian metaphysics into the realm of ethics. In a brief but incisive analysis, Rosenberry, *Comic Spirit,* 168–70, confirmed Oliver's major points, including the reliance on *Nature* and the Egbert–Thoreau connection. Hershel Parker, "Melville's Satire," espoused Foster's view of Winsome's Emersonian characteristics but conceded that the Egbert–Thoreau connection was more likely than Foster acknowledged. More recently, Trimpi, *Melville's Confidence Men,* 200–08, 212–20, has adduced additional biographical evidence of the Winsome–Emerson and Egbert–Thoreau connections (with some residual hesitation over the latter), although her attempt to fit them both into her political argument is necessarily fallacious. For a useful overview of Melville's ambivalent response to Emerson's thought based on his annotations of Emerson's essays in the early 1860s, see Braswell, "Melville as a Critic." Hershel Parker, "Transcendentalists: A Chronology," provides a useful outline of Melville's actual and possible knowledge of Emerson and Thoreau. Sealts, "Emerson's Rainbow," has provided an authoritative overview of Melville's familiarity with Emerson as both lecturer and thinker. Williams's study of Emerson's influence on Melville, on the other hand, pays only perfunctory notice to the caricature of Emerson in *The Confidence-Man.* Regrettably, his revisionist reassessment distorts both the extent and the nature of Emerson's influence on Melville. Braswell and Sealts offer more reliable estimates.

37. The consistency of Melville's criticisms can be seen in the fact that he made nearly identical remarks while reading Emerson over a decade later. Annotating Emerson's "The Poet" in 1862, Melville wrote: "His gross and astonishing errors and illusions spring from a self-conceit so intensely intellectual and calm that at first one hesitates to call it by its right name. Another species of Mr. Emerson's errors, or rather, blindness, proceeds from a defect in the region of the heart" (quoted in Hershel Parker, "Transcendentalists: A Chronology," 263). Barring his criticisms, Melville's enthusiasm for Emerson in 1849 may have been partly due to the congeniality of what would appear to be Emerson's subject that night, "Natural Aristocracy" (later published as "Aristocracy"), a discourse that argued for an aristocracy of merit, lauded the nobility of failure, and was relatively restrained in its expression of antinomianisms and idealisms. See Sealts, "Emerson's Rainbow," 257–61. In this regard, it is interesting to note that Winsome–Emerson appears directly after a character named Charlie *Noble.* Whether Melville heard Emerson lecture at a later date is not known; the fact that Mark Winsome is about forty-five, close to Emerson's age in 1849, might indicate that this first exposure was definitive and not repeated. On the other hand, Emerson's lecture appearance in Pittsfield on March 13, 1856 (von Frank, 314) may have provided a memory jog, if Melville was in attendance.

38. Critics have disagreed on whether Plinlimmon is modeled on Emerson; some have argued that Hawthorne is an equally likely model. For a useful comparison of Plinlimmon and Emerson, see Wilmes, 160 ff. On Plinlimmon as a caricature of Hawthorne, see Murray, *Pierre,* lxxvii–lxxix; Lueders; Watson, "Estrangement," 395–96; and Brodhead, *School of Hawthorne,* 44–46. It seems clear that the optimist core of Plinlimmon's teachings, his cult of transcendental apostles, and many of his personal traits, including the Emersonian associations of his name, are largely derived from Emerson. Yet based on his manifest similarities to both Emerson and Hawthorne, we may conclude that Plinlimmon is a fictionalized *blend* of both writers and

an explicit caricature of neither. Mark Winsome, on the other hand, is a satirical clone of Emerson who exists in a state of dramatic tension with a character modeled on Hawthorne. It should be noted that Winsome's contradiction of the Sermon on the Mount, noted in Chapter 3 of this study, matches a similar subversion by Plotinus Plinlimmon. See Murray, *Pierre,* lxxi–lxxiii. Higgins, "Mark Winsome," discusses the similarities between Winsome's teachings and Plinlimmon's pamphlet.

39. The New York delivery of these lectures was reported in the *Literary World* on February 21, 28 and March 6, 1852. In "Power," for example, Emerson argued: "Success was not accidental but mathematical. In looking at the machinery of a mill, we see the machine more moral than ourselves. The imperfect thread is traced through a web of muslin, two hundred yards, to the attendant whose wages is reduced in consequence. We, too, should thus regard our responsibilities in the web of life" (*Literary World,* February 21, 1852). As Matthiessen remarks, "The sentiments of such essays as those on 'Wealth' and 'Power,' working on temperaments less unworldly than their author's, have provided a vicious reinforcement to the most ruthless elements in our economic life" (4).

40. It is not known when Melville read *Nature,* which was reissued in *Nature, Addresses and Lectures* in September 1849, shortly before Melville went to England and the Continent for three months. During his absence, the Duyckincks published a review of this volume in the *Literary World* on November 3, 1849. The reviewer, identified by Perry Miller as George Duyckinck (*Raven and the Whale,* 262), found reason to praise Emerson for his poetic feeling for nature, but spent most of the review attacking the ethical implications of Emerson's teachings in a manner that anticipates Melville's critique of Winsome–Emerson and Egbert–Thoreau.

41. Winsome's use of the rattlesnake example here may also recall Emerson's essay on "Napoleon": "We like to see every thing do its office after its kind, whether it be a milch-cow or a rattlesnake; and if fighting be the best mode of adjusting national differences, (as large majorities of men seem to agree,) certainly Bonaparte was right in making it thorough" (*Representative Men,* 135–36; noted in Foster, 356n). A similar formulation can be found in Emerson's lecture on the "Transcendentalist": "Now every one must do after his kind, be he asp or angel, and these must" (*Nature,* 207). Graulich discusses the rattlesnake's power to charm its victim in relation to Emerson's potential ability to charm and subsequently victimize his converts.

42. At the conclusion of *Nature* ("Prospects"), Emerson similarly wrote: "A correspondent revolution in things will attend the influx of the spirit. So fast will disagreeable appearances, swine, spiders, snakes, pests, mad-houses, prisons, enemies, vanish; they are temporary and shall be no more seen" (*Nature,* 45). In "New England Reformers" he wrote: "Nothing shall warp me from the belief, that every man is a lover of truth. There is no pure lie, no pure malignity in nature. The entertainment of the proposition of depravity is the last profligacy and profanation" (*Essays: Second Series,* 163). In "Swedenborg" he argued: "Evil, according to old philosophy, is good in the making. That pure malignity can exist, is the extreme proposition of unbelief. It is not to be entertained by a rational agent; it is atheism; it is the last profanation" (*Representative Men,* 77).

43. In *Nature,* Emerson asked, "What is a day? What is a year? What is summer? What is woman? What is a child? What is sleep?" (*Nature,* 44). Emerson's assertion in *Nature,* "A man is fed, not that he may be fed, but that he may work" (12), is also parodied in Winsome's claim that "man came into this world, not to sit down

and muse, not to befog himself with vain subtleties, but to gird up his loins and to work" (*CM*, 198). (Both parallels were first noted by Oliver.) Another possible borrowing from *Nature* is the image of Winsome after his drink of ice water, "gently wiping from his lips the beads of water freshly clinging there as to the valve of a coral-shell upon a reef" (*CM*, 194). After lamenting the lack of a "*metaphysics* of conchology," Emerson goes on to bewail the fact that man is a mere shell of his former grandeur: "But, having made of himself this huge shell, his waters retired; he no longer fills the veins and veinlets; he is shrunk to a drop. He sees, that the structure still fits him, but fits him colosally" (*Nature*, 40, 42).

44. It is amusing to compare Winsome's knowledge that Charlie Noble is a "Mississippi operator" with Emerson's report of the riverboat gamblers he encountered during his first trip on the Mississippi River in the spring of 1850. He described the scene to his wife: "Then a knot of gamblers playing quite ostentatiously on the cabin-tables, & large sums changing owners rapidly, and, as we Yankees fancied, with some glances of hope aimed at us that we should sit down with these amiable gentlemen who professed to be entire strangers to each other, &, if asked any question respecting the river, 'had never been on these waters before' " (*Letters*, 3:211).

45. Another consideration here is Emerson's contempt for most modern fiction, which included that of his Concord contemporary. Emerson noted in his journal: "N. Hawthorne's reputation as a writer is a very pleasing fact, because his writing is not good for anything, and this is a tribute to the man" (quoted in Mellow, 205; see also 116, 160–61, 445, and 570).

46. On Poe and Duyckinck, see Roche, Ch. 2. For a recent study of Poe's life, see Silverman. Poe had previously been caricatured as the critic Austin Wicks, a caddish drunk in Charles F. Briggs's *The Trippings of Tom Pepper* (see Note 15 above). Poe also appeared as another offensive drunk, Marmaduke Hammerhead, in Thomas Dunn English's *1844, or, the Power of the S.F.*, which was published in the fall of 1846 during Poe's libel suit against English and Hiram Fuller's New York *Mirror;* both *Tom Pepper* and *1844* first appeared in the *Mirror*. On this phase of Poe's life, see Silverman, 300–31.

47. The conclusion to Poe's *Eureka* is particularly Emersonian: "The utter impossibility of any one's soul feeling itself inferior to another; the intense, over whelming dissatisfaction and rebellion at the thought;—these, with the omniprevalent aspirations at perfection, are but the spiritual, coincident with the material, struggles towards the original Unity—are, to my mind at least, a species of proof far surpassing what Man terms demonstration, that no one soul *is* inferior to another—that nothing is, or can be, superior to any one soul—that each soul is, in part, its own God—its own Creator" (*Complete Works*, 16:312–13). Significantly, the reviewer of *Eureka* in the *Literary World* associated Poe's treatise with Transcendentalism's heresy of the divinity of the self. See Silverman, 338–42. Strickland suggests that the beggar's tract is based on Poe's lecture, "The Poetic Principle"; but this overlooks the numerous implicit resemblances between the beggar's literary offering and *Eureka*, the most outstanding being that *Eureka* was sold as a "tract" while "The Poetic Principle" was not published until *after* Poe's death and then was included in Poe's collected works.

48. Melville borrowed *A Week* from Duyckinck some time in mid-1850 (Sealts, *Melville's Reading*, no. 524). In 1847 Duyckinck had read the manuscript for Wiley and Putnam, which declined to publish the book unless Thoreau paid expenses; the

Literary World later gave *A Week* a friendly if guarded review. See Harding, 244–45, 249–50. An overview of Melville's possible sources of information about Thoreau is available in Hershel Parker, "Melville's Satire," 65, and "Transcendentalists: A Chronology." Lang and Lease, " 'Practical Disciple,' " claim that Egbert is modeled on the writer, editor, and Emerson admirer, George W. Curtis, but their evidence for this is not persuasive. They trace the name Egbert to Tieck's "The Fair-Haired Eckbert" in Carlyle's edition of *German Romance,* which Melville borrowed from Duyckinck in 1850 (Sealts, *Melville's Reading,* no. 121); but there would seem to be no special reason for Melville to draw on this character for Egbert. The ultimate historical source for the name is the ninth-century king of the West Saxons and first king of the English.

49. See Neufeldt for an extensive examination of Thoreau's appropriation and transformation of his culture's business vocabulary and ideology. Franklin, *The Confidence-Man,* 280n, also considers Egbert's business identity as drawn from *Walden.* On Thoreau's relation to the literary market, see Gilmore, Ch. 2.

50. Higgins, "Mark Winsome," provides a useful discussion of the implicit comparison with New Testament doctrine here, although without reference to Melville's parody of the Christ–Paul relationship. In addition to "Friendship," Melville probably had the "Philanthropy" section from *Walden* in mind when he conceived of the debate between "Charlie" and "Frank," for here again Thoreau is especially antipathetic to the idea of Christian charity: "A man is not a good *man* to me because he will feed me if I should be starving, or warm me if I should be freezing, or pull me out of a ditch if I should ever fall into one. I can find a Newfoundland dog that will do as much" (*Walden,* 74).

51. Hawthorne enjoyed Thoreau's company during his first residence in Concord and wrote about him in both "The Old Manse" and "The Custom-House." (The boat ride described in "The Old Manse" was taken in the boat that Thoreau built for his excursion on the Concord and Merrimack rivers and then sold to Hawthorne.) In the fall and winter of 1848–1849, Hawthorne twice arranged for Thoreau to lecture at the Salem lyceum. Hawthorne saw Thoreau occasionally during his subsequent residence in Concord in 1852–1853 and again after his return in 1860. Thoreau provided the legend that became Hawthorne's uncompleted *Dolliver Romance;* Hawthorne planned to write a commemorative essay on his younger contemporary, who died in May 1862, for this volume. See Mellow, 208–10, 289–90, 546, 559.

52. A number of other literary figures took an equally dim view of Thoreau. Lowell penned a damning indictment of him in a notorious 1865 *North American Review* article. Whitman thought Thoreau "a very aggravated case of superciliousness." Henry James, Sr., called Thoreau "literally the most childlike, unconscious and unblushing egotist it has even been my fortune to encounter in the ranks of manhood." Julian Hawthorne claimed that "his nature was bitter, jealous and morbid. His human affections were scarcely more than rudimentary" (quoted in Harding 374, 150, 309).

53. In this context it is ironic to note that in February 1857, just before publication of *The Confidence-Man,* Emerson and Thoreau experienced an important "rupture" in their friendship, following a previous loosening of ties at the time of Thoreau's publication of *A Week.* See Harding, 302–303.

54. Elkin provides a survey of eighteenth-century satirical defenses; see especially

Ch. 7, "Personal Reference": "As in their discussion of most aspects of satire, Augustan critics changed their minds concerning personal reference according to the needs of the moment and the particular satirical work under discussion. Their dilemma was that they did not really approve of personal satire, yet felt that it alone was effective. . . . Sometimes writers would declare themselves all for general satire, sometimes they would argue the need for personal satire in a degenerate age, and sometimes they wanted to have it both ways. On occasion, a work might be judged too personal by some critics, and too general by others" (138–39). For a recent discussion of the potential impact satire has on its audience, see Griffin, Ch. 6.

CHAPTER 7

1. See, for example, Matterson: "Overall, the result of these strategies is to call attention to fiction itself. If we lose belief in God or in any myth assigning meaning and purpose to the universe, then we fall back on fiction to make temporary sense and order, or we make a masquerade of identity. If we do not have myths we at least have fictions" (xxxiv).

2. See "Melville's Goneril." Foster, 311–14n, contested Oliver's identification, basing her argument on three points: first, the time lag between Melville's only recorded comments on Kemble in 1849 and his later caricature; second, some of the more salient differences between Goneril and Kemble; and third, the seeming improbability of Melville caricaturing an alleged marital martyr like Kemble as a human she-devil. Kemble's most recent biographer, however, asserts that "the case for intended identification is plausible" (Furnas, *Fanny Kemble*, 468n). Most of the basic similarities between Goneril and Fanny Kemble have been provided by Oliver; I add the sexual dimension to the caricature and adduce additional evidence. Oliver overstates his case in an effort to match every detail of Goneril to Fanny Kemble; he also improbably claims that Melville "stops just short of burlesque" (490).

3. For an account of Kemble's divorce, see Furnas, *Fanny Kemble*, Ch. 17. An idea of the national prominence of this case may be gathered from the fact that Pierce Butler hired George M. Dallas, the vice president, to be one of his attorneys; Daniel Webster accepted a retainer. Fanny Kemble hired Rufus Choate as her principal attorney. The case was settled before it came to trial.

4. A modern edition of Fanny Kemble's *Journal* supplies the names designated by initials in the original. Despite its freshness and candor, Fanny's *Journal* belongs to the tradition of disparaging English travelers. Indeed, some of her judgments are worthy of Mrs. Trollope: "The mixture of the republican feeling of equality peculiar to this country, and the usual want of refinement common to the lower classes of most countries, forms a singularly felicitious [*sic*] union of impudence and vulgarity to be met with no where but in America" (106). Regarding Fanny's chauvinism, her husband wrote: "Another topic, which not unfrequently embittered out fireside intercourse, was the spirit of unwise comparison, constantly indulged, between my country and her own. She came to the United States with a prejudice amounting to hatred. Almost every thing which she found different from what she was accustomed to, was pronounced to be inferior and wrong. As I never visited England until some years after my marriage, I was unable to controvert many of her unfavourable comparisons, which now, since I have resided in England, I know to be unjust and

unfounded. Oftentimes when she would express opinions and pronounce judgment, in her accustomed tone of infallibility, disadvantageous to America, I could only sit by and listen in mortified silence, for then I knew only my own country" (*Statement,* 20–21).

5. For the influence of Spenserian character types on Melville's fiction, see Moses. A revealing analogue to Melville's misogynistic caricature of Fanny Kemble was his reaction to Mrs. Lawrence, the wife of the American ambassador, when in London in November 1849: "Such a sour, scrawny, scare crow was never seen till she first saw herself in the glass. I do not fly out at her for her person—no, but her whole air & manner. God deliver me from such horrors as Mrs. Lawrence possesses for me.—Her skinny scrawny arms were bare—She talked of Lady Bulwer—said that—but there is no telling how she managed so well her veiled & disgusted air, without being at all uncivil or meaning any incivility. She belongs to that category of the female sex, there are no words to express my abhorrence of. I hate her not—I only class her among the persons made of reptiles & crawling things" (*J,* 23). Melville later regretted this outburst (*J,* 29) and the passage at some point was crossed out. Karcher, "Philanthropy," 87–89, makes the improbable claim that the story of Goneril is actually a satire on antifeminism; but this discounts both the pervasive evidence of personal satire and distorts the story's larger moral and metaphysical implications.

6. As Rudwin remarks, "The legend of Lilith is an intriguing revelation of old Semitic superstitions and persists to this very day in various forms. The personality of the Hebrew Lilith has been generally derived from the Babylonian-Assyrian Lilit, Lilu or Lilitu, an evil spirit. . . . this personification was a sort of fusion of the Roman Lamia, Greek *hetaera,* and the Turkish vampire" (94). For a summary of the Lilith legend and some examples of its extensive use in nineteenth-century literature by Rossetti, Browning, de Vigney, Hugo, and France, see Rudwin, Ch. 9.

7. Porte notes that "just as the description of Goneril, with a shrewdly humorous mixing of archetypes, presents that heroine in the image of the dark lady as cigar-store Indian, so the secret truth about her revealed in the tale is a black-comic parody of the Melvillian romance theme . . . of natural depravity" (*Romance in America,* 163). We need not follow Porte's suggestion that Goneril's ultimate secret is that she is a transvestite homosexual; her "secret" is that she embodies one of the unspecified archetypes Porte refers to.

8. For a comparison of Hall's chapter on Moredock in *Sketches of History, Life, and Manners in the West* (1835) with its rhetorically heightened retelling in *The Confidence-Man,* see "Melville's Indian-Hating Source" in *CM,* 501–10. For the most complete study of the life and writings of James Hall, see Randall. On Melville's adaptation of the literary figure of the Indian-hater, see Pearce.

9. For allegorical readings of the Indian-hating sequence, see Shroeder, 312–15; Foster, *The Confidence-Man,* lxv–lxviii; Parker, "Metaphysics"; Bowen, 413–15; and Chai, 94–97. For historicist readings, see Pearce; Fussell, 318–25; Grejda, 129–34; Drinnon, Ch. 15; Adler, Ch. 7; Palmeri, 100–05; and Bryant, *Melville & Repose,* 251–58. Those pointing out the story's incongruities and ambiguities include Ramsey, "Moot Points"; Bell, 235–37; Kaetz; and Bellis, "Melville's Confidence-Man," 551–57, and *No Mysteries,* 175–78.

10. This account was published by Moncure Conway in an introduction to an 1898 English edition of *The Blithedale Romance* and was based on Conway's conversations with Melville's widow. In his book *Literary Shrines* (1895), Theodore F.

Wolfe also commented on Hawthorne's visit with Melville in mid-March 1851: "March weather prevented walks abroad, so the pair spent most of the week in smoking and talking metaphysics in the barn,—Hawthorne usually lounging upon a carpenter's bench. When he was leaving, he jocosely declared he would write a report of their psychological discussions for publication in a book to be called 'A Week on a Work-Bench in a Barn,' the title being a travesty upon that of Thoreau's then recent book, 'A Week on Concord River' " (*Log,* 1:407).

11. Melville's melding of Hawthorne and Hall in the figure of Charlie Noble might have also been facilitated by the fact that both Hawthorne's *Mosses from an Old Manse* and Hall's *The Wilderness and the Warpath* were published in 1846 in Wiley & Putnam's Library of American Books, edited by Duyckinck. Melville had himself used the legendary Black Steed of the Prairies from *The Wilderness and the Warpath* to create his White Steed of the Prairies in Chapter 42 of *Moby-Dick* ("The Whiteness of the Whale").

12. Andrews notes Melville's punning allusion to the hero of "The Dragon of Wantley" and goes on to suggest that Melville is also punning on the name of his Pittsfield neighbor, the Morewoods, who in 1850 bought the mansion belonging to Melville's uncle's family and subsequently named it "Broadhall." She also points out that Frank Goodman's query as to whether Moredock's family seat is in Northamptonshire recalls the fact that the county adjoining Pittsfield is Hampshire, with its county seat at Northampton.

13. Fussell, 323–24, first argued that Melville was attacking Hall. Drinnon, Ch. 15, subsequently performed what can only be described as a hatchet job on Hall's character, grossly distorting both his life and writings to conform to Drinnon's larger historical diatribe. Adler, 116, assumes that Melville is criticizing Hall, although she focuses on the larger cultural implications of the Indian-hating material. Foster, on the other hand, argues that "throughout Hall's work, his sympathy for the Indian victims of the determined and heartless aggression of the whites is clear. His attitude is reiterated so often that Melville's change to the antipodal interpretation must have been made with definite purpose. . . . He disclaims personal responsibility for the views in *The Confidence-Man* by putting them in the mouth of the Mississippi operator, who in turn specifically disclaims them and attributes them, quite unjustly, to Judge Hall" (lxii–lxviii). Northcutt also takes a more positive view of Hall's character while drawing attention to the popular clichés inherent in the Indian-hating sequence: "Melville shows his disdain for the Western stereotypes inherent in the Moredock story by this transformation of the real-life narrator, the humanely progressive Judge James Hall, into the garrulous poseur Judge Hall. . . . The movement of the Moredock story from history to popular culture illustrates the fictionalization and distortion of the facts of the Western frontier from reality to entertainment" (47–48).

14. Randall, 219, 310n, lists Hall's five different historical and fictionalized accounts of the figure of the Indian-hater in his writings from 1828 to 1835, noting that "Hall was followed in his studies of the type by Timothy Flint, James Kirke Paulding, Robert Montgomery Bird, William Gilmore Simms, William Joseph Snelling, and Charles Fenno Hoffman, some of whom, if not all, based their descriptions on Hall's stories. The Indian-hater became—along with the scout, the bee hunter, and the white renegade—one of the bizarre characters which the frontier contributed

to American fiction" (219). Pearce, 943n, provides an extensive list of novels in which the figure of the Indian-hater appeared.

15. Ramsey, for example, claims that "Noble's interpolation collapses in upon itself, locating evil in no specific home whatsoever" ("Moot Points," 235). Bell similarly notes that "we may well wonder whether Moredock exists at all. We should reflect, in any case, on the sort of 'colonel' one might expect to find in a 'corn-loft' and on whether there is any 'kernel' of truth in this narrative" (237). Adler asserts that the view of Moredock shows that he is "the stuff of myth and fable. The supposedly material basis for him, in the 'back view' that history takes, turns out to be a moss-ball (a growth whose substance accumulates with the passage of time) or a pile of leaves built up by the wind" (117).

16. Parker, "Metaphysics," discusses Indian-hating as a satire on "nominal Christianity" in which the Indian-hater is a type of Christian ascetic who demonstrates the impracticability of Christian doctrine. Chai, 94–97, also comments on some of the religious aspects of Indian-hating.

17. As Palmeri notes, "In the Indian-hating chapters, Melville makes use of Swift's favorite satiric strategy, as he ironically celebrates action that he deplores by exaggerating only slightly attitudes already present in its defenders" (103). Both Palmeri, 103, and Adler, 115, compare the Indian-hating chapters to "A Modest Proposal."

18. Likening Noble's story to a series of "Chinese boxes," Kaetz remarks that it "explodes outward into a multiplicity of interpretive possibilities, all of which can be validated by the text, but only up to a certain point before the interpretations themselves collapse under their own weight" (11).

19. Charlemont's history even suggests that of Irving himself, for Irving was a bachelor who left New York for England in 1815, experienced the bankruptcy of his family business, resided on the Continent for several years, and in 1832 finally returned to the United States where he reestablished himself as perhaps the most beloved American author of his time. As critics have noted, Charlemont's experience of bankruptcy also bears comparison with that of the hero of Melville's story, "Jimmy Rose," published in *Harper's* in November 1855.

20. A few other possible associations of the name "Charlemont" may be mentioned here. The best known historical individual of this name is the Anglo-Irish peer, James Caulfield, fourth viscount and first earl of Charlemont (1728–1799), a prominent Irish political figure with literary interests: During a residence in London (1764–1773), he associated with Burke, Johnson, Reynolds, Goldsmith, Beauclerk, and Hogarth. *Charlemont* was also the title of a novel by William Gilmore Simms, published about March 1, 1856. See Simms, 2:366n. Bypassing the problem of chronology, Duban, *Melville's Major Fiction,* 211n, suggests a thematic association between Simms's novel and Melville's "Charlemont." It is perhaps mere coincidence that Simms's *Charlemont* carried a dedication dated December 1855 to James Hall, who is characterized as "ONE OF THE ABLEST OF OUR LITERARY PIONEERS; A GENUINE REPRESENTATIVE OF THE GREAT WEST; WHOSE WRITINGS EQUALLY ILLUSTRATE HER HISTORY AND GENIUS."

21. A more detailed summary of the Agatha story can be found in *C,* 621–25. In *Moby-Dick,* Melville described the chief ethical idea of Christ as "the mere negative, feminine one of submission and endurance, which on all hands it is conceded, form the peculiar practical virtues of his teachings" (*MD,* 376).

22. Karcher, "Melville's Concepts," has indicated some of the parallels between

Charlemont and Christ; I offer a slightly different set, including the central idea of the Atonement. Karcher relates "Charlemont" to the novel's three interpolated essays, which allegedly "identify the fictional representation of human reality with the mythical representation of divine reality" (75).

23. In his discussion of the theme of Timonism in the interaction of Goodman and Noble, Wenke adduces the name Charlemont as a play on the names of Charlie and Timon: "Charlemont presents variations on the thematic conflict between philanthropy and misanthropy. . . . Charlemont is actually noble and a false Timon, Charlie is falsely noble and an actual Timon. It is significant that, throughout *Timon of Athens,* the protagonist is repeatedly referred to as 'noble Timon,' a point that was probably not lost on Melville" ("No 'i' in Charlemont," 271, 273). For another discussion of Timonism in the novel, see Watson, "Theme of Timonism," 180–87.

24. Neufeldt, 129–30, notes that Thoreau owned a copy of *The Life of Dr. Benjamin Franklin* (1796), which consisted of the first quarter of Franklin's later, more famous *Autobiography* (1868), together with a continuation by a Dr. Stuber of Philadelphia. In a discussion of the "confidence game" in Franklin and Thoreau, Lindberg writes: "This is how the model selves in *Walden* and Franklin's *Autobiography* are most revealingly alike. They live in competition. Holding out their own procedures as examples for others, they nevertheless find themselves surrounded by incompetents, and in a hundred ways each illustrates his own practical superiority to the timid and the trapped" (177).

25. Heidmann, 208–12, discusses the parallels between Job and China Aster. The flower symbolism of "China Aster" is also appropriate in the context of Job: "Man that is born of a woman is of a few days, and full of trouble. He cometh forth like a flower, and is cut down: he fleeth also as a shadow, and continueth not" (Job 14: 1–2).

26. See Hoffman, "China Aster," 146; Franklin, *The Confidence-Man,* 291–92n; and Sussman, 46–47. Melville's use of flower names for his two main characters also reflects the nineteenth-century idealization of same-sex friendship as found, for example, in both Emerson's and Thoreau's essays on Friendship. See *Essays: First Series,* 117; *A Week,* 285–86.

27. Hershel Parker speculates on some of the autobiographical implications of "The story of China Aster," claiming that "it may be more *jeu d'esprit* than *cri du coeur*" ("China Aster," 356). Watson, "Theme of Timonism," 186, notes the parallels between Melville's writing of *Mardi, Moby-Dick,* and *Pierre* and China Aster's three ventures in spermaceti candles. It is worth pointing out that in the early 1850s Tertullus Stewart was involved in the sugar trade in New York City, and by 1853–1854 he was living in Astoria, New York (*C,* 182): Melville's punning name for China Aster's friend "Orchis" may thus obliquely recall Stewart's trade in a tropical agricultural product, while Stewart's residence in "Astoria" presents another biographical irony.

CHAPTER 8

1. For a survey of satirical defenses in eighteenth-century satire, see Elkin. For useful critical examinations of the interpolated essays in *The Confidence-Man,* see Hayman; Dryden, 154–95; Alter, 127–37; and Kirby, 129–31. None of these critics

discusses the essays in connection with satire. Commenting on the resemblance between the interpolated essays in Melville's novel and Fielding's fiction, Alter complains that "The explicit imitation of Fielding invites comparison and points up a formal deficiency, for the one thing this novel lacks is precisely what Fielding worked out so splendidly—a way of writing about the fictional events absolutely continuous with the theorizing, where in the narrative itself there is a seamless connection between narration and wide-ranging reflection, where at every moment the ostentatiously manipulated fictional materials are set in an elaborate grid of convention, genre, literary allusion, authorial intention" (134). The ostensible formal deficiency Alter points out would be less noticeable if one considered *The Confidence-Man*'s interpolated essays from the perspective of satire.

2. In his defense of his literary methods here, Melville also may have had in mind Spenser's defense of his imaginative "fairyland" in the prologue to Book II of the *Fairie Queene*. Here Spenser defends his work by adducing the example of the New World as proof that man's limited knowledge does not encompass all of reality: "Why then should witlesse man so much misweene / That nothing is, but that which he hath seene?" This portion of Spenser's poem, which Melville scored in his edition, also plays a part in the general Spenserian backdrop to "The Piazza," which Melville wrote in early 1856 while composing *The Confidence-Man*. See Moses, 156.

3. See Perosa, Chs. 2 and 3, for a record of the attempt by antebellum writers of "romance" to establish a privileged imaginative status for their fiction. He notes that the claims being made in Chapter 33 "look forward to James's definition of romance in his 1907 Preface to *The American,* but above all they emphasize Melville's idea of fiction as 'rival creation': fiction not only inhabits, it creates, another world, a different world from everyday life, where a dislocation from actuality has taken place" (64).

4. Melville's preoccupation with literary "originality" dates from the writing of *Mardi* in 1847–1848. In Chapter 75, for example, Melville anticipated the tenor of his later remarks on originality in *The Confidence-Man:* "In all the universe is but one original; and the very suns must to their source for their fire; and we Prometheuses must to them for ours; which, when had, only perpetual Vestal tending will keep alive" (*M,* 229). Melville continued to ponder the issue of originality in early 1849, when he first heard Emerson lecture (*C,* 121).

EPILOGUE

1. For a full account of the contemporary reception of *The Confidence-Man,* see the "Historical Note" in *CM,* 316–30; see also Foster, xxxiii–xxxvii, and Hetherington, 255–64. For a comprehensive selection of reviews, see Parker, *The Confidence-Man,* 269–79, and Branch, *Critical Heritage,* 369–86.

2. Ketterer, "Mark Twain," goes so far as to claim that *The Mysterious Strange* was, in part, inspired by *The Confidence-Man*—this despite the lack of evidence that Twain ever read Melville. He proposes that the numerical designation of Satan in the fourth and final version of Twain's story, "No. 44, The Mysterious Stranger," is derived from Melville's remarks on the original character in Chapter 44 of *The Confidence-Man.*

Works Cited

Abzug, Robert H. *Cosmos Crumbling: American Reform and the Religious Imagination*. New York: Oxford University Press, 1994.

Adler, Joyce Sparer. *War in Melville's Imagination*. New York: New York University Press, 1981.

Agnew, Jean-Christophe. *Worlds Apart: The Market and the Theatre in Anglo-American Thought 1550–1750*. New York: Cambridge University Press, 1986.

Alter, Robert. *Partial Magic: The Novel as a Self-Conscious Genre*. Berkeley: University of California Press, 1975.

Andrews, Deborah C. "A Note on Melville's Confidence-Man." *ESQ: A Journal of the American Renaissance* 63 (Spring 1971): 27–28.

Arvin, Newton. *Herman Melville*. New York: William Sloane Associates, 1950.

Baim, Joseph. "The Confidence-Man as 'Trickster.'" *American Transcendental Quarterly*, No. 1 (1st Quarter 1969): 81–83.

Baritz, Loren. *City on a Hill: A History of Ideas and Myths in America*. New York: John Wiley, 1964.

Barker-Benfield, G. J. *The Horrors of the Half-Known Life: Male Attitudes Towards Women and Sexuality in Nineteenth-Century America*. New York: Harper & Row, 1976.

Barney, Stephen A. *Allegories of History, Allegories of Love*. Hamden, Conn.: Shoe String Press, 1979.

Baym, Nina. "Melville's Quarrel with Fiction." *PMLA* 94 (October 1979): 902–23.

Bell, Michael Davitt. *The Development of American Romance: The Sacrifice of Relation*. Chicago: University of Chicago Press, 1980.

Bellis, Peter J. "Melville's *Confidence-Man:* An Uncharitable Interpretation." *American Literature* 59 (December 1987): 548–69.

———. *No Mysteries Out of Ourselves: Identity and Textual Form in the Novels of Herman Melville*. Philadelphia: University of Pennsylvania Press, 1990.

Bercovitch, Sacvan. *The American Jeremiad*. Madison: University of Wisconsin Press, 1978.

Bergmann, Johannes Dietrich. "The Original Confidence Man." *American Quarterly* 21 (Fall 1969): 560–77.

———. "The Original Confidence Man: The Development of the American Confidence Man in the Sources and Backgrounds of Herman Melville's *The Confidence-Man: His Masquerade*." Ph.D. diss., University of Connecticut, 1969.

Bernstein, John. *Pacifism and Rebellion in the Writings of Herman Melville*. The Hague: Mouton, 1964.

Blackburn, Alexander. *The Myth of the Picaro: Continuity and Transformation in the Picaresque Novel 1554–1954*. Chapel Hill: University of North Carolina Press, 1979.

Blair, John G. *The Confidence Man in Modern Fiction: A Rogue's Gallery with Six Portraits*. New York: Barnes & Noble, 1979.

———. "Puns and Equivocations in Melville's *The Confidence-Man*." *American Transcendental Quarterly*, No. 22 (Spring 1974): 91–95.

Bloom, Edward, and Lillian Bloom. *Satire's Persuasive Voice*. Ithaca, N.Y.: Cornell University Press, 1979.

Bode, Carl. *The Anatomy of American Popular Culture, 1840–1861*. Berkeley: University of California Press, 1959.

Bowen, Merlin. "Tactics of Indirection in Melville's *The Confidence-Man*." *Studies in the Novel* 1 (Winter 1969): 401–20.

Branch, Watson G. "*The Confidence-Man: His Masquerade:* An Edition with Introduction and Notes." Ph.D. diss., Northwestern University, 1970.

———. "The Genesis, Composition, and Structure of *The Confidence-Man*." *Nineteenth Century Fiction* 7 (March 1973): 424–48.

———, ed. *Melville: The Critical Heritage*. Boston: Routledge & Kegan Paul, 1974.

Braswell, William. "Melville as a Critic of Emerson." *American Literature* 9 (November 1937): 317–34.

———. *Melville's Religious Thought*. Durham, N.C.: Duke University Press, 1943.

Brodhead, Richard. *Hawthorne, Melville and the Novel*. Chicago: University of Chicago Press, 1976.

———. *The School of Hawthorne*. New York: Oxford University Press, 1986.

Brooks, Van Wyck. *The Times of Melville and Whitman*. New York: E.P. Dutton, 1947.

Brouwner, Fred E. "Melville's *The Confidence-Man* as Ship of Philosophers." *Southern Humanities Review* 3 (Spring 1969): 158–65.

Brown, Jerry Wayne. *The Rise of Biblical Criticism in America 1800–1870: The New England Scholars*. Middletown, Conn.: Wesleyan University Press, 1969.

Brumm, Ursula. *American Literature and Religious Typology*. Trans. John Hoagland. New Brunswick, N.J.: Rutgers University Press, 1970.

Bruner, Margaret Reed. "The Gospel According to Herman Melville: A Reading of *The Confidence-Man*." Ph.D. diss., Vanderbilt University, 1972.

Bryant, John. "Citizens of a World to Come: Melville and the Millennial Cosmopolite." *American Literature* 59 (March 1987): 20–36.

———, ed. *A Companion to Melville Studies*. Westport, Conn.: Greenwood Press, 1986.

———. "*The Confidence-Man:* Melville's Problem Novel." In Bryant, ed., *Companion to Melville Studies*, 315–50.

———. *Melville & Repose: The Rhetoric of Humor in the American Renaissance*. New York: Oxford University Press, 1993.

———. " 'Nowhere a Stranger': Melville and Cosmopolitanism." *Nineteenth-Century Fiction* 39 (December 1984): 275–91.

Buell, Lawrence. "The Last Word on *The Confidence-Man?*" *Illinois Quarterly* 35 (November 1972): 15–29.

———. *New England Literary Culture: From Revolution Through Renaissance.* New York: Cambridge University Press, 1986.

Butler, Pierce. *Mr. Butler's Statement.* Philadelphia, 1850.

Carothers, Robert Lee. "The Search for the Father in the Writings of Herman Melville: A Study of the Novels." Ph.D. diss., Kent State University, 1966.

Carter, Everett. *The American Idea: The Literary Response to American Optimism.* Chapel Hill: University of North Carolina Press, 1977.

Cawelti, John G. "Some Notes on the Structure of *The Confidence-Man.*" *American Literature* 29 (November 1957): 278–88.

Cayton, Mary Kupiec. "The Making of an American Prophet: Emerson, His Audiences, and the Rise of the Culture Industry in Nineteenth-Century America." *American Historical Review* 92 (June 1987): 597–620.

Chabot, C. Barry. "Melville's *The Confidence-Man:* A 'Poisonous Reading." *Psychoanalytic Review* 63 (Winter 1976–1977): 571–85.

Chai, Leon. *The Romantic Foundations of the American Renaissance.* Ithaca, N.Y.: Cornell University Press, 1987.

Chambers, Robert, ed. *The Book of Days.* 2 vols. Rpt. Detroit: Gale Research Co., 1967.

Charvat, William. *The Profession of Authorship in American, 1800–1870.* Ed. Matthew J. Bruccoli. New York: Columbia University Press, 1992.

Chase, Frederic Hathaway. *Lemuel Shaw: Chief Justice of the Supreme Judicial Court of Massachusetts, 1830–1860.* Boston: Houghton Mifflin, 1918.

Chase, Richard. *Herman Melville: A Critical Study.* New York: Macmillan, 1949.

Clark, Thomas D. *The Rampaging Frontier: Manners and Humors of Pioneer Days in the South and Middle West.* Bloomington: Indiana University Press, 1964.

Cochran, Thomas C., and William Miller. *The Age of Enterprise: A Social History of Industrial America.* Rev. ed. New York: Harper & Row, 1962.

Cohen, Hennig, and Donald Yannella. *Herman Melville's Malcolm Letter: "Man's Final Lore.*" New York: Fordham University Press, 1992.

Combs, Barbara Sue. "*The Confidence-Man* as Apocalyptic Vision." Ph.D. diss., Ohio State University, 1972.

Cook, Jonathan A. "From 'Myth' to 'Mystery': A Possible Emendation of *The Confidence-Man.*" *Melville Society Extracts* (forthcoming).

———. "Melville's Man in Gold Sleeve Buttons: Chief Justice Lemuel Shaw." *ESQ: A Journal of the American Renaissance* 34 (4th Quarter 1988): 257–81.

———. "New Heavens, Poor Old Earth: Satirical Apocalypse in Hawthorne's *Mosses from an Old Manse.*" *ESQ: A Journal of the American Renaissance* 39 (4th Quarter 1993): 209–52.

———. "Rabelais' Solar Lamp: A Source for *The Confidence-Man.*" *Melville Society Extracts* No. 97 (June 1994): 1, 4–7.

Crews, Frederick. *The Sins of the Fathers: Hawthorne's Psychological Themes.* New York: Oxford University Press, 1965.

Daniels, George H. *American Science in the Age of Jackson.* New York: Columbia University Press, 1968.

Derks, Scott, ed. *The Value of a Dollar: Prices and Incomes in the United States 1860–1989.* Detroit: Gale Research, 1994.

Dichmann, Mary E. "Absolutism in Melville's *Pierre.*" *PMLA* 67 (September 1952): 702–15.

Dillingham, William. *Melville's Later Novels.* Athens: University of Georgia Press, 1986.

———. *Melville's Short Fiction 1853–1856.* Athens: University of Georgia Press, 1977.

Dimock, Wai-chee. *Empire for Liberty: Melville and the Poetics of Individualism.* Princeton, N.J.: Princeton University Press, 1989.

Dolan, Marc. "Four Faces of *The Confidence-Man:* An Academic Blind Man's Zoo." *ESQ: A Journal of the American Renaissance* 39 (2nd and 3rd Quarter 1993): 133–60.

Drew, Philip. "Appearance and Reality in Melville's *The Confidence-Man.*" *ELH* 31 (December 1964): 418–42.

Drinnon, Richard. *Facing West: The Metaphysics of Indian-Hating and Empire-Building.* Minneapolis: University of Minnesota Press, 1980.

Dryden, Edgar A. *Melville's Theatrics of Form: The Great Art of Telling the Truth.* Baltimore, Md.: Johns Hopkins University Press, 1968.

Duban, James. *Melville's Major Fiction: Politics, Theology, Art.* Dekalb: Northern Illinois University Press, 1983.

———, and William J. Scheick. "The Commodious Life-Preserver in Melville's *The Confidence-Man.*" *American Literature* 62 (June 1990): 306–309.

Dubler, Walter. "Themes and Structures in Melville's *The Confidence-Man.*" *American Literature* 33 (November 1961): 307–19.

Eberwein, Jane Donahue. "Joel Barlow and *The Confidence-Man.*" *American Transcendental Quarterly,* No. 24 (Fall 1974): 28–29.

Elkin, P. K. *The Augustan Defense of Satire.* London: Oxford University Press, 1973.

Elliott, Robert C. *The Power of Satire: Magic, Ritual, Art.* Princeton, N.J.: Princeton University Press, 1960.

Emerson, Ralph Waldo. *The Collected Works of Ralph Waldo Emerson.* Gen. eds. Alfred R. Ferguson and Joseph Slater. 4 vols. to date. Cambridge, Mass.: Harvard University Press, 1971–.

———. *Essays: First Series.* Eds. Joseph Slater, Alfred R. Ferguson, and Jean Ferguson Carr. *Collected Works,* Vol. II, 1979.

———. *Essays: Second Series.* Eds. Joseph Slater, Alfred R. Ferguson, and Jean Ferguson Carr. *Collected Works,* Vol. III, 1983.

———. *The Letters of Ralph Waldo Emerson.* Vol. 3. Ed. Ralph Rusk. New York: Columbia University Press, 1939.

———. *Nature, Addresses, and Lectures.* Eds. Robert E. Spiller and Alfred R. Ferguson. *Collected Works,* Vol. I, 1971.

———. *Representative Men: Seven Lectures.* Eds. Wallace E. Williams and Douglas Emory Wilson. *Collected Works,* Vol. IV, 1987.

Erlich, Gloria C. *Family Themes and Hawthorne's Fiction: The Tenacious Web.* New Brunswick, N.J.: Rutgers University Press, 1984.

Fisher, Marvin. *Going Under: Melville's Short Fiction and the 1850s.* Baton Rouge: Louisiana State University Press, 1977.

Fletcher, Angus. *Allegory: The Theory of a Symbolic Mode.* Ithaca, N.Y.: Cornell University Press, 1984.

Flibbert, Joseph. *Melville and the Art of Burlesque.* Amsterdam: Rodopi, 1974.

Foster, Elizabeth S., ed. *The Confidence-Man: His Masquerade.* By Herman Melville. New York: Hendricks House, 1954.

Franklin, H. Bruce, ed. *The Confidence-Man: His Masquerade.* By Herman Melville. New York: Bobb-Merrill, 1967.

———. *The Wake of the Gods: Melville's Mythology.* Stanford, Calif.: Stanford University Press, 1963.

Frederick, John T. *The Darkened Sky: Nineteenth-Century American Novelists and Religion.* Notre Dame, Ind.: University of Notre Dame Press, 1988.

Freeman, John. *Herman Melville.* New York: Macmillan, 1926.

Frye, Northrop. *Anatomy of Criticism: Four Essays.* Princeton, N.J.: Princeton University Press, 1957.

Furnas, J. C. *Fanny Kemble: Leading Lady of the Nineteenth-Century Stage.* New York: Dial, 1982.

———. *The Life and Times of the Late Demon Rum.* New York: Capricorn, 1973.

Fussell, Edwin. *Frontier: American Literature and the American West.* Princeton, N.J.: Princeton University Press, 1965.

Galbraith, John Kenneth. *Money: Whence It Came, Where It Went.* Rev. ed. Boston: Houghton Mifflin, 1995.

Garner, Stanton. "Allan Melvill to Martin Van Buren, On Major Melvill's Removal." *Melville Society Extracts* No. 47 (September 1981): 4–5.

———. *The Civil War World of Herman Melville.* Lawrence: University of Kansas Press, 1993.

———. "The Picaresque Career of Thomas Melvill, Junior." *Melville Society Extracts,* No. 60 (November 1984): 1–10; No. 62 (May 1985): 1, 4–10.

Gaudino, Rebecca K. "The Riddle of *The Confidence-Man.*" *Journal of Narrative Technique* 14 (Spring 1984): 124–41.

Gaustad, Edwin S., ed. *The Rise of Adventism: Religion and Society in Mid-Nineteenth Century America.* New York: Harper & Row, 1974.

Gilman, William H. *Melville's Early Life and Redburn.* New York: New York University Press, 1951.

Gilmore, Michael T. *American Romanticism and the Marketplace.* Chicago: University of Chicago Press, 1985.

Glaser, Lynn. *Counterfeiting in America: The History of an American Way to Wealth.* New York: Clarkson Potter, 1968.

Graulich, Melody. "Melville's Most Fascinating Confidence-Man." *American Transcendental Quarterly,* No. 52 (Fall 1981): 229–36.

Greenspan, Ezra, "Evert Duyckinck and the History of Wiley and Putnam's Library of American Books, 1845–1847." *American Literature* 64 (December 1992): 677–93.

Grejda, Edward S. *The Common Continent of Men: Racial Equality in the Writings of Herman Melville.* Port Washington, N.Y.: Kennikat, 1974.

Grenberg, Bruce. *Some Other World to Find: Quest and Negation in the Works of Herman Melville.* Urbana: University of Illinois Press, 1989.

Grey, Robin Sandra. "Surmising the Infidel: Interpreting Melville's Annotations of Milton's Poetry." *Milton Quarterly* 26 (December 1992): 103–13.

Griffin, Dustin. *Satire: A Critical Reintroduction.* Lexington: University Press of Kentucky, 1994.

Griffith, Frank Clark "Melville and the Quest for God." Ph.D. diss., State University of Iowa, 1952.

Guilhamet, Leon. *Satire and the Transformations of Genre.* Philadelphia: University of Pennsylvania Press, 1987.

Haberstroh, Charles, Jr. "Melville, Marriage, and *Mardi.*" *Studies in the Novel* 9 (Fall 1977): 247–60.

Halttunen, Karen. *Confidence Men and Painted Women: A Study of Middle-Class Culture in America, 1830–1870.* New Haven, Conn.: Yale University Press, 1982.

Harding, Walter. *The Days of Henry David Thoreau.* New York: Knopf, 1965.

Hartman, Jay H. "*Volpone* as a Possible Source for Melville's *The Confidence-Man.*" *Susquehanna University Studies* 7 (1965): 247–60.

Hauck, Richard Boyd. *A Cheerful Nihilism: Confidence and "The Absurd" in American Humorous Fiction.* Bloomington: Indiana University Press, 1971.

———. "Nine Good Jokes: The Redemptive Humor of the Confidence Man and *The Confidence-Man.*" In Thompson and Lokke, eds., *Ruined Eden,* 245–82.

Hawthorne, Julian. *Nathaniel Hawthorne and His Wife.* 2 vols. Boston: James R. Osgood, 1884.

Hawthorne, Nathaniel. *The Centenary Edition of the Works of Nathaniel Hawthorne.* Gen. eds. William Charvat, Roy Harvey Pearce, and Claude M. Simpson. 20 vols. Columbus: Ohio State University Press, 1962–1988.

———. *American Notebooks.* Ed. Claude M. Simpson. *Centenary Edition,* Vol. VIII, 1972.

———. *The Blithedale Romance and Fanshawe. Centenary Edition,* Vol. III, 1964.

———. *The House of the Seven Gables. Centenary Edition,* Vol. II, 1965.

———. *The Letters 1843–1853.* Eds. Thomas Woodson, L. Neal Smith, and Norman Holmes Pearson. *Centenary Edition,* Vol XVI, 1985.

———. *Mosses from an Old Manse. Centenary Edition,* Vol. X, 1974.

———. *The Scarlet Letter. Centenary Edition,* Vol. I, 1962.

Hayford, Harrison. "Hawthorne and Melville: A Biographical and Critical Study." Ph.D. diss., Yale University, 1945.

———. "Poe in *The Confidence-Man.*" *Nineteenth-Century Fiction* 14 (December 1959): 207–18. Rpt. in Parker, ed., *The Confidence-Man,* 344–53.

Hayford, Harrison, and Merrell Davis. "Melville as Office-Seeker." *Modern Language Quarterly* 10 (June and September 1949): 168–83, 377–88.

Hayman, Allen. "The Real and the Original: Herman Melville's Theory of Prose Fiction." *Modern Fiction Studies* 8 (August 1962): 211–32.

Heidmann, Mark. "Melville and the Bible: Leading Themes in the Marginalia and the Major Fiction, 1850–1956." Ph.D. diss., Yale University, 1979.

Hetherington, Hugh W. *Melville's Reviewers: British and American 1846–1891.* Chapel Hill: University of North Carolina Press, 1961.

Hick, John. *Evil and the God of Love.* New York: Harper & Row, 1966.

Higgins, Brian. "Mark Winsome and Egbert: 'In the Friendly Spirit.' " In Parker, ed., *The Confidence-Man,* 339–43.

Higgins, Brian, and Hershel Parker, eds. *Critical Essays on Melville's "Pierre; Or, The Ambiguities."* Boston: G. K. Hall, 1983.

Hillway, Tyrus. *Herman Melville.* New York: Twayne, 1963.

Hirsch, P. L. "Melville's Ambivalence Toward the Writer's 'Wizardry': Allusions to Theurgic Magic in *The Confidence-Man.*" *ESQ: A Journal of the American Renaissance* 31 (2nd Quarter 1985): 100–15.

Hoffman, Daniel. *Form and Fable in American Fiction.* New York: Oxford University Press, 1961.

———. "Melville's Story of China Aster." *American Literature* 22 (May 1950): 137–49.

Horlick, Allan Stanley. *Country Boys and Merchant Princes: The Social Control of Young Men in New York.* Lewisburg, Penn.: Bucknell University Press, 1975.

Horsford, Howard C. "Evidence of Melville's Plans for a Sequel to *The Confidence-Man.*" *American Literature* 24 (March 1952): 85–89. Rpt. in Parker, ed., *The Confidence-Man,* 356–60.

Horth, Marilyn Jeanne. "Melville's Confidence-Man: A Diminished Devil." Ph.D. diss., Northwestern University, 1986.

Hovenkamp, Herbert. *Science and Religion in America, 1800–1860.* Philadelphia: University of Pennsylvania Press, 1978.

Howard, Leon. *Herman Melville: A Biography.* Berkeley: University of California Press, 1951.

Humphreys, A. R. *Herman Melville.* New York: Grove Press, 1962.

Hunter, Louis C. *Steamboating on the Western Rivers: An Economic and Technological History.* Cambridge, Mass.: Harvard University Press, 1949.

Imbert, Michel. "Cash, Cant and Confidence: Of Paper Money and Scriptures in *The Confidence-Man.*" In Viola Sachs, ed. *L'Imaginaire-Melville: A French Point of View.* Paris: Press Universitaires de Vincennes, 1992.

Irwin, John T. *American Hieroglyphics: The Symbol of the Egyptian Hieroglyphic in the American Renaissance.* New Haven, Conn.: Yale University Press, 1980.

James, Henry. *The American Scene.* Bloomington: Indiana University Press, 1968.

Jones, Buford. "Some 'Mosses' from the *Literary World:* Critical and Bibliographical Survey of the Hawthorne–Melville Relationship." In Thompson and Lokke, eds., *Ruined Eden,* 173–203.

Jones, Dale. "The Grotesque in Melville's *The Confidence-Man. Colby Library Quarterly* 19 (December 1983): 194–205.

Kaetz, James P. "Layers of Fiction: Melville's 'The Metaphysics of Indian-Hating.' " *Melville Society Extracts* No. 79 (November 1989): 9–12.

Karcher, Carolyn. "Philanthropy and the Occult in the Fiction of Hawthorne, Brownson, and Melville." In Howard Kerr, John W. Crowley, and Charles L. Crow, eds. *The Haunted Dusk: American Supernatural Fiction, 1870–1920.* Athens: University of Georgia Press, 1983.

———. *Shadow over the Promised Land: Slavery, Race, and Violence in Melville's America.* Baton Rouge: Louisiana State University Press, 1980.

———. "The Story of Charlemont: A Dramatization of Melville's Concepts of Fiction in *The Confidence-Man: His Masquerade.*" *Nineteenth-Century Fiction* 21 (June 1966): 73–84.

Kearns, Michael S. "How to Read *The Confidence-Man.*" *ESQ: A Journal of the American Renaissance* 36 (3rd Quarter 1990): 209–38.

Kemble, Fanny. *Journal of a Young Actress.* Ed. Monica Gough. New York: Columbia University Press, 1990.

Kemper, Steven E. "*The Confidence-Man:* A Knavishly-Packed Deck," *Studies in American Fiction* 8 (Spring 1980): 23–35.

Kennedy, Joyce Deveau, and Frederick James Kennedy. "Herman Melville and Samuel Hay Savage, 1847–1851." *Melville Society Extracts* No. 35 (September 1978): 1–10.

Kenney, Alice. *The Gansevoorts of Albany: Dutch Patricians in the Upper Hudson Valley.* Syracuse, N.Y.: Syracuse University Press, 1969.

Kern, Alexander C."Melville's *The Confidence-Man:* A Structure of Satire." In O. M. Brack, ed. *American Humor.* Scottsdale, Ariz.: Arete, 1977.

Kernan, Alvin B. *The Cankered Muse: Satire of the English Renassiance.* New Haven, Conn.: Yale University Press, 1959.

———. *The Plot of Satire.* New Haven, Conn.: Yale University Press, 1965.

Ketterer, David. "Melville, Mark Twain, and 'No. 44': The Source of a Name." *Melville Society Extracts* No. 71 (November 1987): 2–5.

———. *New Worlds for Old: The Apocalyptic Imagination, Science Fiction, and American Literature.* Bloomington: Indiana University Press, 1974.

Keyser, Elizabeth. " 'Quite an Original': The Cosmopolitan in *The Confidence-Man." Texas Studies in Language and Literature* 15 (Summer 1973): 279–300.

Kirby, David. *Herman Melville.* New York: Continuum, 1993.

Kuhlmann, Susan. *Knave, Fool, and Genius: The Confidence Man As He Appears in Nineteenth-Century American Fiction.* Chapel Hill: University of North Carolina Press, 1973.

Lane, Lauriat, Jr. "Entering Jerusalem: The Date of *The Confidence-Man.*" *Melville Society Extracts* 67 (September 1986): 12.

Lang, Hans-Joachim, and Benjamin Lease. "Melville's Cosmopolitan: Bayard Taylor in *The Confidence Man.*" *Amerikanstudien* 22 (1977): 286–89.

———. "Melville and 'The Practical Disciple': George William Curtis in *The Confidence-Man.*" *Amerikanstudien* 26 (1981): 181–91.

Lathers, Richard. *Reminiscences of Richard Lathers: Sixty Years of a Busy Life in South Carolina, Massachusetts and New York.* Ed. Alvan F. Sanborn. New York: Grafton, 1907.

Lenz, William E. *Fast Talk & Flush Times: The Confidence Man as a Literary Convention.* Columbia: University of Missouri Press, 1984.

Levine, Bruce C. *Half Slave and Half Free: The Roots of Civil War.* New York: Hill and Wang, 1991.

Levy, Leonard W. *The Law of the Commonwealth and Chief Justice Shaw.* Cambridge, Mass.: Harvard University Press, 1957.

Lewis, R.W.B. "The Confidence-Man." In Lewis, *Trials of the Word,* 61–76.

———. "Days of Wrath and Laughter." In Lewis, *Trials of the Word,* 184–235.

———. *Trials of the Word: Essays in American Literature and the Humanistic Tradition.* New Haven, Conn.: Yale University Press, 1965.

Leyda, Jay. "From the New *Log:* The Year 1821." *Melville Society Extracts* No. 62 (May 1985): 1–4.

Lindberg, Gary. *The Confidence Man in American Literature.* New York: Oxford University Press, 1982.

The Literary World: A Journal of American and Foreign Literature, Science, and Art. New York: 1847–1853.

Long, Raymond. "The Hidden Sun: A Study of the Influence of Shakespeare on the Creative Imagination of Herman Melville." Ph.D. diss., University of California at Los Angeles, 1965.

Lucid, Robert, ed. *The Journal of Richard Henry Dana, Jr.* 3 vols. Cambridge, Mass.: Harvard University Press, 1986.

Lueders, Edward G. "The Melville–Hawthorne Relationship in *Pierre* and *The Blithedale Romance.*" *Western Humanities Review* 4 (Autumn 1950): 323–34. Rpt. in Wilson, ed., *Hawthorne and Melville Friendship,* 138–49.

McDermott, John Francis, ed. *The Western Journals of Washington Irving.* Norman: University of Oklahoma Press, 1944.

McHaney, Thomas L. "*The Confidence-Man* and Satan's Disguises in *Paradise Lost.*" *Nineteenth-Century Fiction* 30 (September 1975): 200–206.

McIntire, Mary Beth. "The Buried Life: A Study of *The Blithedale Romance, The Confidence-Man,* and *The Sacred Fount.*" Ph.D. diss., Rice University, 1975.

McWilliams, John P., Jr. *Hawthorne, Melville and the American Character: A Looking Glass Business.* New York: Cambridge University Press, 1984.

McWilliams, Wilson Carey. *The Idea of Fraternity in America.* Berkeley: University of California Press, 1973.

Madison, Mary K. "Hypothetical Friends: The Critics and *The Confidence-Man.*" *Melville Society Extracts* No. 46 (May 1981): 10–14.

Magaw, Malcolm O. "*The Confidence-Man* and Christian Deity: Melville's Imagery of Ambiguity." *Explorations of Literature: Louisiana State University Studies* 18 (1966): 81–99.

Mani, Lakshmi. *The Apocalyptic Vision in Nineteenth-Century Fiction: A Study of Cooper, Hawthorne, and Melville.* Washington, D.C.: University Press of America, 1981.

Mason, Ronald. *The Spirit above the Dust: A Study of Herman Melville.* London: Lehmann, 1951.

Matterson, Stephen. Introduction. *The Confidence-Man: His Masquerade.* By Herman Melville. New York: Viking Penguin, 1990.

Matthiessen, F. O. *American Renaissance: Art and Expression in the Age of Emerson and Whitman.* New York: Oxford University Press, 1941.

May, John R. *Toward a New Earth: Apocalypse in the American Novel.* Notre Dame: University of Notre Dame Press, 1972.

Mellow, James R. *Nathaniel Hawthorne in His Times.* Boston: Houghton Mifflin, 1980.

Metcalf, Eleanor Melville. *Herman Melville: Cycle and Epicycle.* Cambridge, Mass.: Harvard University Press, 1953.

Meyer, D. H. "American Intellectuals and the Victorian Crisis of Faith." *American Quarterly* 27 (1975): 585–603.

Miles, Edwin Arthur. *Jacksonian Democracy in Mississippi.* Chapel Hill: University of North Carolina Press, 1960.

Miller, Douglas T. *The Birth of Modern America 1820–1850.* New York: Pegasus, 1970.

———. *Jacksonian Aristocracy: Class and Democracy in New York, 1830–1860.* New York: Oxford University Press, 1967.

Miller, Edwin Haviland. *Melville: A Biography.* New York: Braziller, 1975.

Miller, James E., Jr. *A Reader's Guide to Herman Melville.* New York: Farrar, Straus & Cudahy, 1962.

Miller, Perry. *The Life of the Mind in America: From the Revolution to the Civil War.* New York: Harcourt, Brace, 1965.

———. *The Raven and the Whale: The War of Words and Wits in the Era of Poe and Melville.* New York: Harcourt, Brace, 1956.

Mitchell, Edward. "From Action to Essence: Some Notes on the Structure of *The Confidence-Man.*" *American Literature* 40 (March 1968): 27–37.

Mize, George Edwin. "The Contributions of Evert Duyckinck to the Cultural Development of Nineteenth-Century American Literature." Ph.D. diss., New York University, 1955.

Montaigne, Michel de. *The Essays of Montaigne.* 3 vols. Trans. Charles Cotton. London, 1902.

Moorhead, James H. "Between Progress and Apocalypse: A Reassessment of Millennialism in American Religious Thought, 1800–1880." *Journal of American History* 71 (1984): 524–42.

Moses, Carole. *Melville's Use of Spenser.* New York: Peter Lang, 1989.

Mumford, Lewis. *Herman Melville: A Study of His Life and Vision.* Rev. ed. New York: Harcourt Brace, 1962.

Murray, Henry A., ed. *Pierre; Or, The Ambiguities.* By Herman Melville. New York: Hendricks House, 1949.

Murray, Henry A., Harvey Myerson, and Eugene Taylor. "Allan Melvill's By-Blow." *Melville Society Extracts* No. 61 (February 1985): 1–6.

Mushabac, Jane. *Melville's Humor: A Critical Study.* Hamden, Conn.: Shoe String Press, 1981.

Neufeldt, Leonard N. *The Economist: Henry Thoreau and Enterprise.* New York: Oxford University Press, 1989.

Nichol, John W. "Melville and the Midwest." *PMLA* 66 (September 1951): 613–25.

Nitzsche, Jane Chance. *The Genius Figure in Antiquity and the Middle Ages.* New York: Columbia University Press, 1975.

Norris, William. "Abbott Lawrence in *The Confidence-Man:* American Success or American Failure." *American Studies* 17 (Spring 1976): 25–38.

Northcutt, Mary Jean. "No Philosophy: Melville's Confidence-Man and American Thought." Ph.D. diss., Miami University, 1987.

Numbers, Ronald L., and Jonathan M. Butler, eds. *The Disappointed: Millerism and Millenarianism in the Nineteenth Century.* Bloomington: Indiana University Press, 1987.

Nye, Russell B. *Society and Culture in America, 1830–1860.* New York: Harper & Row, 1974.

Oliver, Egbert S. "Melville's Goneril and Fanny Kemble." *New England Quarterly* 18 (December 1945): 489–500.

———. "Melville's Picture of Emerson and Thoreau." *College English* 8 (November 1946): 61–72.

Olmsted, Frederick Law. *The Cotton Kingdom: A Traveler's Observations on Cotton and Slavery in the American Slave States.* Ed. Arthur M. Schlesinger. New York: Knopf, 1953.

Osgood, Samuel. *Evert Duyckinck: His Life, Writings and Influence.* Boston, 1879.

Otto, Walter F. *Dionysus: Myth and Cult.* Trans. Robert B. Palmer. Bloomington: Indiana University Press, 1973.

Palmeri, Frank Anthony. *Satire in Narrative: Petronius, Swift, Gibbon, Melville, and Pyncheon.* Austin: University of Texas Press, 1990.

Parker, Hershel. "Biography and Responsible Use of the Imagination: Three Episodes from Melville's Homecoming in 1844." *Resources for American Literary Study* 21 (1995): 16–42.

———, ed. *The Confidence-Man: His Masquerade.* By Herman Melville. New York: W. W. Norton, 1971.

———. "*The Confidence-Man* and the Use of Evidence in Compositional Studies: A Rejoinder." *Nineteenth-Century Fiction* 28 (June 1973): 119–24.

———. "Herman Melville's *Isle of the Cross:* A Survey and a Chronology." *American Literature* 62 (March 1990): 1–16.

———. "Melville and Politics: A Scrutiny of the Political Milieux of Herman Melville's Life and Works." Ph.D. diss., Northwestern University, 1963.

———. "Melville and the Transcendentalists: A Chronology." In Parker, ed., *The Confidence-Man,* 255–62.

———. "Melville's Satire of Emerson and Thoreau: An Evaluation of the Evidence." *American Transcendental Quarterly* No. 7 (Summer 1970): 61–67 and No. 9 (1971): 70.

———. "The Metaphysics of Indian-Hating." *Nineteenth-Century Fiction* 18 (September 1963): 165–73. Rpt. in Parker, ed., *The Confidence-Man,* 323–30.

———. " 'The Story of China Aster': A Tentative Explication." In Parker, ed., *The Confidence-Man,* 353–55.

Parker, Theodore. *Sins and Safeguards of Society.* Ed. Samuel B. Stewart. Boston: American Unitarian Association, n.d.

———. *The Slave Power.* Ed. James K. Hosmer. Boston: American Unitarian Association, n.d.

Patrides, C. A., and Joseph Wittreich, eds. *The Apocalypse in English Renaissance Thought and Literature: Patterns, Antecedents and Repercussions.* Ithaca, N.Y.: Cornell University Press, 1984.

Paulson, Ronald. *The Fictions of Satire.* Baltimore, Md.: Johns Hopkins University Press, 1967.

Pearce, Roy Harvey. "Melville's Indian-Hater: A Note on the Meaning of *The Confidence-Man.*" *PMLA* 67 (December 1952): 942–48.

Perosa, Sergio. *American Theories of the Novel: 1793–1903.* New York: New York University Press, 1983.

The Pittsfield Sun. Pittsfield, Mass., 1800–1906.

Poe, Edgar Allan. *The Complete Works of Edgar Allan Poe.* 17 vols. Ed. James A. Harrison. 1902. New York: AMS Press, 1965.

Porte, Joel. *Representative Man: Ralph Waldo Emerson in His Time.* New York: Columbia University Press, 1988.

———. *The Romance in America: Studies in Cooper, Poe, Hawthorne, Melville, and James.* Middletown, Conn.: Wesleyan University Press, 1969.

Puett, Amy Elizabeth. "Melville's Wife: A Study of Elizabeth Shaw Melville." Ph.D. diss., Northwestern University, 1969.

Putnam's Monthly Magazine of American Literature, Science and Art. New York, 1853–1857.

Quirk, Tom. *Melville's Confidence Man: From Knave to Knight.* Columbia: University of Missouri Press, 1982.

———. "Two Sources in *The Confidence-Man.*" *Melville Society Extracts* No. 39 (September 1979): 12–13.

Railton, Stephen. *Authorship and Audience: Literary Performance in the American Renaissance.* Princeton, N.J.: Princeton University Press, 1991.

Ramsey, William McCrea. "*The Confidence-Man:* Melville and the Reader." Ph.D. diss., University of North Carolina at Chapel Hill, 1977.

———. "Melville's and Barnum's Man with a Weed." *American Literature* 51 (March 1979): 101–104.

———. "The Moot Points of Melville's Indian-Hating." *American Literature* 52 (May 1980): 224–35.

———. " 'Touching' Scenes in *The Confidence-Man.*" *ESQ: A Journal of the American Renaissance* 25 (1st Quarter 1979): 37–62.

Randall, Randolph C. *James Hall: Spokesman for the New West.* Columbus: Ohio State University Press, 1964.

Randolph, Mary Claire. "The Structural Design of Formal Verse Satire." *Philological Quarterly* 21 (1942): 368–84.

Reed, Walter L. *An Exemplary History of the Novel: The Quixotic Versus the Picaresque.* Chicago: University of Chicago Press, 1981.

Reeves, Paschal. "The 'Deaf Mute' Confidence Man: Melville's Imposter in Action." *Modern Language Notes* 75 (January 1960): 18–20.

Reynolds, David S. *Beneath the American Renaissance: The Subversive Imagination in the Age of Emerson and Melville.* New York: Knopf, 1988.

Richardson, James F. *New York Police, Colonial Times to 1901.* New York: Oxford University Press, 1970.

Roche, Arthur John, III. "A Literary Gentleman in New York: Evert A. Duyckinck's Relationship with Nathaniel Hawthorne, Herman Melville, Edgar Allan Poe, and William Gilmore Simms." Ph.D. diss., Duke University, 1973.

Rogin, Michael Paul. *Subversive Genealogy: The Politics and Art of Herman Melville.* New York: Knopf, 1983.

Rorabaugh, W. J. *The Alcoholic Republic: An American Tradition.* New York: Oxford University Press, 1979.

Rosenberry, Edward H. *Melville.* London: Routledge & Kegan Paul, 1979.

———. *Melville and the Comic Spirit.* Cambridge, Mass.: Harvard University Press, 1955.

———. "Melville's Ship of Fools." *PMLA* 75 (December 1960): 604–608.

Rosenheim, Edward. *Swift and the Satirist's Art.* Chicago: University of Chicago Press, 1963.

Roundy, Nancy. "Melville's *The Confidence-Man:* Epistemology and Art." *Ball State University Forum* 21 (Spring 1979): 3–11.

Rowe, John Carlos. *Through the Custom House: Nineteenth Century American Fiction and Modern Theory.* Baltimore, Md.: Johns Hopkins University Press, 1982.

Rudwin, Maximilian. *The Devil in Legend and Literature.* LaSalle, Ill.: Open Court, 1931.

Russell, Jeffrey Burton. *The Devil: Perceptions of Evil from Antiquity to Primitive Christianity.* Ithaca, N.Y.: Cornell University Press, 1977.

———. *Mephistopheles: The Devil in the Modern World.* Ithaca, N.Y.: Cornell University Press, 1986.

Sandeen, Ernest. "Millennialism." In Gaustad, ed., *The Rise of Adventism,* 104–18.

Sattelmeyer, Robert, and James Barbour. "A Possible Source and Model for 'The Story of China Aster' in Melville's *The Confidence-Man.*" *American Literature* 48 (January 1977): 577–83.

Scharnhorst, Gary. "Melville's Authorship of 'Hawthorne and His Mosses': The First Attribution." *Melville Society Extracts* No. 73 (May 1988): 1–3.

Schultz, Donald Diedrich. "Herman Melville and the Tradition of the Anatomy: A Study in Genre." Ph.D. diss., Vanderbilt University, 1969.

Sealts, Merton M., Jr. "The Ghost of Major Melville." In Sealts, *Pursuing Melville,* 67–77.

———. "Melville and Emerson's Rainbow." In Sealts, *Pursuing Melville,* 250–77.

———. *Melville's Reading.* Rev. ed. Columbia: University of South Carolina Press, 1988.

———. *Pursuing Melville, 1940–1980: Chapters and Essays.* Madison: University of Wisconsin Press, 1982.

———. "Thomas Melvill, Jr. in *The History of Pittsfield.*" *Harvard Library Bulletin* 35 (Spring 1987): 201–17.

Seelye, John. Introduction. *The Confidence-Man: His Masquerade.* By Herman Melville. San Francisco: Chandler, 1968.

———. *Melville: The Ironic Diagram.* Evanston, Ill.: Northwestern University Press, 1970.

———. "Timothy Flint's 'Wicked River' and *The Confidence-Man.*" *PMLA* 78 (March 1963): 75–79.

———. "Ungraspable Phantom: Reflections of Hawthorne in *Pierre* and *The Confidence-Man.*" *Studies in the Novel* 1 (Winter 1969): 436–43. Rpt. in Wilson, ed., *The Hawthorne and Melville Friendship,* 192–99.

Seltzer, Alvin J. *Chaos in the Novel—The Novel in Chaos.* New York: Schocken, 1974.

Seltzer, Leon F. "Camus's Absurd and the World of Melville's Confidence-Man." *PMLA* 82 (March 1967): 14–27.

Sewell, David R. "Mercantile Philosophy and the Dialectics of Confidence: Another Perspective on *The Confidence-Man.*" *ESQ: A Journal of the American Renaissance* 30 (2nd Quarter 1984): 99–110.

Shapiro, Samuel. "The Rendition of Anthony Burns." *Journal of Negro History* 44 (1959): 34–51.

Shepherd, Gerard W. "The Confidence Man as Drummond Light." *ESQ: A Journal of the American Renaissance* 28 (3rd Quarter 1982): 183–196.

Shroeder, John W. "Sources and Symbols for Melville's *The Confidence-Man.*" *PMLA* 66 (1951): 363–80. Rpt. in Parker, ed., *The Confidence-Man,* 298–316.

Silverman, Kenneth. *Edgar A. Poe: Mournful and Never-Ending Remembrance.* New York: HarperCollins, 1991.

Simms, William Gilmore. *The Letters of William Gilmore Simms.* Vol. 3. Eds. Mary C. Simms Oliphant, Alfred Taylor Odell, and T. C. Dunean Eaves. Columbia: University of South Carolina Press, 1954.

Slotkin, Richard. *Regeneration Through Violence: The Mythology of the American Frontier, 1600–1860.* Middletown, Conn.: Wesleyan University Press, 1973.

Smith, J.E.A. *A History of Pittsfield from 1800 to the Year 1876*. Springfield, Mass.: 1876.

Smith, Richard Dean. *Melville's Complaint: Doctors and Medicine in the Art of Herman Melville*. New York: Garland, 1991.

Smith, Timothy L. *Revivalism and Social Reform In Mid-Nineteenth-Century America*. New York: Abingdon, 1957.

Spann, Edward K. *The New Metropolis: New York City, 1840–1857*. New York: Columbia University Press, 1981.

Stafford, John. *The Literary Criticism of "Young America": A Study of the Relationship of Politics to Literature*. Berkeley: University of California Press, 1952.

Stein, William Bysshe. "Melville's *The Confidence-Man:* Quicksands of the Word." *American Transcendental Quarterly*, No. 24 (1974): 38–50.

———. *The Poetry of Melville's Late Years: Time, History, Myth, and Religion*. Albany: State University of New York Press, 1970.

Sten, Christopher W. "The Dialogue of Crisis in *The Confidence-Man*." *Studies in the Novel* 6 (Summer 1974): 165–85.

Stone, Geoffrey. *Herman Melville*. New York: Sheed & Ward, 1949.

Stowe, Harriet Beecher. *Three Novels: Uncle Tom's Cabin, The Minister's Wooing, Oldtown Folks*. Ed. Kathryn Kish Sklar. New York: Library of America, 1982.

Strickland, Edward. "The Ruins of Romanticism in *The Confidence-Man*." *American Notes and Queries* 22 (November/December 1983): 40–43.

Summers, Mark W. *The Plundering Generation: Corruption and the Crisis of the Union, 1849–1861*. New York: Oxford University Press, 1987.

Sumner, D. Nathan. "The American West in Melville's *Mardi* and *The Confidence-Man*." *Washington State University Research Studies* 36 (March 1968): 37–49.

Sussman, Henry. "The Deconstructor as Politician: Melville's *The Confidence-Man*." *Glyph* 4 (1978): 32–56.

Tanner, Tony. Introduction. *The Confidence-Man: His Masquerade*. By Herman Melville. New York: Oxford University Press, 1989.

Tanselle, G. Thomas. "Herman Melville's Trip to Galena." *Journal of the Illinois State Historical Society* 53 (Winter 1960): 376–88.

Tave, Stuart M. *The Amiable Humorist: A Study of the Comic Theory and Criticism of the Eighteenth and Early Nineteenth Centuries*. Chicago: University of Chicago Press, 1960.

Taylor, George Rogers. *The Transportation Revolution*. New York: Harper & Row, 1951.

Test, George A. *Satire: Spirit and Art*. Tampa: University of South Florida Press, 1991.

Thomas, Brook. *Cross-Examinations of Law and Literature: Cooper, Hawthorne, Stowe, and Melville*. New York: Cambridge University Press, 1987.

Thompson, G. R., and Virgil L. Lokke, eds. *Ruined Eden of the Present: Hawthorne, Melville, and Poe*. West Lafayette, Ind.: Purdue University Press, 1981.

Thompson, Lawrance. *Melville's Quarrel With God*. Princeton, N.J.: Princeton University Press, 1952.

Thoreau, Henry David. *A Week on the Concord and Merrimack Rivers*. Ed. Carl Hovde. Princeton, N.J.: Princeton University Press, 1980.

———. *Reform Papers.* Ed. Wendell Glick. Princeton, N.J.: Princeton University Press, 1973.

———. *Walden.* Ed. J. Lyndon Shanley. Princeton, N.J.: Princeton University Press, 1971.

Ticchi, Cecelia. "Melville's Craft and the Theme of Language Debased." *ELH* 39 (December 1972): 639–58.

Tolchin, Neal L. *Mourning, Gender, and Creativity in the Art of Herman Melville.* New Haven, Conn.: Yale University Press, 1988.

Toll, Robert C. *Blacking Up: The Minstrel Show in Nineteenth-Century America.* New York: Oxford University Press, 1974.

Trimpi, Helen P. "Daumier's Robert Macaire and Melville's Confidence Man." In Christopher Sten, ed. *Savage Eye: Melville and the Visual Arts.* Kent, Ohio: Kent State University Press, 1991.

———. "Harlequin-Confidence-Man: The Satirical Tradition of Commedia Dell' Arte and Pantomime in Melville's *The Confidence-Man.*" *Texas Studies in Language and Literature* 16 (Spring 1974): 147–93.

———. *Melville's Confidence Men and American Politics in the 1850s.* Hamden, Conn.: Shoe String Press, 1987.

———. "Three of Melville's Confidence Men: William Cullen Bryant, Theodore Parker and Horace Greeley." *Texas Studies in Language and Literature* 21 (Fall 1979): 368–95.

Turner, Arlin. *Hawthorne As Editor: Selections from His Writings in the American Magazine of Useful and Entertaining Knowledge.* Port Washington, N.Y.: Kennikat, 1972.

———. *Nathaniel Hawthorne: A Biography.* New York: Oxford University Press, 1980.

Turner, James. *Without God, Without Creed: The Origins of Unbelief in America.* Baltimore, Md.: Johns Hopkins University Press, 1985.

Tuveson, Ernest. "The Creed of *The Confidence-Man.*" *ELH* 33 (June 1966): 247–70.

———. *Redeemer Nation: The Idea of America's Millennial Role.* Chicago: University of Chicago Press, 1968.

Tyler, Alice Felt. *Freedom's Ferment: Phases of American Social History from the Colonial Period to the Outbreak of the Civil War.* New York: Harper & Row, 1962.

Tyrrell, Ian. *Sobering Up: From Temperance to Prohibition in Ante-Bellum America.* Westport, Conn.: Greenwood Press, 1979.

Van Cromphout, Gustaaf. "*The Confidence-Man:* Melville and the Problem of Others." *Studies in American Fiction* 21 (1993): 37–50.

von Frank, Albert J. *An Emerson Chronology.* New York: G.K. Hall, 1994.

Wadlington, Warwick. *The Confidence Game in American Literature.* Princeton, N.J.: Princeton University Press, 1975.

Walters, Ronald G. *American Reformers, 1815–1860.* New York: Hill & Wang, 1978.

Watson, Charles N., Jr. "The Estrangement of Hawthorne and Melville." *New England Quarterly* 46 (September 1973): 380–402.

———. "Melville and the Theme of Timonism: From *Pierre* to *The Confidence-Man.*" *American Literature* 44 (November 1972): 398–413.

———. "Melville's *Israel Potter:* Fathers and Sons." *Studies in the Novel* 7 (Winter 1975): 563–68.

Weaver, Raymond M. *Herman Melville: Mariner and Mystic.* New York: George H. Doran, 1921.

Weiner, Susan. *Law in Art: Melville's Major Fiction and Nineteenth-Century American Law.* New York: Peter Lang, 1992.

Weissbuch, Ted N. "A Note on the Confidence Man's Counterfeit Detector." *Emerson Society Quarterly,* No. 19 (2nd Quarter 1960): 16–18.

Wells, Daniel Arthur. "Evert Duyckinck's *Literary World,* 1847–1853: Its Views and Reviews of American Literature." Ph.D. diss., Duke University, 1972.

Wenke, John. "Melville's Masquerade and the Aesthetics of Self-Possession." *ESQ: A Journal of the American Renaissance* 28 (4th Quarter 1982): 233–42.

———. "No 'i' in Charlemont: A Cryptogrammic Name in *The Confidence-Man.*" *Essays in Literature* (Macomb, Ill.) 9 (Fall 1982): 269–78.

Wicks, Ulrich. *Picaresque Narrative, Picaresque Fictions: A Theory and Research Guide.* Westport, Conn.: Greenwood Press, 1989.

Williams, John B. *White Fire: The Influence of Emerson on Melville.* Long Beach: California State University Press, 1991.

Wilmes, Douglas Robert. "The Satiric Mode in Melville's Fiction: *Pierre, Israel Potter, The Confidence-Man,* and the Short Fiction." Ph.D. diss., University of Pennsylvania, 1976.

Wilson, James C., ed. *The Hawthorne and Melville Friendship: An Annotated Bibliography, Biographical Essay and Critical Essays and Correspondence Between the Two.* Jefferson, N.C.: McFarland, 1991.

———. "Melville at Arrowhead: A Reevaluation of Melville's Relations with Hawthorne and with His Family." *ESQ: A Journal of the American Renaissance* 30 (4th Quarter 1984): 232–44. Rpt. in Wilson, ed., *Hawthorne and Melville Friendship,* 200–14.

Wright, Natalia. "The Confidence Men of Melville and Cooper: An American Indictment." *American Quarterly* 4 (Fall 1952): 266–68.

———. *Melville's Use of the Bible.* Durham: University of North Carolina Press, 1949.

Yannella, Donald. "Writing the '*Other* Way': Melville, the Duyckinck Crowd, and Literature for the Masses." In Bryant, ed., *Companion to Melville Studies,* 63–84.

———, and Hershel Parker. *The Endless Winding Way in Melville: New Charts by Kring and Carey.* Glassboro, N.J.: Melville Society, 1981.

———, and Kathleen Malone Yanella. "Duyckinck's 'Diary': May 29–November 8, 1947." In Joel Myerson, ed. *Studies in the American Renaissance: 1989.* Boston: Twayne, 1978.

Young, James Harvey. *The Toadstool Millionaires: A Social History of Patent Medicines in America Before Federal Regulation.* Princeton, N.J.: Princeton University Press, 1961.

Young, Philip. *The Private Melville.* University Park: Pennsylvania State University Press, 1993.

Index

About the Author

JONATHAN A. COOK has a Ph.D. from Columbia University. He has been a lecturer at Boston University and has published articles on Irving, Hawthorne, and Melville.

ISBN 0-313-29404-6
90000>
EAN
9 780313 294044
HARDCOVER BAR CODE